FROM TRUST TO TERROR

THE ONSET OF THE COLD WAR, 1945–1950

FROM

THE ONSET OF

Herbert Feis

TRUST TO TERROR

THE COLD WAR, *1945-1950*

W · W · NORTON & COMPANY · INC ·
New York

327
F299f

Contents

Photographs follow page 204.

Preface

The span and design of this narrative were set by events and not by choice. In these crucial years the pattern of our present era was formed—although, it may be hoped, not fixed. By 1945 the war was won and hopes were high. By the end of 1949 these hopes had crumpled. The Western Allies and the Soviet Union were glaring at each other, both grasping atomic weapons. China had fallen to the Communists. The lines of division in Europe were trenched. The United Nations was stricken by dissension. Mutual trust had gone, mutual terror was becoming the decisive restraint, and tempers were in constant tension. Arms were to the fore, spies in their cubbies, bombs in their brackets, statesmen splenetic; venom in the air waves. How and through what circuit of chance and action did this change come about?

I have written this narrative without the conscious benefit of and explicit resort to the analytical techniques which cram so many professional productions; I mean such methods as systems analyses, multiple regression, bargaining and conflict theories, causal modeling, integrative social processes based on the concepts of exchange of functions, curve fitting, cybernetic analyses—the abstruse black arts of the searchers for a science of international politics.

But I hope I have absorbed any original insights that these pretentious techniques may thus far have produced. I would like to learn that I have grasped their meaning, without using their lingo—to be surprised as was Monsieur Jourdain in Moliere's *Bourgeois Gentilhomme*, on learning that he spoke prose. Who remembers that dialogue?

M. Jourdain (questioningly): What? When I say: "Nicole, bring me my slippers and night cap," that is prose?

The Master of Philosophy: Yes.

M. Jourdain: By heavens! For more than forty years I have been speaking prose without knowing it. . . .

Our account is almost contemporary. But the moral for our times is the same as that discussed by the gods in Hesiod's *Works and Days*.

PREFACE

Zeus to Prometheus: "Son of Iapetus, surpassing all in cunning, you are glad that you outwitted me and stolen fire—a great plague to yourself and to men that shall be. But I will give men as the price for fire evil (?) things in which they may all be glad of heart while they embrace their own destruction."

Prince Perses: "But you lay up these things within your heart and listen to the right, ceasing altogether to think of violence. For the son of Cronos (Zeus) has ordained this law for men, that fishes and beasts and winged fowls shall devour one another, for right is not in them but to mankind he gave right which proves the best."

All historical tales are tinted by the light of the times in which they are written. Just so this interpretation, no doubt, is colored by the smog and frequent storms in the atmosphere. Perhaps before too long another version of the same historical passage can be written in calmer, clearer days and in a more tranquil environment.

Extant sources of information pertinent to this narrative are ample. However, regrettably, historians are not permitted to consult some of the official records of this determinative period. All major governments refuse to allow them to learn for themselves what is in those hoarded records—the better to find out and tell what happened, and why. I, like others, have had to make do with what governments have chosen to release, memoirs and official histories, and other published accounts and parliamentary or congressional debates. Apropos of this narrative, for example, historians are still denied, on the score of national security, the opportunity to read the whole of the relevant presidential papers and diplomatic correspondence. The memoirs of public figures are their privileged castles; their reputations are surrounded by a moat for a generation.

But the historian can enlist the interest, seek the aid of the numerous other participants and witnesses who shared the experiences, prodding them to search their memories, or even to produce their papers. Many who were active and well-informed observers have helped me in the search for the facts, in the effort to distinguish between the essentials and minor occurrences, and to get to know the characters. Among those whom I wish to thank particularly for such aid are the Hon. W. Averell Harriman, former Secretary of State James F. Byrnes, Clark Clifford, Paul Nitze, Thomas Finletter, David E. Lilienthal, Ernest Gross, Mark Chadwin, Richard Neustadt, George F. Kennan, John D. Hickerson, James Dunn, Desmond Donnelly, M. P., Sir Frank Roberts, Alan Bullock, the Hon. Lester Pearson, Lord Oliver Franks, Lord Avon (Anthony Eden), and Jean Monnet.

The Ford Foundation provided a grant to pay expenses of research and travel. The Charles Warren Center of American History of Harvard

University took on the chore of doling it out and of assisting in practical arrangements for carrying on the work. Libraries and librarians, as always, patiently and with unfailing willingness, enabled me to study the papers and documents of which they are the custodians. I wish particularly to acknowledge the assistance of Alexander P. Clark, of the Manuscript Division of the Princeton University Library, for the use of the papers of Bernard M. Baruch and Arthur Krock; Mr. Gordon Wasson and Miss Janet Rigney of the Library of the Council on Foreign Relations; the Oral History Project of Columbia University for the William Clayton papers; and the Library staffs of the University of New Hampshire, the University of Miami, the Institute for Advanced Study in Princeton, Chatham House in London, the London School of Economics (custodian of the diary of Hugh Dalton) the Ecole des Sciences Politiques in Paris; the Library of Congress in Washington (custodian of the diary of Admiral William Leahy).

For a thorough and corrective inspection of several drafts of the manuscript, and for taking on himself much of the task of checking quotations and citations, I am grateful to Mr. Giora Kulka, a graduate student in history at Harvard. I am also grateful to Mrs. John F. Rowe of Newington, New Hampshire, for the exhausting work of typing and retyping, and to my wife, Ruth Stanley-Brown Feis, for sustenance of all kinds, including literary suggestions, "in sickness and in health, for richer or poorer."

Principal Personages
as They Figure in the Narrative

ACHESON, DEAN. Undersecretary of State of the United States, August 1945–June 1947. Secretary of State of the United States, January 1949–January 1953

ADENAUER, KONRAD. Chairman of Christian Democratic Union, Germany, 1946. Chairman of Parliamentary Council (to write *Basic Law*), 1948. Chancellor of Federal Government of West Germany, 1949

ALLEN, GEORGE V. American Ambassador to Iran

ANTONOV, ALEXEI (GEN.). Chief of Staff of Army of U.S.S.R., 1945

ATTLEE, CLEMENT. Prime Minister of Great Britain, 1945–51

AURIOL, VINCENT. President of Fourth Republic of France, 1947–54

AUSTIN, WARREN. Senator from Vermont (Republican) and U.S. Representative on Security Council of the United Nations

BARUCH, BERNARD M. U.S. Representative on Atomic Energy Commission of the United Nations

BENEŠ, EDUARD. President of Czechoslovakia

BEVIN, ERNEST. Secretary of State for Foreign Affairs of British Government

BIDAULT, GEORGES. Minister of Foreign Affairs, Provisional Government of France, 1945; Premier and Foreign Minister of France, 1946; Minister of Foreign Affairs 1947–48; Premier, 1949–50

BILLOTTE, PIERRE (GEN.). Formerly General de Gaulle's Chief of Staff; Member of French Mission to United Nations, 1947

BLUM, LEON. Distinguished French Socialist political figure. Foreign Minister–Prime Minister of France, December 1946–January 1947

BOHLEN, CHARLES E. Special Assistant to Secretary of State, 1946; Counselor, Department of State, 1947

BRADLEY, OMAR (GEN.). Chief of Staff of U.S. Army, February 1948–August 1949. Chairman of Joint Chiefs of Staff, August 1949

BRAND, SIR ROBERT (later LORD BRAND). Representative of British Treasury in Washington; negotiator of loan agreement

BRIDGES, STYLES. Senator (Republican) from New Hampshire

BRUCE, DAVID. American Ambassador to France; participant in negotiations concerning Marshall Plan program, NATO, and German affairs

BULLARD, SIR READER. British Minister; later, Ambassador to Iran

BULLITT, WILLIAM. Former American Ambassador to France and the Soviet Union; influential adviser to President Roosevelt

BURGESS, GUY. British diplomat who was Soviet agent and defected to the U.S.S.R.

BUSH, VANNEVAR. Chairman of Research and Development Board 1941–48. Adviser on scientific matters to President Franklin D. Roosevelt, especially on atomic bomb

BYRNES, JAMES F. U.S. Secretary of State, July 1945–January 1947

CADOGAN, SIR ALEXANDER. Foreign Office official, representative of British Government on Atomic Energy Commission of the United Nations

CAFFERY, JEFFERSON. U.S. Ambassador to France

CHENNAULT, CLAIRE (GEN.). Commander of 14th U.S. Air Force in China (the Flying Tigers)

CHIANG KAI-SHEK (GEN.). President of Nationalist Republic of China

CHURCHILL, WINSTON S. Prime Minister of Great Britain, 1940–45

CLARK, MARK (GEN.). Commanding General of U.S. forces in Italy, 1944–45, later of U.S. forces in Austria. U.S. Representative on Control Council for Austria

CLARK, THOMAS CAMPBELL. Attorney General in President Truman's Cabinet

CLARK-KERR, ARCHIBALD (LORD INVERCHAPEL). Ambassador of United Kingdom in Moscow and in the United States

CLAY, LUCIUS D. (GEN.). Military Governor of American Zone of Occupation in Germany. U.S. member of Control Council for Germany

CLAYTON, WILLIAM L. Assistant Secretary of State for Economic Affairs, later Undersecretary of State for Foreign Affairs

CLIFFORD, CLARK. Lawyer and Special Counsel to President Truman

COHEN, BENJAMIN. Counselor, State Department, adviser to Secretary of State Byrnes

CONANT, JAMES B. President of Harvard University, Adviser to President Roosevelt on scientific matters, member of State Department Committee on Atomic Energy, 1946

CONNALLY, TOM. Senator from Texas, senior Democratic member of Senate Committee on Foreign Relations

COOPER, ALFRED DUFF (VISCOUNT NORWICH). British Ambassador in Paris

COUVE DE MURVILLE, MAURICE. Senior official in Foreign Office of France

DALTON, HUGH. Chancellor of the Exchequer in British Government, 1945

DAVIES, JOSEPH E. Former Ambassador to Moscow. Member U.S. delegation to Potsdam Conference

DEANE, JOHN (GEN.). Head of the U.S. Military Mission in Moscow

DE GASPERI, ALCIDE. Prime Minister of Italy

DE GAULLE, CHARLES (GEN.). Head of Provisional Government of French

Republic. Then, Premier, Government of Fourth French Republic; resigned January 1946

DEWEY, THOMAS E. Governor of New York. Republican Candidate for President, 1948

DJILAS, MILOVAN. Yugoslav official

DONOVAN, WILLIAM J., THE HONORABLE. Head, Office of Strategic Services. Commander-in-Chief, European Theater.

DOUGLAS, LEWIS. U.S. Ambassador to Great Britain, 1947–50. Adviser in negotiations about Marshall Plan program, NATO, and German affairs

DRAPER, WILLIAM. Chief of the Economic Division of the Control Council for Germany; later, Undersecretary of the Army

DRATVIN, MIKHAEL I. Deputy Governor of Soviet zone of occupation in Germany

DUCLOS, JACQUES. One of leaders of Communist Party of France, member of the Assembly

DULLES, JOHN FOSTER. Adviser to Republican members of Senate and to Presidential aspirant Governor Thomas Dewey, and member of American delegation in various international conferences

DUMAINE, JACQUES. French diplomat, head of Protocol to French President and Foreign Office

DUNN, JAMES. Assistant Secretary of State, later U.S. Ambassador to Italy

EDEN, SIR ANTHONY (LORD AVON). Secretary of State for Foreign Affairs of Great Britain, 1940–45; 1951–55

EISENHOWER, DWIGHT D. (GEN.). Commander-in-Chief of Allied Expeditionary Force in Western Europe; Commander, American Zone of Occupation in Germany; Chief of Staff, U.S. Army, 1945–48

ETHRIDGE, MARK. Publishing Executive, Chief of special Mission sent by State Department to investigate and report on political and economic developments affecting Greece and the Balkans, 1945; member, United Nations Commission to study Greek border disputes, 1947

FIERLINGER, ZDENEK. Ambassador of Czechoslovakia, in Moscow

FORRESTAL, JAMES. Secretary of the U.S. Navy, later first Secretary of Defense

FRANÇOIS-PONCET, ANDRÉ. French diplomat. French High Commissioner for Western Germany

FRANKS OLIVER (LORD). British Ambassador in Washington, Chairman of Committee of Sixteen for Marshall Plan

FUCHS, KLAUS. Physicist who worked on atomic weapons at Los Alamos and in Great Britain, and transmitted secret information to government of Soviet Union

FULBRIGHT, JAMES WILLIAM. Senator (Democrat) from Arkansas

GHAVAM, AHMAD. Prime Minister of Iran 1946–47

GOTTWALD, KLEMENT. Prime Minister of Czechoslovakia

GOUZENKO, IGOR. Member of staff of Soviet diplomatic Mission in Canada, defector to West

GRISWOLD, DWIGHT. Chief of U.S. Mission in Greece. Administrator of U.S. aid program in Greece

GROMYKO, ANDREI. Soviet Ambassador to the United States, 1943–46. Soviet representative on United Nations Security Council, 1946–48. Deputy Minister of Foreign Affairs, 1946–49

GROSS, ERNEST. Legal adviser of State Department

GROVES, LESLIE R. (GEN.). Commandant of the Manhattan Project (atomic weapons)

GRUBER, KARL. Foreign Minister of Austria

GRUENTHER, ALFRED M. (GEN.). Director of Joint Staff of Joint Chiefs of Staff, 1948

GUSEV, F. T. Ambassador of Soviet Government to Great Britain. Soviet Member of European Advisory Commission

HANDY, THOMAS T. (GEN.). Deputy Chief of Staff, U.S. Army

HARRIMAN, W. AVERELL. American Ambassador in Moscow, 1945–46. Special Assistant to President Truman. Chairman, President's Committee on Foreign Aid (Marshall Plan)

HENDERSON, LOY. State Department official. Chief of Division of Eastern European Affairs, later Ambassador to India

HICKERSON, JOHN D. State Department official. Head of Office of Western European Affairs

HILLDRING, JOHN (GEN.). Head, Division of Civil Affairs, War Department, 1943–45. Assistant Secretary of State for Occupied Areas, 1945

HILLMAN, WILLIAM. American journalist, friend of President Truman

HOOVER, HERBERT. Formerly, President of the United States, 1928–32. Special representative of President Truman, report on conditions in Germany

HOPKINS, HARRY. Special adviser to President Roosevelt. Head of special mission to Stalin, 1945

HOWLEY, FRANK (COL.). Commander, U.S. Forces in Berlin. American representative on the Kommandatura, Berlin

HULL, CORDELL. U.S. Secretary of State 1933–44

INVERCHAPEL, LORD (ARCHIBALD CLARK-KERR). Ambassador of British Government to the United States

JEBB, GLADWYN (LORD). British diplomat. The United Kingdom representative on the Brussels Treaty Permanent Commission; participant in NATO Negotiations

JESSUP, PHILIP C. U.S. Ambassador, Deputy U.S. representative to United Nations. Acting member of Security Council

JOHNSON, LOUIS A. U.S. Secretary of Defense, March 1949–September 1950

JOLIOT-CURIE, FREDERIC. Physicist; in charge of work of French government on atomic energy

JONES, JOSEPH. State Department official

Judd, Walter. Member of House of Representatives from Minnesota (Republican)

Kardelj, Edvard P. Vice Premier of Yugoslavia

Kennan, George. State Department official. Member of American Diplomatic Mission in Moscow. Adviser to Ambassador Winant on European Advisory Commission. Head Policy Planning Staff, 1947–49

Keynes, John Maynard (Lord). British economist. Representative of Government of United Kingdom on loan negotiations, 1945–46

Khrushchev, Nikita. Member of Politburo. Subsequently became head of the Government of the Soviet Union

King, Ernest J. (Adm.). Commander-in-Chief, U.S. Navy. Member, Joint Chiefs of Staff

King, W. L. Mackenzie. Prime Minister of Canada

Koenig, Pierre (Gen.). French representative on the Control Commission for Germany

Leahy, William D. (Adm.). U.S. Ambassador to Vichy Government, France, 1940. Chief of Staff to the Commander-in-Chief (Franklin D. Roosevelt), 1942–49

Lie, Trygve. Secretary General of the United Nations

Lilienthal, David E. Chairman of the Tennessee Valley Authority. Chairman, Board of Consultants on Atomic Energy to Secretary of State, 1945

Lovett, Robert A. Assistant Secretary of War, 1943–45. Undersecretary of State, July 1947–January 1949. Deputy Secretary of Defense, September 1950

Lippmann, Walter. American columnist and author

Maclean, Donald. Foreign Office official. First Secretary of the British Embassy in Washington. Agent of Soviet Government

McCloy, John J. Assistant Secretary of War. U.S. High Commissioner for Germany

McMahon, Brien. Senator (Democrat) from Connecticut. Chairman of Senate Committee on Atomic Energy Policy

McNarney, Joseph (Gen.). Commander of U.S. forces in Europe, briefly, 1946. U.S. representative on Control Council for Germany

McNeil, Hector, (M.P.). Minister of State in Labor Government of Great Britain

MacVeagh, Lincoln. U.S. Ambassador in Greece

Malenkov, Georgi. Member of Politburo, U.S.S.R.

Malik, Jacob. Representative of Soviet Government in United Nations

Marshall, George Catlett (Gen.). Head, Presidential Mission to China. Later Secretary of State, later Secretary of Defense

Martin, Joseph. Speaker of House of Representatives (Republican)

Masaryk, Jan. Secretary for Foreign Affairs, Czechoslovakia

Massigli, René. Permanent official, Foreign Office of France; French Ambassador to Great Britain

MATTHEWS, H. FREEMAN. United States State Department official

MAY, ALAN NUN. Canadian official who provided secret intelligence to Soviet Government

MIKOYAN, ANASTAS. Member of Politburo of Soviet Union

MOCH, JULES. French socialist, Minister of the Interior

MOLOTOV, V. M. People's Commissar for Foreign Affairs, U.S.S.R., 1939–46. Foreign Minister of Soviet Government, 1946–49

MONNET, JEAN. French banker, student of public affairs, adviser of Marshall Plan, author of Monnet Plan for economic reconstruction of France

MONTGOMERY, BERNARD L. (VISCOUNT). Commander-in-Chief of British Army on Western front

MORGAN, FREDERICK, (GEN.) SIR. Head of COSSAC, British Military planning group for invasion of France

MORGENTHAU, HENRY, JR. U.S. Secretary of the Treasury

MURPHY, ROBERT. State Department official; chief civil affairs adviser on Eisenhower's staff; U.S. Political Adviser for Germany, 1944. Director, Office of German and Austrian Affairs, 1949

MURRAY, WALLACE. State Department official; U.S. Ambassador to Iran

NITZE, PAUL. Contributor to Marshall Plan. Member of Policy Staff of State Department. Deputy Assistant Secretary of State for Economic Affairs, 1948–49. Director, Policy Planning Staff, State Department, 1950–53

NOIRET, (GEN.). French Member of Control Council for Germany

NORSTAD, LAURIS (GEN.). Air Force officer. Deputy Chief of Operations, U.S. Air Force

NOSEK, VACLAV. Minister of Interior in the Government of Czechoslovakia formed after *coup d'état* in 1948

OPPENHEIMER, J. ROBERT. Physicist. Chairman, Advisory Scientific Panel to Interim Committee on atomic energy problems

OSBORN, FREDERICK. American representative on United Nations Atomic Energy Commission

PATTERSON, ROBERT. Undersecretary of the Army. U.S. Secretary of War, September 1945–July 1947

PEARSON, LESTER (HON.). Secretary for External Affairs of Canada

PÉTAIN, HENRI PHILIPPE (MARSHAL). Prime Minister of Vichy Government of France

PIECK, WILHELM. Chairman of the Socialist Unity Party (Communist)

PRICE, BYRON. Head of Mission sent by President Truman in 1945 to investigate and report on relations between the American Forces in occupation in Germany and the German people

QUEUILLE, HENRI. Prime Minister of France, September–October 1948

RAMADIER, PAUL. Prime Minister of France, January 1947–November 1947

REALE, EUGENIO. One of leading officials of Communist Party of Italy

REUTER, ERNST. Former Communist who left that group and returned to the Social Democratic Party; had been elected Mayor of Berlin

RIDDLEBERGER, JAMES. State Department official

RIDGWAY, MATTHEW B. (GEN.). U.S. Army officer. Senior Army member, Military Staff Committee of United Nations, 1946–48

ROBERTSON, SIR BRIAN (GEN.). Deputy Military Governor of British zone of occupation in Germany. British representative on Control Council for Germany

ROOSEVELT, FRANKLIN D. President of the United States, 1933–45

ROYALL, KENNETH. Undersecretary of War, later Secretary of the Army

RUEFF, JACQUES. Official of French Treasury. President of the Interallied Reparation Agency

RUSK, DEAN. Assistant Secretary of State for United Nations Affairs

ST. LAURENT, LOUIS STEPHEN. Prime Minister of Canada

SCHUMACHER, KURT. Leader of Social Democratic Party in Germany

SCHUMAN, ROBERT. French statesman. Minister of France, Bidault Government, 1946, and Ramadier Government, January–November 1947. Prime Minister of France, November 1947–July 1948. Minister of Foreign Affairs, Marie Government, July 1948, Queuille Government, September 1948–49, Bidault Government, 1949

SEARLS, FRED. Adviser to Bernard Baruch on negotiations in U.N. about agreement to control atomic energy

SMITH, WALTER BEDELL (GEN.). U.S. Ambassador to the Soviet Union

SMYTH, HENRY DEWOLFE. Physicist. Member of the U.S. Atomic Energy Commission. Author of *Report on Atomic Energy for Military Purposes: The Official Report on the Development of the Atomic Bomb under the Auspices of the United States Government* (1945)

SNYDER, JOHN. Secretary of the Treasury in Truman Cabinet

SOKOLOVSKY, VASILI D. (MARSHAL). Soviet representative on Control Council for Germany

STALIN, JOSEPH. Chairman of the Council of Ministers, U.S.S.R.

STEINHARDT, LAURENCE. U.S. Ambassador to Soviet Union, later to Czechoslovakia

STETTINIUS, EDWARD R. U.S. Secretary of State, November 1944–June 1945. Head, U.S. delegation to meeting at San Francisco to formulate charter of United Nations, 1945

STIMSON, HENRY L. U.S. Secretary of War, January 1940–September 1945

STRANG, SIR WILLIAM. Undersecretary of State in British Foreign Office. British representative on European Advisory Commission

SWOPE, HERBERT BAYARD. Public relations adviser to Bernard Baruch on atomic energy policy

TAFT, ROBERT A. U.S. Senator (Republican) from Ohio.

THOREZ, MAURICE. One of top officials of Communist Party of France

TITO (JOSIP BROZ). Prime Minister of Yugoslavia, 1945–53; President, 1953–

TOGLIATTI, PALMIRO. Secretary of Communist Party of Italy

TRUMAN, HARRY S. President of the United States, 1945–52

TSALDARIS, CONSTANTINE. Head of Popular (pro-royalist) party in Greece. Prime Minister of Greece 1946–47. Deputy Prime Minister and foreign minister to September 1947

VANDENBERG, ARTHUR H. Senator from Michigan. Senior Republican member of Senate Foreign Relations Committee. Member of several American delegations to international conferences

VANDENBERG, HOYT S. (GEN.). Chief of Staff of U.S. Air Force April 1948

VAN KLEFFENS, EELCO. Ambassador of the Netherlands to the United States

VINSON, FRED M. Secretary of the Treasury. Justice of U.S. Supreme Court

VISHINSKY, ANDREI. Soviet jurist and diplomat. Permanent representative of Soviet Union to United Nations, 1946. Foreign Minister, March 1949

VON STUELPNAGEL, OTTO (GEN.). The Nazi commandant who had ruled over occupied France

WALLACE, HENRY A. Vice President under Roosevelt 1941–45. Secretary of Commerce in Truman Cabinet 1945–46

WEDEMEYER, ALBERT C. (GEN.). U.S. Army officer. Chief of Staff to Chiang Kai-shek and Commander of U.S. forces in China, 1944–46. Sent to China and Korea to make special survey of situation for President Truman, 1947

WEEKS, SIR RONALD (GEN.). British representative in negotiations with Marshal Zhukov in regard to zones of occupation and access to Berlin

WIGNER, EUGENE P. American physicist

WILSON, EDWIN. U.S. Ambassador to Turkey

WINANT, JOHN. U.S. Ambassador to Great Britain. American member of European Advisory Commission

WRONG, HUME. Canadian Ambassador to the U.S. Member of Committee for formulation and negotiation of NATO pact

ZHDANOV, ANDREI. Important member of Politburo of Soviet Communist Party

ZHUKOV, MARSHAL GEORGI. Commander in Chief of the Soviet armies on Eastern Front in Europe

ZORIN, VALERIAN. Deputy Commissar of Foreign Affairs of Soviet Union. Soviet manager of *coup d'état* in Czechoslovakia, 1948

PART ONE

History Grimaces

Mise-en-Scène

How History, in his dark and bloody lair, must have chuckled when listening to the avowals of the Allies at the end of the war against the Axis that henceforth they would remain friends! "How great is the evidence that national states cannot long live in comity," he muttered. "Humph! I shall be astounded if they do so now. Just look at the situation in which I've left them as they enter the postwar era. Still, it would not displease me if they should manage to surprise me by good and wise behavior."

The American people had long thought that there was no need, and no sense, in becoming involved in the quarrels between the countries of Europe. However, fear of the peril to their liberty and tranquillity, excitement over Japanese transgression in China, and hatred of the cruel baseness of Nazi Germany in 1941 had induced them to enter the wars in Europe and in the Pacific. That war was fought with their usual gusto and moral enthusiasm. When it was won there nested in the spirits of most Americans the belief that they had saved China, rescued the beleaguered European democracies and enabled the Russians to withstand, and presently conquer, the German invaders. They expected appreciation and cooperation in the service of their ideals which the war was deemed to have proved were best. They were hopeful that deference to personal liberty, political freedom, and self-government would spread to other lands. They had eagerly striven to give form to the conception of a new organization which might keep order and peace among the whole society of nations. Was it not natural for them to think that, after its great suffering, even the formerly self-enclosed, thrusting, suspicious Union of Socialist Soviet Republics would conform to the same rules of international conduct as the West?

The British people were proud of the way they had borne their ordeal, but greatly fatigued. They had the same desire as the Americans, that out of the blood and agony of the war a better world might be conceived. However, their statesmen had less hope that the Russians would curb their claims in Europe to keep the friendship of their allies; and greater doubts whether they would subordinate their will to any international association or rule of principle.

The French, bitter and vengeful against Germany, were too absorbed in their own grievances and still too shaken by their defeat to contribute to the creation of a new society. Many were repairing their pride by denying their debt to the British, disliking the Americans, admiring the Russians, and hating each other.

In great contrast to the American evaluation was that of the Soviet ruling authorities. In their retrospective view, the Western democracies, when Neville Chamberlain was the Prime Minister of Britain, had tried to turn the Nazi hatred and fury to the East against Russia. True, after the German attack, Churchill's Britain and Roosevelt's United States had given the Soviet Union enough essential economic and military supplies to enable it to continue to fight the Germans. Yet virtually all Soviet historians and propagandists were still repeating in unison that their Western Allies, even after entering the war, had willfully let the Soviet people bear for over two years the main brunt and suffering of the war before landing in France. Their patriotic publicists counted up the number of German divisions engaged on the Eastern and Western fronts and tended to belittle and, when in bad humor, to denigrate the great Western effort.[1] Thereby, they justified their claim to the right to extend their influence over adjoining territories in Europe and the Pacific, as protection for the Soviet Union against possible future assaults.

History, continuing his ruminations, might well have asked the winds of time: "Can these countries, with such different visions and opinions as I have allowed to shape in their hearts and minds, really settle their respective claims, adjust their respective visions, and maintain a lasting friendship?" To make this the more unlikely, on one lovely day in April 1945 he broke with the tip of his finger an artery in Franklin Roosevelt's brain.

---

[1] As one of thousands of instances of such expressed opinions, this excerpt from an article by D. Zaslavsky, circulated in its Information Bulletin by the Soviet Embassy on June 7, 1945, may serve: ". . . In 1941 the Germans hurled 170 divisions against the Soviet Union; in 1942, 240 divisions; and in 1943, 257 divisions—all of which perished under the hammer blows of the Red Army. In 1944, only after "super-total" mobilization, the Hitlerites were able to place 204 divisions on the Eastern front, leaving only 75 for the Western and Southern fronts. And when the Allies accomplished their march across France and had reached the borders of Germany, the Hitlerite command used its main forces in an attempt to check the advance of the Red Army. Even during the last months of the war the German command continued transferring troops from the West to the East, leaving the Western Front without a defense." This, of course, contains several misstatements of fact, as do all Soviet official statements on the subject.

To the Americans, their ability to raise, equip, and transport such great combat forces as they had and to provide Lend-Lease supplies to the allies was proof of the potentiality of the system of private capitalism and free enterprise. Our valor in combat was deemed proud proof of the vitality and capacity of the spirit of free men and women. Despite what the Russians did during the war, communism, in contrast, was judged to be an oppressive and less productive system.

In contrast, the way in which the Russian people bore the great suffering and strain of the most powerful German assaults was deemed by the Russian leaders evidence of their loyalty to the ideals and institutions of Communism, as well as proof of the firmness of the unity among the many different peoples grouped in the Soviet Union.[2] The performance, they thought, clearly demonstrated the great latent productivity of the Communist system. While mistrust and hostility of Western capitalism had been subdued during the war, the basic belief that by nature it must be rapacious and aggressive lingered deep in Soviet thought—ready to sprout and grow into hideous accusations when quarrels arose.

These differences sundered the bonds formed during the war. How, and in an operative sense why, we shall strive to tell. Our narrative will compass and comment on only the more crucial situations and actions in the swirling rapids of these years. In retrospect, some may be seen clearly as under a good student lamp; others still only dimly as in a marsh light. The historian must find his way as best he can with a lantern that leaves corners of this past in shadow and various explanations connoted by the available records, conjectural.

---

[2] It is significant that while elsewhere this war was known as the Second World War, the Soviet Government usually designated it as "The Great Patriotic War of 1941–1945," as in the published *Correspondence of Stalin with Churchill, Roosevelt, and Truman.* (Moscow: State Political Book Publishing House, 1957).

2

The Ordeal of Decision

The situations of which we shall tell were shaped, or misshaped, by the impact of many countries upon each other. The individuals cast by chance or destiny in roles of decision makers were constrained by circumstances, internal and external; and their responses were affected by impressions of the acts and intentions of others. Each in his own way, within the bounds of power and responsibility bestowed on him, went through the ordeal of decision.

In the United States the task of ultimate decision rests on the President. Let us, therefore, before entering upon the narrative, peer briefly into the chasm of decision in which all our presidents are compelled to plunge. In its depths each of them must ultimately walk alone, often unable, because of the murk over the land of decision, to see clearly the ground ahead.

Public opinion can inspire or frustrate a President. He can neither ignore nor yield supinely to it. He must be its judge, not its servant. Congress can prod, restrain him, or at times even reverse his decisions. Informants and advisers—particularly the Secretary of State and the heads of the armed forces—may propose and persuade. But when peace or war is at issue, the President cannot leave the decision to others without forfeiting the responsibilities of his office. Although the rod of fire may be passed about, in the end it comes back to him. As President Truman was fond of saying—pointing to his desk—"The buck stops here." The credit or blame is ultimately the President's.

Each decision is fateful; it cradles the next one or rocks its cradle. It is hard to abort or even change the seeded progeny of past decisions.

Let us recall how some earlier presidents bore their ordeal—Abraham Lincoln, Woodrow Wilson, and Franklin Roosevelt.

"Lincoln is a man of heart. Aye, as gentle as a woman's and as tender —but he has a will strong as iron." So spoke Herndon, the young law partner with whom Lincoln long shared his thoughts. That tender heart and iron will were flung into anguished encounter. After his election in 1860 he watched with dismay the movement toward secession. Friends during this interim thought him often to be walking in a troubled dream. To one he said, in Biblical parallel: "I see the duty devolving upon me. I have read upon my knees the story of Gethsemane. I am in the garden of Gethsemane now and my cup of bitterness is flowing over."

Before leaving his home in Springfield for Washington Lincoln had a vision which troubled him: while lying on his lounge in his law chambers he saw two separate images of himself in the long mirror opposite, one of the faces a little paler than the other. This, he thought, forebode tragedy for himself. But once in Washington and in control of the powers of the Presidency, he aroused himself. He got ready to meet the crisis of secession. But he continued to strive with the full force of his spirit to persuade the wavering states to stay within the Union. In his inaugural address that longing shaped his appeal: "I am loathe to close. We are not enemies but friends. We must not be enemies. Though passion may have strained, it must not break our bonds of affection."

The appeal failed; the dreaded war came closer. The crisis of decision came before he had been a month in office. After day-long discussion as to whether or not to relieve Federal forts which the Confederates were besieging or allow them to be seized in the hope that patience might soothe the South, he could not sleep. His judgment alone would have to guide, his soul would have to decide what would best serve and save his country. Within the next week his decision was made. Expeditions were prepared to relieve Fort Sumter. It was clear that if they were resisted —and it was almost certain that they would be—he would have to issue the call to arms. Most regretfully, he did.

During the four agonizing years that followed, he took the suffering of the war deep unto himself. His grief was borne in the certainty that he could have done nothing else than what he had done; that the choice before him and his fellow citizens was whether to . . . "Nobly serve or meanly lose the last, best hope on earth."

A half century later the same tormenting issue of peace and war came before Woodrow Wilson. His was a fighting Scotch–Irish nature. But since youth he had put it to school. To his instructed mind American entry into the First World War meant suffering, chaos, brutality all over the world. He was beset by a sense of the futility of war and the hazards of victory. But neither his mind nor his spirit allowed him to tolerate German victory.

His conclusions imposed upon him the need for ultimate decision.

After breaking diplomatic relations with Germany he fell ill and for the next ten days lived within his room, mostly alone, debating with himself. That evening (April 1, 1917) before he asked Congress to declare war, Frank Cobb, the famous editor of the *World*, was with him. Cobb later gave an account of the last pang of decision. "If there is any alternative, for God's sake, let's take it." But Wilson, rightly or wrongly, could see none. His anxiety was dominated by his determination that German arrogance must not be allowed to prevail and master Europe. In perspective that decision continues to command assent. But if the historian had any tears left in him, they would be shed because the two combatant sides did not reach a compromise and make peace *before* Wilson had to make this fateful decision. For that war deeply fractured Western European civilization, greatly weakened its physical constitution, killed many of its best young men, and depressed the spirit of the survivors.

The calamitous consequences of the First World War compelled another President, Franklin D. Roosevelt, to lurch once again in the dark and dreadful chasm of decision. Roosevelt concluded that we must support Britain through thick and thin at any risk. When early in 1941 he proposed to Congress that we extend essential Lend-Lease aid, he announced that it was the end of any attempt at appeasement ". . . The end of compromise with tyranny and the forces of oppression."

The struggle that tried that blithe spirit most was not within himself but with those who continued to oppose his decision to intervene. It was worst during the first half of that year. During that period he spent more time than usual in bed, and went to his office less often. His perceptive secretary made a diagnosis. "What he is suffering most of all is a case of sheer exasperation."

But Roosevelt's resilient spirit bore him up as with expert, and sometimes tortuous, political skill he pursued his determined purpose.

For him the anguish was not in the imminent war. It came later, when victory was in sight, with the ominous first signs of blight upon the possibility of agreements which could give lasting meaning to the war and victory.

President Harry S Truman, as I shall tell, bore his ordeal of decision with less trepidation than those who before him had to weigh the dreadful chances of war and peace. He did not look at them as long or as often, to the right and to the left, in front and behind. Despite his awareness that there was much to learn, he went forward with confidence, seeming seldom to waver. His assurance was perhaps at times a subconscious cover for insecurity. During the crucial first years he mistook rapidity of decision for firmness. He sometimes did not make enough effort to plumb the depths of the questions which crowded upon him. Later, as he learned the hazards of decision and the difficulty of making American aims effective, he tended to wait until his advisers formulated policies and proposed actions. Proudly, he came to conceive his part to be that of judge of others' opinions and suggestions, and to be an unfailingly reliable backer of the advisers and decisions which he approved. He did not seem to worry, and the strain of war did not deeply disturb the regular tenor of his life. But it may be surmised that at times ultimately he took release in faith—and perhaps, in a measure, in fatalism—reflecting, as had Lincoln: "I do the very best I know how—the very best I can; and I mean to keep doing so to the end. If the end brings me out all right, what is said against me won't amount to anything. If the end brings me out wrong, ten angels swearing I was right won't make any difference." [1]

President Truman kept this quotation in a leather portfolio upon his desk. It must still be left to later historians to discern in what respects the end brought him out right or wrong.[2]

---

[1] Lincoln, in response to the suggestion that he answer an attack made on him by the Committee on the Conduct of the War. Quoted in F. B. Carpenter, *Six Months at the White House With Abraham Lincoln* (Boston: Hurd and Houghton, 1866) pp. 258–9.

[2] In this connection a note I have preserved from a talk with President Truman on November 20, 1950, might be of interest. The period covered by this volume was over. The United States had been at war since the previous June. "[I] went to see President Truman in an effort to get him to tell what he felt and thought about the 'ordeal of decision' through which he was going (title of article sent to *New York Times* for magazine section). Two weeks before—through Ross [Press Secretary Charles Ross]—an engagement had been arranged for 11:15 A.M. I forgot the time, was careless, and turned up, to my consternation, at 3:15, bringing along two autographed copies of *The Road to Pearl Harbor* [a book I had just completed], one for him, one for Ross. I wrote a letter of apology and asked him for another chance and in a few days had a friendly response from him saying that he was finding the book of interest.

"The President stood up to greet me and directed me to the chair on the same side of the desk as his. He was in a pearl-gray suit, well cut, with white shirt and blue and white moiré bow tie, neat and pleasing tailoring, without easy drape. His eyes are better, bigger, more thoughtful in their setting than I had known. The chin and jaw are solid. His color alive, pink, perhaps slightly vivified by massage. His gestures and movement vigorous and decided and towards the quick. He had a small paunch—fine silk socks and shoes almost on the elegant side.

"We fell into talk at once. I explained to him how, in the doing of *The Road to Pearl Harbor*, my mind had been drawn to the subject of the article, and explained that in brief review I was trying to tell of the ordeal that Lincoln, Woodrow Wilson, and FDR had gone through. And other Presidents, he quickly added. Jefferson, who was almost flung from office, and Jackson.

"At Ross's suggestion I gave him a carbon copy of the article as it stood, expecting him to read bits and hand it back. But deliberately he read it through, page after page, commenting often—particularly on the part about Lincoln. 'Need never have been, never,' he said, picking up the lines in the text, 'if Buchanan had done what he should have. There was something failing in him, I don't know what.' 'Lack of guts,' Ross put in. The President agreed with a vigorous shake of the head and lift of the hand, and went on,

More awesome than the decisions that any of these predecessors had to make was one that faced John F. Kennedy. His was the strength to be able to face unblinkingly and courageously all possibilities. Harvard had developed his natural intelligence and fostered the habit of careful and painstaking analysis. His career and his experiences gave him assurance without overconfidence, assurance that enabled him to consider advice without being impressed by rank or uniform or august Senators. His youth gave him stamina.

Still, let us read again what his brother recalled of those hours of waiting to learn whether the Russian missile-carrying ships would stop at the quarantine barrier that had been set by us around the island of Cuba or whether they would have to be forcefully intercepted. "I think

---

'Hard to understand—he had great experience in public affairs—Ambassador to Russia —Secretary of State. Something lacking . . . hard.'

"Then a bit later, while still on the Lincoln part, 'Oh, the whole Civil War was in good part the result of the McCarthyism of the day, the wild demagoguery . . . why, in our parts of Missouri, my parents used to tell and half believe, Lincoln intended to force Negroes to social equality—the black and hated Negro-lover—the idea hung on in "Black Republicanism." You'll find the story and others like it in Polland's (?) *President and the Press.*'

"I tried by direct question to tell what he had thought and felt that weekend of June 25–27 [the outbreak of the Korean War], but was ineffective, and failed either to get him to go over the schedule of his movements or actions or thoughts—but some points of significance came out in his talk.

"1) He had felt the weight and threat of Soviet aggression steadily during his five years of office. Twice before he had stood up to it—come what might—when Communists were about to march into Trieste and when they were about to go after Iran; in that case he had 'laid down an ultimatum.'

"2) The Russians had not wanted, still did not want, to get into real war with us. They were not ready for it—for example, the difference in gauge in the railways of Western Europe would make it impossible to keep big armies along the Channel supplied; they could take Western Europe but not hold it, and knew it.

"3) He had first heard the news from Dean Acheson over the telephone—heard also that [Acheson] had already called for a special meeting of the Security Council of the U.N.

"4) [He] had, from the airfield, before starting back [from home in Independence] for Washington, telephoned not only Dean Acheson but Marshall, Bradley, Sherman.

"5) That the only real question on the eve of the 27th was not whether to act if we could, but could we act in time to save the Republic of Korea.

"I rose before he gave a signal. As he went a few steps to the door, he went back and got out of his desk a colored photo of Potsdam—self, Stalin, Churchill, and others. I asked about Stalin. 'I like him,' he began, 'but he is cruel, ruthless and in charge of a ruthless machine.'

"In all this, there was a subdued but still real note both of assurance and self-assurance; assurance that current U.S. policies were working out well; self-assurance about his judgment and willingness to act.

"He did not deny those passages in the article which said that the ordeal lurked for him day and night. But he did say that he dismissed his worries—turned them off. The closing lines of the article repeated Lincoln's statement that he did the best he could, etc. The President reverting to these, said, 'that's the way I feel too; I have these lines written out and keep them here'—the large, thick, tooled Italian leather portfolio on his desk, two inches thick with papers."

these few moments were the time of gravest concern for the President. Was the world on the brink of a holocaust? Was it our error? A mistake? Was there something further that should have been done? Or not done? His hand went up to his face and covered his mouth. He opened and closed his fists. His face seemed drawn. His eyes pained, almost gray. We stared at each other across the table. For a few fleeting seconds it was as though no one else was there and he was no longer the President." [3]

And then, after the news was received that the Russian ships had stopped dead in the water, "For a moment the world had stood still and now it was going around again."

But the conflict was still unresolved, the danger of war still imminent. While deciding how to respond to two quite divergent letters from Khrushchev, "He [President Kennedy] talked about Major Anderson [Major Rudolph Anderson, Jr., one of the pilots who had flown the photo reconnaissance missions over Cuba and had been shot down], and how it was always the brave and the best who die. The politicians and officials sit home pontificating about great principles and issues, make the decisions and dine with their wives and families, while the brave and young die. He talked about the miscalculations that lead to war. . . .

"He wanted to make sure that he had done everything in his power, everything conceivable, to prevent such a catastrophe. . . . The great tragedy was that if we erred, we erred not only for ourselves, our futures, our hopes, and our country but for the lives, futures, hopes and countries of those who had never been given an opportunity to play a role, to vote aye or nay to make themselves felt." [4]

And then, when the news finally came that Khrushchev accepted his proposal for the resolution of the crisis, "It was quite a different meeting from the night before. I went back to the White House and talked to the President for a long time. . . . As I was leaving, he said, making reference to Abraham Lincoln, 'This is the night I should go to the theater.' I said, 'If you go, I want to go with you.' As I closed the door, he was seated at the desk writing a letter to Mrs. Anderson . . ." [5]

[3] Robert F. Kennedy, *Thirteen Days: A Memoir of the Cuban Missile Crisis* (New York: W. W. Norton, 1969), pp. 69–70, 105–6.
[4] *Ibid.*
[5] *Ibid.*, p. 110.

PART TWO

What Was
To Be Done?

3

Truman Takes Over

Harry S Truman entered office April 12, 1945, un-
groomed and untutored. Little attention had been paid to the Vice-President. In casual mention Roosevelt had tended to disparage him. He had
not been asked to take part in conferences about foreign affairs, or
brought in touch with foreign statesmen and military leaders. Truman,
however, had not been offended by Roosevelt's disregard. He had not
complained or asked to be admitted into the inner circle of advisers. He
was not one to go looking for trouble.

Being so suddenly summoned to take over the Presidency, he was allowed very little time to reflect on the multiple hard questions that were
unsettled when Roosevelt died. Under the same sort of pressure as an
unprepared student suddenly called upon to take his final examination,
he had been compelled to "bone up" in haste the record of previous negotiations and accords about our international relations. Aides hurried
to put on his desk thick files on crucial current issues in all the hemi-
spheres. He studied them industriously.

Truman's initial response to all foreign problems was shaped by the
pledge he made to himself, the country, and the world—to carry on the
policies and the programs Roosevelt had advocated. He felt obligated to
carry out the international agreements and engagements into which
Roosevelt had entered. He adopted without question the principle of
unconditional surrender. He took up the project for forming an organization for international peace with more fervor and less doubt than the
sick Roosevelt may have had after the Yalta Conference.

Since some of the Rooseveltian policies were in a state of flux when
Truman took office, as for example those in regard to Germany, he had
striven to do his best rapidly to condense confusion into decision.

Since the phrasing of some of the agreements into which Roosevelt
had entered about postwar settlements, such as those about Poland and
the former German satellites, was vague or wrinkled, he had to turn to
Roosevelt's helpers for explication when the Russians argued over their
meaning, as will be shown. Their interpretations were more closely

fitted to American wishes than to admitted Russian understanding. Thus he quickly formed the impression that the Soviet refusal to accept our interpretations was dishonest. This conclusion animated his serious brush with the Soviet authorities. In April 1945, in his first talk with the Soviet Foreign Minister, Vyacheslav Mikhailovich Molotov, who was on his way to the U.N. Conference in San Francisco, he stated that he intended scrupulously to fulfill the international agreements into which the American Government had entered, all of them, and would expect the Soviet Government to do the same. Their dealings must be based on "the mutual observation of agreements" and not be, as he expressed it, "a one way street." He was soon to find out that this peremptory manner of speech did not cause the Soviet arguments to crumble.

Despite his inexperience, Truman did not seem to doubt that he could row the American oar well. To serve and support his diplomacy were the most powerful American armed forces in history, with a superb record of performance in Europe and the Far East, the great productive achievement of American industry and agriculture demonstrated enormous financial capacity, and in prospect, the stupendous achievement of our scientists, engineers, and industrial plants in producing the atomic bomb. Thus it could easily have seemed to him—as it had seemed to Woodrow Wilson and most Americans at the end of the First World War—that the United States would be able to decide what was done about most questions of primary concern to us. With this American strength to support him, with American energies to provide the lead toward a better world, and with knowledge that we would soon have awesome atomic weapons, he was not intimidated by the great Churchill or by Stalin, the dictator who had led Russia in the war.

He sometimes did not know what he did not know. This enabled him to simplify problems and decisions, and have fewer qualms and doubts in forming judgments and passing judgment.

Within the Circle of Decision

Truman sought to maintain the association with almost all of the persons whom Roosevelt had used as his chief diplomatic agents, among them Edward R. Stettinius, Jr., the Secretary of State. Stettinius was most presentable, but of mediocre mind and shallow—at a time when the world situation required a diplomat of greatest capability and when Truman most needed a skillful guide. Still, Truman might have left him in charge of our foreign policy—if the Vice-Presidency had not been vacant and Stettinius had not, therefore, been in line for the Presidency should he die. For whatever reasons, the President decided quickly to replace him as soon as practicable with someone else who had greater political experience and standing, James F. Byrnes.

While waiting to do so, he sent Stettinius out to San Francisco to head the American Delegation at the conference which met to write the Charter of the United Nations, opening at the end of April.

The hustle and bustle of talk during this long and huge conference over provisions of the Charter was better suited to Stettinius' talents than tough and exhausting negotiations about hotly contested issues in postwar settlements. Arguments in San Francisco were over hypothetical situations, not immediately urgent ones. There Stettinius achieved a general accord upon a Charter the provisions of which contemplated peaceful settlement of all disputes. But it was not a very hard job since the Charter accorded each of the permament members of the Security Council a veto over decisions of consequence. Few commentators at the time—or during the first season of rejoicing and applause—led by the American sponsors, emphasized that the dove of peace had clipped wings and therefore might not be able to fly in stormy weather. Or, to change the metaphor, that it would not be able to soothe the turbulence of nations, nor cause them to care more for peace and less for power. Acceptance of the Charter was obeisance to principles, but not conversion of all into disciples of those principles.

Byrnes had been Truman's colleague in the Senate, a member of the Supreme Court, and a helpful and close assistant to Roosevelt. Moreover, Byrnes had believed until the final turn in 1944 that Roosevelt favored him for Vice-President. But he accepted with good grace his displacement in favor of Truman. The former Senator and Justice was a skillful practitioner of the arts of conciliation and legislation, likable, diligent, self-assured. When Truman appointed him Secretary of State in July, just before they set off together for the Potsdam Conference, it is doubtful whether Truman realized that Byrnes expected to conduct American foreign relations without having to seek approval for any and all turns of decision made in the course of negotiation with foreign diplomats.

Harry L. Hopkins had been closest of all to Roosevelt. But he was mortally ill. After a trip to Moscow at Truman's behest, in May–June, in an effort to obtain from Stalin a more conclusive statement of his intentions and claims, he had been compelled by ill health to retire.

At the opposite end of the circuit of opinion, Truman maintained a close relation with Joseph E. Davies, a former Ambassador to the Soviet Union. Davies was disposed to explain every Russian demand, no matter how forward, on the ground that capitalist countries had caused the Soviet Union to feel a need for ample security; he regarded Stalin as a person of good will and fair intentions, who would respond fairly to generous treatment. Truman sent Davies to London before the Potsdam Conference to moderate Churchill's opposition to the Russians. Then he took Davies along with him to that Conference, where he was present at every plenary session and had the ear of Truman and Byrnes.

In contrast, Truman and Byrnes, during this crucial summer of 1945, paid little heed to the views of their Ambassador in Moscow, Averell Harriman. For by then he was advocating firmer resistance to Russian wishes, and urging that the American Government not give in to them unless the Russian Government was more regardful of our wishes. Byrnes thought Harriman, a liberal, to be prejudiced against him, and Harriman thought Byrnes set against his admission into the top circle of presidential advisers.

In this brief list of officials consulted by Truman about foreign affairs, two others should be included. One was Fred M. Vinson, Secretary of the Treasury. For that crony Truman had glowing admiration and trust, although Vinson was conservative and short-sighted, with little belief in new ideals of international cooperation.

Then there was William L. Clayton, the Assistant Secretary of State for Economic Affairs. His deftness as trader in international commerce had enabled him to amass many millions. His personal charm and friendly manner made it pleasant for others to follow his lead. His ideals and the conduct of international affairs conjoined with the ideals animating the United Nations. Yet until experience in office educated him, his comprehension of political behavior was poor. He was a dogmatic believer in the recuperative power of private enterprise and free international trade—for all societies and circumstances; these were his remedies for wars, and weaknesses and troubles caused by wars. Experience (and fear of Communism) was to convert him from a trader and dogmatist into a more knowledgable and flexible diplomat.

For the character, directness, and repute of elderly Henry L. Stimson, Secretary of State under Herbert Hoover, Secretary of War under Roosevelt, the President had respect and liking. But the President did not seek Stimson's views about current politico-economic matters or about strategy. The energies of an aging and very tired Stimson during the short period he served under Truman (April–September 1945) were concentrated on the culminating effort to create atomic weapons; and after their testing, upon decisions in regard to their use in the war against Japan; and at the very end, upon the ways of bringing this most destructive power under international control.

Very close to Stimson and active in all areas where diplomacy and arms met, was Assistant Secretary of War, John J. McCloy. A conservative corporation lawyer, he was unafraid of responsibility, clear-headed, and positive. By these qualities he acquired the lead in coagulating the diffuse and unstable views of the State, War, and Navy Departments into plans for the direction of the occupation of Italy, Germany, and Japan.

Among professional military men in Truman's inner circle, the influence of General George Catlett Marshall, first as Chief of Staff of the Army, later as Secretary of State, and still later as Secretary of Defense, was supreme. Truman regarded him as the greatest military strategist of our time, the most capable and stalwart director of our foreign policies. He looked uncritically to Marshall for guidance and decision, seldom questioned his opinions, and still more seldom acted contrary to his recommendations. Truman never attributed fault or failure to him. Conjointly, Marshall's prestige in Congress and the country was helpful to the "upstart" President. Marshall's self-assurance gave him confidence. And crucially, despite his earlier fumbling mistakes, Marshall's support enabled Truman to secure and hold the consent of Congress and the American people to the connected series of acts and treaties that allied us closely with Western Europe. Of all this, much more later.

Close to the President's side, as the President's representative on the Joint Chiefs of Staff, was retired Admiral William D. Leahy, former Ambassador to Vichy France (who had gotten on well enough with Marshal Henri Philippe Pétain and prejudiced Roosevelt against General Charles de Gaulle). He took the standard salt-water admiral's view of foreign situations and movements; and like so many retired top admirals, was cranky.

These were the men to whom Truman, while he was becoming aware of the many decomposed situations which the diplomats had inherited from the victorious generals, looked for help and advice. Diffident rather than wavering during this crucial period of initiation, he readily adopted the views and policies suggested in the "position papers" prepared by the various departments. Being stubborn, once he had been led to adopt an opinion of a situation or policy, he seldom reconsidered it.

It is essential to an understanding of the period during which Truman was in office, and of his performance in office, to recall—with brief analytical comment—several of the main agreements about postwar settlements which had been made before he took office. For on these much of the acrimony which was to divide the Allies was to swirl.

19

4

The Porous Accords: Poland

While the war in Europe was still being fought, the Allies had subscribed to several accords. These were loosely stitched fabrications rather than sturdily woven compromises. They were porous; arguments about their meaning could seep through them without coming up against ledges of indisputable and conclusive language. Hence, as soon as difference of purpose and power arose between the Western Allies and the Soviet Union, partisans could the more easily contend that their country was observing an accord, and its adversary was not. Thus accusations of bad faith and deception gradually clustered about them —the barnacles of diplomacy. These scratched away the varnish of trust.

To explain the genesis of the disputes that arose, it is well to recall, albeit briefly, the main features of three accords.

The Declaration on Liberated Europe

One had been conceived at the Yalta Conference in February 1945, to avert rivalries and quarrels over the nature of the governments of some of the Axis satellites from which German forces had been or were being expelled. This was the Declaration on Liberated Europe.

Churchill, veteran student of Continental policies and alliances, had little faith in the potency of principles to determine the treatment of the territories in eastern and central Europe from which the enemy was being expelled. So when in Moscow in October 1944, he had entered into an informal agreement with Stalin about the allocation between Great Britain and Russia of spheres and proportions of "predominance" in the direction of the affairs of the various countries which were being "liberated"—Romania, Yugoslavia, Bulgaria, Hungary, and Greece. He had thought this advisable to avert confusion and clashes; and the best way to assure that the West would have some influence in the region after the Red armies were in occupation.

To Cordell Hull, this rough and ready "split" had seemed a reversion to worn-out practices and a threat to a just and peaceful future; and his fervent objections had caused Roosevelt to limit the time span of a previous arrangement of the sort which Churchill and Stalin had contemplated. But by October 1944, Hull had retired and Roosevelt had adopted a noncommittal stance. For he tended to regard the decisions about Balkan affairs as lying between Britain and Russia and wanted the American Government to keep clear of them. The State Department had retained an attitude of critical reserve toward any and all "spheres of influence" arrangements—reposing its hope and faith in the powers of the future United Nations to avert or settle all disputes.

As the American–British authorities had extended their control over the sections of Italy from which the armies were being driven, they dealt offhandedly with the Russian Mission which was assigned to a presumptive Advisory Council. While still engaged in a tough fight and beset by the need to create stable political order and to alleviate distress, they did not dare to allow the Russians to encourage the Italian Communists, and perhaps embolden them to start a revolution in the North.

The Soviet Government, as its armies gained ground in central and southeastern Europe, was going to cite the Western management of Italian affairs as precedent for its actions. It rejected the contentions of critics that while Western control over Italy would be soon relinquished, Russian Communist domination of countries that came within their grasp would be lasting.

Roosevelt and his advisers had set out for the Yalta Conference in February 1945, with minds bedazzled by the prospectus for the United Nations organization. But they were beginning to worry lest it should be expected to maintain boundaries and regimes formed by might, not right; by power politics, not principles.

The studies in the Briefing Book composed by the State Department, which was taken to Yalta, had marked the onset of anxiety lest the chance of fostering democratic, independent governments in countries bordering on Russia be lost. For wherever the Russian armies went, regimes submissive to Communist control were favored; and resistance to them was construed as a mark of hostility to the Soviet Union.

As an antidote Roosevelt had sought another Joint Declaration. Its high-sounding language could be construed as obligating the three signatory governments *jointly to assist* the peoples in any of these "liberated" states to solve, by democratic means, their pressing economic and political problems; and to form interim representative administrations pledged to establish by free elections governments responsive to the will of the people.[1] So the text was interpreted by American authorities. But how was this to be done? The Declaration stipulated merely, "When, in the opinion of the three governments conditions . . . make such action necessary" they would consult at once on the measures needed to discharge these responsibilities. This left the effectuation of the accord subject to the future inclination of each.

Why did Stalin subscribe to this Declaration? One often-repeated explanation is that he could and did do so with honest intention, because his conception of the nature and meaning of its provisions was different from that of a Western statesman—he had a different conception of "representative government," "democratic parties," and "free elections." This is not convincing.

Those scrutineers of the sayings and doings of the Russian Government—called Kremlinologists—offer other diverse explanations or conjectures. Perhaps Stalin reckoned that when the time came and the Red army was in occupation of the countries bordering Russia, he could interpret the lofty language in any way that served his purpose, without effective reprisals? Perhaps he believed that despite their professions of belief in these principles, the Western Allies would also take advantage of their flexibility—as they had in Italy.

Or—and this is a likely surmise—perhaps the Soviet rulers expected that the majority of the people in these "liberated" countries—the masses of workers and peasants—would welcome the Soviet officials as "liberators" and be so grateful to and admiring of the Russian state and the Communist cause that they would freely form governments companionate to Moscow.

It is even harder in retrospect to explain why Americans in authority reposed as much faith as they did in the potency of this Declaration, or why they professed to do so. Was this merely because they appraised it through the gauze of their wishes? Or because it was the most satisfactory accord, the clearest restraining promise that the Russians would give?

In any event, as we shall see, the insistence of the Western governments that the Russians honor the principles and procedures they had tried to enshrine in this Declaration was to engender ill will, without bringing satisfaction.

---

[1] To quote text, the three Heads of Government affirmed ". . . their mutual agreement to concert during the temporary period of instability in liberated Europe the policies of their three governments in assisting the peoples liberated from the domination of Nazi Germany and the peoples of the former Axis satellite states of Europe to solve by democratic means their pressing political and economic problems."

The Accord About Poland

On the marble spire of the Polish Military Cemetery at Monte Cassino philosophers of the vagaries of war and politics can reflect on this inscription:

> We Polish soldiers
> For our freedom and yours
> Have given our souls to God
> Our bodies to the soil of Italy
> And our hearts to Poland

The future and fate of Poland were of genuine and deep concern to the British and American Governments. Of all the ploys by which the Soviet Government brought its neighbors into subjection, Stalin's distortion of promises given regarding Poland was to hurt the most. That left a black and blue mark upon relations between Russia and the West that would not fade.

It had been to honor its guarantee to defend Poland that Great Britain had gone to war. The Government had, even in its darkest hour, continued to aver that the resurrection of Poland, which had been divided between Nazi Germany and the Soviet Union, was one of its prime war aims. Polish fliers had been among the brave repulsers of the German air attacks on Britain in the crucial period of 1940; and Polish soldiers had fought valiantly in Italy, the Middle East, and France. Connectedly, the British Government felt an obligation to be loyal to the Polish Government-in-Exile to which it had given refuge. To be asked to abandon it seemed to most Britons not only unfair but base.

The American Government was not tied to Poland by as strong bonds of common cause and experience. But other strands moved it to uphold the independence of Poland and the tenure of the Polish Government-in-Exile. Most Poles were Orthodox Catholics and the Catholic clergy in the United States cherished the connection and the flock. Also millions of Americans of Polish origin were excitedly intent on the restoration of Polish independence, and had deep personal, or transmitted memories of Russian oppression of their former home. Thus the cause of Poland was popular. The strategists and combat commanders valued Poland as a weight in the balance of power. Polish plains stretched East and West.

These reasons, as well as devotion to principle, had impelled the American Government to make a sustained—tense and tenacious—

23

WHAT WAS TO BE DONE?

diplomatic attempt before Yalta to assure that the Poles would be genuinely free to live their own lives and form their own attachments.[2]

As one immediate reward for entering into an agreement with Hitler in 1939, the Soviet Union, it will be recalled, had taken in the large Eastern portion of what had been Poland.

The Russian rulers were aware that the Polish prewar government had feared and disliked Russia. They regarded the Polish Government-in-Exile as a dangerous opponent of both Russia and Communism, and some of its leading personalities so reactionary and hostile that they were scheming to reclaim their lost territory and more from Russia, which they expected would be exhausted by the war. And so Moscow had taken steps to supplant the Government-in-Exile with a subservient one. It had founded in April 1943 the Union of Polish Patriots as a rival government, and almost concurrently severed its relations with the Polish Government-in-Exile—explaining its action by the espousal of this Polish Government of an inquiry by the International Red Cross about the unexplained disappearance of thousands of Polish officers known to have been in territory captured from the Nazis by the Russians. Next, in July 1944, as the Red army was advancing into Polish territory, the Soviet Government had entrusted a Communist-dominated "Committee on National Liberation," which had been formed behind the Russian lines at Lublin, with the administration of all liberated Polish territory (and subsequently with a portion of Germany that was to have remained in the Soviet zone of occupation).

The discussions between the Western Allies and the Soviet Union during this period centered on two main questions: What were Poland's boundaries to be and who would govern liberated Poland?

Churchill had tried hard to get the Polish Government-in-Exile to agree in principle to Stalin's territorial proposals; that Russia retain the large eastern parts of Poland it had absorbed and that Poland be compensated in the West by acquiring German territory. Roosevelt had striven to remain uncommitted before the elections of 1944.

This, summarily sketched, had been the diplomatic setting of the discussions at the Yalta Conference. By this time the question of Poland's frontiers had become more jagged, for the Soviet Government was claiming for the Poles areas of Germany greater than the British and American Governments had anticipated, or thought justified or wise.

---

[2] Since those efforts to check the stern and inflexible advance of Communist control over Poland have been recounted in many histories and articles, I shall not here go over this much-trampled ground again. See Herbert Feis, *Churchill, Roosevelt, Stalin: The War They Waged and the Peace They Sought* (Princeton: Princeton University Press, 1957).

Equally intense was argument with Stalin over what the government of Poland was to be. Churchill had earnestly and eloquently defended the Government-in-Exile, and contended that the Lublin (Communist) Government must be replaced by one more broadly representative of all Polish political parties. Roosevelt had pleaded with Stalin to accept some such arrangement. He had promised that if he would, the American Government would transfer recognition from the Polish Government in London to the new one. Stalin and Molotov contended that the Lublin Government must continue to rule in Poland. As a gesture of compromise, he was willing to agree that it might grant important offices to a few representatives of other parties.

Roosevelt had indicated he might accept this proposal on condition that it was agreed that there should be "free" elections in Poland as soon as possible. Stalin and Molotov had thereupon averred that his anxiety was excessive because their mutual differences concerned the composition of the government only *during the short period before the whole of Poland was liberated and general elections could be held.* How long, the President had asked Stalin on February 8, 1945, at Yalta, did he think the interval would be? Stalin's answer was: "In about one month unless there is a catastrophe on the front and the Germans defeat us." Adding with a grin, "I do not think this will happen." [3]

Roosevelt had tried to get Stalin to accept a formula which read: "That the present Polish Provisional Government be reorganized into a fully representative government based on all democratic forces in Poland and including democratic leaders from Poland abroad . . ." But he and Churchill had given their resigned consent to one that was much less conclusive: "The Provisional Government which is now functioning in Poland should therefore be reorganized on a broader democratic basis with the inclusion of democratic leaders from Poland itself and from Poles abroad. . . ." [4]

Thus the lineaments of the reorganization and the genuineness of the share of power to be granted to members of non-Communist groups had been undetermined. Stalin's insistent demand that the Lublin Government should be "the basis," the "kernel," the "nucleus" (all expressions were used) prevailed. Although the American Government was later to argue to the contrary, I believe that Roosevelt understood that the Communists would retain dominant authority—until the Lublin Government might be replaced by one chosen by the Poles in free elections.

In the light of what happened later it is natural to wonder, as George Kennan does in his Memoirs, how Churchill and Roosevelt could have

[3] *Ibid.*
[4] *Ibid.*

believed that the Communist-controlled Provisional Polish Government would permit other Polish elements, as a result of elections, possibly to acquire power and perhaps oust it. Or that the Soviet Government would permit this to happen, as it thought back to Polish policy before the war and the German invasions through Poland.

They, I believe, were not really trusting. But, the Red army was in occupation of Poland, and its agent, the Lublin Government, with Soviet tanks in front and behind, was exercising authority throughout the country. The alternative—a major confrontation with the Soviet Government while the war with Germany was still being fought—was dismaying to both the Western military and diplomatic leaders.

To the Western allied troops engaged in combat, the push of the Soviet armies provided sustaining hope that the struggle would soon be won, their lives preserved, and their quick return home assured. Were they to be kept on in the bleak plains of Central Europe, stand entrenched against the Red armies, for the sake of Poland?

Besides these cautionary considerations, conceptions were current that made the differences over Poland seem transient and secondary. Should they be allowed to abort the birth of the new international organization of nations which, it was conceived, would in time reconcile conflicting national claims and political dogmas?

To venture a most summary verdict, I think it would have been better to risk a break with Stalin at Yalta. But even Churchill, although distressed and angered, did not then dare to do so. Roosevelt, sick and near exhaustion, was clinging to the hope that if the Soviet Government was reasonably satisfied, it would be a well-behaved associate of the Western Powers for the maintenance of enduring peace. Thus they had balked at the possibility of leaving a deep gash in the lines of alliance while the war was still being fought. But I think that if they had taken that risk, Stalin would have given in slightly about Poland.

5

The Porous Accords: Germany

More crucial still were the consequences of the two accords about German affairs.

About Occupation Zones in Germany

The first accord delineated the respective zones that each of the four
Allies was to occupy in Germany and the sectors in divided Berlin. The
tale of the conception of this determinant accord should not be scanted.

Well before the war had been won, a zonal system of occupation had
been conceived. Proposals for the combined unitary, multinational administration for the whole of Germany had been discarded as unworkable. Sufficient coordination could be achieved, it was thought, if the
zonal authorities of each occupying power were directed to pursue the
same policies in all but local matters.

The planners of the invasion of Normandy had thought it advisable,
foresighted, and useful to fix zonal boundaries before that operation was
well under way: advisable, since it would lessen the temptation to warp
military moves in order to secure future political advantage; foresighted,
in order to avert confusion and encounters between forces advancing
from opposite directions; and useful, in treatment of civilian populations. In short, the zonal divisions were regarded as temporary arrangements of convenience.

The accord made about zonal boundaries had been affected by three
anticipations which turned out to be wrong.

Its Western sponsors misjudged where in Germany the armies of the
Western Allies and the Soviet Union would be when the war ended.

They did not foresee how drastically the West and the Soviet Union
would differ about the unsettled situations in Europe or that the positions of armies and pulsations of power and ideologies would separate
them in Germany.

They chose Berlin, deep within the zone to be assigned to the Soviet Union, as the center of the Allied Control Authority for the whole of Germany, the city to be divided into national sectors. High school juniors with a history book, a map, and a set of toy soldiers could have devised a better arrangement.

In its consideration of zonal boundaries, the American Government stuttered and stumbled.

In late 1943 the efforts of the Chief of Staff of the presumptive Supreme Commander (COSSAC) residing in London, headed by a British General (Sir Frederick Morgan), was drawing up the comprehensive plans for the invasion of the Continent. While it was at work, a Committee of the British War Cabinet, chaired by Clement Attlee, Churchill's deputy, had begun to consider arrangements for the occupation of Germany. It had to make some assumptions about probabilities. One that influenced the Committee, as recalled by Gladwyn Jebb (who was then head of the Economic and Reconstruction Department of the Foreign Office) was ". . . that there was absolutely no guarantee that Germany might not succumb to the Russians before she was 'knocked out' by a Cross-Channel blow—the success of which could not be guaranteed. It therefore seemed desirable to work out a plan whereby Germany would be divided into three zones equal from the point of view of population; for if by an ill chance we ourselves never got any further than say, the Rhine, we would at least have strong legal arguments for pushing the Russians from the west toward the east of Germany. . . ." [1]

The division proposed by this Committee assigned the northwest section of Germany, including the Ruhr area and the ports of Bremen and Hamburg, to the British forces; the southwest section to the Americans; and the rest of Germany to the Russians—except Berlin, which was to be jointly occupied. The Russian zone would comprise about 40 percent of German territory and a third of the German people. The zones demarcated in this plan did not converge at any central points; the boundaries followed those of the German states, except that Prussia was divided between British and Soviet zones.

The British Cabinet approved this scheme. General Morgan had given a copy to General Marshall. He and other members of the American Joint Chiefs of Staff had discussed it with President Roosevelt while en route on the U.S.S. *Iowa* to the Conference at Teheran in November 1943. The President had assented to the basic conception of zonal divi-

[1] H. M. Gladwyn Jebb (now Lord Gladwyn), *Halfway to 1984* (New York: Columbia University Press, 1966), pp. 9–10.

sions.[2] But he had been displeased by the British plan, believing that it had been shaped by political rather than by military calculations.[3] He wanted American forces to be in the northwest zone, not the southwestern one. For if in the south, they would be dependent on movement of supplies through French ports, and he thought France might be in turmoil when the war ended. While if they were in the northwest, "We can get out ships into such ports as Bremen and Hamburg, also Norway and Denmark and we should go as far as Berlin. . . . the United States should have Berlin." [4]

General Marshall and Admiral Ernest J. King had pointed out that if the proposed zonal positions were reversed, as the President wanted, military dispositions and plans would have to be changed. For the British divisions were assigned to the left, the northern sector of the combined drive through France and Germany and the American divisions to the right, the southern sections of the front. The President did not think the relocation of forces, either before or after the fighting was over, would be too hard. Moreover, he said that he thought that the northwest zone should be extended eastward to include Berlin, and that "We may have to put the United States divisions in Berlin as soon as possible." [5] On a handy small map he had marked out an alternative zonal division into three large wedges. The American zone was to be enlarged and to be in the northwest of Germany; its eastern boundary line was to run through or very close to Berlin and then on to Stettin.[6] (See map, page 30.)

[2] To the best of my knowledge the only senior American officer, military or civil, who objected to the plan for dividing Germany into zones of occupation was General Dwight Eisenhower. When he visited Washington in January 1944, shortly before he assumed the post of Supreme Commander, he told Roosevelt that he thought it wise to attempt a joint occupation of the entire undivided Germany, through the administration in which American, British and Russian officials would be associated. He thought this practicable, and that in any case it would quickly test the possibilities of continuing the wartime alliance. As told by Stephen E. Ambrose in *Eisenhower and Berlin, 1945* (New York, W. W. Norton, 1967), pp. 41–2. Roosevelt, who did not even want the Combined Chiefs of Staff (U.S.–British) to be maintained after the war, was not persuaded, or, apparently, even interested.

[3] *Foreign Relations of the United States. The Conferences at Cairo and Teheran*, pp. 253 ff.

[4] *Ibid.*

[5] William L. Franklin, "Zonal Boundaries and Access to Berlin," in *World Politics*, October 1963.

[6] The map with Roosevelt's markings and initials was taken by Marshall to Washington and turned over to General Thomas T. Handy, Marshall's deputy on the Joint Chiefs of Staff. Where thereafter, within the Pentagon, it rested in neglect is still not known. The map is reproduced in one of the studies published by the Government Printing Office, *Strategic Planning for Coalition Warfare, 1943–1944*, by Maurice Matloff and E. M. Snell, p. 341.

Cornelius Ryan in his book *The Last Battle*, pp. 147–48, gives a detailed account of the discussions between Roosevelt and the Joint Chiefs of Staff on board

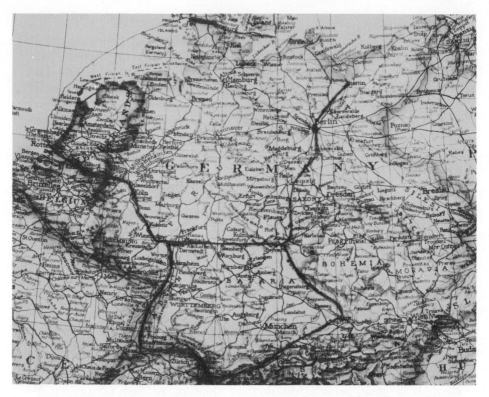

Shortly thereafter, the American Joint Chiefs of Staff had given the British Chiefs of Staff a plan drawn roughly in accord with Roosevelt's ideas, though it did not include Berlin in the American zone. When General Morgan and his aides at COSSAC read this paper, they were upset.

For reasons not of record, when Roosevelt met with Churchill and Stalin at Teheran, he had not pursued the question of zonal allocations.

---

the U.S.S. *Iowa*. In a footnote on page 148 he writes, "The account of events aboard the *Iowa* comes from handwritten minutes which were made by General George C. Marshall. The actual memo (in which the Joint Chiefs asked for guidance on Morgan's revised plan) contains no direct quotes, only notes made on points of reference. I have directly quoted the President and others where it was clearly indicated that a sentence was being attributed to them."

I have tried to identify and procure the source of Ryan's account. Dr. Forrest C. Pogue, who is completing the official biography of General Marshall, has informed me that the inquiries he made of the historical section of the Department of the Army and the Military Records Center in Alexandria led him to the conclusion that the only notes which exist in Marshall's handwriting were a few lines in the Executive File containing General Handy's report and that these few lines consist only of points in a boundary. Moreover, Pogue informs me that although Mr. Ryan promised to send him a Xerox copy of Marshall's notes, he has never done so.

I requested Mr. Thomas Hohmann of the National Archives to permit me to consult the Executive File, but have received no reply.

30

But the three had agreed to ask the European Advisory Commission to develop plans of occupation. It was to meet in London. The British Government selected Sir William Strang of the Foreign Office as its representative. The American and Soviet Governments, their Ambassadors to the United Kingdom, John G. Winant, and F. T. Gusev.

At the first meeting of this Commission (EAC) on January 14, 1944, Strang had presented a scheme essentially the same as the one which the President had rejected.

The location of the dividing boundaries between the Western and Soviet zones reflected Churchill's pessimistic misjudgment of the prospects of advance of the Allied force that was to land in Normandy. He feared grim holdups and did not foresee the rapid progress of the armies commanded by Eisenhower.[7]

Winant, who had not been informed of Roosevelt's ideas, or of the fact that the British and American Chiefs of Staff were acquainted with them, had been mute. About a month later Gusev had submitted a scheme in which the lines of division between Western and Soviet zones was the same as those in the scheme submitted by Strang, except that Gusev's included all of East Prussia in the Soviet zone. Gusev explained that the Soviet Government was willing to have the British and the Americans decide between themselves which was to have the northwest and which the southern zone.

The British and Soviet proposals had been sent on by Winant to Washington. But they had evoked neither response nor instruction. For at this time (early 1944) the views of different divisions of the State Department were so dispersed and divergent that it could not provide guidance to Winant. Hull was ill and unwilling to face up to any of the hard unsettled situations of Europe; Stettinius, the Undersecretary, was scatterbrained. Moreover, the Civil Affairs Division of the War Department had resented and opposed State Department "interference" in the question of zones, since it regarded this as a military matter.

As for Roosevelt—when the State Department had sent word informing him that the British and Russians had reached an agreement on zones, he was surprised. He sent a query to Acting Secretary of State Stettinius, "What are the zones in the British and Russian drafts and what is the zone we are proposing? I must know this in order that it conform to what I decided on months ago." [8]

The State Department, in ignorance of the plan which Roosevelt had

[7] This is attested in various accounts, the most recent of which to come to my attention is the article by Cyrus Sulzberger in *The New York Times* of June 6, 1969, largely derived from conversations with Eisenhower.

[8] Quoted in Ambrose, *Eisenhower and Berlin*, p. 39.

sketched out on the way to Teheran, had not been able to make the comparison; and it did not seek elucidation at the White House. In any event, the President seems to have let the main questions of the arrangement and location of zonal boundaries slip from his mind; or perhaps Marshall persuaded him not to pursue it.

But he remained set against acceptance of the southern zone. He thought the American Government would be burdened with the task of reconstituting France, Belgium, Italy and the Balkans; that was, he thought, Britain's responsibility. In a jocular mood he had wired Churchill on February 29, 1944, "I denounce in protest the paternity of Belgium, France and Italy. You really ought to bring up and discipline your own children. In view of the fact that they may be your bulwark in future days, you should at least pay for their schooling now." [9]

Then, out of the blue, a hint having most tardily percolated from somewhere, members of the Civil Affairs Division of the War Department had begun to advocate that Winant be instructed to get the EAC to put aside the British-Soviet proposals and secure approval for the much different scheme of division which Roosevelt had outlined. Under a covering letter there was sent to Winant on March 8th a paper which was merely a copy of a memo which the U.S. Chiefs of Staff had presented to the British Chiefs of Staff at the Cairo Conference the previous December. [10]

Two State Department officers, James Riddleberger and H. Freeman Matthews, who were concerned with German affairs, had asked General John Hilldring, head of the Civil Affairs Division in the War Department, to accompany the paper with a brief explanation, substantiating the plan. But the Civil Affairs Division had been unwilling. A reason may be surmised; this ancillary branch of the Army General Staff did not want to risk presidential wrath by ignoring Roosevelt's views; but it was loathe to incur the wrath of Marshall and other members of the Joint Chiefs by seeming to sponsor the plan.

Winant had been even more perplexed than usual. He had concluded that it would not be advisable to introduce this upsetting plan into the EAC so late, the invasion being so imminent. [11] He was afraid of arous-

---

[9] *Ibid.*

[10] Franklin, "Zonal Boundaries."

[11] When Robert Murphy, Political Adviser to Eisenhower, had raised the question with him, Winant said: "You have no right to come along at this late date and make such a proposal after we have agreed upon a draft." Winant thought it would disturb the whole accord on zonal occupation, prevent other agreements, and intensify Russian mistrust. Franklin M. Davis, Jr., *Come as a Conqueror: The U.S. Army's Occupation of Germany, 1945–1949* (New York: Macmillan, 1967), p. 87.

ing Russian displeasure at this juncture. So, uneasily, he had bumbled along, tensely tugging at his knuckles under the table at EAC meetings till one was disjointed.

He had asked George Kennan, the Counsellor of the American Embassy, who deputized for him on the EAC, to go to Washington and explain to the President the rumble that would be caused if the American Government insisted on its plan of zonal division. On doing so Kennan pointed out various objections to the geographic division the President had favored. By then the advance of the Russian forces from the East had so much momentum it is probable that the Soviet Government would have rejected the revised plan of triangulation.

The President had given way to the pleas of his advisers "not to rock the boat." On May 1st an instruction, approved by both the President and the Joint Chiefs, had been sent to Winant authorizing him to accept the boundaries between Soviet and Western zones on which the Russians and the British had agreed. When Winant visited Washington soon thereafter, Roosevelt had confirmed his acceptance of that line.

The Ambassador, accordingly, at the next EAC meeting in June had so stated. The Committee left the question of whether the British or the Americans were to have the northwestern zone for Roosevelt and Churchill to decide. When they met at Quebec in September, Roosevelt gave in. He consented to having the British in the North after Churchill agreed that the Americans should have control of the port area of Bremen and Bremerhaven, and have free access to these ports through the British zone.

The EAC arrangement was confirmed at the Yalta Conference. There Stalin gave grudging assent to the American and British wish to grant France a zone, provided it was formed out of the Western zones. A refusal would have been in defiance of geography and an insulting denial of the aspiration of France to have its suffering, its service, and its grandeur recognized. None of the three arbiters seemed to have realized that in doing so they were giving France, so wounded in body and spirit, the chance to thwart their program for control of Germany unless it got what it wanted.

The Russian armies had gone forward so far and so fast that by then they were only about thirty-five miles from Berlin. Yet the Soviet staff feared that the Germans would mass almost all their forces against them to protect Berlin. Since Roosevelt and Churchill were eager to have the Red army resume its assault, and Stalin wished the West to hurry on with its offensive, they did not chaffer over the boundaries of postwar occupation zones.[12] The wish to complete the defeat of Germany, as soon and with as little unnecessary loss of life, was paramount.

Thus the geographic realms within Germany over which, respectively, the Western Allies and the Soviet Union were going to be able to exercise decisive power were, by guess and misguess, determined. But at the end of the war, to repeat, all the Allies, including Russia, regarded them as useful markers of the bounds within which each would have the authority and responsibility for effectuating common policies for the whole of Germany.

Berlin was encapsulated in these zonal plans for Germany, but how is best kept in escrow until we travel to the time when the rights of access from the Western zone to Berlin were denied and Berlin was blockaded (see Part Nine).

[12] As latter affirmed by Eisenhower, "This future division of Germany did not influence our military plans for the final conquest of the country." Dwight D. Eisenhower, *Crusade in Europe* (New York: Doubleday, 1948), p. 396.

6

The Agreement on German
Occupation Policies

Until the war was nearly over Roosevelt and Stalin had inclined toward partitioning Germany into several independent states. This was one of the notions which had caused American advanced planning to wobble.

How deal with a nation so formidable, so domineering and brutal when aroused, so responsive to vicious leadership? So many Germans had blood on their hands, evil in the depths of their spirits! The prevailing wish to punish and suppress did battle with the view that policy, though strict, should be quieting and corrective. Determination that Germany should never again be strong enough to start a war had to be reconciled with the wish that it be self-supporting and peacefully busy. The plan devised had to be acceptable to all three (or four) of the powers who were going to share in the occupation of the country, each with its own memories, fears, interests, and ideals.

So hard a task would have taxed the talents of a Solon, and there was none among the policy makers of Washington—or London—or Moscow.

Neither the Secretary of State, Cordell Hull, nor his successor, Edward R. Stettinius, Jr., had given clear guidance to their plagued staffs. William L. Clayton, Assistant Secretary of State in charge of economic affairs, had clung to his simplicities of doctrine amid the ruins. Henry Morgenthau's counsel (that German basic industries be abandoned and the country forced to become mainly a producer of food and raw materials) was still potent, Stimson dissenting, because of worry lest the army be required to carry out a policy that went against the grain. Thus, within the American Government the task was shuttled around by committees and subcommittees who strove to condense and stabilize the protean ideas of their members.

Out of the swirl of interdepartmental memos, Assistant Secretary of War, John J. McCloy, the positive-minded and prudent lawyer, had managed to compound a Directive for Eisenhower. This, No. 1067, had been sent to the Supreme Commander of the Allied Expeditionary Force, General Dwight D. Eisenhower, on April 26, 1945. It had borne the impress of the drastic program that had originated in the Treasury.

The American and British military commanders and presumptive staff members of military governments in Germany had been busy during the sixty-day interval between the German surrender and the Potsdam Conference installing themselves and arranging for the transfer of most of their troops, either for home or the Pacific. Except to set about eradicating all Nazi and military formations, and revoking all laws derived from Nazi doctrines, the Western occupants in this formative interval (May–July 1945) had not undertaken to change the basic character of German life and society.

In the Eastern zone the Russians had at once begun to impose economic, political, and social changes, and to seize German stores of goods and machines as reparations.

Almost certainly Stalin and his Bolshevik company had hoped that the beaten and disillusioned German masses in *all* of Germany, not merely those in the Eastern zone, might, in the chaos and distress, turn to Russia. Would the revolutionary veterans in Moscow have forgotten that call to revolution—of which Stalin had been one of the cosigners—sent to the leaders of the militant section of the German Social Democratic Party in 1918, or the affirmation in Lenin's Farewell Letter to the Swiss workers, written just before he entrained for Russia: "The revolution will not stop at Russia. The German Proletariat is the most faithful and reliable ally of the Russian and world-wide proletarian revolution." German Communist politicians who had been living in Russia had been brought back to their country in the train of the Red army. They were to serve as agents of the Soviet Government in the direction of civilian affairs in the Eastern zone.

Germany, still under the stigma of Hitler, stricken and shocked, was limp when in July 1945 the three heads of state, at the butte of authority, met at Potsdam. Of all the problems which confronted them, none was as crucial or as difficult to compass as that of formulating principles to govern their contemplated joint control of Germany. Of this momentous conference and of the statement setting down *The Principles To Govern the Treatment of Germany in the Initial Control,* many have written in much detail elsewhere.[1]

---

[1] My version is in my book *Between War and Peace: The Potsdam Conference* (Princeton: Princeton University Press, 1960). The White House released the communiqué containing this statement about Germany on August 2d. It was printed in the State Department *Bulletin* for August 5, 1945.

Thus, in this transitional account of it, our purpose is served by noting merely a few of the main elements around which discussion pivoted, commenting on its faults and frailties that were to become evident.

The professed general aims of the three Great Powers could be mistaken to be the same. All averred that they wanted a weakened and harmless Germany. All were determined that the German people should be disarmed, de-Nazified and "democratized." But the Americans and British thought that after the country was so transformed it might be reembraced within the European power configuration as an independent neutral. As such, it would be obligated not to align itself with any combinations or take sides in any disputes. But the Russians did not believe that such a course would ensure that Germany would not again become a menace. They thought that it would be necessary not only to demolish the influence of the Nazis, but also to subordinate (or subdue) the conservative industrialists, the clerical parties, and even the moderate liberals and socialists. That is what Moscow meant by "democratization."

About economic and financial issues the Western Allies and the Soviet Union were far apart in their aims and priorities.

These and other differences had been discernible at Potsdam. But the negotiators, in their wish to reach an accord rather than separate in anger, had fooled themselves and the world; they had obscured or evaded the antithesis by three devices of diplomacy. One was by recourse to ambiguous language. Another was by adopting countervailing provisions. The third was by relegating some of its most disputed and unsettled questions to the Four-Power Control Council which they were creating, to exercise joint control over Germany. By these ruses the baffled and harried delegations at Potsdam got out of the clinches into which they fell, and informed the world that they had reached an accord. How the thistles were to sprout in the field they averred they had ploughed and harrowed! [2]

The Control Council was to be composed of the Commanders-in-Chief of the armed forces of the four occupying powers. They were "so far as is practicable" to treat the Germans in their zones uniformly. However,

[2] But I do not share the scorn of George Kennan in his *Memoirs 1925–1950* (Boston: Little, Brown, 1967) for the American and British approval of these "unreal" and "unworkable" arrangements—which they were—and of their acceptance of provisions which the Soviet Government was sure to interpret differently than we, or ignore (pp. 257 ff.). He does not take into account sufficiently the "corral of circumstances" or fairly face up to the alternatives. The most probable one, one which I believe the American Government was unwise to oppose when Churchill and Stalin suggested it during the war, was the division of Europe into "spheres of influence." But almost certainly the section of Germany adjoining Poland and Czechoslovakia and the East and Southeast satellites would have been left in the Communist sphere. That solution, his *Memoirs* plainly indicates, would have seemed to Kennan most reprehensible.

each of the four members of the Control Council was to be instructed by its own government. Each was to have supreme authority in his zone, subject to agreement in the Control Council. But within the Council decisions could be made only by common accord; it could do nothing without the assent of all its members.

This contrived association might have stood the strain had the Four Powers planned to occupy Germany for the comparatively short time needed to carry out those few primary purposes on which they were genuinely agreed: the destruction of all Nazi and military formations, the arrest and punishment of Nazi leaders, disarmament and the destruction of all plants providing arms, the release of prisoners of war and of the foreigners whom Germany had impressed into its service, and some kind of bond for payment of reparations.

But no; the victorious Allies decided their forces must remain in Germany long enough to make the Germans realize that they were a beaten nation, to reeducate them, and nurture a new social, political, and legal system. Moreover, they feared civil war or chaos if they pulled out before they had settled claims of France, the Soviet Union, Poland, and Denmark for German territory. Then, too, prolonged occupation was deemed necessary to assure collection of reparations under the plan adopted. These considerations ruled out the idea of a brief occupation, to be ended quickly by the imposition of a peace treaty. This locked the Allies into quadrangular occupation of indefinite duration, during which time the West and the Soviet Union would come to mistrust and detest each other.

The provisions about the political and social transformation of Germany seemed clear and simple, deceptively so since the West and the Russians had such different ideas of what should be done to carry them into effect.

The claims about economic affairs were so convoluted and offsetting that even a panel of impartial judges would have been compelled to be policy makers, not merely interpreters. The Control Council, with a newly recruited and inadequate staff, and subject to the need for unanimity, was left to articulate them, to strive to get agreement on facts and to fit them together into a program for all zones acceptable to all the concerned governments.

In the West it was thought that the Germans, if the system of private capitalistic enterprise was retained, would still have the incentive and ability to rebuild a healthy economy. But if, as contemplated, capacity and production in all the basic industries were to be severely limited, and many of the larger plants dismantled, could it be expected that the Germans, capitalists and workers alike, would exert themselves to rebuild and save? Could it be expected that, since the available supply of industrial products would be so reduced, and the value of the currency would decline, that farmers would try hard to supply food and raw materials for the workers in factories, mines, and offices, and for the millions of displaced and unemployed?

These quandries were entangled with the provisions in regard to reparations. The insistent demand of the Russians that the Germans be unconditionally obligated to pay reparations to the total amount of twenty billion dollars, half to go to the Soviet Union, had been refused. In the Potsdam Agreement no precise sum was stipulated. "The reparations claims of the Union of Soviet Socialist Republics," it was stipulated, "shall be met by removals from the zone of Germany occupied by the Union of Soviet Socialist Republics and from appropriate German external assets." It was also given a claim upon a fraction of "disposable" industrial plants in the Western zones—those not needed for the contemplated low peacetime standard of living.

However, it was also predicated that "the determination of the amount and character of the industrial capital equipment unnecessary for the German peace economy and therefore available for reparation shall be made by the Control Council. . . ." To this provision, it may be foretold, the Russian authorities paid no attention. Was it really believed that they might? Since millions of Russians were in greater misery than the Germans, was it really thought that the Russians would wait for the Control Council to tell them what they could take? Or that the Soviet occupants would permit food and coal or other products greatly needed in Russia to be exported from the Eastern to the Western zones of Germany, or beyond? And, as will be seen, soon the Western Allies similarly discarded the Potsdam concept of what the Germans would need, and became callous to Russian demands.

It was around this group of questions that arguments in the Control Council were first to circle. Memory, that indiscriminating instructor, prodded the Americans to resist all proposals that might make it necessary to support the German economy even more expensively. But to the Russians this clearly foreseeable consequence did not seem inevitable or imperative enough to thwart their quest for reparations. They were not disturbed by contingencies that in order to pay them the Germans had to endure misery and that the United States, which they thought to have been spared from the war and enriched by it, would be compelled to meet the deficit. If suffering and revolution resulted, so much better would be the chance that the Germans would adopt the principles of Communism.

How evident, then, in retrospect does it appear that the West and the Soviet Union would soon quarrel over the executions of the filmy agreement they had reached at Potsdam, and that each would begin to twist or disregard some of its promises; and how evident that accusations of bad faith would pour out like lava from the volcanic crust. History, alas, seldom grants a lasting reprieve merely for good intentions, or clears away conflicts of purpose concealed by fair avowals.

PART THREE

Dissensions

Become Evident

7

Potsdam: An Alienating Experience

Even though at its end accords were signed, the conference at Potsdam in July–August 1945 about the deranged situations in Europe was an abrasive experience. It turned into a court of claims rather than a prayer meeting in commemoration of the millions of dead.

Truman and his advisers sought settlements which corresponded to principles and aims that soared beyond the ordinary satisfactions and rewards of victory. They wanted to transmute the wartime alliance with the Russians into a lasting working accord for peace. Their hope had survived the shock of learning how determined the Soviet authorities were to get what they wanted, as their right, and despite signs that these Communists still regarded the Western capitalist democracies as cunning adversaries rather than dependable friends.

At San Francisco the nations, with great fanfare, had just agreed on a charter for a world organization which could not function effectively unless the three Great Powers meeting at Potsdam were in accord (and perhaps France, when she revived, and China when "it recovered her greatness").

But in the negotiations at Potsdam, some of the main decisions—about frontiers, territorial claims, the treatment of the liberated countries and defeated enemy countries—had been shaped to conform to national military position and power. Truman and Churchill had been compelled to reckon with the spread of the Red armies. Stalin had not yielded any ground or advantage won in battle, except for compensation. Britain had clung to its passing preeminence in the Middle East. The United States retained the positions it had gained in the Pacific. The agreements made had not been annealing. And many situations and claims were left unsettled, exposed to the wiles of national diplomacy.

Truman found the experience at Potsdam wearing and disturbing. Though he appreciated the cooperation of Churchill and Attlee, he remained inclined to suspect that British diplomacy was trying to manipulate American power to salvage the Empire, and to regain influence in the European balance of power.

The President's impatient wish for decision came up against Stalin's obduracy. Yet he found Stalin likable and pleasing in his terse directness and seemingly even temper. He did not yet grasp how subtle and unscrupulous were the Marshal's gift of dissimulation; or how ruthless his use of power to impose his will on smaller countries.

Yet, his encounter with the Russians had erased any lingering belief that it was going to be easy to get along with them or achieve a smooth friendship. He learned for himself that the Communist rulers were graspers and crude respecters of power. He immediately formed two conclusions: that the Soviet Union must not be accorded a share in the control of Japan, and that it should not be told how atomic weapons could be made until and unless it agreed to refrain from trying to make them.

It is probable that the policies advocated by Churchill and Truman at Potsdam, and positions maintained by them, caused Stalin to think that the British and Americans did not appreciate the agonizing war efforts of the Russians or recognize that Russian armies on the Eastern front had done most to batter Germany down. He probably regarded the resistance of these Western leaders to Russian requests for a large loan and reparations as proof of their selfish indifference and desire to exact diplomatic advantage from distress. It was to become apparent also that he construed the Western contention that Germans must be permitted to live a tolerable life as a secret design to use Germany to restrain, possibly menace, Russia. Stalin and Molotov, who had signed the notorious nonaggression pact with Hitler, and had been a subservient ally and supplier of Nazi Germany until Russia was invaded, could not rid themselves of the suspicion that the West might well similarly shift alliances. In their guilt it was essential for them to believe that other countries, the capitalist ones, if they had the chance, were likely to act as they themselves would have acted. The guilty need company.

One other grudge bedeviled the Conference and its aftermath. If de Gaulle, as head of the French Provisional Government, had been invited to take part in the discussions, the route to any agreements would have been stonier. He would have been intent solely on restoring French place among the powers and vindicating French reclamations. Yet, who knows whether his superior intelligence might not have produced better settlements?

France was granted an equal place on the Control Council for Germany, with equal veto powers. But not having been consulted in advance, the French Government did not feel obligated to moderate its aspirations or to refrain from weakening the structure of accords about Germany on which Allied cooperation was set. Its hindrance was to be critically divisive.

In short, the Conference frayed the wartime alliance between the West and the Soviet Union. Weakened, its residual bonds were to be broken by the sway and tug of the arduous negotiations that ensued in the months and years after Potsdam.

8

The Accords Begin To Crumble

Poland First

The accords on which the American Government thought American–Russian cooperation could repose thereafter began to crumble faster.

First, and most resented, was the presumed understanding reached at Yalta about Poland (see Chapter 4). To glance back at what had occurred since Yalta: Stalin and his associates had maintained that Roosevelt and Churchill had, in effect, recognized that the country should be governed by Communists and be affiliated with Russia. The acceptance of representatives of other political parties was treated as an old-fashioned formality. They were to be adjunct, and tolerated only as long as they were useful in soothing the West. The Soviet spokesmen had sternly fended off Western proposals that would have turned the government into a broad coalition of all "democratic" political parties.

Brought in and upheld by the huge Red army, the Lublin regime had become strongly entrenched. By April 1945 the Soviet Union had entrusted it with the administration of not only all the territory which it had been agreed would be in Poland, but those parts of Germany which the Poles were claiming—Danzig and much of Silesia (which had been included in the Soviet zone of occupation.)

When the Soviet Government had entered a treaty of mutual assistance with the Lublin Government (now in Warsaw), Truman protested. On April 25, 1945, Stalin had flatly rejected the President's rebuke. The Western Powers, he said, had no business to interfere with the Polish Government; they ought to show the same forbearance that he had shown by not interfering with the governments of Greece and Belgium, which had been helped by the West.

President Truman had tried in May to find out, before he met with Stalin at Potsdam, what the Soviet Government intended, by sending Harry Hopkins to Moscow to talk with the dictator. Probably he wished to make manifest to Stalin that he wanted to continue Roosevelt's policy of friendliness rather than be turned against Russia by Churchill. Hopkins' reports of his talks with Stalin about Poland had left Washington hopeful that Russia would still comply with the main features of the Yalta accord, as wishfully interpreted by American negotiators. For Stalin's cleverly phrased answers and remarks allowed Hopkins to think that the Marshal was honestly willing to have an independent and democratic government emerge in Poland, after free elections, provided it was friendly to the Soviet Union. But these statements were so cunningly qualified as to allow leeway for his deviations.

Truman had accepted the evaluation which Hopkins made of Stalin's avowals. Churchill, feeling he had no alternative, accepted them "for what they were worth." The President and the State Department had been relieved because they thought that a way out of the Polish morass had been sighted.

At Potsdam in July Truman and Churchill had encountered a Stalin who would concede nothing to reconcile them to the regime that was ruling Poland. Byrnes and the Secretary of State for Foreign Affairs for Britain, Anthony Eden, had striven to get from Molotov a clear reaffirmation that the Soviet Government would see that the pledge to hold free elections was carried out under rules of universal suffrage and secret ballot, all democratic and anti-Nazi parties to have the right to take part and put forward candidates. Had not, they pointed out, the new Polish Government itself, as it was being formed, given this pledge? But Molotov argued that the language they proposed was not in the spirit of the Yalta Accord.[1] Concluding that small turns of language would make little difference, Byrnes and Eden had subscribed to a statement which absolved the Soviet Government from direct responsibility for the holding of the elections and the way they would be carried out, placing the responsibility on the Warsaw Government itself. Molotov rejected incisive language with a smirking air of virtue, on the score that since it showed mistrust, it would offend the Polish Government.

When Truman tried to talk over with Stalin the future of the political regime in Poland, the Marshal was bland but unbudgeable. In fact, he had already won Poland—and lost Western good will. The former Polish Government-in-Exile was to be repudiated; its armed divisions (incorporated in the Allied Forces) were to be dispersed; Polish gold reserves were to be turned over to the new government.

[1] The pertinent sentence of that accord read: "The Polish Provisional Government of National Unity shall be pledged to the holding of free and unfettered elections as soon as possible on the basis of universal suffrage and secret ballot." More conclusive language could not have been found.

47

Truman and Churchill, disconsolate, had accepted Stalin's terms as providing as much chance as could be had for a free and independent Poland—friendly to the West as well as to Russia.

During the election campaign in Britain which brought the Labor Party into office in late July 1945, Ernest Bevin, on the stump, had told the voters that he believed the Labor Party could and would get on with the Soviet Union better than the Tories, who had cold-shouldered Russia before the war. He knew from rough experience that Communists were stand-offish and tricky bargainers.[2] Still, he had been determined to try to get along with the Soviet Government, and at Potsdam he had given way over Poland rather than break with Moscow as Churchill might have done.[3] But Bevin did not get over the repulse.

At Potsdam, too, the Western diplomats had found out that the Russians and Poles were determined to exact the utmost territorial gain from the uncompleted settlement discussed at Yalta. Churchill had ardently opposed the transfer to Poland of German territory between the Eastern and Western Neisse rivers. He objected, and Truman had joined him, to Russian action in placing a large segment of the Soviet zone of occupation under Polish administration, pointing out that this would exclude from the authority of the Control Council almost one-fifth of former Germany and deprive the Allies of a source of reparations and supplies. Stalin's justifications had been specious and weak, but the Russian divisions in occupation were many and strong.

There had been no "showdown." A "package deal" had been arranged by Byrnes and approved by Truman because he wanted to get back

[2] Bevin's knowledge of Communist bargaining went back to his early days when he was an organizer for the Dockers' Union. He then used to board ships as they came up the Thames or the Mersey Rivers, and negotiate with the ship captains the terms of unloading and landing on the docks. Usually when he went aboard a ship the Captain or first mate would say to him and the other union delegates, "Come down below and have a drink and we'll talk over terms." But not the Captains of Russian ships. They would always insist on settling terms first, and only then invite the union representatives to have a drink. As related by Sir Frank Roberts, who often heard Bevin reminisce.

[3] Before leaving Potsdam and returning to England to learn the results of the elections, Churchill had made a last try to persuade the Russians and Poles to be less grasping in their acquisitions of German territory. But his animation drew from Stalin only indifferent answers. In his subsequent account of this divisive question, the Prime Minister averred he had intended, if reelected, to come to grips with the Soviet Government over the frontiers of Poland. "Neither I nor Mr. Eden," he wrote, "would ever have agreed to the Western Neisse being the frontier line. . . . I had in view, namely, to have a 'showdown' at the end of the Conference, and, if necessary, to have a public break rather than allow anything beyond the Oder and the Eastern Neisse to be ceded to Poland." Winston S. Churchill, *The Second World War: Triumph and Tragedy*, Vol. 6 (Boston: Houghton Mifflin, 1953), p. 672.

home with an accord in his brief case. The Russians and Poles had their way about Poland's western frontiers. (The famed Oder–Neisse line, but including the territory between the Eastern and Western Neisse Rivers.) In return, the Soviet Government ceased to object to Italy's admission into the United Nations. And the original idea of the nature and scope of the system whereby reparations from Germany were to be procured was changed, with divisive consequences, of which we will tell more later.

"As is well known," to use the shop-soiled phrase of Soviet diplomacy, the elections, the prospect of which had led Roosevelt to accept the Yalta accord, were never held. The representatives of other elements that were included in the government were soon ignored and displaced. During the next two years Poland was turned into a stagnant country, ruled by Communists, living in fear of the Red army under orders from Moscow.

Whenever, in connection with the atomic bomb policy (to which we will devote later chapters), the question of whether and how far to trust the word of the Soviet Government arose, no experience figured as clearly in the thoughts of the American decision makers as the way they thought they had been misled about Poland.

But the Russians thought their course justified by their own experience—the attempt of the Poles at the time of the Bolshevik revolution to invade Russia; the flirtation of the prewar Polish Government with Hitler, and several German invasions of Russia through Poland. Hence the Soviet rulers evidently concluded that since the former Eastern section of Poland was being absorbed into Russia, only a Polish Government subservient to the Kremlin could be trusted not to connive with its Western opponents. Deceit often leaves its practitioners scared and suspicious.

In Italy the Western authorities, while not banning the Communist Party or excluding Communists from public positions and professions, continued to oversee political and social trends in the country. Most Italians accepted this direction, since they were relying on American benefaction to feed and clothe them and to enable them to restore public services and rebuild private industries. Moreover, the American and British Governments were Italy's support against Yugoslavia's territorial claims and sponsors of Italy's wish to get back some of her former Italian colonies in North Africa. Thus, and without need for threats or hard pressures, Italy was being folded within the Western orbit.

The Declaration on Liberated Europe

That statement of intent—the Declaration on Liberated Europe—to direct in unison the affairs of the former German satellites and other liberated countries of Europe, similarly crumpled up during the autumn–winter of 1945–1946. It was thrown in the waste basket of history, in which there is always ample room.

Letting Italy go temporarily, the Soviet Government set about bringing three former German satellites, Romania, Bulgaria, and Hungary, within the Communist community. It was not content with close association; it acted to clamp them hard and fast to its side.

None of these countries had been, between the wars, genuine democracies in fact or in spirit. Fierce political partisanship had debased constitutional forms. Usually they had been ruled over by indifferent kings, queens, or regents; their national life had been controlled by squalid combinations of large landowners, privileged aristocrats of inherited wealth, and army officers. Fascist elements had prevailed, and they had lined up with Nazi Germany during the war and imitated Nazi ways and institutions. Their soldiers had fought the Russians on the Eastern Front until they were beaten and flung back by the Red army.[4] This record diminished their rights of appeal to principles of democracy or tolerance.

Geography placed them within Russia's grasp; and Russian claims of primacy over them were buttressed by the presence of the Red army divisions. In short, the West's defense of their freedom was shaky, and its diplomatic stance weak. Western protests in the name of precepts and practices of political democracy were dismissed by Russia as fraudulent and guileful. Fraudulent because, as remarked in one of the bulletins issued by the Soviet Embassy in Washington, "So tangible an achievement of democracy as the abolition of feudal ownership, and the allotment of the land to the broad mass of the peasantry will weigh more in the scale of history than the numerous abstract effusions on the subject of democracy with which a certain section of the foreign press is

---

[4] An observation of Philip E. Mosely in his essay "Soviet Exploitation of National Conflicts in Eastern Europe" elucidates pithily another element in the situation. "The advance of Soviet power across most of East Central Europe found many long-standing national disputes and a patchwork of conflicting national claims in being; it did not invent them. . . . it has manipulated them ruthlessly to enhance its own monolithic control and to strengthen its chosen instrument of local rule." *The Soviet Union: Background, Ideology, Reality*, edited by Waldemar Gurian, (Notre Dame: University of Notre Dame Press, 1951), pp. 67 ff.

filled."[5] Guileful, the Moscow publicists charged, because they were a cloak for the aims of greedy Western capitalists, and of the desire to keep pro-Fascist groups in power. Why permit the "democratic forces" in these countries to remain split, Moscow asked, to compete with and weaken each other? "Totalitarian democracy" in which all popular elements of a country were united, was "true democracy," for these countries and our times, Moscow argued.

The efforts of the Russians to get the political parties in these countries to adopt Communist doctrines by persuasion, and to effect conformable political and economic revolution, failed. They were compelled to use compulsion, to crush all resistance to their will. Even as they did so, they professed to "adhering to the principle of absolute respect and support for their sovereignty and independence."[6] In no other area did the justifications of the Communist exponents writhe more or lie with more effrontery.

The possibility of leading these beaten people, after the deposition of the men and parties who had formed the alliance with Hitler's Germany, to cast off bad and outworn ways and institutions was diverted into a program for bringing them under Communist control. To this end, the means used during the next two years were unscrupulous and shocking: the suppression not only of reactionary and privileged groups but of moderate democratic ones, brutal restraints on personal and political freedoms.

Again, should I relate at length the tedious diplomatic tussle that occurred about the regime for and alignment of each of these "liberated" countries, I would only be adding a surplus and inadequate account to many thorough studies. So I will forgo doing so.

During the immediate postwar period, the acts of these three countries normally were subject to the orders of Control Commissions. There were American and British members of these Commissions, and the Soviet Government pretended that for this reason the requirements of the Declaration on Liberated Europe were being met. But the Soviet member of each, the commanders of Red army forces stationed in that country, consulted with his Western colleagues as little and as late as he

[5] *Information Bulletin,* October 2, 1945. Or as summed up in an article in the *New Times* with Eastern European countries in mind, May 15, 1946: "In the economic field the substance of progressive democracy consists in the fact that it liquidates the landlord class and transforms the landed estates into private peasant property; that it concentrates the economic key positions (the banks, large-scale industries, the railways), in the hands of the state."

[6] See for example, I. Taigin, "Development of Democracy in the East European Countries," *New Times,* May 15, 1946.

chose, which was usually after the act. Because of American and British protests, the Soviet Government had slightly redressed undue balance of authority but never to the extent of permitting Western opposition on significant matters to be troublesome.

The Russians were able to rejoin that they were affording the Western Allies as much or more of a share in the direction of the affairs of these three countries than had been accorded the Soviet representatives in Italy and Japan. Roughly this was so. The spheres of political domination being established tended to conform to the contours of the military situation at the end of the war. Politicians were heirs of military estates as well as purveyors of political principles.

Western efforts to induce the Soviet authorities to pay more heed to the principle of the Declaration on Liberated Europe, though earnest, were constrained by the wish to accomplish other diplomatic purposes, more primary. One was to progress with the peace treaty with Italy. Another was to secure Soviet acquiescence in American control of the occupation of Japan. These situations became connected in the course of negotiations between the three Foreign Ministers in Moscow in December 1945.

9

Give and Take—December 1945

In the Conference of Foreign Ministers at Moscow in December 1945, after hard haggling, Molotov compromised enough to reach an accord as to how the treaties with Italy and the former German satellites would be drawn up and negotiated.

Connectedly Byrnes and Bevin eased the way toward eventual recognition by their governments of the Communist-controlled regimes in Romania and Bulgaria. Molotov agreed to urge the subsequent regimes to give a few minor posts in their Cabinets to other political elements, and some time after to hold free elections, whereupon the American and British Governments were to recognize them. Byrnes and Bevin must have known by then—they certainly should have known—how frangible these promises were. They were swayed by the thought that these measures would facilitate the conclusion of peace treaties with Romania, Bulgaria, and Hungary; and thereafter Soviet troops would depart and, then, perhaps national elements not subservient to Moscow might reemerge. Stalin, of course, had no intention of allowing this to happen.

Byrnes could conclude with reason that in return for yielding in a part of Europe where the Western diplomacy was at so great a disadvantage, he secured for the United States valuable freedom of action in a part of the world where it had the advantage. Stalin had sought an equal share in control of the occupation of Japan, or at least a chance to veto American decisions. When he realized how firm was American resolution not to share ultimate right to direct the occupation, the Soviet leader settled for the right to be consulted (to agitate inside and outside the control organization), and a provision, tantamount to a pledge, that the United States would not turn Japan into an American satellite hostile to the Soviet Union.[1]

---

[1] An account of these negotiations, based on original sources, may be found in my book, *Contest Over Japan* (New York: W. W. Norton, 1967). The Russian view of the tacit agreement reached is well exemplified by the comment of *The New Times* of January 1, 1946, right after the adjournment of the Moscow Conference of the Council of Foreign Ministers. "The decisions regarding Rumania and Bulgaria will,

Soviet official comment on the outcome of that conference was bland and smacked of satisfaction. The government newspaper, *Izvestia,* set the general tenor: "The decisions of the Moscow Conference witness that a new step has been made toward the development of the collaboration of the Allied states."

In Britain, in contrast, the general appraisal was cold or discouraged. The editors of *The Economist* went so far as to write, ". . . owing to the inexperience of Mr. Byrnes as a negotiator and America's general diplomatic myopia when any area other than the Far East is in question, the Russians have succeeded in separating their two allies and Britain has been left isolated." [2]

That was not so. But Bevin had been glum at the start of the conference and was glummer at the end. Byrnes seemed at times almost to slight Britain's role, and to treat Bevin offhandedly. The Russians were readier to defy the wishes and test the will of exhausted Britain than to oppose the United States. Molotov's caustic references to the presence of British troops in Greece, who were defending its government against Communist-led malcontents, irritated Bevin. The grudging concessions regarding the reform of the governments of Romania and Bulgaria the British Foreign Secretary mistrusted. Unretracted Russian claims on Turkey, their efforts to acquire a Soviet naval base in the Dardanelles, and a trusteeship for one of the Italian colonies seemed ominous threats to the British position in the Eastern Mediterranean and Middle East. Above all else, Molotov's refusal to set a fixed date for the evacuation of Soviet troops in Iran, to which we shall revert, worried him. In sum, neither Bevin and his associates in the British Government nor the Conservative opposition thought that the agreements reached at this Conference of Foreign Ministers at Moscow would bring a surcease in the tension between the Soviet Union and the West. They were disgruntled.

So was President Truman. His nose was also put out of joint by Byrnes. He thought the Secretary of State had not kept him well enough informed about the discussions at Moscow or taken enough pains to find out whether he, the President, approved what he said and did. How keenly conscious Truman was of the prerogatives of his office, and how sensitive to any lapse in deference to his ultimate responsibility for decision! He was, moreover, not indifferent to the criticisms of those in his political circle who were chaffering at Byrnes or to the suspicions of in-

---

it is to be hoped, put an end to the prolonged attempts to interfere in the internal affairs of these countries by imposing on them abstract standards of 'Western democracy' and completely ignoring the real democracy which the people of Rumania and Bulgaria have achieved."

[2] "Diplomatic Balance Sheet," *The Economist,* January 5, 1946.

fluential Senators. Thus Truman was more receptive to Leahy's criticisms that the Secretary had made concessions destructive of the President's announced policies; that the Moscow Conference communiqué was "an appeasement document which gives to the Soviet (Union) everything they want and preserves to America nothing . . . that Byrnes was not immune to the communistically inclined advisers in the State Department." [3]

This is all surmise. But that Truman was dissatisfied because Byrnes had not succeeded in securing the terms which he, himself, had failed to obtain at Potsdam is attested by the letter addressed to Byrnes and printed in Truman's *Memoirs*.[4] In this he said brusquely: "I do not think we should play compromise any longer. We should refuse to recognize Rumania and Bulgaria until they comply with our requirements; we should let our position on Iran be known in no uncertain terms and we should continue to insist on the internationalization of the Kiel Canal, the Rhine-Danube waterway and the Black Sea Straits and we should maintain complete control of Japan and the Pacific. We should rehabilitate China and create a strong central government there. We should do the same for Korea. . . . I'm tired of babying the Soviets."

This was shooting from the hip; or, to be more up-to-date, drawing fire from the atom. Peremptorily, it may be said, that were the objectives set down by Truman as "shoulds" to be the gauge of the success or failure of his administration, it, as this narrative will ruefully attest, would have to be judged in many respects a failure.

This mordant letter of reproof may be testimony of the way Truman's anger and thoughts were surging. But it was never read to or sent to Byrnes. After its publication in the President's *Memoirs*, the Secretary of State explicitly and most incisively denied it.[5]

In sum, the Conference at Moscow in December 1945 left hope that by "give and take," settlements could be reached, and that the war Allies might continue to live together on the same small earth—if not in comity, if not in trust, with dour restraint and common memories of the agonies of war. But that hope was less meaningful because of the way in which policies in and toward Germany were diverging.

[3] Entries in Leahy Diary, December 26 and 28, 1945. Manuscript in Library of Congress.
[4] Harry S Truman, *Memoirs*, Vol. I: *Year of Decisions* (New York: Doubleday, 1955), pp. 551–2.
[5] See Byrnes' article in *Colliers Magazine*, April 26, 1952. Byrnes tends to believe this letter was fabricated for the record by Truman after he, Byrnes, made a speech at Washington and Lee University dissenting from the President's policies.

10

Divergences In and About Germany

By this time—December 1945—the accords about Germany were also beginning to crumble fast.

The difference of attitude between the political and economic branches of the State Department about the treatment of Germany had lingered on even after the Potsdam Agreement had been signed. The officers concerned with political affairs had begun to fear that if the original directives sent to General Lucius Clay (who was General Eisenhower's representative on the Control Council) were interpreted strictly, Western Germany would remain in ruins. Millions of Germans would be kept in aimless idleness and hunger, and unrest would spread. But the officers who dealt with economic policy continued to be intent on preventing Germany from ever again becoming a formidable industrial state able to make war or bid for alliances from strength. The name of the office in the State Department which dealt with German economic affairs signified this primary concern: Office of Economic Security Policy.

General John Hilldring, the former head of the Civil Affairs Division of the War Department, who had been appointed Assistant Secretary of State for Occupied Areas, did his best to reconcile the divergent memos of instructions sent to the American member of the Control Council. But Hilldring was neither bright nor flexible enough to formulate and win acceptance for a definite and stable policy—neither one consistently punitive nor one which would get the Germans back to work. The best efforts of his able staff, among them Ernest Gross, did not quickly produce a well-adjusted program.

Thus, during the first year of occupation, the initiative in American policy making had passed from Washington to Berlin, and was to remain there. General Clay and his subordinates applied the Potsdam Accord in ways that facilitated their assigned tasks and enabled their occupation troops to get along with the Germans. Sometimes Clay acted first, and sought approval for his adaptations of policy later; sometimes he made recommendations to Washington about what he thought should be done in the American zone.

One of the primary questions which had presented itself was whether the Western governments were going to adhere to the stricture of the Potsdam accord that the Germans must get along as best they could with what they had or could themselves produce. This accord contemplated that they should be permitted to have " . . . average living standards not exceeding the average of the standards of living of European countries" (excluding the United Kingdom and Union of Soviet Socialist Republics). Except those Germans who had accumulated spoils from the invaded countries, and those who had been enriched by the war, most were in dire straits as the winter of 1945–1946 came in. In November 1945 Byron Price, who had been sent by the President to study the relations between the American forces of occupation and the German people, reported: "We must decide whether we are going to permit starvation, with attendant epidemics and disorders, in the American zone, or ship the food to prevent it." [1] We had begun to ship food, as had the British into their zone.

Complaints over the way in which the Potsdam Accord was being carried out in the several zones were first aired at the Conference of Foreign Ministers in December 1945. Molotov accused the British of allowing powerful German military units to exist in its zone. Bevin, just as roughly, denied it; a few small units, he explained, were being kept in existence temporarily to be sent to England to replace Italian prisoners of war who would soon be sent home. The Soviet Foreign Commissar also asserted that American and British commanders were detaining several hundred thousand Soviet citizens in their zones who ought to be turned over at once to a Soviet repatriation agency. A new directive issued to General Joseph McNarney (who briefly, in succession to Eisenhower, was the U.S. representative on the Control Council) went far to meet Soviet demands. But the American and British authorities refused to compel Polish soldiers who came from the part of Poland absorbed by Russia to return there against their will.

The members of the Control Council could not reach a genuine agreement on matters essential for joint supervision.[2] During its first year the only measures passed which represented real Four-Power agreement on matters of importance were in the fields of de-Nazification and taxation.

[1] Report of Byron Price, *Relations between American Forces of Occupation and the German People.* The President transmitted the letter to James F. Byrnes, Robert Patterson, and James Forrestal.

[2] The best brief account I know of the record of the Control Council is Anne Whyte's article in *International Affairs* for January 1947. It is entitled *"Quadripartite Rule in Berlin,"* but she observes that a better title might have been "Four-Power Myth and Reality."

Such other agreements as were reached were interpreted differently in the four zones—especially as between the Western zones and the Soviet Union zone.

The attempt to establish uniform arrangements for all Germany was, in this plasmic period, hindered by the negativism of the French member of the Control Council. Intent on detaching from Germany certain areas in the West (the Saar, the Rhineland) and internationalizing the Ruhr, he vetoed every measure for recreating a central administration for the whole of the country. Among the proposals rejected by him were those providing for the formation of national political parties and free passage for Germans between zones.

As succinctly described by Price in his report, "Repeated attempts have been made to set up common policies so that the German railways, the German postal service and other essential facilities could be operated as integral national systems. All of these attempts have failed, due almost entirely to the rigid opposition of the French. As a result of the French attitude, Germany is not being treated as an economic unit. Instead what is happening amounts, to speak plainly, to the economic dismemberment of Germany." [3]

The Soviet officials could not understand why the American and British Governments tolerated French recalcitrance, why they did not use coercive measures to get them to conform. It was thought that de Gaulle was not likely to pay heed to American or British remonstrances. Moreover, the American force of occupation was dependent on communications through France. And there was fear of provoking a deep political crisis in France which the Communists could turn to their advantage.

Still, after Clay's effort to induce his French colleague to be more amenable failed, the American Government did, hesitantly, try to bring pressure on France. In February 1946 Byrnes appealed personally to Georges Bidault, but to no avail. On March 5, 1946, the French Cabinet reaffirmed unanimously its position on the Saar, the Ruhr, and the Rhineland, and the French member of the Control Council maintained his veto. Stumped and resentful, the War Department authorized Clay to go ahead, despite the French, and establish central agencies in cooperation with the Russians and British. But neither was yet ready to take this measure.[4]

France's refusal to permit central economic agencies to operate, France's restrictions on trade between its zone and others, and France's

[3] Price, *Relations between American Forces and German People.*

[4] See John Gimbel, *The American Occupation of Germany: Politics and the Military, 1945–1949* (Stanford: Stanford University Press, 1968), pp. 26–27, 52–53, 57. Clay in October and December of 1945 had made two previous attempts to secure British and Russian acceptance of a three-power program of economic unification, but both had urged postponement.

requisitions of German products, gave the Russians a reason, which they did not need, for defending their refusal to allow exports from the East zone to the West.

Before the French objections were worn down and relaxed, the policies in the Soviet and Western zones had scudded so far apart they could not be reassembled.

Deep contrasts in political views and purposes evinced themselves quickly. In the Eastern zone the Russians forbade independent or anti-Communist parties to operate. In the Western zones the Americans and the British did not ban or exclude parties of Communist persuasion but made it difficult for them to exist. No less different were the policies and practices in the licensing and supervising of the press, the selection of the judiciary, and the exercise of the police power. The Russians in their zones ignored Western standards of freedom and equality under the law, and introduced Communist rules and methods.

In the selection of Germans to carry on work of local government and to re-start industrial plants, the Americans preferred liberal-conservatives or moderate socialists; they favored especially men of firm religious affiliation, many Catholics. The British occupation officials favored members of the Social Democratic Party and circles in sympathy with Socialist aims.

The Russians put in positions of authority in local government and industry Germans willing to accept Communist direction and discipline. They accused the Americans and the British of enabling former Nazis to regain office and power, and implied that they were doing so in order that Germany would, when it regained strength, attempt to destroy the Communist community. In fact, the Russians were readier than the West to use former Nazis if they had the desired technical competence and followed the orders of Soviet bosses. But the Communist commanders were less tolerant of the delays and evasions of the German courts and prosecuting officers to whom the Allies had turned over the duty of judging and sentencing the hundreds of Nazi officials, bureaucrats, and industrial servitors secondary in rank but not in viciousness of deed.

The Western and Soviet occupants differed no less decisively in their direction of economic and social affairs. The Russians confiscated all large farms and estates (over 250 acres)—and all belonging to Nazis— about one half of the arable land in the Eastern zone, over which Junkers had long ruled. This was redistributed among small holders, none more than 40 acres.

In the Western zone farm properties were much smaller and the authorities were averse to confiscation. So they reallocated only small areas, contenting themselves with reducing by half all estates of 750 acres or more, and setting a maximum limit, 375 acres, to the size of individual land holdings. The Americans and British arranged to compensate owners of expropriated land.

The Soviet officials closed all private banks. The Western occupants allowed private banks to continue operation; in the British zone the old Reichsbank was maintained, and in the American zone coordinating financial agencies in each state on the pattern of the Federal Reserve Board. The Russians blocked all private banking accounts; the Western occupants blocked only the accounts of Nazis. There were no agreed values for the dollar, ruble, franc, or pound sterling; they were different in each zone.

The Americans and British, while striving to oust prominent and powerful Nazis from control of German industries and sequestering their property, allowed and depended on private ownership and enterprise. The Russians nationalized most industries in the Eastern zone. In cooperation with the Socialist Unity Party (Communist-directed) and Communist trade unions, they controlled the management of all coal and electricity production, more than half of the output of metals, and almost half of the turnout of machinery. They formulated a two-year plan, and by a combination of compulsion and inducement saw to it that the industries in their zone strove to realize it.

The Four-Power Control Council, after protracted arguments, had managed to formulate on paper a plan designed to carry out the pertinent Potsdam provisions about economic affairs and the connected question of reparations. One of the explicit assumptions, even then contrary to fact, was "that Germany will be treated as a single economic unit."[5]

The limits of industrial production which the Germans were to be allowed to retain were set down. This, it was conceived, would be sufficient to enable them to maintain the standard of living described in the Potsdam Accord; a standard that defied statistical definition.[6]

[5] Plan of the Allied Control Council for Reparations and the Level of Post-War German Economy, March 28, 1946. Text is in *Documents on U.S. Foreign Relations, July 1945–December 1946* (Boston: World Peace Foundation, 1948), pp. 244–49.

[6] The production of all implements of war, aircraft, sea-going ships, and the production of all types of industrial capital equipment essential to their production, including such products as ball-bearings, primary aluminum, heavy tractors, and heavy machine tools of various types, were prohibited. Quantitative limits were set on permissible production of many other industries; metallurgical and basic chemical industries (equal to about 40 percent of 1936 capacity) electroengineering (equal to about 50 percent of 1938 capacity) cement, rubber, and even textiles and boots and shoes.

The requirements of Western Europe had in one field contravened the plans for repression and limitation. American and British were intent on reviving coal pro-

Production of steel was taken to be the decisive regulator of the amount and character of the industrial capital equipment which the Germans would need. All production capacity over that needed to fabricate the allowable output of steel was to be made available for reparations. The British proposed an allowance of 11.5 million tons a year; the Russians, 4 millions; the Americans, a median. The compromise effected permitted Germany to retain a production capacity of 7.5 million tons, with allowable annual production of 5.8 million tons. Moreover, it was stipulated that the steel plants to be left in Germany ". . . should, as far as practicable, be the older ones." This capacity turned out to be far less than Germany needed to be self-supporting—as was envisaged in the Potsdam Accord.

But the actual current rates of production in the several zones and various industries differed greatly. In the basic industries of the Ruhr— coal, steel, machinery, chemicals, and electrical—output was far less than before the war, as was the supply of farm products. But in the Eastern zone the lighter industries had been reactivated rapidly, and the output of diverse products such as optical goods, precision instruments, turbines, and textiles rose to prewar levels. The Russians paid for the goods they wanted in German marks which they printed, and they sent the goods to Russia. The Western authorities believed this to be a violation of the Potsdam Accord, which contemplated that any surplus production in any zone should be permitted to move in trade to other zones.

All the while that the former Allies were, during the early months of 1946, engaged in the effort of formulating a common plan for Germany,

---

duction so that Germany could export enough to meet urgent needs of the worn-down industries and power plants of Britain and Western Europe. No supplies could be expected from Silesia, because that region had been ceded to Poland. And in the West miners were not getting enough food to enable them to work a long day, or enough purchasable goods to make them want to work more than a minimum. The equipment in many of the mines was in need of repair, and necessary parts and mining supplies were not to be had.

Even before the war ended, the Western commanders, Eisenhower and Montgomery, had been instructed to do everything they could to make 25 million tons of coal available for export by the end of April 1946. At Potsdam Truman had asked Stalin to cooperate in measures for increasing production. But the Russian representative on the Control Council did not advance any positive proposals. The French Government was indifferent to measures for improving the conditions and incentives of German coal miners, so production continued to be far less than the quantities needed in Germany and Western Europe.

In this plan adopted by the Council, American and British insistence prevailed. It was stipulated that "coal production will be maximized as far as mining supplies and transport will allow . . . The necessary supplies and services to this end will be arranged to give the maximum production of coal."

they were quarreling over other several claims of the Soviet Government, especially those upon Iran and Turkey. These occurrences should be fitted into the cursive, cavorting course of history before we return our memories to the primary scene and cause of discord—Germany.

11

The Russian Intrusion into Iran

Hardly had each of the three Foreign Ministers, in their respective addresses about their conference in Moscow in December 1945, assured their fellow countrymen that peace with justice was what they sought and craved, than the governments of the Western Allies and the Soviet Union fell afoul of each other over crafty Russian efforts to acquire a segment of scraggy, but possibly oil-containing, land in northern Iran. For this Stalin threw away the residue of good will there remained in London and Washington. What swamps there are that never dry up along some historical boundaries!

The Genesis of the Dispute

The war had given Russia the opportunity to extend its power over the province of Azerbaijan in the north of Iran, and perhaps to force expulsion of its traditional rivals, the British, from the south. It had given the Russians reason for stationing troops in the north. The control of the Iranian Government in that region was shaky; people who lived there were close kin to those in the Soviet province of Azerbaijan. Moreover, the Azerbaijans living in northern Iran had cause for disaffection; they were miserably poor and neglected by the Government at Teheran.

The British, in order to protect both the oil fields and their military situation, had stationed troops in the south.

Britain and Russia had, in January 1942, concluded a treaty with Iran in which they promised ". . . to respect the territorial integrity of Iran." It had been stipulated that "the forces of the Allied Powers shall be withdrawn from Iranian territory not later than six months after all hostilities between the Allied Powers and Germany and her associates have been suspended by the conclusion of an armistice or armistices, or the conclusion of peace between them, whichever date is earlier." [1]

In December 1943, at the Teheran Conference, Roosevelt had joined Stalin and Churchill in a Declaration which reaffirmed the "desire" of the Allies to maintain the independence, sovereignty, and territorial integrity of Iran. The American Government, having declared the country eligible for Lend-Lease, had been sending to Iran civilian advisers, military missions, technicians, and supplies.

Stettinius, then Lend-Lease Administrator, had explained our purpose. ". . . The United States can contribute substantially to world security by assisting to create a strong Iran, free from internal weakness which invites foreign intervention and aggression."

But what availeth such good intentions in the face of propinquity and petroleum! The first clear sign that the Russians would try to exact payment from Iran before evacuating the country was a request for exclusive mineral rights in northern Iran—believed to contain great oil deposits—in return for technical assistance. The Iranian Government had suspended negotiations with foreign oil interests until after the war. The Russians had kept their troops in Iran after Germany had surrendered.

By the time Truman took office, Russian tactics in northern Iran were agitating the State Department and British Foreign Office. Soviet troops had closed the region to all foreigners except Russians; they had tried to direct and administer various local economic activities; they had disseminated Soviet propaganda; they had released Communists from prison; and they had fostered the formation of the Tudeh (Masses) Party, which advocated drastic economic, social, and political reforms. Russian agents were also stirring up the restless and disaffected Kurdish tribes of Iran, Iraq, and Turkey. The British Government had upheld the Central Iranian Government as a counterpoise.

At Potsdam Eden had proposed that British and Soviet forces be withdrawn at once from Teheran, the capital, and then in several gradual stages from all of Iran. Stalin had demurred. He was willing to agree to the prompt exit of all forces from Teheran, but he wanted to let the troops remain elsewhere in Iran for a while longer, perhaps until six months after the end of the war against Japan. Churchill not being averse, it was agreed to let the situation rest until the Foreign Ministers met in September. After Truman said abruptly that he expected to have all American troops—they were service troops not combat troops—out

---

[1] The treaty defined the expression "Associates" of Germany as meaning "all other powers which have engaged or may in the future engage in hostilities against either of the Allied Powers."

of Iran in sixty days, Stalin remarked: "So as to rid the United States of any worries, we promise that no action will be taken by us against Iran."

But Soviet publicists were diffusing critical descriptions of Iran. It was not, they averred, really a unified country, but merely a poor assortment of different tribes and nationalities; it was ruled by feudal lords and tribal heads who made and broke laws with impunity; these were all reactionary and many just "placemen" for British imperialists. Consequently the Iranian people were oppressed and miserable. The wonder is that these assertions did not gain more supporters in Iran, for there was some validity in all of them.

Insurrections and tribal revolts in the province of Azerbaijan had spread thereafter.

The British and American Embassies in Teheran were speculating whether the Soviet Government was seeking merely to obtain oil concessions in Northern Persia or/and to annex Iranian Azerbaijan. Or/and, so far did the suspicions of Russian aims course, was Moscow trying to foster a subservient government in Teheran and extend Soviet interests to the Persian Gulf; and therefrom, to frighten the Turkish Government to accede to its terms for a treaty of friendship? The American Ambassador in Iran, Wallace Murray, a splenetic individual, was particularly worried lest the Soviet Union was determined to extend Communist control over the whole of Iran; and his messages to Washington aroused similar fears in others.

The Iranian Government had appealed to the subscribers to the tripartite Declaration that had been made at Teheran in 1943. The Soviet Government did not answer its notes, and the Soviet press denied the truth of reports that it was interfering in the insurrection in Azerbaijan and supplying arms to the rebels. Soviet publicists portrayed this revolt as a democratic movement against oppression and the denial of the rights of natives of this province to have schools in which they used their own language, and to publish books and newspapers in their own language. In short, the Soviet Government averred that the rebellion was local in inspiration and direction, with democratic objectives; and it accused the Western press of concealing that truth.

On November 24, 1945, Byrnes had instructed our Ambassador in Moscow to make a formal presentation. Molotov was to be told that the American Government was convinced that it would be in the common interest if all foreign troops were taken out of Iran at once. It was to be pointed out that the number of American forces which had been sent to Iran during the war in order to manage the transport of supplies through Iran to the Soviet Union over the railways and roads had already been reduced from about 28,000 to less than 6,000; and those re-

65

maining were under orders to evacuate by the first of January 1946. Why should not the Soviet and British Governments give similar instructions to commanders of their forces? They were obligated by treaty to take their troops out before March 2, 1946, at the latest (as agreed by all in the London Conference of Foreign Ministers); and there seemed to be no compelling reason to wait until then. Harriman had sent a note along these lines to Molotov on November 27th.

On the next day the British Ambassador, Archibald Clark-Kerr, had given Molotov a protest against the refusal of Soviet troops to permit the Iranian Government to send troops into the northwestern region of the country.

The formal Russian answer to the American and British notes had been given a week later. It had again portrayed events in northern Iran as merely a local movement for democratic rights and national autonomy within the limits of the Iranian state. It denied that the Soviet military command in Iran was hindering these Iranian army or police units which were already in northern Iran. But it admitted that it was preventing new troop movements into the region since, it asserted, that would increase the disorder and compel the Soviet Government to introduce more Soviet troops "for the purpose of preserving order and of assuring the security of Soviet garrisons." It saw no reason for considering anew the question of the time limit for the stay of foreign troops in Iran.

By September the insurrectionist group had formed what it called the National Government of Azerbaijan at Tabriz. At its head was a veteran Communist agitator, Jaafar Pishevari. This regime adopted a program calling for autonomy and local independent armies.

The Determined Diplomatic Resistance

The Iranian Government urged the British and American Governments to get Molotov, at the prospective meeting of the Foreign Ministers in December 1945 in Moscow, to realize that they regarded Soviet intrusion into Iran as a serious offense and breach of promise. The briefing papers written in the State Department for the guidance of Byrnes had taken a grave view of the danger to the independence of both Iran and Turkey, and perhaps Iraq, of Soviet-sponsored and -protected rebellious and separatist activism in the North. They recommended that the American Government should give a stern reproof and warning.

Getting no clear reassurance from Molotov, Byrnes while in Moscow turned to Stalin. He had sought to secure a promise that Soviet troops would be withdrawn within a designated period. He professed to be perplexed because the Soviets had refused to allow 1500 Iranian Government troops to go North, and had averred that this movement could endanger the position of the 30,000 Soviet troops that were in Iran.

But Stalin, in their first talk, was just as impermeable as Molotov, and just as unashamed in his excuses. Since the Iranian Government was hostile to the Soviet Union, it might, he said, send saboteurs to set fire to the Baku oil fields. Moreover, he denied, as had Molotov, that these Soviet troops were interfering in local developments; and he asserted that the reason why the Soviet Government would not allow the Iranian Government to send more troops into the area was fear that they would clash with the local people, and this might involve Soviet forces.

To these subterfuges Stalin added a commentary. He enlarged on the way in which small nations tried to foster friction between the large powers, some with complaints to the Soviet Government about England and America, and some to the English and American Governments with complaints about the Soviet Union. It was wise to take a skeptical view of such laments.

In short, Stalin concluded, the Soviet Government would keep its troops in Iran as long as conditions were disturbed and there was a possibility of danger; how long that would be depended in a large measure on the way in which the Iranian Government behaved.

Why, the Marshal asked—and this was a significant clue to his thinking—did the American Government make such a fuss about this situation, since it had troops in so many other foreign countries? It was not clear to him how they got there or what they were doing there. Byrnes's response was that every American soldier wished he were back home and every American citizen wished to get him back home.

Later that same day Bevin had also talked with Stalin. He had been more forthright in explaining that his government feared that the Soviet Government was trying to bring the province of Azerbaijan into the Soviet Union or make it into a dependency. The British Government could not regard such a change in the international position of the region without great qualms; its valuable oil properties in the south of Iran, and the bearing of the country on the routes to India and the East, made the preservation of its independence and integrity a primary British interest. Stalin had repeated the assurance he had given Byrnes, that "he had no claims against Iran, no idea of incorporating any part of Iran in the Soviet Union, and no intention of impairing the sovereignty of Iran." But these verbal assurances did not carry conviction; how Stalin had used clever language to disguise intentions in regard to Poland was well remembered.

The British Ambassador in Iran, Sir Reader Bullard, was of the opinion that the Russians would not, under present circumstances, get out of

Iran and let the Iranian Government settle the situation by itself. Therefore he thought it expedient to enlist Soviet cooperation to put into effect local reforms and create local governments, rather than merely to continue to insist that Soviet forces pull out. Bevin had been impressed. Accordingly, he suggested to Stalin that the Soviet, British, and American Governments set up a joint commission to advise and assist the Iranians in forming a provincial government in Azerbaijan and in carrying out reforms in the province. Stalin had said that he would take the idea under consideration.

The American officials had been dubious of this procedure. Alternatively they urged through the American Embassy in Teheran that the Iranian Government proceed at once on its own to satisfy such local wishes in Azerbaijan as were feasible without impairing its sovereign control over the province, such as allowing the use of the Turkish language in the schools, along with Iranian, to make various desirable social and economic reforms, and to foster the creation of a provincial council, as provided in the Iranian constitution.

On December 22d the Iranian Prime Minister told the American Ambassador that steps to these ends would be taken quickly. However, he said that the Iranian Government could not accept the "Parliament" and "Government" which had been formed in the province of Azerbaijan by elements in revolt; that it was illegal and had been largely organized by aliens who had entered Iran illegally. He reaffirmed the intention of the Iranian Government to put down the rebellion by force if necessary once Soviet interference was ended. The American Ambassador advised both the Shah and the Prime Minister to settle the Azerbaijan problem without bloodshed, by negotiation with local elements in Azerbaijan.

Byrnes, in a second talk with Stalin on December 23d, had said that the Iranian Government had indicated that it was planning to bring an accusatory complaint to the first meeting of the U.N. Assembly, and that the American Government, though sorry to have to do so, might have to support it. Since neither his talks with Molotov nor his appeals to Stalin had brought forth definite promise of withdrawal, Byrnes had concluded the situation could not be settled at this Conference. But Bevin was reluctant to drop the subject. He told Molotov that if he signed a protocol which did not even mention Iran, there would be great perturbation in Britain. Molotov answered gruffly that that was Bevin's worry. So it was. Before departing he warned Molotov that the British Government did not want to be faced with an accomplished fact, which he thought was being prepared.

Thus Bevin instructed the British Embassy in Teheran to urge the Iranian Government to let it be known that it had accepted the plan for a three-power commission; and that the British Government would lend its full support to the idea. Byrnes, adopting the British protest, sent similar instructions to the American Embassy in Teheran. But the Iranian Government preferred to argue its case before the U.N., with the expected support of the American and British Governments, rather than to take the risk of interference in its affairs by the proposed commission—on which the Soviet member would have much to say.

Truman, as mentioned earlier, concluded Byrnes had not been firm enough. The American Government got ready to fight the next round in and out of the U.N. By then it was becoming more suspicious and fearful of Communist purposes in Greece, Turkey, and elsewhere.

Iran Appeals to the Security Council

On January 1, 1946, the United States brought out the last small contingent of American troops that remained in Iran. The British Government reaffirmed that it would evacuate its troops from the south before or at the end of the period defined in the Declaration, March 2, 1946. The Soviet Government continued to refuse to set a term on the stay of its forces in the country.

On January 19, 1946, the Iranian Government brought a formal complaint before the first session of the Security Council of the United Nations. It alleged that the Soviet Government was interfering in its internal affairs in violation of the Three-Power Declaration of December 1943, and the Charter of the U.N. It accused the Soviet Government of preventing it from suppressing disorders, disrupting the economic life of the country by setting up at the frontier of the so-called Soviet zone, barriers to the passage of goods, civilians, and troops, and of encouraging and supporting disloyal agitators who were demanding autonomy for Azerbaijan. The Iranian Government asked that, since its efforts to ease this situation by direct negotiation had failed, the Security Council look into it and recommend what action was to be taken.[2]

The Russian representative repeated the refutations with which we are familiar. Therefore, he argued, there was no ground for the Iranian request that the Security Council take cognizance of the trouble. Concurrently he entered a formal complaint against the presence of British troops in Greece and against the Dutch attempt to reassert its authority in Indonesia—as threats to peace and security.

The American representative firmly justified the Iranian request for the mediation of the Security Council on the score that continued presence of Soviet troops in Iran was a threat to world peace.

[2] Letter from the Iranian Government to the Presiding member of the Security Council, January 25, 1946.

After hearing views of British, French, and other governments, on January 30, 1946, the Security Council resolved that since both the Iranian and Soviet Governments affirmed their readiness to seek a solution by negotiations, they should proceed to do so, keeping the Security Council informed of the results.

12

Three Impinging Occurrences:
Early 1946

Here I will briefly interrupt the account of the Iranian crisis in order to bring into the circle of historical attention other occurrences during these early months of 1946 which, though not as immediately critical, were more broadly consequential. Of the many—for history flings into flight at the same time, each week and month, more bolts than the historian can follow—I shall tell of only three which marked —and left their mark on—the trend of relations between the Soviet Union and the West.

A Loan for the Soviet Union?

Stalin, more openly than ever before, indicated that the Soviet Union would like to get a large American loan. His inquiry was left to languish.

The granting of a large loan to the Soviet Union had long been bruited about and touched on at various times in discussions between American and Soviet officials about their postwar relations. The possibility had been discussed by Harriman with Molotov early in 1943, and at the Teheran Conference. Subsequently the pivotal matter had been taken over from Molotov by Anastas Mikoyan, Soviet Commissar for Foreign Trade. It had become entangled with the question of obtaining wanted information from the Soviet Government in justification of current requests for Lend-Lease goods.

The American officials were becoming annoyed because the Soviet Government would not provide adequate information on the uses being made of our Lend-Lease aid. They were, perhaps, not sufficiently cognizant of the difficulties of doing so while the whole of Russia was staggering under German assault. But why was the Soviet Government so remiss in letting their own people know how much we were helping? Why were they in every way belittling this?

These annoyances evolved into an opinion that if the Russians wanted us to help them after the war, they should be less peremptory and more mindful of our wishes. But Stalin and his Marxist advisers thought there was no need to be. They were convinced the United States would have to grant large foreign loans to avoid a deep depression after the war. Moreover, that belief was fostered by forecasts made by visiting American businessmen, to whom the prospect of the end of the great flow of exports, financed as Lend-Lease, was dismaying. It may have been also buoyed up by the knowledge that Secretary of the Treasury Henry Morgenthau, Jr., and Assistant Secretary Harry White were urging that a large loan be made to the Soviet Union. They based their recommendation on dual grounds: that the loan would provide a valuable market for American products and a valuable source of raw materials, and that it would be an unguent in our relations with Russia during the period of peacemaking. Moreover, projects for an International Monetary Fund and International Bank for Reconstruction were being shaped up by the Treasury, and Russian participation in both institutions was desired.

When in January 1945 Molotov had presented a definite Soviet proposal for a long-term credit, its tenor had been chilling. It implied that the Soviet Union was willing to accept a credit in order to satisfy American wishes for Russian business. The suggested terms were deemed much too easy. But these features might well have been overlooked or adjusted had it not been for the emergent fear that the Soviet Government was going to be pushing and demanding in postwar settlements. Roosevelt was about to meet with Stalin and Churchill at Yalta. Thereafter we might be able to gauge whether the Soviet Union would be reasonably cooperative with the West or on the rampage. The State Department had advised the President that the Russians would not of their own volition defer to American wishes in return for a loan, once they had it. Hence he had hesitated to dispense with any diplomatic use which our power to assist Russian reconstruction might have. He did not raise the question at Yalta; neither did the waiting Stalin.

The American Government had allowed it to remain dormant. Both Harriman and the influential head of the American Military Mission in Moscow, General John Deane (later the author of *The Strange Alliance*),[1] were then advising Washington that all deals with the Soviet Union should be on a quid pro quo basis. The conclusion they had reached is signified by a terse comment of Harriman's in his message to the State Department in April. "Our experience has incontrovertibly

[1] John R. Deane, *The Strange Alliance: The Story of Our Efforts at Wartime Cooperation with Russia* (New York: Viking, 1947).

proved that it is not possible to bank general good will in Moscow, and I agree with the Department that we should retain current control of these credits to protect American vital interests in the formulative period immediately following the war." [2]

What chance there might have been that the American Government would strive to persuade a critical Congress to approve a loan to Russia faded when, as told, the Soviet Government showed itself determined to impose permanent Communist control on Poland. Truman had been in no mood to buy restraint and compromise if it could be bought. Then Stalin's tough demeanor and demands at the Potsdam Conference had further withered any disposition to believe that if the United States relieved the Russian distress and assisted Russian reconstruction it would become more moderate or reasonable.

Thus, the American Government had left the matter swinging in the breezes of diplomacy. Finally Stalin, who probably had been confident it would be handed to him, inquired about it.

When on January 23, 1946, after the Moscow Conference of the Council of Foreign Ministers, Ambassador Harriman paid a farewell call on Stalin, the Marshal sounded him out. A large American Government credit for Great Britain was being negotiated. The Marshal was careful. Was his impression, Stalin asked, correct, that if the Soviet Government raised the question of a loan the American Government would meet it halfway?

Harriman, after some rather unconvincing explanations of our passivity, remarked that the American Government would want to discuss at the same time a settlement of Russia's Lend-Lease obligation and the basis of economic collaboration between the two countries. But to the main obstacle he alluded only indirectly, observing merely that there was in the United States a perplexed feeling and fear that the differences between the two countries were irreconcilable. This had "a definite bearing" on what the administration in office could do in regard to a loan and its terms. Stalin had not pursued this aspect of the subject. He had said that the Soviet Government was ready to start negotiations, but not on terms that had been put forward by congressmen who had visited Moscow; some of these were offensive and could not even be discussed.

Not until April 1946, when the crisis over Iran was past, did the American Government invite the Russians to begin negotiations about conditions and terms for a loan. The Secretary of State, on informing the press that it had done so, said that among the subjects which the American Government would want to discuss in connection with a loan were

[2] Harriman to Secretary of State, April 11, 1945. *Foreign Relations of the United States* (1945), vol. 5, p. 996.

the Russian trade pacts with the Balkan countries and peace treaties with the satellites (which was on the agenda of the Conference of Foreign Ministers, soon to begin).[3] This indication of what the American Government would expect in return for a loan snuffed out the possibility.

The American decision not to make a loan to the Soviet Government —despite Russian transgressions and threats—may have been unwise. For it may have seemed to confirm Communist belief that the United States did not care about the suffering of the Russian people. If the West had demonstrated that this was not so, and had supplied the Russian people and industry with essentials they still lacked because of the German assault, might the Soviet Government have relaxed its demands for reparations from Germany; and might it have taken a less embittered view of the suspension of shipments of industrial equipment from the Western zones? If so a loan might have planed down one of the main causes of friction over Germany.

But those with most experience in negotiating with the Russians thought the chances of so affecting these matters very slight. They anticipated rather that our motives would be misinterpreted by the ideologists as an act of self-interest to enrich some American millionaires, and our generosity would not be reciprocated. True, apropos Russian treatment of Germany, memories of the suffering and ruins of Leningrad would not have been softened by American wheat and machines. Still the United States could have spared the resources wagered for combined humanitarian and diplomatic purposes—without serious deprivation.

These conjectures are not meant to be a corroboration of the theme first forcefully propounded by Henry A. Wallace when he broke with the Administration (of which we shall tell); that our response to Stalin's request for a loan was one of the prime reasons for the onset of hostility and the sequential actions of the Soviet Union.

To pass judgment authoritatively on this hypothesis, it is necessary to consider the whole historical movement and explore illusions and dogmas. After doing my best to do so, my definite opinion is that this supposition about the inception of the "cold war" is ill-founded and superficial. Soviet Communist ways, the principal Soviet Communist aims, were too firmly fixed to have been deflected by the receipt of a loan, except in secondary ways and in situations in which Russia was at a disadvantage.

[3] *New York Times*, April 20, 1946.

No simple conclusion can dispose of the whole of the subject. With these surmises I return it to others who think it more important than I do, and tell of two utterances which, I am fairly sure, did leave more of a black and blue mark on the countenance of the powers.

Stalin Speaks Out

Just before the start of direct negotiations between the Iranian and Soviet Governments, which is recounted in a later section, Stalin made a speech which caused the American and British authorities to wonder whether the Soviet Union was not going to turn its back on the U.N. and its former Allies.[4] True, it was an election speech. But still, Stalin's stress on Marxian doctrines and his vaunting of the strength and merits of the Communist system and failure to mention the war efforts of Russia's allies, or the United Nations, were taken to indicate his real view of relations with the Western democracies. Marxians knew, he declared, that the capitalist system of world economy conceals elements of crisis and war, and that its development does not follow a steady and even course forward but proceeds through crises and catastrophes. Thus, his interpretation continued, the splitting of the capitalist world into two camps had brought about two world wars, and—the implication was— might cause another. In his historical review he did not mention his deal with Hitler, or Great Britain's valorous struggle against the Axis while the Soviet Union was nurturing and appeasing Hitler. The point he wanted to make was: "The entry of the Soviet Union into the war . . . could only strengthen and did strengthen the anti-Fascist and liberating character of the Second World War." [5]

The Marshal referred to the assertions in the foreign press that the Soviet system was " . . . a risky experiment doomed to failure . . . a house of cards without roots in real life, and imposed on the people by the organs of the Cheka [secret police]. . . . The war has refuted all [these] assertions . . . [it] has shown that the Soviet social system is a truly popular system, issued from the depths of the people and enjoying its mighty support." It also showed how "ridiculous" were statements, not only in Germany, but also in France, Britain, and America, that the Red army, if struck a hard blow, would fall to pieces; and it showed that it was "a first-class modern army with completely up-to-date armament, most experienced commanders and high morale and combat qualities." [6]

---

[4] It was broadcast over the Moscow radio on February 9th, and appeared in the *New York Times*, February 10, 1946.

[5] *Ibid.*

[6] *Ibid.*

Thus it was wholly capable of defending the country.

Stalin did not allude to the impending crisis over Iran. But the Soviet commentators did, aligning it with other situations in which the British and French and Dutch imperialisms were in trouble—Syria, Lebanon, India, Egypt, Palestine, Indonesia, and Greece.

Churchill's Iron Curtain Speech

Former Prime Minister Churchill had been brooding over the active efforts of Russia to extend its great domain and foment disturbance and civil strife near and far. He began to compose the famous condemnatory speech (The Iron Curtain Speech) he was to make at Fulton, Missouri on March 5th.

President Truman had invited the former Prime Minister to deliver an address at the degree-conferring ceremonies of the small Westminster College.[7] Churchill had spent several weeks in the United States. He had talked with the President. He had read drafts of his speech to Byrnes and Leahy.[8] The Secretary of State had told the President of its general nature and said he thought the President should look it over.[9] Truman had ridden on the President's special train with Churchill to Fulton and introduced him.

Churchill began his speech by saying he wished to make it clear that he had no official mission and he spoke only for himself. "There is nothing here but what you see." [10] This did not greatly lessen its import or impact. But it left the British Labor Government free either to associate itself with Churchill's stand or suggest that it was just an outburst of the old Tory and that it did not harbor the same animus. It allowed those members of the Labor Party who still were eager to keep on good terms with the Soviet Union to condemn the speech as irresponsible and provocative.

A few brief extracts from this declamatory address will suffice to convey its tone and import, its ominousness and warning. Waxing eloquent

[7] A memo made by an experienced reporter for the *New York Times* later in the spring of 1946 has come to my attention. It relates that Truman told him breezily that he, Truman, had also invited Stalin to visit the United States on that occasion; and that Stalin had answered that his doctors would not permit it (his "ticker"). In response to my letter of inquiry, President Truman replied that although he remembered inviting Stalin several times to come to Washington, he did not recall having done so on this occasion. Perhaps when, if ever, the correspondence with Stalin and other pertinent records are opened, this interesting question can be definitely answered.

[8] Leahy Diary, March 3, 1946.

[9] Byrnes to the author, personal communication.

[10] Winston S. Churchill, *Sinews of Peace: Post-War Speeches* (Boston: Houghton Mifflin, 1949) p. 94.

against the two great dangers confronting all peoples—War and Tyranny—Churchill advocated that the United Nations be equipped at once with an international force. And then coming to what he called " . . . the crux of what I have travelled here to say," [11] he pleaded for a continuance of intimate military association and joint defense arrangements between the United States and the British Commonwealth. This fraternal association of the English-speaking peoples would, he averred, play its part in steadying and stabilizing the foundations of peace. "There is the path of wisdom. Prevention is better than cure." For "Nobody knows what Soviet Russia and its Communist international organization intends to do in the immediate future, or what are the limits, if any, to their expansive and proselytising tendencies. But the facts about the present situation in Europe are clear.

"From Stettin in the Baltic to Trieste in the Adriatic, an iron curtain has descended across the Continent. Behind that line lie all the capitals of the ancient states of Central and Eastern Europe. Warsaw, Berlin, Prague, Vienna, Budapest, Belgrade, Bucharest, and Sofia, all these famous cities, and the populations around them lie in what I must call the Soviet Sphere, and all are subject in one form or another, not only to Soviet influence but to a very high and, in many cases, increasing measure of control from Moscow. . . .

"Turkey and Persia are both profoundly alarmed and disturbed at the claims which are being made upon them and at the pressure being exerted by the Moscow Government. An attempt is being made by the Russians in Berlin to build up a quasi-Communist party in their zone of Occupied Germany . . .

"At the end of the fighting last June, the American and British armies [in Germany] withdrew westwards, . . . to a depth at some points of 150 miles upon a front of nearly four hundred miles, in order to allow our Russian allies to occupy this vast expanse of territory which the Western Democracies had conquered.

"If now the Soviet Government tries, by separate action, to build up a pro-Communist Germany in their areas, this will cause new serious difficulties in the British and American zones, and will give the defeated Germans the power of putting themselves to auction between the Soviets and the Western Democracies. Whatever conclusions may be drawn from these facts—and facts they are—this is certainly not the Liberated Europe we fought to build up. Nor is it one which contains the essentials of permanent peace."

And veering toward the conclusion that resounded in Moscow, "I do not believe that Soviet Russia desires war. What they desire is the fruits

[11] *Ibid.*

77

of war and the indefinite expansion of their power and doctrines. . . . Our difficulties and dangers will not be removed by . . . a policy of appeasement. . . . I am convinced that there is nothing they [the Russians] admire so much as strength, and there is nothing for which they have less respect than for weakness, especially military weakness. . . . If the population of the English-speaking Commonwealths be added to that of the United States with all that such cooperation implies in the air, on the sea, all over the globe and in science and in industry, and in moral force, there will be no quivering, precarious balance of power to offer its temptation to ambition or adventure. On the contrary, there will be an overwhelming assurance of security."

When Truman was asked by the press whether he had seen a copy of Churchill's address in advance, he said he had not. Byrnes, when asked whether the United States associated itself with the address, said: "The United States had nothing to do with it." [12]

These denials stretched credulity and evoked chuckles. It has since become known that Truman read a mimeographed copy of the final draft on the train. And, according to the message which Churchill sent to Attlee and Bevin on March 7th, the President had remarked " . . . "he thought it was admirable and would do nothing but good though it would make a stir." [13]

The President and Byrnes wanted to be in the lee of the storm in the public press and Congress which the speech might provoke. They wanted to avert the inference that American policy was being governed by these Churchillian views and ideas even though we were firmly opposing Communist subversion and demands in Iran, Turkey, Greece, and elsewhere. They thought it time that Russia be challenged and warned, while diverting the anticipated Soviet kick-back from the American Government to that veteran anti-Bolshevik, Churchill.

So it was. *Pravda* informed its readers that "Churchill convulsively grabs for the coat-tails of Uncle Sam in the hope that an Anglo-American military alliance would enable the British Empire. . . . to continue its policy of imperialist expansion."

Stalin answered a series of questions asked by a well-drilled publicist:

Q: "How do you assess the last speech of Mr. Churchill?"

---

[12] *New York Times,* March 8, 1946.

[13] The substance of this telegram is contained in Francis Williams' (Attlee's press secretary) book *A Prime Minister Remembers: The War and Post-War Memoirs of the Rt. Hon. Earl Attlee* (London: Heinemann, 1961), pp. 162–4. In this same message Churchill informed his colleagues that Truman had told him that he had decided to send the body of the Turkish Ambassador to the United States, who had just died, back to Turkey in the battleship *Missouri*, accompanied by a strong task force which would remain in the Eastern Mediterranean.

A: "I assess it as a dangerous act calculated to sow the seeds of discord among the Allied Governments and to hamper their cooperation."

Q: "Can one consider that Mr. Churchill's speech is damaging to the cause of peace and security?"

A: "Undoubtedly yes. In substance, Mr. Churchill is now in the position of a firebrand of war. And Mr. Churchill is not alone here. He has friends not only in England but also in the United States of America. . . . There is no doubt that the set-up of Mr. Churchill is a set-up for war, a call for war against the Soviet Union."

Q: "How do you assess that part of Mr. Churchill's speech in which he attacks the democratic regimes of the European countries which are our neighbors, and in which he criticizes the good-neighborly relations established between these countries and the Soviet Union?"

A: ". . . . It needs no special effort to show that Mr. Churchill rudely and shamelessly libels not only Moscow but also the States neighborly to the U.S.S.R. . . . One may ask . . . what can be surprising is the fact that the Soviet Union, in a desire to ensure its security for the future, tries to ensure that these countries should have governments whose relations to the Soviet Union are loyal? How can one, without having lost one's reason, characterize these peaceful aspirations of the Soviet Union as expansionary tendencies . . . ?

". . . . I do not know whether Mr. Churchill and his friends will succeed in organizing, after the Second World War, a new crusade against 'Eastern Europe.' But if they succeed in this, which is not very probable, since millions of 'common people' stand guard over the peace, that one may confidently say they will be beaten just as they were beaten twenty-six years ago." [14]

In these replies, Stalin did not conceal the fury which he and his Communist supporters felt. In part because they knew Churchill was disposed, if he could, to challenge Soviet advances in Central and Eastern Europe, in part because they really thought that in the European countries linked to the Soviet Union they were establishing true democracies, while Churchill longed to bring back the reactionary kings, politicians, and landowners—Fascists all.

The reemerging animosities and differences of belief were brought out by this speech as by a streak of lightning. The heads of the Labor Party in Britain neither rebuked nor applauded Churchill. Truman, having thought that this candid statement was timely and beneficial, kept aloof. When asked by the press on March 14th to comment, he refrained from answering questions about Churchill's views. However, he allowed

[14] The complete text of this long interview, of which I have given only extracts, was printed in the *Information Bulletin*, distributed by the Embassy of the U.S.S.R. in Washington, March 19, 1946.

the press to quote him to the effect that he was not alarmed. "I am sure," he said, "we will work it out."

But in Iran he was not going to risk the outcome if the Russians and Iranians were left alone to settle Iran's complaints against the Soviet Union. In that situation he was about to speak and act in accordance with Churchill's dicta.

13

"We May Be at War...
Over Iran"

While Churchill's speech was brewing, the new Iranian
Prime Minister, Ahmad Ghavam, was in Moscow dickering with Stalin.
He stayed there until March 11th. Stalin told him that Soviet troops
would remain in Iran until the Iranian Government recognized the "autonomy" of Azerbaijan. He proposed the creation of a joint company to
develop the oil resources of the five northern provinces, the Soviet Government to have 51 percent of the stock.

Intimations of what Russia was going to exact from Iran, then definite
information of what was being asked of Ghavam, found its way to
Washington and London. They evoked outspoken American and British
protests.

Byrnes, on February 28th, in a speech to the Overseas Press Club had
in effect put Russia on notice that no matter how the talks went in Moscow, the American Government would keep the Iranian situation before
the U.N. "Only an inexcusable tragedy of errors could cause serious conflict between us [the United States and the Soviet Union]. . . . But . . .
we must make plain that the United States intends to defend the
Charter. . . . We will not and we cannot stand aloof if force or the
threat of force is used contrary to the purposes and principles of the
Charter." [1]

On March 1st, the day before Russia was obligated to take its troops
out of Iran, the Moscow radio announced that the Iranian Prime Minister had been told that evacuation had begun from certain "relatively
quiet" districts in Eastern Iran but Soviet troops would remain in Northwestern Iran "until the situation had been elucidated." Our Embassy in
Iran reported that, to the contrary, Soviet troops were moving into
hitherto unoccupied areas.

[1] *New York Times*, March 1, 1946.

Instructed by Bevin, the British Ambassador in Moscow presented a vigorous protest to Molotov on March 3d. This was two days before Churchill made his Iron Curtain speech. An entry in the Diary of Hugh Dalton, the Chancellor of the Exchequer, noted, "I ran into E.B. . . . and found him in a great state, saying that the Russians were advancing in full force on Teheran, that 'this means war' and that the United States was going to send a battle fleet to the Mediterranean." [2] Dalton and Prime Minister Attlee thought Bevin was "strung up," presumably too strung up.

Kennan, the American Chargé d'Affaires in Moscow, also handed in a protest written in Washington; this reaffirmed that the American Government would not calmly acquiesce in the decision of the Soviet Government to keep its troops in Iran contrary to the principles of the Charter.[3]

The wily Prime Minister of Iran did not cave in. Ghavam was an elderly man who owned property in the part of Iran over which the Russian troops were roaming. He was thought to be predisposed to Russia and therefore might be able to convince the Soviet leaders that the Iranian Government was not unfriendly and so persuade them to leave Iran alone. But finding the Russians designing hagglers, he temporized. Outwitting them, he departed from Moscow on March 11th, without leaving his signature behind. And all the while he had left the Iranian complaint before the United Nations.

Reports—whether correct or not—that Soviet troops were advancing toward Teheran and the border of Turkey and Iraq caused the American Government to make known that it would bring the dispute before the Security Council even if Iran refrained.[4] It wondered whether the Soviet Government would show its displeasure by refusing to take any further part in that session of the U.N. It did not for a time. But it sent tanks, artillery, and cavalry into Iran, possibly with the thought of extorting what it wanted from the Iranian Government before the Security Council met.

Truman let his anxieties be known in close official circles. It was about then, if not just then, in persuading Ambassador Harriman (who, having left Moscow, wished to remain in the United States) to go to

[2] The entry in Dalton's Diary is dated March 22d, but it refers to a talk with Bevin "a fortnight ago." Was this statement of Bevin about American intentions based on the telegram from Churchill relaying what Truman had said to him about sending the U.S.S. *Missouri* and a strong task force into the Mediterranean?

[3] The American Government released its text, and it is in the *New York Times* of March 8, 1946.

[4] On March 13th, the headlines of the *New York Times* read: "Heavy Russian columns move west in Iran. . . . Red Army . . . believed 25 miles from Teheran." The Soviet official press agency denied these reports. *New York Times*, March 15, 1946.

London as Ambassador, he said, "It is important. We may be at war with the Soviet Union over Iran." [5]

But in public the President kept a cool demeanor and told the press that he saw no reason to become alarmed over the international situation, saying, "I do not think it is as fraught with danger as a lot of people seem to think it is." [6] Undersecretary of State Dean Acheson suddenly canceled his engagement to deliver one of the welcoming addresses at the dinner which New York City was giving for Churchill.

These soothing signals were offset by an ambiguous one. The American press informed the world that at the instigation of the State Department, the Navy Department had shelved the plan to have a large part of the Eighth Fleet, including the aircraft carriers *Franklin D. Roosevelt* and *Midway* and the battleship U.S.S. *Missouri,* cruise in the Eastern Mediterranean. Instead, the U.S.S. *Missouri* would take the body of the Turkish Ambassador to the United States, Mehet Munir Ertegun, to Istanbul, visiting various places in the Mediterranean.[7]

On March 18th, despite Soviet warnings that it would be regarded as an unfriendly act, the Iranian Government petitioned the Security Council again to take cognizance of the dispute, stating that it imperiled peace.

Moscow may have thought that Iranian capitulation was near. Ambassador Andrei Gromyko (Mar. 19th) asked that the discussion of Iran's complaint in the Security Council be postponed to April 10th.

President Truman let it be known that he was against postponement and thought that the U.N. must prove itself on this first test.[8] Prime Minister Ghavam was reported, in the press and in an information bulletin circulated by the Soviet Embassy in Washington, as having said on the 23d that a "satisfactory" solution would be found for Iran's dispute with Russia, and as having rebuked the Iranian Ambassador to the U.N., Hussein Ala, for urging immediate U.N. action.[9] It may be noted that when the actual words used by Ghavam were officially obtained by the State Department, their meaning was ambiguous, and within a few days he was to deny that he had given any such instruction to the Iranian Ambassador.[10] On the 25th, Stalin, in reply to a cabled inquiry from Hugh Baillie, President of the United Press, stated that an agreement had been reached. "As to what concerns the question of withdrawal of

[5] Exact date not recorded in Harriman memo.
[6] *New York Times,* March 15, 1946.
[7] *Ibid.,* March 7, 1946.
[8] *Ibid.,* March 22, 1946.
[9] *Ibid,* March 24.
[10] On March 30th Ghavam told the United Press representative in Teheran that he was not repudiating any of Ala's charges before the Security Council.

Soviet troops from Iran, it is known that this has been decided in a positive way by an understanding reached by the Soviet Government and the Government of Iran." [11]

On the 26th, speaking in the Council, Gromyko explained his request for delay. He averred, as had Stalin, that the discussions with the Iranian Government had resulted in an understanding whereby evacuation of the Soviet troops had begun on March 2d, and that those remaining in Iran would be brought out within five or six weeks "unless unforeseen circumstances arise." [12] But the Iranian representative objected to the delay and denied that any understanding about evacuation had been reached. Byrnes, who had stepped in over the head of Stettinius, speaking in the U.N. for the American government, opposed the Russian proposal vigorously. He urged that the Council consider the dispute over Iran as its first business. After the Council refused Gromyko's request for postponement, he walked out of the meeting, and absented himself from subsequent ones.

The Security Council Takes Cognizance of the Dispute

Of what happened at this juncture, of the order of events, and the connection between them, the historian, lacking uncontested information, cannot be sure. In particular he is left uncertain as to whether Truman sent a personal peremptory message to Stalin, and whether this impressed the Marshal.[13] In any case, the Security Council rejected the Russian motion to take the Iranian issue off the agenda. It did so although Gromyko said (after Byrnes and the British representative, Sir Alexander Cadogan, expressed doubts as to whether an agreement had

[11] *New York Times*, March 26.

[12] *Ibid.*, March 27, 1946.

[13] The President, in *Memoirs*, Vol. II: *Years of Trial and Hope*, (New York: Doubleday, 1956), page 95, states—without giving a precise date—"Then I told Byrnes to send a blunt message to Premier Stalin. On March 24 Moscow announced that all Russian troops would be withdrawn from Iran at once."

Professor Herbert Druks, in his book *Harry S. Truman and the Russians, 1945–1953* (New York: Speller, 1966), page 125, writes that in a talk he had with Truman on August 1, 1962, the former President related that he had sent a note to Stalin saying he expected the Russians to withdraw all their forces. "He warned that unless their withdrawal did commence within a week's time and was completed within six, he would move the fleet as far as the Persian Gulf and he would send American troops back into Iran."

I have seen no other reference to such a personal message from Truman, and Loy Henderson, Chief of the Division of Eastern European Affairs at the time, has told me that as far as he knows, Truman never sent an admonitory message to Stalin. It may be that the President had in mind the note he had instructed Byrnes to send, which is referred to cryptically in *Years of Trial and Hope*, page 95.

been reached with the Iranian Government), "I would make it quite clear that such doubts are absolutely unjustified." [14]

On March 29th the Security Council adopted a suggestion by Byrnes that both Russia and Iran be asked to report by April 3d on the state of their negotiations, and whether Russia was imposing conditions on its evacuation.

The Soviet official press denounced this Resolution as unjust and contrary to the Charter. But when April 3d came round, the Russian Government advised the Secretary General that an agreement had been reached whereby the evacuation of Soviet troops, already begun, would be completed in six weeks; that this action was unconditional; and that the question of the oil company was quite separate.

This latest Russian assurance could not, however, allay the Council's concern because the Iranian side of the situation, explained in a letter from Ambassador Hussein Ala, dated April 2, was quite different; no positive results had been achieved in the Iranian–Russian talks. In retrospect it almost seems as if Ghavam, while negotiating with the Russians at home, let his ambassador maintain stubborn resistance in the Security Council. Besides, the Russian reports to the Council seem to have preceded by several days the events which they were presumably reporting. The Council puzzled over this contradiction during the April 3d and 4th sessions (Gromyko absent), and then resolved to defer further proceedings on Iran until May 6th, by which date it hoped Russian troop withdrawal would have been completed. Then, on April 4th, an agreement was reached, contained in notes exchanged between Ghavam and the Soviet Ambassador in Teheran, Ivan Sadchikov. The three points of the announced agreement were: (1) that all Soviet troops were to be out of Iran by early May; (2) that a joint Iranian–Soviet oil company would be formed, of which the Soviet Government would be majority stock owner, but—and this turned out to be the clause by which the Iranian Government later winkled out of the project—it had to be validated by a treaty to be submitted to a newly elected Majlis (the Iranian parliament) within seven months; and (3) "with regard to Azerbaijan, since it is an internal Iranian affair, peaceful arrangements will be made between the Iranian Government and the people of Azerbaijan for carrying out reforms in accordance with existing laws and in a benevolent spirit toward the people of Azerbaijan." [15]

Who can match the Soviet publicists for piety? In a *Pravda* editorial quoted in the issue of the *Information Bulletin* distributed by the Soviet Embassy in Washington on April 11th, referring to this agreement, it was written that, "Once again the Soviet Union objectively demon-

[14] *New York Times*, March 27, 1946.
[15] *Documents on American Foreign Relations*, 1945–6, pp. 858–9.

strated its inflexible desire to come to mutual understanding with other countries, to establish good-neighborly friendly relations with other states and to consolidate international cooperation for the benefit of general peace and security."

The State Department (and Foreign Office) feared that this Soviet–Iranian agreement would allow the consolidation of the autonomous Azerbaijan regime.[16] Thus, the American and British Governments wanted the Iranian situation to remain on the Council's agenda until the Soviet Government proved its intentions by its actions, even though the Iranian Government on April 15th had withdrawn its complaint. Because the majority of the Council resolved to keep the question before it until all Russian troops were out of Iran, Gromyko accused the American and British Governments of using Iran as a pawn in power politics.

After weeks of inconclusive and confusing reports, the Iranian Ambassador to the U.N. informed the Secretary General that the Iranian Government had been able to inspect all Azerbaijan, and no Soviet troops or equipment remained. Whereupon, on May 22d, the Council suspended further consideration of the situation. But the Iranian Government continued to be nervous. Later in the year it wanted the American Government to arrange for U.N. supervision of elections in Azerbaijan. It was advised to postpone elections until it was in firm control of the provinces and promised "strong support" should the Soviet object to the entry of Government troops in the region.[17] By the end of the year 1946 the Iranian army had suppressed the separatist movement in the North, and all members of the Tudeh Party were expelled from the Cabinet.

This out-in-the-open skirmish with the Soviet Union left a lasting impression on Truman's disposition. It convinced him that the Soviet Communists were bent on trying by subterfuge and subversion to extend Soviet rule or influence, not only over northern Iran but down to the Persian Gulf and into the Eastern Mediterranean. He concluded that while the Soviet Government would grab whatever it could in this region without war, it did not want to engage, for the time being anyhow, in another war. Hence, if firmly resisted and faced, it would "back down." This cast of Truman's judgment and temper was to show itself more clearly and consequentially later on.

Jumping far ahead of other sections of this narrative, I shall point out how nearly complete—for the time being, at least—was the frustration of the Soviet designs upon Iran. Russia did not even manage to extract

---

[16] Dean Acheson, *Present at the Creation: My Years in the State Department* (New York: W. W. Norton, 1969), p. 197.

[17] *Ibid.*

out of the coils of Iranian diplomacy the right to develop oil resources in northern Iran. By one ruse or another, the election for and convening of the Majlis was repeatedly deferred until July 1947. Then, taking its lead from Ghavam, that Assembly loitered before considering the provisional accord about the oil company.

Washington encouraged its rejection. The American Ambassador to Iran, George V. Allen (who had succeeded Wallace Murray), on September 11, 1947, announced publicly: "Our determination to follow this policy (opposition to all threats of aggression) as regards Iran is as strong as anywhere else in the world. . . . Patriotic Iranians, when considering matters affecting their national interest, may therefore rest assured that the American people will support fully their freedom to make their own choice." [18]

The Majlis rejected the agreement almost unanimously. The Soviet Government did not rage or even protest. Probably it did not attach much importance to the oil project except as a center of political subversion. It had managed to debar American or British oil concessions in the north, near Soviet frontiers, and it had enlivened Iranian criticism of the great British oil undertakings in the south.

To revert to our main order of narration: while the Iranian dispute was exciting the diplomats, the American Government was formulating a plan for the control of atomic energy to be presented to the U.N.—a matter of far greater and more lasting consequence. Thus, before proceeding with the course of other unsettled political situations which were evolving with an irregular pulse of accord and discord I believe that an account of the formulation of this plan and its reception in the U.N. should be given in this retrospective attempt to understand this period as fully as it figured at the time in the reckoning of governments.

[18] *New York Times*, September 12, 1947.

PART FOUR

The Intruder:
The Atomic Bomb

14

The American Quandary

While the Conference at Potsdam was assembling, the American Government, after five years of gigantic effort, had successfully tested an atomic bomb, of destructive power, explosive and radiating, far greater than any weapon hitherto known.

In releasing atomic power to national states, history—with science and engineering as its favorite agents—played one of its grimmest and most impish tricks. For, such being the virus in their marrow, many of these states were likely to prize the potential destructiveness of atomic power more than its potential serviceability. Henceforth this intruder was to be a presence in every international crisis.

History sired this weapon at a time when the war alliance—between the Western democracies and the Soviet Union—was beginning to crumble. It gave the Americans supreme power, of a kind, for a few years, and a false sense of lasting security. It caused the Soviet Union to subordinate all other scientific and engineering efforts to extort the same power from nature and knowledge.

The American authorities stood in awe of this super-human force and wanted to imprison it; releasing it only for peaceful civilian purposes. They strove to devise and innovate a system of control which would safeguard the world against the demoniac energy compacted in the atom. But this effort was always haunted by fear that some other country—most probably the Soviet Union—would, by deception, procure the same weapon and use it to impose its will on others.

As soon as it seemed likely that the bomb could be made, some of the eminent men who had pried open this Pandora's box had begun to formulate ideas about the connected consequences of their achievement. In their vision, lit up by fore-glimpses of radiant fires, immense questions burst, and bold conclusions flickered.

Most immediately, whether and how to bring this new power to bear upon our relations with the Soviet Union, which were becoming touchy and cloudy. Connectedly, could reliable controls over the production or/and use of atomic energy be contrived and made effective?

As the discussions of these matters which took place before the bomb was used at Hiroshima have been fully told elsewhere, I shall not review at length twice-told tales.[1]

Roosevelt had briefly seemed all but persuaded to inform the Russians what we had accomplished before the bomb was demonstrated and used; to get started on direct discussions with them of what should be done, as a matter of common concern, before the Communists could suspect that the bomb was going to be used in the service of national diplomacy, and therefore conclude that they must make a breakneck effort to emulate us. But Churchill had rejected this course as naïve; naïve because it would nullify this great weapon which power-bent Communists would respect, and certainly seek to secure. In September 1944 Roosevelt had abruptly changed his mind and agreed with Churchill that no knowledge about the atomic bomb project should be disclosed before a permanent policy was determined.

Truman, who had known nothing about the bomb project, had been compelled to reckon with the coming event in a great hurry. The first informing memo which Secretary of War Stimson, who had been the supervising mentor of the whole effort, gave him (Apr. 25th) should have been startling. "Within four months we shall in all probability have completed the most terrible weapon ever known in human history, one bomb of which could destroy a whole City." The new President had been impressed but not astounded. Unlike Stimson, he was not flung into sleepless nights of anxiety about problems of policy.

The wish to know whether we actually possessed this awesome weapon may have been, and probably was, one of the reasons why Truman deferred his meeting with Churchill and Stalin to discuss postwar settlements. The question of whether, when, and how much to tell the Russians had been left in abeyance. There lurked in everyone's mind the thought that when Truman met Stalin at Potsdam, he might open up on the subject.

The impressions formed at Potsdam by Truman, Byrnes, Stimson, and Marshall of the harsh ways of a Communist police regime and of the

---

[1] Among the various books on the decision to use the bomb against Japan and preliminary suggestions for its control is my book, *The Atomic Bomb and the End of World War II*, rev. ed. (Princeton: Princeton University Press, 1966). More exhaustive accounts of the discussions are in the official American history *The New World 1939–1946*, Vol. I: *A History of the United States Atomic Energy Commission* (University Park: Pennsylvania State University Press, 1962), by Richard G. Hewlett and Oscar E. Anderson, Jr., and the official British history by Margaret Gowing, *Britain and Atomic Energy 1939–1945* (London: Macmillan, 1964).

sprawl of Russian aims, caused them to decide that the Russians should be told only enough to avert future accusations of malevolent deception, until they had a clearer idea of what the Russian policy would be.

Truman had waited a week after learning of the successful test in New Mexico to tell Stalin about the bomb, and then casually and laconically. To Truman's surprise, Stalin's response was equally off-hand; he had not shown any curiosity about the nature of the weapon, or given any hint that he perceived it might affect the contest for national advantage and position. The President inferred that Stalin did not grasp the significance of what he had been told. But later revelations make it seem far more probable that Stalin was dissimulating; that he did not wish by quiver or inquiry to allow Truman and Churchill to conclude that Soviet diplomacy would be affected by the fact that the West now had a supreme weapon. We know now that by the time of Potsdam Soviet scientists and engineers with capable knowledge of the theory of atomic structure and fission were hard at work designing laboratory apparatus to produce a chain reaction.[2]

In short, the evasions at Potsdam now seem clearly to forecast the devious direction that subsequent discussions about the control of atomic energy would take. The nations were to be frightened tenants in a house that at any time might be blown to pieces by a monstrous force rather than trust each other as caretaker.

Here the narrative may be briefly interrupted to take note of accusations that our primary purpose in using the bomb against Japan was not to shock the Japanese leaders into acceptance of our demand for unconditional surrender, but to end the war before the Soviet Union entered. And conjunctively to impress and frighten the Soviet Government so that it would be more yielding to American and British diplomatic designs and wishes.[3]

Rather careful study seems to me amply to justify dismissal of these allegations. They are distorted inferences from the acknowledged fact that after American negotiators at Potsdam knew they had the weapon, they no longer thought it necessary to worry over whether the Soviet Government would enter the Pacific War in time to save American lives, or to offer additional inducements to do so. His knowledge that the

[2] See mimeograph study by M. J. Ruggles and A. Kranish, *The Soviet Union and the Atom: The Early Years* (Santa Monica, Calif.: Rand Corporation Publication, 1956).

[3] This opinion was first boldly and ably advanced by a British scientist of Communist persuasion, Professor Patrick Blackett, who wrote that the use of the bomb should be regarded not as a last act of the Pacific War but the first act of the cold war. The opinion was quickly espoused by the Russians. At present it has several convinced expositors among the American and British historians who seek to supplant prevailing versions of the course of the "cold war" with new ones.

bomb had been tested did make Truman firmer in his refusal to cede some of the more grasping Soviet claims at Potsdam and after. But the American Government did not change its policies or expand its claims because it had acquired the bomb; it faithfully followed the course defined by officials who had known nothing about the bomb until it was exploded on Hiroshima.[4]

As the news of the bomb dropped on Hiroshima astounded and upset the world, both the President and Stimson had issued statements about our efforts to create the bomb that were exultant, awesome, and somber. The genie—good or evil—was out of the bottle.

In the report to the nation which Truman made about the Potsdam Conference, he merely stated that the Government was preparing plans for the future control of the bomb so that it would serve only purposes of peace.

Since the scientists who had conceived the bomb seemed so sure and almost unanimous in their opinion that the basic scientific knowledge and technique needed for atomic fission was known in professional circles of all countries, the President, and even Secretary Byrnes and General Leslie R. Groves, the director of the Manhattan project and a military lion who roared at any notion of relaxing security, were half convinced of the fact. But they thought the span of "know-how" and industrial performance between such "theoretical" knowledge, and the "harnessing" of atomic energy tremendous, so great it could not be quickly, if ever, traversed by a country as hard hit as the Soviet Union. Hence the view that was to govern our policy: secrecy while we sought a satisfactory system that would protect us—and every other nation— against the terror of the bomb.[5]

[4] This conclusion may be tested by anyone with enough patience to compare policies contained in the Position Papers written for guidance of the President and the American delegation to the Potsdam Conference, and those sustained by Truman at Potsdam and thereafter—until the cold war had really set in. (See U.S., Department of State, *Potsdam Papers: a Collection of Papers Concerning the Potsdam Conference.*) Will qualified Ph.D. aspirants please consider whether these issues are not of enough importance to investigate?

[5] In order to quell the impulse of scientists or engineers who had contributed to the creation of the bomb to tell what they knew, Truman, on August 15, 1945, directed the Secretaries of State, War, and Navy, the Joint Chiefs of Staff, and the Director of the Office of Scientific Research and Development ". . . to take such steps as are necessary to prevent the release of any information in regard to the *development, design or production of the atomic bomb* [underlining mine]; or in regard to its employment in military or naval warfare, except with the specific approval of the President."

But the American Government, wanting to preclude the circulation of incorrect and indiscreet versions, authorized publication of a history of the discoveries and processes that enabled us to produce the bomb, written by the physicist who had been officially instructed to keep that record. This was entitled *Atomic Energy for*

Boldness or Caution

Byrnes had discouraged what he thought to be undue haste in formulation of any agreement that might too quickly cancel our achievement. For he was about to leave for London to meet with Molotov and Bevin, and he believed that the exclusive knowledge of how to make atomic weapons might abet him in sustaining American diplomatic policies. Moreover, he doubted whether any promises we might obtain from the Soviet Government could be trusted.

However, cognizance of the fact that the presence of atomic weapons in national arsenals would later, if not sooner, torment all of mankind would not let Stimson, that veteran worker for just law and order in the international world, rest. He detested the crushing, thrusting, conspiring nature of the Soviet state. Yet, weighing all aspects of this dilemma that would face the world until met, his spirit reverted to that working maxim which had stood him in such good stead—that the way to win trust was to show trust. Thus he advocated that it was best to take the risk of exposing the United States to atomic competition in order to bring that awesome force under international control. Despite weariness of age, illness, his last exhausting stint in office was to compose a statement of his views of what should be done.

On September 11th he presented this to the President with a covering letter.[6] No other official recommendation went so far in its bid for Soviet cooperation. Stimson first remarked that the Soviet Government must surely sense the tendency in many American quarters to regard our exclusive possession of the atomic weapons as a counter to Soviet ambitions in Europe. This would almost certainly, he predicted, cause the Soviet Government feverishly to seek to develop these weapons, to enter a secret and desperate race to possess them. "Whether," he continued— and this was the fulcrum of his arguments—"Russia gets control of the necessary secrets of production in a minimum of four years or a maximum of twenty years is not nearly as important to the world and civilization as to make sure that when they do get it they are willing and cooperative partners among the peace-loving nations of the world. . . . if we fail to approach them now and merely continue to negotiate with them, having this weapon rather ostentatiously on our hip, their suspi-

---

Military Purposes: The Official Report on the Development of the Atomic Bomb Under the Auspices of the United States Government 1940–1945 by Professor Henry deWolfe Smyth.

[6] The memorandum is printed in Henry L. Stimson and McGeorge Bundy, *On Active Service in Peace and War* (New York: Harper, 1948), pp. 642 ff.

cions and their distrust of our purposes and our motives will increase." [7]

Thus Stimson recommended that after clearing with London, the Russian Government be told *directly* that the American Government was ready to enter into an agreement to control the production and use of the bomb. We should, he urged, offer to stop work on the improvement or manufacture of the bomb as a military weapon provided the Russians would agree to do likewise; and to impound the bombs we had, provided it was agreed with us that in no event would they or we use the bomb as an instrument of war unless all three governments approved. This would have been a great gamble on Soviet good faith.

Stimson added and italicized, "I emphasize . . . the importance of taking this action with Russia as a proposal of the United States—backed by Great Britain but peculiarly the proposal of the United States. Action of any international group of nations, including many small nations who have not demonstrated their potential power or responsibility in this war would not, in my opinion, be taken seriously by the Soviets." [8]

But at the last meeting of the Cabinet (on Sept. 21st) attended by Stimson before he departed from Washington its members sharply differed.[9] Stimson made a heartfelt, impressive plea for initiating discussions with the Russians along the lines of his memorandum. To him human destiny—nothing less—was in the crucible of this decision. Acting Secretary of State Acheson supported his recommendation, as did Undersecretary of War Robert Patterson, and the strongly inclined internationalist, Secretary of Commerce Henry A. Wallace. But Fred M. Vinson, the obtuse Secretary of the Treasury, took strong issue. He said he thought the step ill-advised and sure to get the President in hot water. Why, he asked, if we wanted to share any part of our knowledge of atomic energy, should we not also want to share all the military secrets? He was afraid that exchange of information about atomic matters would be a one-sided affair, the United States receiving nothing in return for what it gave. Attorney General Thomas Campbell Clark agreed with Vinson. Secretary of the Navy James Forrestal, most dubious, advised against any precipitate decision.

At this point in the Cabinet discussion Truman interrupted to point out that they were not discussing the question of giving the secret of the bomb to Russia or anyone else, but the best method of controlling bomb warfare and the exchange of scientific information. Here again was the attempted distinction between theoretical knowledge of how to split the

[7] *Ibid.*
[8] *Ibid.*
[9] The most comprehensive account of the discussions at this Cabinet meeting is in Truman's *Year of Decisions*, pp. 525–7. Other versions generally corroborate it.

atom and produce a chain reaction, and the practical knowledge of how to produce a bomb. The President's remarks diverted the discussion from the essentials of Stimson's proposal. The comments of others scattered all around.

The comment in his *Memoirs* with which President Truman ended his account of this momentous Cabinet meeting is inane: "The discussions had been lively and it was this kind of interchange of opinion that I liked to see at Cabinet meetings. This Cabinet meeting showed that honest men can honestly disagree, and a frank and open argument of this kind is the best form of free expression in which a President can get all points of view needed for him to make decisions. The decisions had to be mine to make." [10] A decision with an explosive core!

Truman Hesitates

Hesitation followed. Members of Congress were agitated by rumors, emanating from this Cabinet meeting, that the American Government was about to give away important secrets to the Russians. The scent of supersecurity was beginning to pollute judgment.

In the message which the President sent to Congress on October 3d, urging enactment of a national policy for atomic energy into law, he said: "The hope of civilization lies in international arrangements looking, if possible, to the renunciation of the use and development of the atomic bomb . . . The difficulties in working out such arrangements are great. The alternative to overcoming these difficulties, however, may be a desperate armament race which might well end in disaster. Discussion of the international problem cannot be safely delayed until the United Nations Organization is functioning and in a position adequately to deal with it."

Therefore, he told Congress, he proposed to initiate discussions first with our associates in this discovery, Great Britain and Canada, and then with other nations. It was against this slower but presumably safer order that Stimson had warned in his notable memo.

About a week later (on Oct. 8th) the President, in a relaxed mood, ruminated aloud in the company of members of the press, as they sat on the front porch of a fishing lodge at Tiptonville in Tennessee. He remarked that he thought it idle to try to withhold scientific knowledge diffused throughout the world. Thus, he continued, the only secret we had was "our know-how in the construction of the bomb." Being asked whether under proper conditions we might impart this to the Russians,

[10] *Ibid.*, p. 527.

he answered: "I don't think it would do any good to let them in on the know-how, because I don't think they could do it anyway. You would have to have the industrial plant and engineering ability to do the job. . . . If they catch up with us on that, they will have to get it on their own hook, just as we did." [11]

As the authors of the official history of American atomic policy remark, the President's comment on this informal occasion seemed to downgrade the urgency of international control. This impression was strengthened because Truman made it known that he intended to leave the discussion with the British and Canadian missions chiefly to Secretary Byrnes.[12]

Retrogression Starts

Another interjection at this point is apropos. Curiosity still hovers over several remarks Molotov had made at the London Conference of Foreign Ministers which had just ended.

Molotov had said to Bevin that if Britain would not agree to allot one of the former Italian colonies in Africa to Russia, it would be content to have the Belgian Congo. Was there a hidden meaning in this professional jest? Bevin had thought so; he inferred that the Russians were more interested in obtaining uranium than anything else. And how was the remark made by Molotov to Bevin at a reception at the Soviet Embassy to be taken? Molotov, drinking "rather much, even for him," according to Bevin, had raised his glass and said: "Here's to the Atom Bomb," and added, "We've got it." [13]

The Russians did not have the bomb, but they did know how it might be made. As soon as the Soviet Government heard of the explosion at Alamogordo, "it had called upon its scientists and engineers to produce their own atomic bomb as soon as possible. . . . Work was being conducted at a feverish rate; under orders of regional and party committees,

[11] Truman *Year of Decisions*, p. 534. This opinion of Truman's that the Russians would not be able for a long time to master the engineering and construction problems faded slowly. How slowly is shown by the remark Truman made as late as 1949 to Admiral Dennison. In the course of explaining why he thought the United States should proceed to start work on the hydrogen bomb, Dennison referred to Russian success in achieving an atomic explosion as proof of their capabilities. Truman agreed that we ought, whereupon Dennison and his colleague gathered up their papers and started to leave. As they reached the door the President looked up from his desk and, glancing over his spectacles, said: "But I still don't believe it." As told by Admiral Dennison to Richard Neustadt, as told to me.

[12] Hewlett and Anderson, *The New World 1939–1946*, p. 456.

[13] Dalton Diary, entries dated October 5, 1945, and October 17, 1945. Diary in custody of London School of Economics.

special institutes, created for the purpose, were mobilizing their best workers, technicians, designers and production managers for the task." [14]

Truman and Byrnes appeared inclined to want more time to consider what lead to take. But Prime Minister Clement Attlee was eager to secure, without further delay, validation of a secret agreement into which Churchill and Roosevelt had entered at Quebec on August 19, 1943. That agreement had specified ". . . the arrangements [that] shall be made to ensure full and effective collaboration between the two countries in bringing the [Manhattan] project to fruition." It was construed by the British authorities as a promise to give them all information that would be helpful if they decided also to make atomic bombs. The agreement had also stipulated: "Thirdly, that we will not either of us communicate any information about Tube Alloys except by mutual consent." [15]

With discussions with Attlee in prospect, Truman, on October 17th, conferred with Byrnes about atomic policy. He asked his representative on the Chiefs of Staff, Admiral Leahy, to be present. Leahy was even more convinced than Byrnes that ". . . our safety demands effective secrecy in regard to the manufacture of the atomic weapon, and continued effort to keep ahead of foreign developments." [16]

When next Truman expounded his ideas publicly, in an Army–Navy Day speech of October 27, 1945, he had sailed clear away from Stimson's idea of bidding for trust by disclosure, and of discussing the problems of control first of all with the Russians. He had decided to toss them to the still unorganized United Nations.

In anticipation of Attlee's projected visit to Washington, Undersecretary of State Acheson and the Counsellor of the State Department, Benjamin Cohen, urged that a plan for the international control of atomic energy be formulated. But their efforts encountered complacency at the top. Thus none was drafted until Vannevar Bush took the task unto himself and, having received Byrnes's approval, composed (over the November 3–4 weekend) a plan envisaging it. As tentatively suggested in his draft, in roughest summary, the progression would be first, free exchange through the U.N. of fundamental scientific information about atomic energy and atomic fission; then, if others gave as well as got, the extension

[14] Igor Golovin, *I.V. Kurchatov: Biography of the Soviet Nuclear Scientist*, trans. William H. Dougherty (Bloomington, Ind.: Selbstverlag Press, 1968). Kurchatov was the physicist in charge of the Soviet atomic bomb project.

[15] *Articles of Agreement Governing Collaboration Between the Authorities of the U.S.A. and the U.K. in the Matter of Tube Alloys*, August 19, 1943. For an account of the discussions preceding the agreement and its drafting, see Hewlett and Anderson, *The New World*, pp. 277–80.

[16] Leahy Diary, entry dated October 17, 1945.

of the exchange of information to production of atomic energy for industrial uses, to be coordinated with the inauguration of a reliable international inspection system; and when that was operative, a mutual arrangement not to make atomic weapons, and the conversion by the American Government of the nuclear element in the bombs it had, into material for power plants.[17] Essentially this idea of moving from stage to stage, leaving the United States in exclusive possession of the bomb during the progression, was to be the basic American approach throughout the subsequent debate in the U.N.

While Prime Ministers King and Attlee were getting ready to leave for Washington, Molotov (on Nov. 6th) made a fiery speech in St. Andrew Hall inside the Kremlin. After giving warning against the creation of an anti-Soviet bloc, he declared ". . . there can be at present no such technical secrets of great importance as could remain in possession of any single country or any narrow group of countries. Therefore the discovery of atomic energy should encourage neither fancies concerning the utilization of this discovery in the international play of forces nor a carefree attitude toward the future of peace-loving nations." And in a peroration which brought the audience to its feet, he had shouted: "The enemy interfered with our peaceful constructive work. But we shall catch up to everything as it should be. . . . We shall have atomic energy too, and many other things." [18] Most scientists who worked in this field thought the prophecy well founded, but most American and British politicians and military officials thought it a statement of hopeful purpose.

The Americans took the lead in the discussions with the British and Canadians which began on November 10th. These were rambling and inconclusive. The Conference went along smoothly since all three—Truman, Attlee, and King—thought their countries ought to be cautious, and since all decisions of immediate consequence were deferred.

Although he had not been present when the three chieftains talked, and therefore had only a second-hand idea of what had been said, Bush was asked by Byrnes to prepare the communiqué. Grumbling, he agreed to try. His production (a composite of American, British, and Canadian drafts) was an acceptable basis for the statement which the world awaited.

This was called a Three Power Agreed Declaration. Truman read it aloud to the press as dramatically as his flat Missouri manner of speech allowed. Its four most important principles were to become hardened

[17] Hewlett and Anderson, *The New World, 1939–1946*, pp. 459 ff.
[18] *Information Bulletin,* Embassy of the U.S.S.R., November 27, 1945. Washington, D.C.

later in the oven of negotiation. In summary, it stated: (1) The three governments were in favor of full freedom of interchange of basic scientific information. (2) But they were not convinced of the wisdom of disclosing detailed information concerning the practical applications of atomic energy. ". . . before it is possible to devise effective, reciprocal and enforceable safeguards acceptable to all nations." (3) A special Commission should be created within the U.N. which would be asked to convert this general aim into a plan and program. These should contain "effective safeguards by way of inspection and other means to protect complying states against the hazards of violations and evasions." (4) The program was to be carried out in separate and successive stages, as the successful accomplishment of one created mutual confidence, and so justified further sharing of knowledge and acceptance of controls.

The two senior members of the Foreign Relations Committee, Senators Tom Connally and Arthur H. Vandenberg, both vain and voluble men, had not been consulted in the course of the talks with the Canadians and British. But they were invited to be present when the three Heads of Government announced their accord to the press. The Senators chose to be affronted. Connally told Byrnes bluntly that the Executive did not have the authority to propose "sharing atomic energy" without the consent of Congress. They stood stony-faced during the ceremony and left in a huff, without waiting to pose for photographs.

This first augury of what attitude the Soviet Government would adopt toward the Truman–Attlee–King plan and procedure was estranging. The official Soviet press tended to compress their impressions of the Declaration into two leading accusations: that the Declaration meant that means and methods of producing atomic weapons were going to be kept secret; and that the three signatories, armed with the atomic bomb, were going to array themselves against the Soviet Union.

Byrnes was eager to try again to reach agreement about procedure for preparing peace treaties with former German satellites—the issue that had disrupted the previous session of the Council of Foreign Ministers. In a message to Molotov he proposed that they and Bevin renew discussion of this and other pending questions. Stalin thereupon invited the Council to meet in Moscow on December 15th, or thereabouts. The American Government decided that at this meeting the Foreign Ministers should resolve to ask the U.N. to consider and devise a plan for the control of atomic energy.

The Senators Alarmed

Before Byrnes left for Moscow a large and capable interdepartmental group had developed the text of the proposal which Byrnes could put forward.

The memorandum followed the line of the Truman–Attlee–King Declaration. It was, however, hazy about the stages of performance during which disclosure and control were to be geared together. Within the complicated interstices of the program outlined, there might lurk the chance that the American Government would disclose important segments of knowledge about the processes of production of the fissionable materials before the clamps of control were tightly fastened.

General Groves protested hotly. Secretary of the Navy Forrestal backed him up; he was adverse even to any discussion of what sorts of information the United States should release until there was a guarantee of genuine reciprocity.

Influential Senators, on learning of the memo, became equally alarmed lest Byrnes, in order to induce the Soviet Government to join in the work of the United Nations Atomic Energy Commission, impart information—or promise to impart information—which they thought vital. When, shortly before leaving, Byrnes read to them a draft of the proposal which he had in mind to make in Moscow, Connally, noting James B. Conant's presence (he was to go with Byrnes to Moscow as adviser), was sure that dangerous influences were circling about Byrnes. He grumbled loud enough for all to hear about bringing in "college professors." The Senators' response is recorded in an entry in Vandenberg's Diary for December 10: "His [Byrnes] plan was a great shock to the entire Committee. . . . We [the Senators] agree that Russia can work out this atom science in perhaps two years; but we are unanimously opposed to hastening the day unless there is absolute and effective agreement for world-wide inspection and control. . . . We are opposed to giving any of the atomic secrets away unless and until the Soviets are prepared to be 'policed' by U.N. in respect to this prohibition. We consider an 'exchange' of scientists and scientific information as sheer appeasement because Russia has nothing 'to exchange.' " [19] There was to be no chink left open as a beckoning entry to the conference table.[20]

[19] Entry *Private Papers of Senator Vandenberg* (Boston: Houghton Mifflin, 1952), dated December 10, 1945, p. 228.

[20] To the testimony of most American scientists who had worked on the bomb, the Senators preferred to accept the judgment of other experts such as the eminent Dr. Irving Langmuir (Associate Research Director for General Electric Company), who

Soviet physicists had in fact learned much from the reports received from various secret agents in the atomic projects and in the British diplomatic service, and from the Smyth report. Perhaps most helpful, they had been briefed by French scientists. Working under Frédéric Joliot-Curie, like their professional colleagues in Germany and England, they had as early as 1938 fastened on the possibility of a chain reaction in fission of uranium; and some had worked at the atomic energy installation in Canada—part of the Manhattan Project; they knew that their theories were essentially correct and they were acquainted with the processes used for making uranium and the bomb.

Whether vitally helped by information procured from abroad or not, the Soviet scientists and engineers had, despite the interruption of the war and the shortage of material and equipment, by the end of the war against Germany, worked out the basic principles and methods of atomic fission and were procuring from their own plants their first large supplies of pure graphite and uranium.[21] But the guardians of American security knew nothing of these beginnings.

Byrnes left for Moscow on December 12th. Members of the Senate Committee on Atomic Energy, being unsure that he had taken their admonitions to heart, called on the President. Connally and Vandenberg spoke for the group. As recorded in Connally's biography, "I told the President flatly 'we must have an inspection system *before* we exchange information about the atomic bomb and atomic energy.'"[22] The President was soothing. He said he agreed with the agitated Senators and that they must have misunderstood Byrnes. The Secretary had no intention of disclosing even "scientific" information at Moscow; all he *might do* was to explore the possibility of exchanging information. The Senators wanted to be sure that this was so; they asked to see the instruction which had been given Byrnes. The President let them read it. Whereupon Vandenberg said he and his colleagues were "amazed." This seemed to them to give Byrnes authority to give away half of our "trad-

---

told the MacMahon Committee (the Senate Special Committee on Atomic Energy): "When you go to Russia and you find that Kapitza, Fersman, Frenkel and Joffee—all of those men . . . working on problems that have nothing to do with atomic energy—when Joffee tells me and shows me the cyclotron started in 1938, work on which was discontinued during the war and is now just starting again, and tells me the cyclotron will be finished in December of this year—and he is the most prominent physicist that has had anything to do with nuclear physics—when you see that, you are convinced they are not carrying through a Manhattan Project." Hearings before the Senate Special Committee on Atomic Energy, pursuant to Senate Resolution 179, November 30, 1945, part I, p. 118.

[21] Golovin, *Kurchatov*.

[22] Tom Connally, as told to Alfred Steinberg, *My Name is Tom Connally* (New York: Thomas Y. Crowell Co., 1954).

ing stock" in the course of the process of getting others to consent to controls.[23]

The Senators asked the President to change the Directive to Byrnes. This he evaded. But he instructed Under-Secretary Acheson to send Byrnes a full report of what had been said. After the President had approved the message, it was sent. Byrnes's discreet acknowledgment said merely that any proposal he would make would be within the framework of the Truman–Attlee–King Declaration.

The Assignment Is Passed to the U.N.

When, in Moscow, the Foreign Ministers discussed their order of business, the Russians asked that the topic be changed from first to last on the conference list of business. This was done.

Byrnes and Bevin on December 19th asked Molotov to join in recommending that the United Nations Assembly set up an Atomic Energy Commission. This, Byrnes proposed, should inquire into all elements of the subject, including those four objectives designated in the Truman–Attlee–King Declaration as primary ones.

Two days later Byrnes informed Molotov and Bevin that he wished to add a paragraph to the American proposal. This, which merely repeated a section of the Truman–Attlee–King Declaration of November 15th, probably was put forward because of reports from Washington of the Senators' criticism. It read: "The work of the Commission should proceed by separate stages, the successful completion of each one of which will develop the necessary confidence of the world before the next stage is undertaken. Specifically it is considered that the Commission might well devote its attention first to the wide exchange of scientists and scientific information, and as a second stage to the development of full knowledge concerning the natural resources of raw materials."

Molotov told Byrnes he did not object to the supplement. But he thought the U.N. Commission ought to be allowed to determine its order of discussion. No, said Byrnes, this was the very heart of the American proposal. Molotov dropped the point without further objection.

[23] Hewlett and Anderson, *The New World, 1939–1946*, p. 474.

Vandenberg wrote in his Diary (entry incorrectly dated December 11, 1945, *Private Papers of Senator Vandenberg*, p. 229), "To our amazement we found that the 'directive' would fully justify the precise sort of plan which Byrnes told us he intended to pursue. It listed four consecutive steps (with 'inspection' and 'control' last); and it then specifically asserted that our government considers it quite proper to proceed 'a step at a time.' We pointed this out to the President—and showed him that—under the 'directive' it would be possible for the Secretary to prematurely give away, while in Moscow, at least half of our 'trading stock' when we seek essential control."

The Soviet Foreign Minister asked only one significant change; that the Commission report directly to the Security Council rather than through the Assembly. Byrnes and Bevin hesitated, pointing out that the Commission was to be authorized only to make recommendations and that the Security Council would have the decisive say about what was done about them. Stalin himself urged them in a spirit of compromise to acquiesce, and they did. It was agreed that the Commission should submit its reports and recommendations to the Security Council, and that these should be made public unless the Council, with the concurrence of all permanent members, ruled otherwise. In appropriate cases the reports were to be submitted by the Council to the Assembly.

All that had been agreed on was that the U.N. Assembly should strive to develop a plan that would eventuate in a well-safeguarded system of control by steps which the U.N. Commission, the formation of which was contemplated, would define in its deliberations. But Senators Vandenberg and Connally detected a chance that the professors or diplomats might somewhere along this route give away vital secrets. In his Diary Vandenberg recorded that when he read the communiqué of the Foreign Ministers he almost resigned the appointment he had accepted as a member of the American delegation to the coming meeting of the Assembly which would designate and instruct the U.N. Atomic Energy Commission. The order in which the four stages were listed in the communiqué he took to mean that the American Government was going to follow the policy of "give away first," about which he had so volubly protested to Byrnes and Truman.[24]

The listing had no such significance. What the Senator, and those who thought like him, were seeking to do was to prevent in advance any attempt to ease the way toward control by agreeing to an exchange of basic scientific information even though the scientists said most of it was common professional knowledge.

[24] *Private Papers of Senator Vandenberg*, pp. 232–3.

15

The Ardent Conception

The resolution to create a special U.N. Commission on Atomic Energy had been sponsored in the first meeting of the U.N. Assembly in January 1946 by all five of the permanent members of the Security Council. It was identical with the text which had been agreed on at the Moscow Conference of Foreign Ministers.

While the Assembly readily adopted this resolution, the American officials who had been formulating a proposal to be put before the U.N. Commission, defining how it was to be carried into effect, were most perplexed. They were becoming aware how squeezed any proposal would be between the Senators and the Russians; how hard to convince the Senators that it would protect the advantage we had acquired, and yet be negotiable.

With many other serious issues on his desk, Byrnes had turned over with alacrity the task to a special Committee formed for the purpose. Acheson, then Undersecretary of State, was designated as Chairman. Acheson, whose swift insight had by then no doubt perceived the difficulties, asked to be let off. But Byrnes had disregarded his demurrer; he hurried to catch the plane for London for the first meeting of the U.N. Assembly. The other members of the Committee were General Leslie R. Groves, the apostle of strictest secrecy, and two scientists and directors of official scientific research, Bush and Conant. They had entertained, perhaps sporadically, the thought that the free flow of professional knowledge between scientists could open the way toward an international control agreement. The fifth was John J. McCloy, former Assistant Secretary of War, who had worked with Stimson on his memo to the President.

But the real question was—as it so often is in foreign affairs—not who was going to mind the store, but who was going to do the thinking. This eminent group, in effect, turned over that hard job to another group to conceive. They appointed a Board of Consultants, a panel of five—David E. Lilienthal, head of the Tennessee Valley Authority, was

106

induced to act as Chairman; Robert Oppenheimer, former director of the Los Alamos Laboratory was also asked to serve. The three other members were experienced in the construction of the plants and manufacture of the components necessary to produce the materials of which the bomb was formed, and the bomb itself.

The Board of Consultants had undertaken the job with a sense of foraging through untraveled country. In order to try better to determine the nature and scope of a plan to be recommended, each member took upon himself to draft a section of the report. The two papers that made the greatest impression on the group were those of Robert Oppenheimer and Charles Thomas, Vice President of the Monsanto Chemical Company and an expert on plutonium chemistry. Both advocated that there be established a *World Authority with positive as well as negative functions.* [my underlining] For they did not believe that attempts of nations to produce atomic weapons would be deterred by mere agreements or detected by inspections. They thought it unlikely that nations would allow foreigners to inspect all the operations of the laboratories, workshops, and factories, where such effort might be conducted and concealed. What an irritant any roving board of inspectors, and the international bureaucrats to whom they would report, would be, they thought; how suspect as agents of foreign powers and saboteurs!

Thus the Board of Consultants had felt compelled to adopt bold astounding conclusions. They were allured by the great aim of creating a real international community by cooperation in the control and use of this wild force of nature. At the end of February they produced a draft report which was not merely a vague, general discussion "but a detailed analysis of the mechanics of international control . . ." [1]

The Board of Consultants had recommended that all activities essential to production of atomic weapons should be entrusted to an international agency (called the Atomic Development Authority). This by treaty should be given exclusive jurisdiction over all these activities, and any or all national initiatives would require its assent.

Specifically, it was contemplated that this Authority (1) should acquire ownership or lease of all mines containing atomic materials, of all stocks of uranium and thorium, and operate all refineries that converted them into metal, (2) be authorized to construct and operate all plutonium production and separation plants which yielded the materials for weapons—and potentially—for peaceful "safe" uses, (3) be free to engage in all research deemed necessary to carry out its assignment, and (4) be authorized to inspect and license all activities in the atomic energy field which were not directly managed by it.

[1] Hewlett and Anderson, *The New World, 1939–1946*, pp. 538–9.

"We have concluded," they stated unanimously, "that there is no prospect of security against atomic warfare in a system of international agreements to outlaw such weapons controlled *only* by a system which relies on inspection and similar police-like methods. . . . " [2] [underlining in original]

The Board of Consultants kept in constant touch with the Acheson group; mainly by converse between Lilienthal and Oppenheimer of the consultant group and Herbert Marks (Acheson's assistant) and Carroll Wilson (Bush's assistant).

Acheson had suggested inclusion of a section which the Consultants had thought it best to leave for later discussion. . . . as to how the nations got through a transitional stage into international control.[3]

Would the Secretary of State's Committee approve or object to the scope and emphasis of the Consultants' report? That was presented formally to it in early March, as winter's traces were beginning to fade from the lovely grounds at Dumbarton Oaks. That Committee discussed them section by section, raised many questions, some complex and involved, technically and administratively. Few now would persist in reading an adequate account or analysis of them.[4] They have become part of the midden of memos which now marks their grave.

But to foretell, neither then, nor in all the later watchful, involved discussions within the American Government or the U.N. of stages in this program of progression did it prove possible to define the timing and linkage of the sequence of actions and responses that the Americans thought safe and the Russians thought advantageous. Using what I trust may not be an offensive figure of speech, no one could devise a schedule and itinerary for this contemporary journey along the stations of the Cross. It was much easier to perfect a rocket that would go to the moon.

General Groves was more worried than any other member at the possibility that the United States might lose exclusive possession of the bomb before complete controls were operative.

Acheson, summarizing his Committee's conclusion in as far as it had coagulated, said: "The consultant's plan risked shortening the time other nations needed to overtake the United States against the chance of achieving a system of controls, operation and management. This system would not make atomic warfare impossible, but it promised to warn the American people if another power started developing nuclear arms." Acheson thought the full plan should go into effect as rapidly as possible, but he recognized it would take time—"five or six years perhaps." [5]

[2] *Ibid.*
[3] *Ibid.*
[4] The most thorough one, explaining as simply as scientific validity permitted, is that in *ibid.*, chap. 15.
[5] *Ibid.*, p. 548.

But since the Committee did not think it advisable—or perhaps even possible—to identify with finality the conditions and schedule of progression, they agreed that this section of their report should be suggestive rather than detailed. It was a pentacle of provisions whose location along the trail of negotiation could be rearranged. As phrased, the United States was not to be required to give up its stocks of nuclear materials and bombs or shut down its plants until the whole plan was operative and tested. Thus the United States could not be endangered were the plan to break down during the transition from any stage to the next.

Acheson, himself, drafted the letter transmitting (on March 18th) the Consultants' report to Byrnes, recommending it as a "framework within which the best prospects" of international control might be found. He urged Byrnes to release it as soon as the President approved. Three days later the Secretary sent it on to the President, the Secretaries of War and Navy, and others. Acheson had also sent a copy to the McMahon Committee. It quickly seeped out to the press.

Its publication followed the first major revelation of Soviet success in espionage about the bomb. The Canadian Government in February 1946 made known that a spy ring, directed by a member of the Soviet Embassy in Ottawa, Igor Gouzenko, had obtained comprehensive information about the American undertaking from Alan Nun May (a British atomic scientist who had worked on the atomic project in Montreal) and other Communist agents in Canada.[6] The disclosure did not cause American officialdom to question the value of our security strictures. It was taken rather to prove the need to bolt them down more tightly. The world was by then beginning to live in the era of James Bond, fascinated by practices and tales of espionage and conspiracy. Stalin and Beria were most at home in it.

Any slight chance that the American plan might be negotiable was lessened by the choice of the man to present it to the U.N. When Acheson had turned over the Consultants' report to Byrnes, the Secretary told him that he would recommend to the President that Bernard Baruch be chosen to translate " . . . the various proposals stimulated by the Acheson–Lilienthal report into a workable plan." Acheson protested, since he doubted whether the translation would be an improvement and because he did not share Byrnes' high regard for Baruch's abilities. Nor, it may be surmised, did he think Baruch's political influence so val-

---

[6] *Report of the Royal Commission . . . to investigate the Facts Relating to and Circumstances Surrounding the Communications by Public Officials and other Persons in Positions of Trust of Secret and Confidential Information to Agents of a Foreign Power.* Ottawa, 1946. The even more striking revelation of Fuchs's services to the Soviet Government were still to come.

uable as to put the whole proposal to hazard. As he later succinctly recorded, "My plea was useless." [7] Baruch was a close and old friend of Byrnes and various senators whom he had entertained at his luxurious plantation in South Carolina,[8] and had contributed to their campaign funds. His appearance was impressive and his self-esteem impervious. His popular image was that of a canny man, an experienced adviser of presidents, a keen analyst whom idealistic advisers could not lead astray, or cunning foreign diplomats outwit. This image was skillfully burnished by Baruch's aide in public relations and speech writer, Herbert Bayard Swope. Only a few caustic observers of his career knew that his reputation grew out of shrewd publicity rather than actual achievement, and that he was vain, stiffly assertive, and hard of hearing.

When Baruch, while his nomination was still before the Senate, first heard about the Acheson–Lilienthal Report, he was aggrieved and asked that his nomination be withdrawn. His judgment of various main features was adverse. He had rushed down to Washington; Byrnes was at the meeting of the Council of Foreign Ministers in Paris, so he talked with Acheson, asking whether the government was going to sponsor the report. When the Acting Secretary so affirmed, Baruch, as recorded in notes he made, remarked " . . . the Western Union doesn't take messenger boys at 76—that was my age—he would have to get some other messenger boy." [9]

Baruch had plied Byrnes, after his return from Paris, with questions about the prospective proposal. Byrnes admitted that he could not answer the questions conclusively. But he assured Baruch that he would be given ample chance to reconsider the proposal before its presentation to the U.N. Moreover, he promised Baruch that he need not be dependent on the State Department or the Board of Consultants for aid and advice; he could be free to choose his own corps of assistants.[10]

The President, although annoyed by Baruch's craving for credit and penchant for the limelight, wanted him to serve. What a tall, esteemed, influential lightning rod!

Truman states in his *Memoirs* that he made clear whatever proposals Baruch might be asked to present in the U.N. would have to be made

[7] Acheson, *Present at the Creation*, p. 154.

[8] His business office was in the Wall Street district, his home in the affluent section of the East side in New York, but his photographs featured in the press located him on a bench in Lafayette Park across the street from the White House, dispensing wisdom and feeding the pigeons and squirrels.

[9] Baruch memo entitled *Notes on Bernard M. Baruch* in Baruch papers, Princeton University.

[10] He chose men from the hard-headed circles of downtown banking and investment world, except Swope, who glided smoothly through all worlds—financial, political, journalistic. The others were John M. Hancock, Ferdinand Eberstadt, Fred Searls, and Thomas Farrell.

under Byrnes' direction and subject to presidential approval. [Truman] averred that he had no intention of giving Baruch a different role from that of other American delegates to the U.N.[11] But according to Baruch, when he asked Truman who would draft the proposals to be put before the U.N., the President answered: "Hell, you are." [12]

Whatever the nature of the understanding reached—or not reached— Baruch agreed to have his nomination go forward, and it was speedily approved by the Senate. Byrnes subsequently, in a talk on April 18th, gave Baruch still further assurance that his advice would be sought and heeded.[13]

There now ensued further weeks of intensive consultation between Baruch and his group, and Acheson and his associates. On May 17th and 18th Baruch and his group of advisers met at Blair-Lee House with Acheson and all of the Board of Consultants. There, while Oppenheimer stressed his opinion that the plan as conceived by the Consultants would give advance warning of any violation of its terms and thus eliminate risk of a surprise attack, Baruch's group held to the belief that any accord must provide automatic and inescapable penalties; that a law without a penalty was useless.[14] The Acheson group failed to persuade the Baruch group that the suggested provisions for punishment for violation—not subject to Russian veto in the U.N.—would rule out any chance that the Soviet Union would accept the U.S. proposal.[15]

The Baruch group, after all the churning about, decided to adopt the concept of an international agency with positive functions rather than any plan that just controlled or prohibited production of atomic weapons. But it demurred at the proposal in the Lilienthal–Acheson plan that an international agency have "dominion" over uranium and thorium.[16]

[11] Truman, *Years of Trial and Hope,* p 9.

[12] Bernard Baruch, *The Public Years* (New York: Holt, 1960). Also recalled in Baruch memo just cited.

[13] A letter which Byrnes wrote Baruch on April 19th summarizing for the record their conversation of the day before is printed in Truman's *Years of Trial and Hope,* pp. 9–10. It is genial and stressed the belief that they would be able to cooperate without difficulty. In fact, Baruch was to have virtual control over the presentation to the U.N.

[14] Memo of Conference, Baruch papers, Princeton University.

[15] In *Present at the Creation,* chap. 17, p. 155, Acheson wrote, ". . . the 'swift and sure punishment' provision could be interpreted in Moscow only as an attempt to turn the United Nations into an alliance to support a United States threat of war against the USSR unless it ceased its efforts [to develop nuclear weapons] . . ." That is true, but the Consultants' proposal contemplated that all national efforts to develop nuclear materials and reactors should be ended.

[16] The difference of judgment was most clearly expressed at talk on the evening of May 31, 1946, between Byrnes, Baruch, and Hancock. As recorded in the memo which John Hancock wrote, he, and presumably Baruch, wanted ". . . the International Authority to be the only owner of the ore from 'birth to death' from the mine

In the proposal ultimately developed and presented to the U.N., both possibilities, "dominion" or "managerial control," by the International Authority, were presented for consideration.

On June 7th Baruch maintained that he thought the Acheson-Lilienthal prospectus was defective in other main respects. It left some essential matters for determination by unpredictable negotiations within the U.N. Worse still, it did not foreclose all chance that again any party should be able to violate it with impunity; therefore he insisted verdicts of the Atomic Energy Authority should not be subject to veto by any permanent member of the Security Council. As stated in the memo which Baruch prepared for this talk: "As far as atomic energy is concerned there cannot be a veto, because while you debate you can be destroyed." [17]

After their talk, Baruch and Byrnes went to the White House together to settle Baruch's instructions. Up to then Truman had not ruled over the matters in question. Baruch gave Truman a copy of a memo, entitled *Statement of United States Policy* (a revised Acheson-Lilienthal Plan). As the President read along, he initialed most of the paragraphs in the margin. Next to the paragraph stating the procedure should be by stages, he jotted "most important." At the end he wrote: "Above principles approved June 7, 1946, Harry S Truman." [18] Moreover, he gave a letter to Baruch, assuring him again that the proposal, even as revised, was general in character and solely for Baruch's guidance. ". . . I want you," the President wrote, "to have authority to exercise your judgment as to the method by which the stated objectives can be accomplished." [19]

Thus the way was cleared for Baruch to direct our negotiations in the U.N. It may be surmised that the President had concluded that public opinion, especially in Congress, would demand the same presumptive protection of our security which Baruch was bent on procuring. A clear indication of this was the response of the Special Senate Committee on Atomic Energy (the McMahon Committee) after Baruch explained to its members the proposal he intended to make in the U.N. The Senators

mouth on." But he (and presumably Baruch) thought Russia more likely to object to international ownership than to international inspection; he could not conceive of Russia turning over State property to an international agency. This long memo covers many other points of difference. It is dated June 1, 1946, and is in Baruch papers, Princeton University.

[17] Baruch memo dated June 1, 1946, Baruch papers, Princeton University.

[18] Hewlett and Anderson, *The New World*, p. 574.

[19] Baruch's account of this meeting in his memo already cited is conformable. It states that Truman was ". . . particularly strong about the veto." Both this account and Truman's letter to Baruch dated June 7, 1946, are in the Baruch papers, Princeton University.

were highly pleased with Baruch's presentation, especially what he said about the veto. General Eisenhower and the Joint Chiefs of Staff also upheld him.[20]

Negotiations were quickly to demonstrate that the requirement in the original draft that all stages and sectors of development of atomic energy be owned, controlled, or directed by an international authority, and all national activities in this field be (eventually) prohibited was unrealistic. The Soviet press was commenting caustically on statements made during the Senate Committee Hearings on the McMahon Bill, on the report of the Committee of Consultants, and above all on the advance notices of tests that were to be made in May and July at the Bikini atoll to determine the effect of atom bombs on naval vessels. A typical example was the special article in the *New Times* for March 15th, which said that these tests were being publicized with an "inordinate amount of trumpet blowing . . . (and) talks about defending the United States' new interests" in all parts of the globe, including the Mediterranean, and the necessity of taking advantage of the present situation to establish a "new atomic imperialism" and atomic dictatorship.

"Not even by the widest stretch of the imagination can all of this be regarded as likely to create the chance . . . for the success of measures taken to control atomic energy." [21]

But most Americans complacently concluded that the knowledge that the United States intended to enlarge its atomic arsenal would cause the Russians to be more receptive to the proposals in mind. They had been brought up on the maxim, "Put your trust in God . . . and keep your powder dry."

[20] As stated in a letter from Eisenhower for the Joint Chiefs of Staff to Baruch June 14, 1946, the three paragraphs of the summary in this letter were: a.) "The existence of the atomic bomb in our hands is a deterrent, in fact, to aggression in the world. We cannot at this time limit our capability to produce or use this weapon. b.) We must move, by steps, toward international control of atomic energy if we are to avoid an atomic war. . . . A first step is to *prove* a system of inspection. c.) . . . To control atomic weapons, in which field we are pre-eminent, without provision for equally adequate control of other weapons of mass destruction can seriously endanger our national security." Baruch papers, Princeton University.

[21] This was a precursor of standard Communist interpretations and appraisals of American foreign policy during this period, as being coercive and aggressive because of our possession of atomic bombs.

PART FIVE

Unsettlement in the Center of Europe

16

The Deepening Divergence
over German Affairs

During these same months of 1946, even as the dispute about Iran was subsiding, and the American proposal for control of atomic energy was being worked over, the policies of the Allies about German affairs were becoming more discomposed.

The dismal plight of the country had disturbed the military commanders in the Western zones more and more and caused the sponsors of the Potsdam program in Washington to conclude that the provisions must be moderated.

Various tendencies in American life and feeling were at work toward a relaxation of American policies toward the conquered nation: religious affiliations between Catholic groups and some Protestant groups in the United States and Germany; reviving commercial attitudes; and remembered former business and banking connections. These had begun to challenge and upset the impulse to punish the Germans for the suffering they had caused. But perhaps the most cogent reason for reconsidering the constraints on German economy was the urgent wish of the western European countries to procure German goods—especially coal and iron, machinery, and chemicals.

The Western military officials in Germany were more responsive to these influences because they witnessed each day the distress of the Germans, and were beset by their complaints and appeals. The former Nazi worshippers knew well how to court, comfort, and corrupt through the black market.

Almost all Germans within Western zones were living even more poorly than envisaged in the Potsdam Agreement because of the exhaustion of war; the enormous influx of refugees from the East (about 8 million); the insufficiency of raw materials and fuel for industry; and the shortage of seeds, tools, and fertilizer on farms, and of housing in bombed cities. But it should not be forgotten that food, coal, and raw materials were in very short supply, not only in Germany but in almost all of Western Europe.

As the winter of 1945–1946 wore on, the American and British Governments had found it advisable to respond to recommendations of their military commanders in Germany and provide, at their own expense, large quantities of food and other essentials of life and raw materials for the Germans.

Even so, many Germans in Western zone towns were securing only 1500 calories of rationed food a day, and had to scrounge and sell off their possessions to get more. Workers in factories, mines, and the railways were not being well enough nourished to do a good day's work. Sickness due to malnutrition was widespread.

In December 1945, at the meeting of the Council of Foreign Ministers in Moscow, Molotov had complained that advance deliveries from Western zones to the Soviet Union on reparations accounts had not yet begun, and he had urged that the preliminary work to determine the total amount of deliveries be accelerated and completed by February next. Bevin had explained that the difficulty was to determine how much production should be left in Germany for essential peacetime needs. Byrnes had pointed out that deliveries already scheduled were greater than could be transported. Both Bevin and Byrnes had professed, despite the dust of controversy, that they saw no reason why the Potsdam Agreement about reparations should not be carried out in time. But subsequent deliveries had been small, fewer than the Russians expected, and they thought more could have been made had the Americans and British made an effort to expedite them.

The Russians had, as far as they could, taken care of themselves; without consultation with the Control Council, they had taken out of Berlin and the Eastern zone productive plants, stocks of raw materials, machinery, and spare parts—some as war booty, some as reparations. They had men working day and night to dismantle plants and machinery and to load them on trucks, barges, and trains. They had refused to give any accounting of these levies to the Control Council. The Western Allies computed that in this independent fashion the Russians had secured several billions in reparations in the first postwar year from their own zone alone.

The thought began to spurt, would the Western occupants not be justified in suspending transfer of industrial capital equipment to the Soviet Union? Wouldn't it be justified especially since the conviction was spreading that it might be advisable to initiate measures to stimulate German production, and plants designated as available for reparations might be needed? And then, too, the Russians were preventing any movement of food, coal, or other essentials from their zone to the West, although millions of Germans from the East were now crowded into the still stricken Western zones.

Because of these rising qualifications and doubts, General Clay, early in May 1946, informed the Coordinating Committee of the Control Council that from then on no plants other than those previously allocated and committed would be torn down. He suspended the dismantling of many plants that was under way, and withheld publication of a list of additional plants which had been drawn up by his staff. Clay explained his decision in a press conference on May 27th on the ground that the provision for economic unity in the Potsdam Accord had not been carried out, and the United States was being compelled to subsidize Germany. He stressed the fact that the suspension would affect *all* prospective recipients.

Since France was to receive a substantial share (22.8 percent) of the plants in the American zone deemed by the Inter-Allied Reparations Authority to be in excess of what was necessary for the German economy, it was hard hit by Clay's order. It may be that by this action Clay hoped to sting the French Government into acceptance of the formation of central German administrative agencies and into economic cooperation with other zones,[1] and perhaps to move the Russians to cease engrossing all sparable production in the Eastern zone and to permit trade with the West.

But the position of the French Government remained the same as that which Georges Bidault had explained in the note he had sent to Byrnes on March 1st in response to the Secretary's request that he agree to the creation of central administrative agencies. "It seems [to the French Government] in view of the human potential of that country, that the German menace will subsist as long as a German Government keeps . . . the possibility of utilizing its industrial resources to reconstitute its military power. France is thus opposed while the territorial division of Germany has not been brought about to the establishment of tentacular administrations having power to make decisions." [2]

[1] Gimbel, in his study, *The American Occupation*, p. 61, so construes the decision. This interpretation is consistent with the fact that on May 26, 1946, Clay informed the War Department that he thought the time had come to establish a provisional German Government, that he thought the Russians, though presenting many difficulties in detail, would cooperate, but that the French would strongly resist. *Ibid.*, p. 57.

[2] Note from Bidault to Byrnes, dated March 1, 1946. Quoted in Georgette Elgey, *La République des Illusions 1945–1951, ou, La Vie Secrète de la IVe République* (Paris: Arthème Fayard, 1965), p. 133.

The British authorities soon followed our example and began to hold back all industrial plants in the Ruhr except those which had been definitely designated as destined for dismantling.

The Russian publicists interpreted the trend toward easing the restrictions on German industry and the decision to suspend dismantling as signs that the ruling coterie of Western industrial and banking magnates were trying to salvage the property of their German business connections (friends) and to preserve the economic basis of German military power. Evidence of this intention they saw in the presence of prominent American business and banking executives and their lawyers on the staff of the American Military Government in Germany.[3] And in the fact that German executive and financial magnates who had been active Nazis were being protected and given jobs in German industrial administrations.

Thus, then, the associations of the war Allies in the direction of affairs of Eastern and Central Europe—above all Germany—were fraying fast. Interpretations of these accords were in dispute, and they were being gradually ignored. Avowals of cooperation were being muted; asperity was becoming the negotiating mood.

---

[3] These were, the Russians thought, centered around the great German chemical trust—I. G. Farben Industry—which had had business agreements before the war with DuPont, the Standard Oil of New Jersey, General Electric, General Motors, and various American drug companies. Most Soviet commentators were inclined toward "conspiratorial" interpretation of history, especially of groups of "capitalist exploiters." See, for example, many articles in *The New Times* during the first half of 1946, which almost always were false or exaggerated.

Senator Harley Kilgore of West Virginia made two public statements to the same effect, reported in *New York Times*, November 25, and December 22, 1945. The Senator charged that American representatives on the Control Council were reluctant to carry out the policy of economic and military disarmament of Germany, and that some American officials in OMGUS and in the State Department were connected with German industrialists and financiers—among them former Nazis.

17

The Quest for Peace Treaties

It is hardly surprising then, that the Deputies of the Foreign Ministers who had been discussing the terms of peace treaties to be made with Italy and the satellites had not straddled the differences. These had awaited the Foreign Ministers when they met again in Paris at the end of April 1946. Byrnes, asked about the prospect, had recalled the Negro spiritual, "Standin' in de Need of Prayer."

The patience shown during two long and contentious sessions left ground for the belief that enough common purpose still remained to restore a state of peace in Europe, that is, to conclude peace treaties, though not to heal the cuts.

The start of the first session of the Conference was almost jovial. Molotov agreed to permit the French representative (Bidault) to take part in the discussion of *all* peace treaties—those of Romania, Bulgaria, Hungary, and Finland, as well as Italy. But positions soon froze up. The wearisome and repetitious arguments twirled around two main congeries of questions. One was the terms of peace with Italy and the Balkan countries. The other was what should be done about Germany. Although the discussion swung from one to the other and back again, the issues and decisions stand out more clearly if recounted separately. I will do so, but only summarily, since few would now care to tramp through shrubs of details which have been dried out by time.

What Terms for Italy?

By this time (the spring of 1946) Italy was being treated in most respects not as a former enemy, but as a friendly power. The Facist regime was broken, the Italian army dispersed and disarmed, and the deposition of the remainder of the Italian fleet was being discussed. But about three matters the peacemakers had clashing claims and wishes. How much in reparations should Italy be obligated to pay? What was to be done with the former Italian colonies in North Africa? What were the northern boundaries of Italy to be; and was the seaport of Trieste and the country around it to be returned to Italy or turned over to Yugoslavia?

In general, the American Government was the protector of Italy. The British Government, remembering the "stab in the back" was, except in regard to the colonies, ambivalent. The Soviet Government was demanding. The Yugoslavs were still smarting from the wounds of Italian occupation and angry because they felt that they were being unjustly treated.

For reparations, France and the Soviet Union had presented demands —the Soviet Union for 300 million dollars, one-third for itself, the rest to be divided between Yugoslavia, Greece, and Albania. This amount, Molotov stressed, was very small considering the damage done by Italian armies and occupation forces, which in Russia had advanced as far as the river Don, and had occupied the Donets basin, Kharkov, and Minsk. Wherever they had been, they ruined towns and villages.

Byrnes and Bevin could not dispute the record. But still they objected to the stipulation of any fixed sum on the ground that it was impossible to forecast what the Italians would be able to pay. They maintained that reparations must not be a drain on the poor Italian economy, and that the American and British Governments must not be compelled to increase their relieving outlays in order that Italy might pay reparations. Therefore, they argued, the obligation should be no greater than might be paid by the conveyance of ownership of Italian properties in the countries its troops had occupied, and by the transfer of equipment of Italian war industries that might be dismantled.

To Mussolini's victims, that seemed shockingly little. They thought that British and American solicitude for the welfare of the Italians due to a wish to preserve opportunity for their own capitalists.[1]

Since this difference was still unresolved when the Conference recessed in the middle of May, it was discussed again at the second session in June. Then Molotov dismissed the American proposal that the obligation be discharged by transfer of Italian properties in the Balkans, dismantled war plants, and a few ocean liners, as preposterous. The

[1] As propounded in an article reprinted in the *Information Bulletin* of the Soviet Embassy in Washington (May 16, 1946, issue). "The British and American powers, who removed from Italy at the time of their occupation, values many times greater than the sum of reparations, are now drawing up a peace treaty demanding from that country full compensation for all the damage done to the property of British and American firms, including that property which was destroyed during the war by Allied air forces. . . . They want to inflict on Italy an economic regime which would make her completely dependent on American and British capital."

American estimates of the value of these properties, he charged, were ridiculously high. Let Italy, he argued, be obligated to pay out of current production for some years; this, he contended, would stimulate the Italian economy. But Byrnes and Bevin held out because they thought that such an indefinite lien on Italian production might give the Soviet Government and/or the Italian Communist Party a basis for diverting, perhaps directing, Italian economic effort. In the end they agreed that whatever part of one hundred million dollars to be paid the Soviet Union was not covered by the conveyance of Italian assets in the Balkans should be made by deliveries of goods from future production over a short term of years. Decisions regarding the diverse claims for reparations of the smaller countries that had been cruelly hurt by the Italians were left over for the comprehensive Peace Conference in prospect.

Over the former colonies of Italy in North Africa and along the Red Sea, a Soviet claim hovered.

At the meeting in San Francisco, at which the Charter of the United Nations had been written, Molotov had indicated to Stettinius that the Soviet Government sought, if not sovereignty, at least administrative control, under the U.N., of one of these colonies. Stettinius had sidestepped, saying merely that the American Government considered the Soviet Union "eligible" for such an assignment. Molotov was to profess later that this was a promise that the American Government should honor.

Stalin, during the Potsdam Conference, had suggested that all Italy's African colonies be placed under trusteeship and that Russia should be asked to administer one of them, but the whole question had been left open. Molotov had renewed this proposal at the meeting of the Council of Foreign Ministers in September 1945. Bevin had said he saw no valid ground for the Russian claim, which he described as "A thrust across the throat of the British Empire." Byrnes had upheld Bevin. He repudiated Russia's supposition that the Italian colonies should be treated and disposed of as either spoils of war or compensation for war damages. Their welfare and development, and Italy's residual interest, he thought, should be the determinants of decision.

The question still stared at the Foreign Ministers when in Paris they chaffered over terms of peace with Italy. Molotov introduced a new plan: that these colonies should be granted independence within ten years; but during that period each would be under the dual trusteeship of Italy and one of the four Great Powers. Russia, he averred, needed ports of call and repair for its shipping in the Mediterranean, since its trade with countries along that sea would grow. Bevin had countered by proposing immediate independence for the Mediterranean colonies while temporarily continuing British control over the former Italian possessions in the Red Sea. Molotov dismissed this proposal also; in his accusatory imagination it would establish British hegemony, in fact a commercial and strategic monopoly of a vast basin of vital interest to many countries. Bidault, afraid of the effect on French colonies of granting immediate independence to the Italian colonies, sided with Molotov; he rather favored the reassignment of all the colonies to Italy under trusteeships.

When they met again in June the Foreign Ministers came near accord on other disputed elements in the Italian peace treaty, but, flummoxed about this one, they agreed to postpone decision regarding the disposition of the colonies until after the entry into force of a peace treaty with Italy.

Over the question of where the Italo–Yugoslav boundary was to be, the national feelings of both countries were inflamed. The Foreign Ministers had sent a group of four "experts," each minister having nominated one, to examine the terrain and titles. Each expert had recommended a different line of division. The Russian had thought it just and wise that Yugoslavia—which had played so heroic a part in the war—should have not only the city of Trieste and the adjacent peninsula but also a large part of the northern Italian province of Venezia Giulia. The American expert agreed that the old frontier ought to be shifted in Yugoslavia's favor, but only a small distance, and suggested that the city of Trieste should remain in Italy, its port to be turned into a "free port" administered by its users.

The Italian Government was set against ceding any territory. It was afraid that if compelled to yield that it would be cast out of office by a resentful populace—to be followed by a coalition in which Italian Communists would be influential if not dominant.

The Foreign Ministers for many days pored over maps and argued over rights and wrongs, ethnic and economic considerations. Any settlement they recommended would be resented by Italy or Yugoslavia, or quite likely by both.

On the whole, the arrangement which the four members of the Council, in the very last days, agreed to propose at the Peace Conference, protected Italy better than a defeated ex-enemy country could have expected.

Western troops were in occupation of Trieste; the influence of Americans of Italian origin and Catholic affiliation was active; and the British determination to keep Russian Communist influence out of the Mediterranean, firm. To these facts and sentiments Molotov was compelled to pay deference.

The territory ceded to Yugoslavia was much smaller than Tito had striven to secure. The city of Trieste and the adjacent area were to become an autonomous territory under the watch and protection of the U.N. The Security Council was to appoint the Governor after consulting Italy and Yugoslavia; and the Governor was to report to the Security Council.

The Conclusion of the Peace Treaties

Let us pursue briefly the path toward the completion of the peace treaties with Italy and the Balkan countries, even though we must course in front of other contemporary events.

The dispute over the procedure for determining the terms of the peace treaties with Italy and the satellites had been settled by compromise. The preliminary recommendations of the Foreign Ministers—which we have just given—were to be presented to a conference at which all nations that had fought the Axis in Europe would have the chance to be heard, and to vote upon acceptance of the proposals of the Council, or propose amendments. The Soviet Government, afraid that there would be a pro-Western majority in this larger concourse, had consented to afford the smaller Powers this chance, on the understanding that the decisions of the Peace Conference would be heeded, only if acceptable to all four of the Great Powers.

This larger concourse was called the Peace Conference. On July 29th, at the Luxembourg Palace in Paris, representatives of twenty-one nations met; the five members of the Council of Foreign Ministers and sixteen of the smaller war Allies.[2]

Before Byrnes and Molotov left for this Paris Peace Conference, they knew that the negotiations in the U.N. about control of atomic energy were entering a dark impasse. The knowledge that the United States alone had this weapon was comforting to Byrnes, but it was of little value to him in the negotiations. It may have caused Molotov to accept a few settlements with less bluster than usual, and it probably made him more inclined to construe Western proposals as attempts to "bully" the Soviet Union. Bevin broke down the eve of the Conference, and for a while Attlee had to replace him. Harold Nicolson, being present, thought him "so small, so chetif" (puny).

[2] China was the fifth, passive and almost invisible, member of the Council of Foreign Ministers.

There was still some fire in the arguments over "economic" provisions of the treaties with the smaller German satellites, though it was burning down.

The Russian representatives implied that the Western Allies were trying to obtain rights which would enable them to upset Soviet control of southeastern Europe. They minded most the Western protests against the agreements which Russia had imposed on Romania and Hungary; these provided for the creation of joint companies in which the Russians would be equal partners, to control the industries of these two countries —oil, timber, aviation, and the Danube shipping.

Byrnes proposed that ex-enemy states be required to guarantee equality of opportunity to the trade and enterprise of all United Nations and their nationals. Molotov's rejoinder was: "Nobody can say that the unlimited application of the principle of 'equality of opportunity' is equally suited for . . . great and small powers. . . . It is obvious that the unlimited application of this principle is something which is convenient for those who have the power and the wealth, for those who are trying to use their capital in order to subjugate those who are weaker. If we are going to consider the interests of the people of these countries, then we must be a little more modest in those matters and not apply by force conditions which might stifle the economy of the weaker powers." [3] In other speeches he attributed American policy more explicitly to a wish to make money by penetrating the Danube region, and declaimed that Russia would protect these countries against enslavement and the wiles of dollar diplomacy.

The Western effort to reverse or check Russian domination of this region came to naught. Philip Mosely's terse comment of the outcome corresponded to Washington's conclusion. "By the end of 1946, against unyielding Soviet insistence on transforming East Central Europe into a closed preserve, the American Government had a heap of broken Soviet promises to point to, a reminder that hope, divorced from power, is not

---

[3] Molotov, Speech, August 15, 1946, at Paris Peace Conference. For a slightly different translation see V. M. Molotov, *Problems of Foreign Policy* (Moscow: Foreign Languages Publishing House, 1949).

Some British commentators and officials were less devoted to the abstract principle of equal opportunity than the Americans. Harold Nicolson tells (in Volume III of his *Diaries and Letters: The Later Years: 1945–1962* (New York: Atheneum, 1968), p. 172, of a lunch on August 9th with Gladwyn Jebb, then Assistant Undersecretary of State at the Foreign Office, and Hector McNeil, Parliamentary Undersecretary for Foreign Affairs, at which he, Nicolson, was chided for being too tolerant of the Russians in his BBC broadcasts. Nicolson rejoined: "There is much to be said for the Russian point of view, and we shall achieve nothing by ignoring it." Whereat McNeil—who had even less use for the Communists than Bevin—"hooted."

Ironically, McNeil's private secretary at the Foreign Office was Guy Burgess, the notorious Communist agent who fled to Russia.

a policy." [4] Molotov's defense was that the main spirit of the Declaration on Liberated Europe was on the need to destroy all vestiges of Nazism and Fascism, and so enable the liberated peoples to create institutions of their own choice. That was his portrayal of what Russia was doing.[5] There were no political leaders left free within these countries to contradict him.

About the gore-soaked boundaries between the states of southeastern Europe, over which they had, in folly, fought so many wars, there was only one squabble. Molotov insisted that the transfer of northern Transylvania from Hungary to Romania, as promised by Stalin in the armistice agreement in March 1945, should be confirmed. Since Bevin thought this not unjust, and since conflicting claims were tenable, Byrnes gave in.

The discussions at the Peace Conference were almost free of bitterness and recriminations. Rather, they were matter-of-fact and at times torpid. At the Plenary Meeting on October 14th, Molotov reminded Byrnes and Bevin that while, as he put it, for the sake of cooperation the Soviet Government had agreed that these treaties should be *examined* by the many countries at the Conference, it remained convinced that all issues on which the Conference had not agreed must be settled by the four Great Powers alone.[6] This meant that the Soviet Government did not regard as final any resolution passed by a majority at the Peace Conference against Russia's vote. "All this," Molotov concluded, "places a big responsibility on the Council of Foreign Ministers for the ultimate decisions on which the signing of the treaties will depend." [7]

The Soviet Commissar left the Conference hall suddenly, before the formal adjournment of the final session on October 15th. The Yugoslavs, in demonstration against the Statute for Trieste that had been adopted, left their seats, and the current surmise was that Molotov wanted to be gone before the Conference rejected their protest.

The British delegation went off quietly. But the departure of the Americans at Orly Airport was enlivened by the chatter of wives and secretaries bunched with orchids and Parma violets. Their cheerfulness showed they were glad to get away. Their parting, one sensitive French diplomat, who liked the the Americans, noted in his Diary, "A crisp sep-

---

[4] In the chapter by Philip Mosely in the book entitled *The Fate of East Central Europe: Hopes and Failures of American Foreign Policy*, edited by S. D. Kertesz (Notre Dame: University of Notre Dame Press, 1956).

[5] Speech at Paris Peace Conference, July 31, 1946, in Molotov, *Problems of Foreign Policy*, p. 76.

[6] *Ibid.*, pp. 221–34.

[7] The most important of these was a group of economic articles, some elements of the Statute of Trieste, the regime for the navigation of the Danube River.

aration, nothing more than the colored coils of paper thrown from a steamer to those who remain ashore." [8]

Surprisingly, toward the end of the year 1946, in the next short session of the Council of Foreign Ministers in New York, compromises on all provisions of the treaties left unsettled by the Peace Conference sprouted.

Molotov accepted several recommendations of the Peace Conference against which he had voted. Conversely, in lieu of any genuine lessening of Russian domination of the satellites, Byrnes and Bevin had to be content with a stipulation that an international conference of the riparian states and the Great Powers would be called to establish a system of control of the traffic on the Danube River.

The way was cleared for signature of these treaties early in 1947.

[8] Jacques Dumaine, *Quai D'Orsay (1945–1951)* (Paris: R. Julliard, 1955) entry dated October 16, 1946.

18

But No Peace Treaty
with Germany

Despite the deepening divergence between the West and the Soviet Union, or perhaps in a sense because of it, the American and British Governments were also willing to contemplate the conclusion of peace treaties with Germany and Austria. For then all foreign forces might be brought out of Central Europe and the Balkans. The Soviet Union professed the same wish. But all the sorties of diplomacy had run into fences of barbed wire—West and East.

To Guarantee that Germany Would Be Peaceful

Early in the first session of the Council of Foreign Ministers (on Apr. 29th) at Paris—the Conference which had been convoked particularly to discuss European peace treaties—Byrnes made a proposal prompted by the hope of allaying French and Russian fears of Germany. Thereby he sought to get them to renounce or shrink the claims on Germany which they wished to have validated by the peace treaty. The Secretary thought they might do so, if reassured by a long-term treaty pledging the four main Allies to take combined and effective action to suppress any future tendency of Germany to rearm and be aggressive.

This proposal was not an improvisation. Byrnes had first broached the possibility to Molotov during the meeting of the Council of Foreign Ministers in London in September 1945. The Secretary then had the impression that Molotov was interested. Therefore he had tried to elicit Stalin's support when in December 1945 he had gone to Moscow for the next session of the Council. While coffee was being served after a friendly Christmas Eve dinner given by Stalin, he had remarked to the Marshal that he was disappointed at not having had any response to this suggestion. According to *Speaking Frankly* he said to Stalin: "Such a treaty will give all European states assurance that the United States would not return to a policy of isolation. I have often recalled how you expressed at Yalta your fear of another invasion by Germany. You then asserted that the continued cooperation of the four Allies in keeping Germany demilitarized would relieve your fears and perhaps influence your actions in the Balkan States. . . . The United States has always been reluctant to enter into such treaties, but our experience in trying to stay out of Europe's wars has been so disastrous I am confident our people would support a treaty under which the major powers would join forces to keep Germany disarmed. The Senate will have to ratify such a treaty but I think they will do so and I am willing to make the effort." He remembered Stalin as answering, "If you decide to fight for such a treaty, you can rely on my support." [1]

Thereupon, after his return to the United States, Byrnes had directed that a treaty be drafted. The preliminary text contemplated that "following the conclusion of a peace treaty with Germany, the four major powers should maintain an inspection force . . . to prevent the establishment or conversion of industries capable of producing weapons of war." [2] It defined the procedure for requiring the German Government to comply with the treaty, and reserved the right of the Four Powers— in the last resort—to take whatever steps they thought necessary to secure compliance. However, it also stipulated that action under the treaty could be taken by a majority vote; the purpose of this, Byrnes has explained, "was to prevent any one state from blocking joint action." [3]

President Truman had approved the tender. So had the senior Republican and Democratic members of the Foreign Relations Committee of the Senate, among them Connally and Vandenberg.

Having secured this general concurrence, in February 1946 Byrnes had sent copies of a draft to the governments of the Soviet Union, the United Kingdom, and France, to serve as the basis for discussion. Bevin and Bidault had said quickly that they would recommend acceptance, with minor amendments. Molotov had reserved his comment. The Soviet Government was not convinced of the value of the treaty, and it was certainly not eager enough for it to give up its freedom of action in Germany.

On April 28th, during one of the dinners given at this Conference of the Council of Foreign Ministers in Paris, Molotov gave reasons for the Soviet Government's reserved attitude. In the Postdam Agreement, he said, it had been stated that Germany was to be disarmed at once. But the Western Powers, he alleged, were being laggard. Let the Powers

---

[1] James F. Byrnes, *Speaking Frankly* (New York: Harper, 1947), pp. 171–2.
[2] *Ibid.*
[3] *Ibid.*

first verify that this had been done, before considering a treaty setting up controls in the future. He intimated that he thought Byrnes' proposal a devious move to postpone the disarmament of Germany.

Bidault's response was favorable. But the French Government did not forgo its demands for territorial, economic, and political adjustments. Bidault, aware that the American and British Governments were adverse to the dissection of Germany and did not think France either needed or deserved the acquisition it sought, tried to justify them in a fervid discourse just before the Council recessed in May. He reposed his claims of what was due France on the record embedded in French history books. As paraphrased by Senator Vandenberg, who was sitting at Byrnes' side: France had been invaded by Germany several times in one hundred and fifty years. Political considerations should be decisive though they need not be economically unsound. To quote: "The Ruhr is an immense factory and the first coal basin of Europe. The Rhineland is an agricultural area which has been the usual corridor of German attack. The Saar . . . was taken away from us after the fourth invasion; but France has had it and its coal mines since World War One. The Ruhr is a great European Treasury. We must guarantee that its natural and industrial resources shall never again be used destructively. It must be internationalized both economically and politically. There should be local administration and policing as far as possible. . . . The Rhineland should be under permanent [French] military control. . . . We will agree to any reasonable political regime so long as it does not involve German sovereignty. . . . Its public administration should be detached from the Reich and put under the political and economic control of France. All of these things are vital to France and to the peace of the world." [4]

Bevin was enthusiastic about Byrnes' initiative. As later related by him to the House of Commons on June 4th: "Having regard to what happened at the end of the last war, I must say that these proposals of the United States Government, through Mr. Byrnes, left with me the impression that here at last we had something which would give us peace in Europe, and allow for normal development over a sufficient period to eradicate the war-like spirit of Nazism in Germany."

Thus the British Foreign Secretary had tried to reconcile American, French, and Soviet positions. He remarked first that he shared Bidault's ideas about the Saar and the Ruhr. But he thought they ought to deal first with the Saar. In regard to Russian proposals that the Ruhr be internationalized, he said that it should be considered in connection with decisions made about the whole of Germany. ". . . my attitude has been all through that we must not only know what is happening in the Ruhr,

[4] *Private Papers of Senator Vandenberg*, entry dated May 15, 1946, pp. 281–2.

but what is happening in Saxony, in Thuringia [areas within the Russian zone] and anywhere else." The problem as he saw it ". . . was to achieve security while maximizing production for the whole of Europe. . . . It is dangerous to peace to leave a mass of people in Central Europe on a substandard basis. Let studies of how this was to be done be begun at once."

Byrnes, who had asked General Clay to join him in Paris, took up these themes eagerly. It was imperative to settle policy toward the Ruhr and the whole of Germany quickly. Otherwise next winter there would be chaos in all zones. Answers must be rapidly found for all the main issues. He urged that Special Deputies devote themselves to the task and report to the Council when it reassembled on June 15th.

Molotov was willing to "think it over." But he could not or did not repress accusations. Again, Vandenberg's notation in his journal may be quoted. The Soviets had taken "the initiative at the Berlin [Potsdam] Conference to discuss the Ruhr, but were told they were out of order in the absence of France. Now France is here. But in the meantime events have marched on. We read in the press and we hear rumors about arrangements the British are making to take over Ruhr industry in the British zone. We have sought direct information but we have received none . . . The plans being made by the British and by German trusts and cartels have a great bearing on this military potential. It is obvious that we should discuss Germany as a whole. But I shall not conceal the fact that the Soviet wants to know what goes on in the British Zone and thus in the Rhineland."

Bevin was not one to remain silent under attack. "You can," he stormed back, "have all the information you want about our zone; and meanwhile we should like to find out what goes on in other zones where we can get very little information. I do not propose to have Britain singled out, for propaganda purposes, for attack. I shall insist upon dealing with Germany as a whole." [5]

The Soviet reception of Byrnes's proposal may have been infected by memory of prewar actions. Stalin and Molotov could hardly have forgotten how Soviet Russia had secretly contributed to the rearming of Germany in the nineteen-thirties. Certainly they had not forgotten Munich, or the infamous pact with Nazi Germany signed by Molotov. In the depths of distrust and self-knowledge they were incapable of believing that the American and British Governments would genuinely renounce a chance to turn Germany against Russia, even as they might turn it against the West, if they could.

Despite the proffer of a treaty, the Soviet rulers construed evolving

[5] *Ibid.*, p. 283.

American and British policies as signs of indifference—if not hostility—to Russian Communist security and interests. Did not the wish to stimulate production in the Western zones and in connection therewith to suspend shipments of capital equipment to Russia portend the restoration in Germany of old-style capitalism and social democracy—in the Communist lexicon only variations of Fascism?

This session of the Council of Foreign Ministers recessed in the middle of May without setting a date for the convocation of a Conference to consider terms of peace with Germany. All the delegations flew home, each to justify its stubbornness. Byrnes had been firmer than in any of his previous encounters with the Russians. He had refused to "trade" with either Bidault or Molotov. His performance pleased even Vandenberg—the Republican monitor.

During the recess of the Council session, the prospect of an agreement on measures that would prepare the way for a peace treaty with Germany became bleaker.

By the time the four Ministers met again, Molotov had rigidly aligned Soviet grievances. The Commissar denounced the tendered treaty which Byrnes had proposed as wholly inadequate. He insisted that provision should be made before any such treaty was made, or in the treaty, for fulfillment of the Soviet claims for 10 billion dollars of reparations from Germany—to be paid by deliveries either of existing German capital equipment or of commodities produced in the future. Moreover, he said that before concluding any treaty of the sort, the Soviet Government would want to be sure that the German Government that would come into existence would be "sufficiently democratic" and "sufficiently responsible."

On July 10th the Soviet Commissar released to the press in advance of the Council meeting a statement which was intended, no doubt, to cause the Germans to regard the Byrnes treaty proposal as an insult. After reciting, with all the outraged feeling which the Russians stored up like vintage wine, the accusation of the failure of the Western Allies to be faithful to the principles of Potsdam, he put a different face on Soviet intentions than before.

The Soviet Commissar took a line which, it is safe to surmise, he hoped would conjure up the bogey of the Morgenthau program, cause the Germans to devalue Western measures to improve their condition, and induce them to regard the Soviet Union as its true, unexacting befriender. Now Molotov averred that the Soviet Government would not treat the German people vengefully or harshly. "It would be incorrect," he said, "to adapt to a course of Germany's annihilation as a state or of its agrarianization, including the destruction of its main industrial centers. . . . [that] will result in making Germany a center where dangerous sentiments of revenge will be nourished and will play into the hands of German reactionaries. . . . We should not put obstacles in the way of the increase in the output of steel, coal and manufactured products of peaceful nature in Germany. . . . It should now be admitted that peaceful industries in Germany must be given the opportunity to develop on a wider scale." Consistently, the Ruhr must remain in Germany, but subjected to Inter-Allied Four-Power control; without it Germany could not exist as an independent and viable state under Inter-Allied Four-Power control. No dismemberment of Germany should take place. No territory should be separated from Germany except as a result of a plebiscite.

As for the federal structure envisaged by the Americans and British, the Soviet Government thought it incorrect to impose some one or other evolution of this question. Apropos this affirmation, it may be assumed that the Soviet Government intended to insist that the German administration be "sufficiently democratic" and "sufficiently responsible." This may be inferred from another passage in the statement. ". . . Even when a German Government has been set up, it will require a number of years before it can be verified what . . . [it] represents and whether it can be trusted. The future German Government must be a democratic government which will be capable of extirpating the last vestiges of Fascism in Germany, and at the same time capable of fulfilling Germany's obligations toward the Allies. [above all—make reparations deliveries] Only then will it be possible to speak seriously of concluding a peace treaty with Germany." [6]

Molotov's speech shook Byrnes. He correctly took it to be a bid for the allegiance of the Germans. "I realized at once," he later recorded, "the strength of this appeal. It was clearly calculated to play on the widespread German fear of the so-called 'Morgenthau Plan,' which had been widely discussed in the American press." [7] And which, I may remind, had influenced both the Potsdam Accord and the Directives to Eisenhower and Clay.

Byrnes became convinced that the Soviet High Command and Politburo had concluded that they did not want the American presence in Germany to be as prolonged as it would be under the proposed Four-Power Treaty. Their negativism was thought to justify—if not

---

[6] V. M. Molotov, *Problems of Foreign Policy*, pp. 68–9. A slightly different version or translation of its main parts is given by Byrnes in *Speaking Frankly*, pp. 179–181. George Curry and Richard L. Walker in their book *Edward R. Stettinius, Jr., 1944–1945 and James F. Byrnes, 1945–1947* (New York: Cooper Square Publishers, 1963), p. 233, summarizes and comments lucidly.

[7] Byrnes, *Speaking Frankly*, p. 181.

necessitate—independent action.[8]

Among the American officials who listened to Molotov were General Clay and Robert Murphy, the latter a senior Foreign Service officer who was political adviser to Eisenhower. Clay had brought to Paris in his briefcase a memo in which, after describing the miserable situation in Western Germany, he stressed the need for economic unity. He had been recommending that a provisional German Government be formed, and that the British and American zones be merged if the French and Russians would not agree to the formation of a central German administration of the sort favored by the United States.

The evening of July 10th, after Molotov's speech, the American officials went into a huddle and consulted the Senators who were members of the delegation, Connally and Vandenberg. All agreed that the time had arrived to move forward in the consolidation of the economies of the two zones to the fullest extent possible. The next morning Byrnes informed the Conference that "pending agreement among the Four Powers to implement the Potsdam agreement requiring the administration of Germany as an economic unit, the United States will join with any other occupying government or governments in Germany for the treatment of our respective zones as an economic unit." [9]

One and all of the arguing powers were still asseverating that they wanted the Potsdam Accord to be carried out, while in fact each and all were ignoring any features it regarded as harmful and hindering.

Bevin announced at once that in principle the British Government would respond to Byrnes' offer. Bidault demurred even though Bevin and Byrnes promised to support French claims to the Saar.

The discussion about Germany during the remaining days of the meeting of Foreign Ministers was ragged and repetitive. Molotov once again refused to agree even to the appointment of Deputies to consider, in a preliminary way, the terms of peace treaties with Germany and Austria.

The channels of negotiation about Germany were silted up—tightly, thickly. But what happened is better understood, I think, if we recall how, during this same summer of 1946, the discussions in the U.N. about atomic energy were circling in a whorl around a vacuum.

[8] *Ibid.*, p. 176. Byrnes also believed that it was Molotov who personally undermined the treaty, whereas Stalin had favored it.
[9] *Ibid.* pp. 195–6. Gimbel, in *The American Occupation*, pp. 74–5, draws the curious conclusion that because this reply of Byrnes to Molotov was "limited and cautious. . . . it appears . . . that Washington's primary aim at Paris had been to use the Byrnes 25-year treaty proposal as a wedge to open serious negotiations with France on the issues that had brought a stalemate to Potsdam. . . . that Washington was unprepared to go beyond that."

PART SIX

Opposing Ideas and
Deepening Divergence

19

The Atomic Bomb:
How To Exorcize
the Intruder

While the Peace Conference at Paris was going on, Dalton, Bevin's colleague, told him that he was troubled by the continual difficulties with the Russians. The Secretary said he did not understand why the Russians were so difficult. Molotov, Bevin explained, was like a local Labor Party Communist. "If you treated him badly, he made the most of the grievance and, if you treated him well, he only put his price up and abused you the next day. Soboliev, now gone to the U.N., whom he found the best of the Russians, had told him that 'the bomb has a lot to do with it.' Bevin thought both the Americans and the Russians were too bomb-minded. Each was afraid of the other. . . . Bevin, on the other hand, took the line that 'I won't have the bomb in the Foreign Office.' He would not let his policy be deflected one way or the other by the bomb and its possible uses." [1]

The possession of atomic weapons did not significantly affect the main lines of foreign policy of the Western Allies. But it probably made them more confident and stubborn in the clashes that arose, as in Germany. Conversely, it is probable that the strategems which shaped Western and Russian proposals for control of atomic energy caused the mutual mistrust to become more intense, the spirit of competition more pervasive.

The Commission of the United Nations, set up to consider how to safeguard the world against the awesome weapon, had assembled in June 1946. The United States and the Soviet Union had fixed objectives

[1] Hugh Dalton, *High Tide and After: Memoirs, 1945–1960* (Mullex, 1962), p. 155 (September 10, 1946). Dalton was Chancellor of the Exchequer.

and tactics. The American Government sincerely wished to bring about the elimination of atomic weapons—forever—provided it could maintain its advantage until it was sure that no other country could in the interim obtain them by stealth.

The Soviet Government wanted to nullify our advantage by having a ban imposed immediately on the production and use of the weapons while it strove to secure them. While doing its utmost to convince the Communist supporters that atomic weapons could not decide wars and should not scare them, the Soviet Government had hastened, after Hiroshima, to amass all its scientific and engineering talents to duplicate our feat with utmost priority. Equality with the United States—perhaps superiority—was the well hidden secret at the heart of *its* "atomic diplomacy."

The discussions in the U.N. were earnest. They bulged with professions of determination to dispel the menace of atomic weapons. But the proposals of the main progenitors of policy during the prolonged negotiations—if they may be called that—never meshed; they were lofted past each other by contrary winds of contrary purpose. Mistrust was so great, strategies so opposed, and social structures so divergent, that there was no middle ground on which the Western creators of atomic weapons and the Soviet Union, aspirant rival creator of them, could or did meet.

Only armchair devotees of strategic "gamesmanship" would now find novel instruction or entertainment in a comprehensive and detailed review of the variant proposals and counterproposals presented, the justifications, and the rebuttals. These became standard and repetitious. For purposes of historical understanding and judgment, only the main features of a few presentations need be recalled.[2]

The American Proposal: Conceived in Awe and Mistrust

Baruch, as representative of the host country, was asked to take the chair at the first meeting of the U.N. Commission. He prefaced the presentation of his proposal, a stiffened version of the Acheson–Lilienthal plan, by an explanation written by the fluent Herbert Bayard Swope.

[2] The most valuable sources of information on these are the records of discussions of the subject in the U.N. Commission on Atomic Energy and its subcommissions. The best secondary source is the official American history, *The New World, 1939–1946,* by Hewlett and Anderson, and two volumes published by the State Department entitled: *The International Control of Atomic Energy: Growth of a Policy* (1946) and *The International Control of Atomic Energy: Policy at the Crossroads* (1948).

This averred that the American Government would not be satisfied with a general vow not to make or use atomic weapons. It was imperative to create an international authority that would be empowered to *own, manage or license all activities that used atomic energy.* (Italics mine) It was to have "unhindered access to, and power to control, license and inspect all other facilities which possess, utilize, or produce materials which are a source of atomic energy" and all other activities which utilize or produce or are capable of producing atomic energy.[3]

Another resounding passage in Baruch's utterance was: "If I read the signs aright, the peoples [of the world] want a program not composed merely of pious thoughts but of enforceable sanctions—an international law with teeth in it. It must provide adequate controls and condign punishment for violations." [4]

The American proposal, in essence, meant that all nations would be required to refrain from trying to make atomic weapons. They would have to turn over uranium ores and atomic materials to the international agency and secure permission from that agency to operate plants using atomic energy. They would also have to permit thorough inspection of all activities in this realm by the agency.[5] If it found any member violating the agreement or derelict in obeying the Authority's rule, and if its judgment was upheld by majority vote of the Security Council, it was not to be subject to obstruction by veto power of any permanent members. Defiant offenders were to become subject to collective punitive action. The matter of punishment, Baruch said, was at the very heart of our present security problem—without explaining how a determined violator could be punished without using force.

While this system of ownership and regulatory control was being created in a series of transitional stages, and its reliability tested, the United States was to be allowed to continue to produce and stockpile atomic weapons. However, at some still to be defined stage in the evolution of the system of controls, the United States would desist from production, destroy its stock, and submit to the same supervisory inspection as other subscribers to the accord. In other words, during or at the end

[3] As stated in the first American memorandum presented to the U.N. Commission explaining its proposal.

To carry out its functions, the Authority was to have: (1) unhindered use of established postal, telephone, radio communications; (2) the right to operate its own and exclusive system of radio; (3) unhindered movement of its personnel, supplies and equipment within and between countries, and across national boundaries. Quoted in Bernard Baruch, *Growth of a Policy*, pp. 64–65.

[4] *Ibid.*

[5] The pertinent provision in the Majority Report which the U.N. Committee adopted later stipulated that the International Authority should have the right to enter any country, make land and air surveys, manage mines and plants, appoint inspectors, check accounting, issue licenses, supervise all operations, and demand reports from national governments on atomic energy.

of the period during which nations in unison were installing this great international system of control, the United States would give up whatever national superiority, diplomatic, military, or technical, exclusive mastery of atomic energy might retain. The world would thus be endowed with all the knowledge that the scientists, engineers, and construction men had accumulated.

This American proposal was bold, even revolutionary in its portents. But because of the determination that our veil of secrecy could not be even slightly lifted until we were sure that no aspiring producer of atomic weapons could benefit, and because of the craving for absolute certainty that the agreement could not be evaded, in retrospect it seems to have been almost overbearing. And on some points it was incomplete, unclear. The question of how, by what stages, the transition from the existing situation to the ultimate designated state of control, this first American proposal still left open.

As summed up by Baruch's most influential aide, John Hancock, in an address on July 15th, "The period of negotiation of the treaty is to be sharply distinguished from the series of stages in which the Atomic Development Authority will come into full possession of all information in the field once the treaty is in full force and effect. It is in this latter series of stages that we propose making more and more information available to the Authority in step with the progressive establishment of workable safeguards, proven in operation, to protect ourselves and the world from the misuse of such information by any nation." [6]

In the mazes of that problem—the phasing of steps or stages, to be defined in the treaty, which would govern the nexus between disclosure and the acceptance of control—the discussions in the U.N. Committee got permanently mired. There remained difference of opinion on this point even among the American advocates of the proposal. None was able to master the complexities and delineate a phasing that would be both completely secure and negotiable.

The Soviet official publications at this time were telling their readers that the imperialists were wearing a black cap to scare the Russian people. They reproached the United States for subordinating all work in the atomic energy field to military ends. The lugubrious warnings of the physicists were explained away as ". . . an illustration of what Karl Marx brilliantly foretold . . . that the productive forces of capitalism, including so powerful a productive force as science, at a certain stage of development 'are no longer productive but destructive forces'." [7]

[6] State Department Publication, *Growth of a Policy*, p. 76.
[7] See for example, the article entitled "A Report to the Public on the Full Meaning of the Atomic Bomb" in *New Times*, June 15, 1946, reviewing a symposium of

Needless to remark, the Soviet Government allowed nothing to be learned about the massive effort it was beginning to organize to produce atomic weapons. While deploring American secrecy and pillaging American knowledge through its agents, it was maintaining utmost secrecy about its own activities, and successfully thwarting foreign attempts to learn of them.

The Soviet Proposal: Conceived with Guile

The response which the head Soviet delegate, the stony Andrei Gromyko, made on June 19th, had no ideological tones or overtones.

If the hidden purpose in putting forth the proposal was to gain time, by giving the impression that it was willing to renounce the development of atomic weapons, the Soviet Government chose its spokesman well. For Andrei Gromyko was the most unhesitant and bold-faced dissimulator—as well as liar—in the Communist company which prized these diplomatic abilities. How talented he was the world might never have known, were it not for the record which Robert F. Kennedy has left us of Gromyko's talk with President John F. Kennedy on Wednesday afternoon, October 17, 1962, after the American Government had most convincing evidence that the Soviet establishment was placing in Cuba ground-to-ground missiles with an atomic warhead potential of about one-half the current long-range missile capacity possessed by the entire Soviet Union. I quote from Robert Kennedy's report: "Gromyko said that he wished to appeal to the U.S. and to President Kennedy on behalf of Premier Khrushchev and the Soviet Union to lessen the tension that existed in regard to Cuba. President Kennedy listened, astonished, but also with some admiration for the boldness of Gromyko's position. . . . Gromyko repeated that the sole objective of the USSR was 'to give bread to Cuba in order to prevent hunger in that country.' As far as arms were concerned, the Soviet Union had simply sent some specialists to train Cubans to handle certain kinds of armament, which were only 'defensive.' He then said he wished to emphasize the word 'defensive' and that none of these weapons could ever constitute a threat to the United States." [8]

This was the Russian representative on the U.N. Commission who submitted a counterproposal to the American one, and with utmost show of moral earnestness defended its fairness. This was *that nations*

American physicists held in March 1946—among them Oppenheimer, Wigner, Urey, and Bethe.

[8] Robert F. Kennedy, *Thirteen Days: A Memoir of the Cuban Missile Crisis* (New York: W. W. Norton, 1969), pp. 40–41.

should enter at once into a convention whereunder each and all would resolve to prohibit the production or use of atomic weapons, and to destroy existing stockpiles within three months. [italics my own] Each national subscriber to this vow should further pledge itself to pass legislation banning the production and use of atomic weapons, providing therein severe punishment for violations. But each would be its own judge and warden.

True, he also suggested that after the atomic ban treaty had been signed, a U.N. subcommittee should be created to formulate the ways and means of control and ascertaining that the treaty was not violated. At the end of his speech, Gromyko asserted that the Security Council in its role as sponsor and controller of any international agency that was created, must retain the general rule written into the Charter: that each of the Great—potentially atomic—Powers must retain the right to veto the recommendations of any U.N. agency.

The American authorities did not at once dismiss this first Soviet response as impossible.[9] But it soon became clear that it was irreconcilable with the American approach. Gromyko, in the subsequent discussions (from June 28th to Aug. 6th) in committees and subcommittees, made utterly clear how strict were two Soviet convictions: one was that the *first* step had to be an agreement to ban the production and use of atomic weapons and the destruction of existing ones; and only after an agreement to these ends was signed would the Soviet Government consider participation in an international authority. The other was that there must be added no erosion of the veto power—of the rule of unanimity—of the permanent members of the Security Council in regard to questions of substance.

These positions directly clashed with the American idea that imposition of a ban on production and use of atomic weapons should be one of the more advanced—perhaps the last—step in the sequence of measures leading to the establishment of an unviolable system of control. It was, so the opinion ran in Washington, only fair that the American Government should not give up its advantage until the protective international system was operative; that only then could it be sure that no other power would acquire the deadly weapons it would be renouncing. Moreover, one of the merits of the American plan of proceeding by stages was deemed to be that it would give advance warning of any attempt of other nations to produce atomic weapons. Should any viola-

[9] Ambassador Walter Bedell Smith, in Moscow, feared that this "disingenuous" Russian proposition might enable the USSR to seize "moral leadership" in the field, and obscure the basic issue of inspection. He suggested that the American Government recapture the "moral ascendancy" by expressing readiness to discuss regulation and control of all weapons, provided the United Nations were accorded "unhampered" rights of inspection. Memo Smith to Secretary of State, June 26, 1946.

tions of the treaty occur, the Security Council must not be prevented by a hindering veto from dealing with them promptly.

On July 1st, about two weeks after Baruch presented his proposals, the Americans carried out planned tests at the Bikini atoll of the effect of atomic bombs on naval vessels. These tests had been delayed by the President so that congressmen might be present. It would have been troublesome, once the arrangements had been made, to change the schedule again. It was decided to go ahead, even though the Soviet response in the U.N. negotiations might be affected. Some of the American officials concerned forecast that this display of the weapon should make the Russians more resistant and more determined to have a national atomic force of their own. Others, mainly in the military establishment, thought the demonstration might so impress the Russians that they would be more inclined to accept our proposals. As far as I can tell, without being able to know what is in the Russian records, Soviet policies and intentions had been so nearly determined before the tests at Bikini that they had no effect upon the program under way or the Soviet position in the U.N. Committee. But they did provide handy material for accusations.

President Truman was of Baruch's opinion, that if we acquiesced to the Russian proposals for a ban and they thereafter should stealthily launch an atomic bomb race, our present advantage and security gained by our discovery and initiative would be lost.[10] As he pithily expressed his conclusion in a talk with Baruch about the Soviet proposal, and a confirmatory letter dated July 10, 1946, ". . . We should not . . . throw away our gun until we are sure the rest of the world can't arm against us." [11] Fear of this possibility at the time was the ruling one, ruling over the prediction of the scientists that the Soviet Union would be able within a few years, by its own efforts, to offset our advantage.

What sage, what scientists, what daring public figure would have been able in mid-1946 to convince Congress and the American people that it was sensible, seemingly, to hazard our national security on the good faith of the Soviet Union? Who, especially after Gromyko spoke again on July 24th, condemning the American proposal in principle and practice? He questioned the need for the proposed international control authority; he rejected the idea that it should be authorized to intervene in national affairs in the atomic field as an infringement of national sov-

10 Truman, *Years of Trial and Hope,* p. 11.
11 Baruch papers, Princeton University Library.

ereignty. He avowed that any departure from the principle of sovereignty of states, such as the restriction of veto power in the Security Council, would injure and perhaps destroy the U.N. Therefore, he concluded, the United States' proposals in their present form were not acceptable either as a whole or in their separate parts. Two days later he made the breach more complete by observing that he thought further negotiations useless unless the committee recognized the need first of all to prepare a convention outlawing atomic weapons.

In view of the virtual freeze of the confrontations that set in this early, and never thereafter thawed, I am tempted to end the analytical narrative of the negotiations about international control of atomic energy here. By the end of July 1946 the opposed purposes and positions were so criss-crossed and fixed that all subsequent efforts to reconcile them, or pretensions to that end, were but dismal shouts of orators lost in their own smoke. While the negotiators thrust into many corners, they never met.

The American proposal had been shaped in awe of our scientific and industrial achievement. The Russians recognized that it was a remarkable one requiring great effort; Stalin had said as much to Harriman. But by then the Russian leaders were in all probability confident that their technology and industrial skill would match it, given time—aided by knowledge acquired legitimately and illicitly. What they needed was time—and that, their diplomacy and guile could secure for them.

20

The Atomic Bomb:
How To Exorcize
the Intruder (Continued)

The depth and fixity of the differences having become
even more apparent, Bernard Baruch again asked General Leslie R.
Groves for a surmise in regard to the length of time which the Soviet
Government would need to produce a stock of atomic bombs adequate
for an attack. Groves answered that he thought the four-year estimate
entirely too short and that he still stood by his original estimate of five
to seven years. This took into account, he said, the probability that the
Soviet Union would receive considerable help—presumably illicit—
from the United States. He was influenced by his belief that the high degree of centralization of the Soviet organization engaged in the production of atomic energy, both in research and engineering, would reduce
efficiency and prolong the time the Soviet strivers would need.[1]

By this time the American negotiating group concluded that continuation of the impasse favored the Russians. They thought it was causing a
lag in American efforts to accumulate raw materials and make more
bombs. Moreover, they saw signs of diminishing interest of other nations
in the bold and novel American purpose. They decided that American
initiative should not be allowed to remain stuck in the sludge of discussion in the U.N.

Thus Baruch, on September 17, 1946, asked the President for further
instructions in the light of the discussions up to then. Referring to indications of success of foreign governments in learning about the science
and technology of atomic energy through both legal and illegal methods, he said that made uncertain all surmises as to the period that

[1] Memo for Baruch by Franklin A. Lindsay, dated September 12, 1946. Baruch
papers, Princeton University Library.

147

would be needed by the Soviet Union. He remarked: "While expert testimony suggests a period of at least five years before any other country
will be in a position to produce atomic weapons, we are not ourselves
able to assess accurately the length of this margin of time. It is conceivable that this margin may be cut, especially under the pressure of an
arms race." [2]

In the same communication he said that he could not imagine how
the American Government could reach a compromise with the Soviet
proposal. For, in his opinion, ". . . Preventive measures are the very essence of control. Without them, we do not see how the Security Council
could even have knowledge of prospective violations. In the face of this,
the Soviet Government is apparently proposing that a convention outlawing atomic weapons be signed immediately and that the [United Na-
tions] Commission proceed *later* to a discussion of controls, safeguards
and sanctions, although every indication suggests that such later discussion would be entirely fruitless.

"The U.S. plan includes the Soviet proposal in the sense of also em-
bracing a convention outlawing atomic weapons. But the Soviet plan
stops at this point, while we insist on simultaneous, effective and enforceable safeguards to ensure that the production and use of atomic
weapons is not merely illegal but is in fact prevented.

"We see no possibility of reconciling these views." [3]

How, therefore, Baruch asked, should the American Government act
at this juncture? He assumed that our plans and proposals could not be
—would not be—reconsidered and revised. Should he therefore urge
that the U.N. Atomic Energy Commission submit a report to the Security Council, even though it would be a divided report? To do so, he
recognized, would lessen the chance of an agreement rather than induce
one. Or, he wondered, should the Commission take a recess, allowing for
a continuation of discussions, especially of the scientific and technical
elements of the subject, in subcommittees? Baruch thought this tempor-
izing measure the more advisable. But if that failed, and no new vista of
an agreement opened, then the American Government should have the
Security Council express itself on the divergent proposals.

The President, who had kept aloof, agreed with Baruch's expedient.

Henry Wallace's Dissent

The sag in the discussions within the U.N. did not seem to upset
American opinion. But it did excite Henry Wallace, who had, two

[2] Baruch's Report to the President, September 17, 1946, in Baruch papers, Princeton University Library.
[3] *Ibid.*

months before (on July 23d), written the President a letter explaining his views. This letter had reposed in Baruch's files ever since. But on September 18th, while Baruch and one of his aides, John Hancock, were in Washington for a conference with the President, the substance of this letter was printed on the front page of the newspapers.[4]

Wallace had written that he was deeply troubled by the way in which our people were beginning to think they had no choice but "to arm to the teeth." The arms race that would result, he believed, would end in war, as other national competitions in arms always had. Therefore, he argued, the United States, in its negotiations about the control of atomic energy, should try hard to allay any reasonable basis for the suspicion of the Russians.

The American proposal, in his opinion, gave the Russians reasons for being mistrustful. Did not Baruch's plan mean in effect that we wanted other countries to desist from efforts to make atomic weapons until a system of international ownership and control was operating to American satisfaction? We would be the judge, while in possession of atomic weapons.

This evaluation was, I believe, tenable. But Wallace's interpretation of the American proposals was not. He implied that the American Government was being deceiving; that it harbored the secret purpose of finding out what raw material resources and technological objectives Russia had, and only after learning would it decide whether or not to carry through with the later stages of control. Moreover, he alleged that the American Government intended to retain complete discretion as to *when* (at what juncture in the effectuation of the system of control) to disclose information about the production of atomic weapons and when to decide to destroy its bombs. This, to put the point summarily, was not so. It was contemplated that scheduling of these measures should emerge from the consultations between all the members of the United Nations Commission and be defined in the treaty establishing an Atomic Energy Authority.

Lastly, Wallace had asserted that the American Government should not persist in its attempt to deprive the Soviet Union of the veto power, to which it was entitled as a permanent member of the Security Council.

An adequate analysis of the validity of Wallace's allegations would carry us deeply into the thicket of questions regarding the nature, order, and pace of the program of progression proposed by the United States. The discussion in the U.N. Commission itself was rambling—in confused

[4] *New York Times.* September 18, 1946.

In *The New World*, page 599, Hewlett and Anderson give an explanation of the "inadvertent" publication of the letter in Drew Pearson's column; Charles G. Ross, the White House Press Secretary, "apparently misjudged the President's intention and, despite Truman's express disapproval, he permitted mimeographed copies of Wallace's July letter to reach the Press."

fashion from point to point in this forest. But this should be said, that while Wallace was unsparing in his criticisms of the American concern with security, he had no word of reproof for the self-serving Soviet attitude or for Russia's insistence that its word be trusted and that it should not be required to submit to examination of its good faith.

As soon as Wallace's letter became public, Baruch hastened to complain to the President. Baruch accused Wallace of major errors of fact and interpretation, among them: (1) in his unfair appraisal of what the procedure by stages meant; (2) in his assertion that the United States was asking the right to determine the form, sequence, and timing of the stages in its discretion; and (3) in his assertion that the Soviet Government would be required to agree not to try to make atomic weapons and give us information about its reserves of uranium and thorium, while the United States maintained a monopoly of atomic weapons for an indefinite period. On this last point, I may interject, I found Baruch's rebuttal disputable.

In his defense of the need to abolish the veto, Baruch was repetitive; he did not face up to the difficulties caused by this condition. Baruch's rejoinder in general seems to me more conclusive in its criticisms of the Soviet proposal than in his rebuttal of Wallace's criticisms of the American proposal.[5]

Baruch wanted Wallace to be required to retract his censure; and if he did not, he wanted the President to repudiate it. Otherwise, Baruch said he would have to resign. The President had told him to forbear for a while. He said he was going to talk with Wallace that same afternoon (September 18th) and he thought that Baruch would derive satisfaction from the outcome; if he did not, he could feel free to issue any statement he wanted.

As will be explained later, this difference between the Administration and Wallace over the judgment about proposals in regard to atomic energy was merely one feature—a secondary feature—of Wallace's criticisms of the general course of American foreign policy which led to Wallace's dismissal from the Cabinet (see chap. 21).

This bout of controversy did not make much impression on American opinion. Why, neither print nor memory makes clear. Was it due to complacence because we had atomic weapons and no other nation had? Was it avoidance of the ominous import of the issues? Was it because of a belief that like other questions in the field of armaments, no agreement could be reached? Or was it because of a suspicion—well grounded— that the Soviet Union would, no matter what agreement was signed, go ahead and produce atomic weapons as soon as it could?

[5] The rebuttal is contained in a memo which Baruch sent to Truman on September 24, 1946. Baruch papers, Princeton University Library.

A Mirage of Possible Compromise

On October 2, 1946, while the Western and Soviet proposals were tumbling about in the air like two trapeze artists who had missed their connection, Stalin was asked by a correspondent of the London Sunday *Times:* "Do you believe that the virtual monopoly possession of the atomic bomb by the United States of America is one of the principal threats to peace?" His answer deprecated the importance of atomic weapons. "I do not believe the atomic bomb to be so serious a force as certain politicians are inclined to consider it. The atomic bombs are intended to frighten the weak-nerved, but they cannot decide the outcome of war . . ." [6]

This was pretense. Probably the statement was intended to keep the Russian people calm during the period of maneuver in and out of the U.N.

Truman and Byrnes had continued to hope that the educative probes in the scientific and technical subcommittees of the Atomic Energy Commission might lead the Soviet Union to be more receptive to the American plan for the repression of atomic weapons.

During the prolonged inquiry that went on during the autumn, the American delegation tried to induce the Russians to be less rigid by manifesting readiness to re-examine all elements of the procedure and program for control. Offers were made of graduated disclosures about some of the processes of atomic fission—as a feature of the course of creation of the system of control. But to no avail. The adverse Russian response was not tempered by our professions of flexibility or tempted by proffered tidbits of knowledge. For example, when Robert Oppenheimer, as authorized, offered to tell the Russian physicists who were serving on the Scientific Sub-Committee the identity of a material used to make reactors—which hitherto had been spoken of as Material X—Professor Skobeltzyn smiled half mockingly and said: "Thank you, but I shall continue to refer to it as Material X."

When Molotov next, on October 29th, spoke in the General Assembly, he made a scathing attack on the American plan, and on Baruch personally. The proposal he advanced was substantially the same as the original Soviet one, though more comprehensive. It again put to the fore the need for a convention banning *at once* the production and use of atomic

[6] Printed in the *Information Bulletin* of the Russian Embassy in Washington, October 2, 1946.

151

weapons—in order to create, Molotov said, a favorable atmosphere for conditions of control. The quick American rejoinder was a replica of earlier ones and centered on the point that any plan for atomic and/or general disarmament would have to provide effective safeguards.[7]

Rather to the surprise of the American group, Molotov not long afterward (Dec. 4th) said he would accept a kindred American resolution as a basis of discussion.[8] Moreover, he agreed that in the conduct of its ordinary duties any international agency established by the Security Council should not be subject to the veto; though allegations of violations and the imposition of penalties would be. But there was no accord on what these ordinary duties were to be!

Since the Soviet records are denied to the historian, he is left to conjecture about the reasons for this slight bend in the Russian position, perhaps only an apparent bend. Did the Soviet tacticians think that by professing willingness to consider the American proposal, while not obligating the Soviet Government to any definite action, they would be brightening its image as an advocate of peace and disarmament, or, and this is the most plausible interpretation, to cause the other members to reject any proposal that the Commission proceed to render a formal judgment and report to the Security Council?

However, this round of more amiable discourse in the U.N. had come to nothing. The projects for disarmament and atomic control got no further. Having no firm anchorage in the national policies of either proponent, they blew away in the gale of hostility that was brewing.

Disagreement Is Acknowledged

By early November Baruch concluded that the time for decision should not be put off any longer. He wrote Byrnes that the choice seemed to be to have the U.N. Commission issue a report regarding policy or to adjourn without doing so. If a vote were taken in the near future, a favorable majority of 10 to 2 could be foreseen. But if it were postponed, the effect of the delay would be unpredictable, since there would be new members on the Commission who would want time to study the question. He informed the Secretary that his staff was beginning to prepare a statement of policy to serve as a basis of an interim report to be considered by the U.N. Commission.

On November 21st, Acheson informed Baruch that the President had decided that he should go forward with the report which would clarify the essentials and highlight the differences without forcing the Russians

[7] Hewlett and Anderson, *The New World*, p. 608.
[8] *Ibid.*, p. 611.

at that time to take a public stand against the American proposals. In regard to a resolution which Molotov had offered for general disarmament, the President thought that the American group on the U.N. Commission should not attempt to revise it but rather to attack it directly, saying in effect: "We have already been negotiating for nearly a year in the field in which the Russians are weakest and in which we are the strongest. We had no success whatsoever. Under such circumstances it seems unthinkable that the Russians are sincere in their proposal for general disarmament . . ." [9]

On December 5th, Baruch asked that Commission to endorse a resolution in which he condensed the essentials of the American plan. Undeterred by the fact that almost all instructed observers concluded that it was not negotiable, he again contended that no measures less comprehensive than those that had been put forward by the American Government in its primary proposal would do. Certainly, he repeated, a treaty that merely "outlawed" atomic weapons would not in itself be sufficient to remove the atomic menace and bring trust. He stood fast on a pinnacle of his precepts, saying at one of the Commission's last meetings: "It is either—or. Either you agree that a criminal should have this right [to use the veto to escape punishment] by voting against our position . . . or you vote for this sound and basic principle of enduring justice and plain common sense." [10] He warned that the American people would pull out from the U.N. if there were any possibility that a criminal state would escape the consequence of its acts.

The U.N. Commission, after long discussions which eventuated in only minor changes, had, on December 31, 1946, voted upon the Report to be made to the Security Council. Its findings and recommendations which incised the difference between the Western Powers and the Soviet Union, received ten affirmative votes. The Russian and Polish members abstained. Gromyko's final objections were the same as his first ones. Baruch voiced his satisfaction over "a complete victory." But it was an empty victory.

When the report came before the Security Council two months later (Feb. 1947), Gromyko submitted a number of major amendments, so involved in meaning as only to bewilder—which may have been their intention.

The admission of failure in the negotiations about control evoked only resigned laments in the United States. The Russians' fulminations

[9] Memo of talk, Hancock and Lindsay with Acheson, November 21, 1946. Baruch papers, Princeton University Library.
[10] Hewlett and Anderson, *The New World*, p. 617.

against the Report were generally construed as a sign of frustration and proof of the inferiority of Soviet technical and industrial capacity. No responsible American official publicly expressed any doubt as to the protective value of secrecy for presumed American superior scientific knowledge and industrial proficiency. The scientists who had earlier pleaded for an accord with the Soviet Union had become quiescent. Discouraged at the way in which their views had been ignored, they no longer badgered the American Government with their forecasts that within a few years Russia would have atomic weapons and that all the elaborate arrangements for secrecy and safeguards would become pointless.

Still, to perceptive and concerned observers, the lapse of the discussions in the U.N. had been a sombre omen that there was going to be an atomic arms race. This was to loom like a thundercloud over the political scene during the next two eventful years. It darkened every other controversy—especially that over Germany, which we will discuss next.

21

The Quarrel over
Germany Worsens

As soon as the Conference of Foreign Ministers in Paris had ended, General Sir Brian Robertson, Deputy Military Governor of the British zone, asked Konrad Adenauer, head of the Christian Democratic Union in the West, Jacob Kaiser, leader of that party in Berlin, and Dr. Kurt Schumacher, the leader of the Social Democrats, to meet with him. On July 15th they were told that the British Military Government was going to form a new political Land (State) of the regions of North Rhineland and Westphalia.

Adenauer approved of this step since he thought it necessary to interlock the former Rhine province with other German regions in view of French pretensions. Schumacher preferred a different formation of states of the region. Having ascertained the probable German reaction, the British Military Government announced the creation of a new Land of North Rhine–Westphalia.

The German political party leaders were also informed of the intention to bring about the economic consolidation of the American and British zones.

Adenauer noted that the diverse and permanent consequences of these two measures would prevent the reconstitution of the state of Prussia, they would frustrate French demands for the internationalization of the Ruhr,[1] and, it could be foreseen, they would displease the Soviet Government and affect adversely any remaining chance for German reunification.

In August and September the American and British zone Governors entered into agreements for the formation of bizonal agencies to concern themselves with food and agriculture, transport, finance, and communications.

[1] Konrad Adenauer, *Memoirs 1945–53* (Chicago: Regnery, 1966), pp. 80–1.

Byrnes Makes the Change of Direction Clear

While this step toward the economic merger of the two zones was going forward, Byrnes took leave from the Paris Peace Conference. He traveled from Berlin to Stuttgart on the same private railroad car Hitler had furnished, and there, on September 6th, at the State Opera House, he delivered a major public address to a large German audience. On the stage with him were Senators Vandenberg and Connally and General Joseph T. McNarney (ex officio Military Governor of the U.S. Zone), Commander of American forces in Europe, who introduced the Secretary. One of Byrnes's purposes was to counter Molotov's bid (of July 10th) for favor of the Germans, by stressing the positive measures the American Government intended to take to improve their plight and their prospects.[2]

The Secretary began by repeating the ritual avowal that the United States wanted to carry out "fully" the "principles" outlined in the Potsdam Agreement on demilitarization and reparations. He then went on to justify the relaxation of the economic provisions of the ground that if Germany was not to be administered as an economic unit (because of French and Russian obstruction), the permitted levels of industrial production must be changed. "The conditions which now exist in Germany," he declared, "make it impossible for industrial production to reach the levels which the occupying powers agreed were essential for a minimum German peace-time economy. Obviously, if the agreed levels of industry are to be reached, we cannot continue to restrict the free exchange of commodities, persons, and ideas throughout Germany. . . . We favor the economic unification of Germany. If complete unification cannot be secured, we shall do everything in our power to secure the maximum possible unification."[3]

Among the several reasons for unification, the Secretary stressed also the need for a common monetary and financial policy. This should be

---

[2] Text in James F. Byrnes, *Speaking Frankly*, pages 187–91.

In many respects, Byrnes' address conformed to a statement of policy which Gen. Clay had sent to Washington on July 19th. He had intended to release this statement publicly, but the State and War Departments would not clear it. Among the important reasons why, as related by Gimbel, *American Occupation of Germany*, pp. 78–79, ". . . because it contained statements on the early establishment of a provisional government and on eventual admission of Germany to the United Nations, neither of which was firm and definite U.S. policy." Moreover, committees in Washington were still considering how far and in what ways to revise Directives concerning limits of industrial capacity, dismantling, the frontiers, the Rhineland, and internationalization of the Ruhr.

[3] Byrnes, *Speaking Frankly*.

remembered when later Western initiative in this field brought on a crisis over Berlin. "Runaway inflation accompanied by economic paralysis is almost certain to develop unless there is a common financial policy directed to the control of inflation. A program of drastic fiscal reform to reduce currency and monetary claims, to revise the debt structure . . . is urgently required." [4]

Another noteworthy point, which from then on was to be increasingly stressed, read: "While Germany must be prepared to share her coal and steel with the liberated countries of Europe dependent upon those supplies, Germany must be enabled to use her skill and her energies to increase her industrial production. . . . Germany is a part of Europe, and recovery in Europe, and particularly in the states adjoining Germany, will be slow indeed if Germany with her great resources of iron and coal is turned into a poorhouse." [5]

In regard to reparations, I cannot simplify the filigree of the Secretary's statements. All I can clearly discern is the refusal of the American Government to sanction reparation payments that might deny Germans the chance of improving their lot—certainly to rule out payments to be made out of future production. Keynes' scornful criticisms of the generation-long schedule of reparations envisaged in the Versailles Peace Treaty still stung.[6] Memories of German resistance to exorbitant and prolonged obligations to make such deliveries set at the end of the First World War, of the fiasco of French occupation of the Ruhr, of the wild inflation in Germany, of the lost loans of American investors in Germany during this period—all foreclosed any attempt to appraise the possibilities in the light of potential German ability to pay, if and when its productive capacity was revived. If the Soviet Union and France wanted to obtain more reparations by deliveries of surplus capital equipment from the Western zones, let them agree to the economic unification of all of Germany!

As regards Germany's political future, the Secretary held out an attractive prospect. "It is the view of the American Government that the German people . . . under proper safeguards, should now be given the primary responsibility for the running of their own affairs. . . . [they] should now be permitted and helped to make the necessary preparations for setting up of a democratic German Government. . . . The United States favors the early establishment of a provisional German Govern-

---

[4] *Ibid.*

[5] *Ibid.*

[6] Is this an example of John Maynard Keynes' memorable witticism that "Practical men, who believe themselves to be quite exempt from any intellectual influences, are usually the slaves of some defunct economist."? *The General Theory of Employment, Interest and Money* (New York: Harcourt, 1936), p. 383.

ment for Germany." [7]

He had added a sentence to the text, which pledged "as long as there is an occupation army in Germany, American armed forces will be part of that occupation army." Byrnes had some misgivings about making this pledge; and tried to consult the President by telephone, but getting no response had, in face of Clay's assurance, included this sentence.[8] That either foresaw that American troops would still be stationed in Germany a quarter of a century later is unlikely.

For in another segment of his speech Byrnes related the duration of the occupation regime and the size of the occupation forces to the treaty which he had proposed. The American Government, he stated, did not believe "that large armies of foreign soldiers or alien bureaucrats . . . are in the long run the most reliable guardians of another country's democracy." The Allied occupation forces should be limited to numbers sufficient to see that the rules under which Germany could govern itself, which should be laid down by the Allied governments, were obeyed. Certainly the force needed would be smaller were "our proposal for a treaty with the major powers to enforce for 25 or even 40 years the demilitarization plan [to be] finally agreed upon in the peace settlement" accepted. Unfortunately it had not been.[9]

Probably most unpalatable to the Soviet Union, the Secretary assured the German people that the American Government did not consider Germany's Eastern frontier with Poland as settled; it would support a prewar revision in Poland's favor, but the extent of the area to be ceded to Poland must still be determined.

This statement, inevitably, evoked a counterstatement of Molotov's. The three Great Powers, the Soviet Foreign Minister flatly declared, had passed conclusive judgment on Poland's western boundary when they agreed at Potsdam that the section of Silesia that had been German should be placed under Polish administration. What other response could Byrnes have expected? He, himself, had proposed at Potsdam the "package deal" of which this arrangement was one feature—though nominally only until the boundary was fixed in a peace treaty.

As for French aspirations, the American Government, Byrnes averred, did not feel it could deny the claim to the Saar; however, it was against separating the Rhineland and the Ruhr from Germany.

The concluding paragraphs of this notable address of Byrnes were, "The United States cannot relieve Germany from the hardships inflicted upon her by the war her leaders started. But the United States has no desire to increase those hardships or to deny the German people an op-

[7] Byrnes, *Speaking Frankly*.
[8] Lucius D. Clay, *Decision in Germany* (New York: Doubleday, 1950), p. 79.
[9] Byrnes, *Speaking Frankly*.

portunity to work their way out of those hardships so long as they respect human freedom and follow the paths of peace.[10]

"The American people want to return the Government of Germany to the German people. The American people want to help the German people to win their way back to an honorable place among the free and peace-loving nations of the world." [11]

This address marked the resentment of the American government at Russian behavior, fear that the Communist courtship might win over the Germans. It was a triumph over the feeling that it was just that all Germans should continue to suffer as punishment for their evil acts during the years in which they hailed and served Hitler.[12]

The British Government Similarly Changes Course

Churchill applauded Byrnes' speech. When Bevin expounded British policy toward Germany in the House of Commons (on Oct. 22d), the core of his explanation was the same as Byrnes'. "There are many imperfections in this [Potsdam] Agreement, but we have said many times that we are ready to carry it out in its entirety. What we are not prepared to do is to carry out parts of it which are unfavourable to us, while other parts are not fulfilled. . . . The basic provision of the Agreement is that Germany shall be treated as an economic unit. . . . We and the Americans have had to buy food and other goods to send to Western Germany, while the Russians are taking similar goods from Eastern Germany into Russia. . . . We must either have Potsdam observed as a whole, and in the order of its decision or we must have a new agreement." [13]

The Appeal to the French

Neither Byrnes nor Bevin had much hope that this exposition of their intentions regarding Germany would cause the Russians to reconsider their terms or tendencies. But Byrnes thought that it might impel the French to moderate or renounce claims and practices which were retarding the trend toward unification of the Western zones and providing

[10] *Ibid.*

[11] The change in policy may have been influenced also by a wish to reduce or end the need to provide dollars to support the German people.

[12] The one object of revulsion was gradually yielding to another—Russia, as in a gliding, appalling moving-picture.

[13] *Parliamentary Debates*, House of Commons, October 22, 1946, column 1513.

the Russians with pretext for maintaining the economic separation of the Eastern zone. He tried to sway French opinion in a speech before the American Club in Paris. There, emphasizing the firmness of American opposition to the revival of German military power, he averred that a four-power treaty would provide France with the security it wanted and end the struggle for the control of Germany which might again give it the chance to divide and conquer. The American Government, he said, ". . . does not want to see Germany become a pawn or partner in a struggle for power between East and West." [14]

The Secretary probably shared the prevailing American opinion that the demoralized collapse and surrender of the French armies in 1940 had shown that France was not entitled to a primary part in deciding policy toward Germany and was incapable and indisposed to carry the correlative responsibility. He was less cognizant of the fact that most of the French parliamentary leaders and at least half of the Assembly members, including Georges Bidault, had risked their lives in courageous acts of resistance in the underground. As Theodore White recalled in his shining book, *Fire in the Ashes* "The Gaullists on the Right and the Communists on the Left count scores of heroes who survived the perils of Resistance and Insurrection; some members of the Assembly still carry on their arms the tattooing of German concentration camps." [15] These and the people they represented were not ready to forget and forgive the terrible German brutality and their own suffering under the occupation, or willing to trust the impulses and vows of a beaten and chastened Germany.

Not even the French Socialists were budged by Byrnes' assurances. Bidault, though with less authority, clung to the demands which de Gaulle had formulated. France by then was becoming engaged in the struggle for Indochina, which eight years later was to end in the disaster of Dien Bien Phu.

The dissension over Germany was to continue and become more abrasive.

The Final Falling-Out with Wallace

Soon after Byrnes and Clay returned from Stuttgart to the Paris Peace Conference, former Vice President Wallace—then Secretary of Commerce—publicly dissented from the course the Secretary of State was keeping. Wallace had long been smoldering with the belief that

[14] October 3, 1946. Text of speech is printed in *Speaking Frankly*, p. 193.
[15] Theodore White, *Fire in the Ashes: Europe in Mid-Century* (New York: Sloane, 1953), p. 87.

American policy toward Russia was ungiving and hostile; that Truman was endangering peace in an attempt to appease the Republican Party; and that the policies of the British Labor Government were being warped by the inherited wish to retain imperial interests. These opinions, and their companionable condemnations, burst forth in an address at Madison Square Garden on September 12th.

Wallace warned that "the tougher we get, the tougher the Russians will get. . . . We must not let our policy be influenced by those inside or outside the United States who want war with Russia but this does not mean appeasement." Bracing himself against the wind of hatred of Russia which was gathering force—he said: "The real peace treaty we now need is between the United States and Russia. But we want to be met half-way. We want co-operation. And I believe we can get that co-operation once Russia understands that our primary objective is neither saving the British Empire nor purchasing oil in the Near East with the lives of American soldiers. . . . On our part, we should recognize that we have no more business in the political affairs of Eastern Europe than Russia has in the political affairs of Latin America, Western Europe and the United States. . . . Whether we like it or not, the Russians will try to socialize their sphere of influence just as we try to democratize our sphere of influence." [16]

Wallace was directing his charges largely against the Republican aspirants for office at the coming election, especially Governor Thomas E. Dewey, Senator Vandenberg, and John Foster Dulles. But the fallout descended mainly on Byrnes. And the recoil knocked him, Wallace, out of office.

The speech was the more confounding, at home and abroad, because Wallace stated that it had the approval of President Truman. The President, when quizzed by newspapermen (who had received advance copies) on the afternoon of the evening Wallace spoke, said that he had approved the whole speech, adding that there was nothing in it that departed from Byrnes' policy. "They are exactly in line." [17]

Shortly after this press conference, Acting Secretary of State Will Clayton, having conferred with division heads in the State Department, telephoned Charles Ross, the White House Press Secretary, and said that in his opinion Byrnes "would be very much disappointed" and ". . .

---

[16] Address, Madison Square Garden, New York, Sept. 12, 1946.

[17] For fuller knowledge of this confused and confusing episode read and compare Truman's and Byrnes' books of memoirs: the *New York Times* of September 13, 14, and 15, 1946; the issues of the New York newspaper *PM* of September 18 and 19, 1946; and the pertinent section in the book by George Curry, *James F. Byrnes.* I have been enabled by Secretary Byrnes to read the files of his communications to and from Washington.

would probably feel that the ground had been cut from under him." [18]
Clayton and the Undersecretary of the Navy urged Ross to persuade the
President to withdraw his approval before the speech was given, but re-
ceived only a non-committal answer.

Truman was careless and wavering. He was careless because, as
James Reston, that insidious pursuer of realities, wrote in the *New York
Times* on the following morning, "Mr. Wallace sent him the speech . . .
and Mr. Truman let it go without taking time to study its implications
or think about how it would read here and abroad." [19] Truman in his
Memoirs excused himself by relating that Wallace merely mentioned to
him that he was going to make a speech and said: " . . . that he intended to say that we ought to look at the world through American eyes
rather than through the eyes of a pro-British or rabidly anti-Russian
press. . . . There was, of course, no time for me to read the speech, even
in part." [20] Clark Clifford, the White House Legal Counsel, also has said
that the President had merely "thumbed it through." [21] In fact, Wallace
had read to him diverse short extracts, and the President had nodded
and said "Fine." Moreover, and this the President seems to have forgotten, Wallace had made his views clear in a letter he had written the
President almost three months previously (July 23d).

Truman wavered—and here I am only venturing my own surmise—
because he shared in a degree Wallace's critical displeasure at the attention being paid to the pronouncements of some leading Republicans,
and was regretful at having to heed their views on foreign policy.[22]

[18] From Byrnes' file
[19] New York Times, Sept. 13, 1946.
[20] *Year of Decisions*, page 557.
[21] This explanation comforted—or discomforted—persons close to Truman. Arthur
Krock, then Head of the *New York Times* Washington Bureau, in his reminiscent recording for the Oral History Project of Princeton University, remarked that Harriman, who noted that in response to a reporter's question Wallace retorted, "I tell
you Mr. Truman read that particular sentence and approved it," thought this was a
give-away that the President *had not read the whole speech.*
Sir Pierson Dixon, Secretary to Bevin, relates that Vandenberg confirmed the truth
of the story, then current, that the President had written on the margin of Wallace's
speech, "This will make Jimmy [Byrnes] sore." But this cannot be verified. Pierson
Dixon, *Double Diploma: The Life of Sir Pierson Dixon, Don and Diplomat* (London:
Hutchinson, 1968), p. 227 (Entry of Sir Pierson Dixon in his Diary, dated September
21, 1946).
[22] Ironically, a few months later Truman was to write Byrnes, who had resigned,
"You have noticed . . . the tendency on the part of Vandenberg and our partisan
Republican friend, Dulles, to attempt to implement a Republican foreign policy.
Dulles has made two speeches in which he has made a sincere attempt, with the
help of the Republican press, to take charge of foreign relations, especially as it affects the German settlement and Central Europe. It seems to me if you are inclined
to do it, that you are in a much better position now than at any time in the recent
past to flatten out that sort of approach." Truman to Byrnes, January 27, 1947.
Byrnes papers.

Moreover, he was not averse to securing the votes of the liberals to whom Wallace appealed. There still sounded in Truman's spirit echoes of Roosevelt's wariness of British diplomacy and Roosevelt's wish for friendly relations with the Russians. These briefly diluted his anger at the Russians, though he, himself, had urged Byrnes to be tougher with them.

In Paris, foreign representatives at the Peace Conference quizzed Byrnes, Vandenberg, and Connally about Wallace's address. Byrnes refrained from public comment on the ground that the question could be clarified only by the President himself. Vandenberg and Connally spoke up as defenders of the bipartisan foreign policy that was being maintained. Vandenberg pointedly remarked that this "requires unity within the Administration itself. We can only cooperate with one Secretary of State at a time." Connally declared that while American officials in Paris were "striving desperately for peace in the world there should be no controversy or bickering or strife at home."

The President, who had hoped the excitement would blow itself out, found that he had to issue a public statement. He said at a press conference on the 14th: "It was my intention to express the thought that I approved the right of the Secretary of Commerce to deliver the speech. I did not intend to indicate that I approved the speech as constituting a statement of the foreign policy of this country. There has been no change in the established foreign policy of our Government."

Wallace then issued a statement, in which he took back nothing. "I stand," he said, "upon my New York speech. . . . I intend to continue my efforts for a just and lasting peace. I shall within the near future speak on the subject again."

The President told Clayton, who informed Byrnes, that he was going to talk with Wallace the next day ". . . and if he carries out his present intention the result will be entirely satisfactory to you."

Truman had an earnest talk with Wallace in which both tried hard to scrape through the episode and to avert a rift and separation. Truman did not reprimand the former Vice-President. He tried rather to impress him with the upsetting effects of his remarks, pointing out that if they were not controverted they would give the impression that the American Government was going to change the whole tenor of its foreign policy drastically. Any such inference would mean that Byrnes could not carry out his assignment at the Council of Foreign Ministers then going on.

Wallace did not admit any fault of judgment or behavior. But he did consent to inform the press that after a "friendly" discussion he had reached the conclusion that he "would make no public statements or speeches until the Foreign Ministers' Conference in Paris is concluded."

As reporters crowded around him and asked if everything was patched up, that naïve, stubborn idealist replied: "Everything's lovely." He added —and here was his streak of stubborn conviction—that he "absolutely" still stood upon the New York speech. Then asked finally if he was going to remain in the Cabinet, he said: "Yes, I am."

Prodded by the Senators, Byrnes, after being informed of Wallace's talk with the President and its outcome, on September 18th, notified the President that he would have to resign unless Wallace was repressed. Byrnes said: "If it is not possible for you, for any reason, to keep Mr. Wallace, as a member of your Cabinet, from speaking on foreign affairs, it would be a grave mistake from every point of view for me to continue in office, even temporarily. Therefore, if it is not completely clear in your own mind that Mr. Wallace should be asked to refrain from criticizing the foreign policy of the United States while he is a member of your Cabinet, I must ask you to accept my resignation immediately."

Any chance that the President might have soothed this row between his subordinates by the salve of obfuscation passed when he read an interview with Wallace which appeared in a New York daily which shared Wallace's opinions of our policy. Wallace was reported as having said that the President had asked his help in the coming congressional elections, and that he had told the President that he would not give it if he was not free to discuss foreign affairs.[23]

Wallace did not appreciate how aroused were Byrnes and his senatorial supporters: the Army and Navy officials, whom he had accused of wanting to launch a preventive war against Russia; and Baruch, whose stand on atomic energy he predicted could not bring agreement but only provoke an atomic bomb race (see chap. 20). Even liberal idealists turned against him because in his speech he had in effect advocated a "sphere of influence" deal between the Soviet Union and the United States. Mrs. Franklin D. Roosevelt stood by him and tried to quiet the disturbance by obscuring its cause, remarking inanely at a Liberal Party rally that "Fundamentally Henry Wallace wants what President Truman wants, what Secretary of State Byrnes wants, and what everyone of us want." [24]

The combination of indignant assailants was irresistible. Byrnes' resentment was not to be assuaged, since he was convinced that his efforts and influence would be vitally stricken if Wallace was not repudiated. He had a long teletype talk with the President (on the 19th). In this

[23] This interview appeared in the newspaper *PM*. This sheet was notoriously slanted and frequently dishonest. But Wallace did not deny the interview, as far as I know. It was also in the Washington *Daily News* (Scripps-Howard) afternoon edition of the 18th.

[24] *New York Times,* September 19, 1946.

Byrnes said that Wallace's statement left him and foreign governments in more doubt than ever as to just what our foreign policy would be. The position of the American delegation at the Peace Conference was tottering. He did not want to be confronted by Wallace's criticisms as soon as the Conference ended. "I would then have to insist on being relieved. It is far better for the Administration to let us come home now. . . . [For] I respectfully submit that if Mr. Molotov believed that on October 23rd next, [when the Conference was due to adjourn] there would be a re-examination of the question of permitting Wallace to again attack your policy he would derive great comfort." [25]

The President assured Byrnes that he was not going to leave any doubts about his views. The next day he asked for Wallace's resignation. Wallace, with an air of friendly acceptance of this penalty for having expressed his deep convictions, complied at once. The White House issued an explanatory statement: "It had become clear that between his [Wallace's] views on foreign policy and those of the Administration . . . there was a fundamental conflict. We could not permit this conflict to jeopardize our position in relations to other countries. . . . No change in foreign policy is contemplated. . . . Mr. Byrnes consults with me and the policies which guide him and his delegation have my full endorsement." [26]

In a letter the President wrote to his mother he told her: "I had to fire Henry today." Ruminating, he continued: "If Henry had stayed Secretary of Agriculture in 1940 as he should have, there'd never have been all this controversy, and I would not be here and wouldn't that be nice? . . . . I asked him [Henry] to make no more speeches until Byrnes came home. He agreed to that, and he and Charlie Ross and I came to what we thought was a firm commitment that he'd say nothing beyond the one sentence statement we agreed he should make. Well, he answered questions and told his gang over at Commerce all that had taken place in our interview. It was all in the afternoon *Washington News* yesterday, and I never was so exasperated since Chicago. So—this morning I called Henry and told him he'd better get out, and he was so nice about it I almost backed out." [27]

Thus departed from the Administration the only senior member who was deeply disturbed by the growing rift with the Soviet Union, and willing to hazard the fate of the Western democracies by trusting the Soviet Union.

Perhaps—and this is pure conjecture—his eloquent plea did briefly

[25] Byrnes gives much of the text of this conversation in *Speaking Frankly,* pp. 240–2.
[26] *New York Times,* September 21, 1946.
[27] This letter is in Truman, *Year of Decisions,* p. 560.

churn American and Soviet policies. Truman and Stalin both published denials that there was any danger that there would be war.[28] And during the closing weeks of the Paris Peace Conference each made some concessions to the other that previously they had refused.

It may be permissible to observe that by now—at the time this book is being written—an unacknowledged sphere of influence arrangement has emerged. But it is unstable and subject to frequent tremors.

The Formation of Bizonia

To tell of this dissonance within the American Government, I have interrupted the account of developments in Germany. There, as in the concurrent negotiations about the control of atomic energy in the U.N., the American Government remained firm.

The economic merger of the British and American zones was accelerated because the British Treasury, in sore straits, informed the Americans that it would henceforth have to ask payment in dollars for goods procured from the British zone.[29]

The agreement was signed by Secretaries Byrnes and Bevin on December 2d, while Bevin was in New York.[30] In the preamble it was stated that "The arrangements set out hereunder . . . should be regarded as the first step towards the achievement of the economic unity of Germany . . . The two Governments are ready at any time to enter into discussions with either of the other occupying powers with a view to the extension of these arrangements to their zones of occupation."

American officials continued publicly to deny an imputation that this was a step toward the division in Germany; and to aver that, to the contrary, there was reason for hoping ". . . that it will lead to economic unity of all Germany, and that it will pave the way also for creation of a

---

[28] Stalin in an interview printed in the London Sunday *Times* on September 24, 1946, in his usual stiff prose went so far as to say that the Soviet Union "could not affirm" that capitalist Great Britain and the United States were trying to "encircle" Russia and that it believed "unconditionally" in the possibility of a friendly and lasting collaboration between the Soviet Union and Western democracies.

[29] So Bevin confirmed in the House of Commons on February 27, 1947.

[30] *Memorandum of Agreement Between the United States and the United Kingdom on the Economic Fusion of American and British Zones of Occupation in Germany.* Signed December 2, 1946. The Agreement provided for a pooling of the resources of the two zones, a Joint Export–Import Agency and for the establishment by the Commanders-in-Chief in their two zones of such German administrative agencies as were necessary to the economic unification under the joint control, and for supporting an increase in the present standard of 1550 (to 1800) calories for the normal consumer as soon as the world food supply permitted.

political entity in Germany." [31]

The fusion was nominally only of economic policies and acts. But its authors were not unaware that although each of the signatories retained control over military and political affairs in its own zone, this accord would almost certainly lead to extensive cooperation and coincidence of political and social policies and actions. For that reason, and because it granted to the American authorities an equal part in the direction of the coal and iron and steel resources of the Ruhr, the agreement was of wide consequence.

The Soviet authorities appeared to take a calm view of the economic fusion of the two zones. At long last they agreed in this same month of December 1946 to have the Deputies of the Foreign Ministers begin their studies and discussions of the nature and terms of a peace treaty with Germany. Thereby, perhaps, the Russians hoped to avert the further exclusion of Communist influence in West Germany, and to dull the inclination of the Western majority members of the Control Council to go their own way.

But if the Russians had such hope, it quickly faded. As we shall see, when the Foreign Ministers conferred the following March (1947) about whether and how to proceed to make a peace treaty with Germany, Russian opposition to a merger of the Western zones was most vehement, and their notions of what should be done before a peace treaty was made with Germany were as purposeful as ever. But in the interval there was a short and deceptive spell of amiability—conducive to euphoria.

[31] Letter Secretary of War Robert Patterson to Palmer Hoyt, editor of the *Denver Post*, December 1946. Assistant Secretary of State Hilldring was, as was usually his way, more positive when testifying before the House Appropriations Committee in February 1947. "If we succeed in the program we have instituted now in Western Germany, it will require all our partners in Germany, including the Soviets, to carry out their agreement arrived at at Potsdam." Quoted by Gimbel, *American Occupation*, pp. 112–3.

22

A Brief Spell of Euphoria

Five Peace Treaties Agreed

The Council of Foreign Ministers met next in the elevated elegance of the Waldorf-Astoria in New York City. Sir Pierson Dixon, Bevin's secretary, was sufficiently impressed to describe the setting ". . . In an exotic room on the 27th floor . . . sitting round a circular table of maple wood, the central space being filled with Braque-like flowering plants, and the eau-de-nile walls covered with rather unmodern pictures." [1] Bevin was still in a state of exhaustion, having almost collapsed on the *Aquitania* during the rough Atlantic crossing. Maurice Couve de Murville, substituting for Bidault, was as always antiseptic, assured, and cool to American life; Molotov calm; and Byrnes blithe, as was his wont.

The four first resumed their discussion of those elements of the peace treaties with Italy and the satellite countries upon which they had not been able to agree. [2] Molotov must have come with instructions to be conciliatory, for he quickly joined with his three other colleagues in approving most of the resolutions which had been passed in the Paris Peace Conference, including some that had been adopted in the face of stiff Russian objection.

But Molotov tried to secure Western assent to agree to changes in the Italian treaty that would mollify Yugoslavia. The group was enough at ease to banter without giving offense. As when on November 23d, he said that he thought that if agreement was reached on a contemplated accord on the Austro-Italo boundary, they could agree on the regime of the railroads between Yugoslavia and Trieste.

---

[1] *Double Diploma*, Entry of Sir Pierson Dixon in his Diary, November 4, 1945, p. 235.
[2] This six weeks meeting was a most busy one. The completion of the peace treaties with Italy and the satellites was only one of the difficult matters before the Council. Another was preparations for discussions by Deputies of terms of the peace treaties with Germany and Austria. At the same time Byrnes and Bevin progressed in their negotiations about the merger of their zones in Germany; and they talked over the worrisome situations in Palestine and Greece. The U.N. General Assembly was in session at the same time in New York City.

"*Bevin:* This seems like horse trading to me.

Molotov: I do not know how to horse trade.

Byrnes: Find me a horse trader as hard as you are and I will give him a gold medal.

Molotov: I am learning.

Bevin: God help us when you have learned."

Molotov persisted. In a private meeting with Byrnes on November 26th, he said Byrnes knew that Russia had a troublesome problem with Yugoslavia. Tito was dissatisfied with both the territorial and reparation provisions of the peace treaty with Italy, and unless given some satisfaction there was little chance that the Yugoslav Government would sign a treaty. Soviet authorities thought that the Yugoslav claims, well founded by what they had done in the war, were being slighted. But the only concession which Byrnes and Bevin made was to agree that Italy should be required to pay thirty-five million dollars more in reparations than had been previously designated. Italy's total obligation to pay reparations was increased to $360-million, but the mode of payment and period of payment were adjusted to Western desires.

Into the treaties with the Danubian states a provision was inserted that there should be free navigation on the Danube except for traffic between ports of the same country. Here it may be foretold that when, in a later conference dominated by the Communist states, a regime for the Danube was settled, this principle was discarded.

It was also agreed that the pending discussions regarding peace treaties with Germany and Austria, which loomed over all, would be deferred until the Council of Foreign Ministers next met in Moscow. In the interim, Deputies were to study the moot issues. Molotov, who had been hesitant, stated, in one of the terminal meetings, that the Soviet Delegation did not object to the appointment of Deputies; they could listen to what spokesmen for directly interested countries had to say, in the first place the neighbors of Germany, and learn from them. In haste, out of the shower of suggestions by each of the Foreign Ministers, a list of the elements of a treaty with Germany to be considered by the Deputies, and with what priority, was compiled and adopted. The Deputies would be instructed to submit their report by March 10th, so that the Council could study it when it foregathered in the spring of 1947 in Moscow.

Molotov was almost gracious in his remarks at the closing session on December 12th. "It seems to me that we have finished our work. This being so, permit me as Chairman of the present meeting to congratulate the members of the Council of Foreign Ministers on finishing a long and hard work in drafting the five peace treaties."

He went on to thank the American Government and Mr. Byrnes for their hospitality. Bevin and Couve de Murville added their gratitude and hopes for the meeting in Moscow, to which Mr. Byrnes cordially replied.

To the American public Byrnes spoke cheerfully of the way in which relations with the Soviet Union might develop.[3] In Britain, Bevin's similar impression is clearly expressed in the broadcast he gave on December 22d. "I believe we have entered the first stage of establishing concord and harmony between the Great Powers. What is the ground for that belief? First, we are agreed on the first round of peace treaties, which are the instruments to restore normality after the war. Second, we are shaping the organization to which the United Nations look to guide their relations and keep the peace. . . . Soviet Russia, who is now recovering from the wounds of war, fully realized, I think, in New York that there was a great desire for complete understanding, and that there is throughout the world a readiness to co-operate with her and see her develop her system in her own way, but with the recognition that others equally have the right to their own way of life." [4]

In the Soviet Union, the tone of the press was exemplified by the leading editorial in the *New Times:* [5] "The year 1947 is being ushered in under certain favourable signs in the international arena. The recent session of the UNO General Assembly (October–December 1946) was a definite success for the policy of peace and international cooperation as consistently upheld by the Soviet Union and other democratic countries. . . ." And Stalin himself, when interviewed by Elliott Roosevelt, deprecated the fact that the relations between the American and Russian Governments had been worn down since the death of Franklin Roosevelt. He said: ". . . There have been misunderstandings. Certain deterioration has taken place and then great noise was raised that their relations would even deteriorate still further. But I see nothing frightful about this in the sense of violation of peace or a military conflict. . . . I think that the danger of a new war is not real." [6]

The five peace treaties were signed at Paris on February 10, 1947, to go in force in the following September.

[3] Text of address at Plenary Assembly of United Nations, December 13, 1946, in State Department *Bulletin* issue December 22, 1946.
[4] *The Times* (of London), December 23, 1946, p. 8.
[5] *New Times,* January 1, 1947.
[6] Article by Elliott Roosevelt in *Look,* February 4, 1947. General Montgomery, who had been appointed Chief of the Imperial General Staff, went to Moscow. On his return to Britain he told a colleague who told Dalton, who recorded it in his Diary, that "My visit was a great success. Now that I have done this preliminary work, Bevin . . . can get his extension of the Anglo-Soviet treaty quite easily." Montgomery believed, and let Stalin know he believed, that he thought Britain had not been sympathetic enough with Russian sufferings and devastation. This conversation took place on January 25, 1947. Hugh Dalton, *High Tide and After,* p. 201.

Marshall Succeeds Byrnes

After the completion of the negotiation of the five peace treaties, the brief period of calm that set in was a favorable occasion for Byrnes to resign as Secretary of State. He had wanted to for quite a time—he was tired and anxious about his health. The Wallace row had caused him to think that Truman might at any time let him down. Although the President regretted the ending of their association, he was relieved. Some of his circle had kept telling him that Byrnes, by his indecision, was prejudicing the presidential image. Possibly the President had the sense that Byrnes nurtured a grievance because he, Truman, had been designated by Roosevelt to be Vice-President rather than himself; and that Byrnes believed he was better qualified.

Truman had long since decided to appoint General George C. Marshall, who was giving up his assignment in China, as Secretary of State, and Marshall had said he would be willing to serve. The President was impressed with the great general, as a former captain of artillery might be, and thought his wisdom and stability would make him an able and effective Secretary of State. He liked Marshall's curt decisiveness, a trait —or manner—which the President himself cultivated. Besides, who was so esteemed in Congress? Some qualities in the man—or in his manner —or both—seemed to make him immune to blame or criticism; few thought the less of him because he had fumbled before Pearl Harbor; because he had approved the unworkable setup for Germany; and because he had failed in China. He stood, in public eyes, for controlled strength, just spirit, and soldierly uprightness.

Marshall's reputation snubbed out any misgivings in the United States at the designation of a military man for the sensitive role of Secretary of State. British officials seemed pleased and impressed, though the belief lingered in professional circles that Marshall's strategy in Europe had needlessly prolonged the war and left the Soviet Union in a stronger position than it would have been in had Churchill's ideas prevailed. Bevin had never really liked Byrnes—part Irish, a Southern conservative, and so adroit a compromiser; Bevin probably thought he would be able to get along better with Marshall, rely on him more.

Stalin had professed, when talking with General Montgomery, to be pleased by the change. According to the General, Stalin said he was delighted that Marshall had succeeded Byrnes and he also said: "Marshall will be much better than Byrnes. I always prefer soldiers." [7]

[7] Dalton Diary, entry dated January 27, 1947.

Presumably Stalin was pleased by Marshall's record in the war, his refusal to accept Churchillian strategy, and the faithfulness with which the understandings with Russian military commanders had been carried out.

During this brief spell of euphoria, Britain and France annealed again their association which had been broken when in June 1940 France fell and the Vichy Government entered into an armistice with Germany.

Léon Blum, the veteran Socialist who had defied Vichy and the Nazis, very briefly exercised the powers of both Prime Minister and Foreign Minister of France at the end of 1946. Bevin grasped this favorable circumstance. For two years the idea of an English–French alliance had been under consideration. But it had been unrealizable because of the frequent ministerial crises in France and the British opposition to French demands on Germany. When the British Ambassador to France, Duff Cooper, revived the proposal on December 16, 1946, Blum had at first paused, because he thought that their difference over Germany should be settled first before any alliance was formed. But he changed his mind. On the first of the new year—1947—he wrote Attlee that he was eager to form an alliance while he was still in office, which would probably only be for a few weeks. The Prime Minister at once invited Blum to come to London. There he found Bevin full of the most excellent sentiments, in good form and jovial; and within two days, January 13th–15th, they agreed on their text of the treaty of friendship and mutual assistance in the event of a renewal of German aggression.[8]

Before the formalities were completed, a new election in France beached Blum. But Bidault, who succeeded as Foreign Minister, concluded the accord in March 1947. He, the veteran of the Resistance, suggested that it be signed at Dunkerque, and to be known as the Treaty of Dunkirk. The ceremony was emotional because memories of the despair of the defeat of the Allied armies in 1940, and the courageous defense on the shores of Dunkerque and the rescue of the survivors, stirred in British and French spirits. This treaty betokened that their friendship was stronger than any vicissitude that might befall them.

The French Communists did not venture to oppose the treaty forthrightly. But, although it was specifically designed for joint protection against Germany, they detected that it would hurt their chances of coming into favor in France and be an impediment to Russian efforts to enlarge Communist influence in the whole of Germany. The Soviet authorities were sparse in their comment. The brief season of euphoria was expiring.

---

[8] Duff Cooper, in his book *Old Men Forget* (New York: Dutton, 1954), chap. 22, tells of the course of the negotiations.

23

To The East and South:
Communism Thrusts
and Prods

The Rumble of Dissatisfaction

Despite the completion of peace treaties with Italy and the satellites, and the prospective renewal of discussions about a peace treaty with Germany, the rumble of dissatisfaction over Russian conduct became louder again.

Accords which the American Government had thought to be clear and valid were being distorted. What irritated most was the way in which the Communist Government of Poland prevented the Polish Peasant Party from taking part in the elections, arresting and even killing some of its leaders, dismissing others from employment, searching their homes, suppressing sympathetic newspapers. In a note to Moscow the American Government (on Jan. 5, 1947) asserted that these actions were a violation of the Potsdam Agreement, which called for free and unfettered elections in which all democratic and anti-Nazi parties were to have the right to put forward candidates. The Soviet Government denied the charge, and heaped the usual accusations of criminal and subversive activity against the Peasant Party.

A month later, in February, when the National Assembly in Hungary refused to take away the parliamentary immunity of Bela Kovacs, Secretary of the Small Holders Party, whom the infamous Minister of the Interior accused of conniving in a counter-revolutionary conspiracy, the Russians arrested Kovacs.

During the next six months, while the United States—as we shall tell in a later section—was coming to the support of the Greek and Turkish Governments, the Communists, Russian and local, expelled from power all political leaders in Hungary, Romania, and Bulgaria whom they thought unfriendly or unreliable.

Who, observing such malign actions, the thought ran, could continue to believe that the Soviet Government would permit freedom or democracy in the Western sense, or show regard for any agreements which obligated them to tolerate opposition? Months before, Clark Clifford, then Counsel to President Truman, had written a memo, one section of which contained a list of the agreements which, according to the American reading, the Soviet Government had violated, and an analysis of these violations.[1] The President had kept a copy in his safe and Clifford had added new items from time to time.

The American Government was not yet ready to resign itself to acceptance of Communist domination in East-Central Europe. The United States was the center of emigré political and propaganda activities. The organizations of Americans who had come from the countries which were being compacted under Soviet control, or whose fathers had come from such countries, were insistent in their charges, and petitioned the American Government to challenge every Soviet action, if necessary risking war with the Soviet Union while the United States alone had atomic weapons.

The activities of these organizations were construed in Moscow not only as a threat to its control of that region, but as a proof of conspiracy. The Russians could not get at the emigrés—but they struck down any local objectors to Communist rule. Thus history, through the zealots who are its favorites, distributes its cruelties and injustices, yesterday, today, tomorrow.

In a grave analysis of Soviet foreign policy which George Kennan had sent to Washington a year before, as his term of Counsellor of Embassy in Moscow was ending, he had concluded that the Russian rulers sought security ". . . only in patient but deadly struggle for total destruction of rival power, never in compacts and compromises with it."[2] Ambassador Walter Bedell Smith had stressed the importance of Kennan's essay. Its views had percolated into the thought of many individuals who directed American foreign policy. As remembered by Benjamin Cohen, who was then Counsellor of the State Department, "Policy was then in transition —but certainly directly and indirectly it [the Kennan cable] influenced departmental thinking although the specific decisions it affected or determined might be difficult to pinpoint."[3] The bruising Communist pres-

---

[1] The memo is dated September 24, 1946, and was given to Truman soon after Henry Wallace had made his speech criticizing the stand of the American Government vis-à-vis Russia. Author's talk with Clifford, June 1, 1966.

[2] This was telegram 511, February 22, 1946. Curry, in his book on Secretary Byrnes, tells of the wide distribution in the State Department of this message, and gives Cohen's comment, conveyed in a private letter to Curry. Page 202, and note on pages 368–9.

[3] *Ibid.*

sure on Central and Eastern Europe, and the attempts of the strong Communist parties in France and Italy to exploit the destitution and hatreds within these still broken-down countries, lent more credence to its grim analysis. The conclusion uncoiled that the time had come to accept the "fact" of struggle; and interpose ourselves against any further thrusts of the Communists.

Great Britain neither could nor would be able to parry and check them. The war had drained its resources and vitality. For not only were many of its people at home in distress, but the government was being compelled, by military and financial exigencies, to recognize that British authority must depart from more distant lands, in the defense of which so much effort had been expended during the war: India, Burma, Egypt, and Palestine. The power of Britain, its supplies and resources shrunken, its ability to determine events in foreign lands under assaults of Communism and nationalism, once so great and skillfully used, was rapidly lapsing.

The sag in two situations where the Communists had inserted themselves impelled the American Government to choose between inaction and action. Under stress for years, in the early months of 1947 these slid toward concussion.

The Protracted Internal Struggle in Greece

Of all the countries of Europe, except perhaps Poland, Greece had been the most ravaged. Its people had had to endure first the assault by the Italians, then the onslaught of the Germans and their terrible treatment and deliberate destruction.

Only a breed as tough and hardy and conniving as the Greeks would have fought back and survived. The country from which the invaders had been forced to flee was in great distress and turmoil. Its few industries were short of raw materials and much of their equipment was broken. The despoiled farms lacked seeds and tools. The roads were smashed. Inflation was rampant; the government could only continue to operate by printing great amounts of paper money. War invalids and sick were everywhere, and many of the healthy could not find work. In calamity the Greeks, always disputatious, became more so.

When late in 1944 the German forces had begun to retreat from Greece, British troops had again been sent to enable the Greek Government—which was being challenged by armed groups of dissidents, animated by Communists—to regain control and maintain order. The rebels had then retreated to the Northern hill regions, refused to give up their arms, and defied the Greek Government. They procured weapons and supplies from the adjacent countries of Yugoslavia, Bulgaria, and Albania, and refuge across their frontiers.

In this damaged and disturbed condition even an able government that had popular favor and appeal would have found it very hard to manage. But the Greek Government was under the influence of reactionary elements and interests. It was laggard and incapable of dealing with deep general distress. Despite continued British military and financial support, the condition of the country had not improved, and the danger that the Communist-led antagonists might prevail had seemed imminent.[4] The Soviet press and radio had been raucously critical of British policy in Greece and of the Greek Government. The Soviet authorities, while denying responsibility for what appeared in Soviet journals, had averred that the criticism was due to the fact that reactionary forces in Greece were being more and more offensive.

During the Conference of Foreign Ministers at Moscow in December 1945, Bevin and Molotov had thrown hammers and tongs at each other. Molotov had alleged that the British were the real masters in Greece, maintaining in office a Government of men who had aided the Germans and who persecuted those who had fought the Germans. It was high time, he had concluded, that the Greeks be left to settle their own affairs. Bevin had defended the continued presence of British forces in a country so chaotic and riven by dissension; all Britain was trying to do was to help the Greeks set up a stable and democratic government, so that its troops could clear out. Bevin went on to say that what he would like to see was the exit of foreign troops from all the countries of Central and Southeastern Europe, so that disputes over their presence would not disturb relations between Britain and Russia. Molotov had said he thought the situation in Greece vastly differed from that in Romania, Bulgaria, and Hungary, which had been former enemies and were being occupied under armistice agreements. Moreover, with no twinge of expression, he asserted that the Soviet forces did not intervene in local political questions. A subsequent talk with Stalin had left Bevin with the impression that the Soviet Government might cease to badger the British Government about Greece if the British in turn would agree to grant to the Soviet Union a trusteeship over Tripolitania.

[4] On March 21, 1945, not long before his death, Roosevelt had consulted Churchill about sending a special mission of Americans, British, and a Russian (perhaps Mikoyan) to Greece to help its reconstruction—a nonpolitical mission. Churchill had said he was attracted to the idea but doubted whether a Soviet representative should be included because no help could be expected from the Russians. Roosevelt had thereupon dropped the idea lest, if an Anglo-American mission were sent, they might be accused of disregarding the Declaration of Liberated Europe. He had thought of having a Greek economic mission come to Washington, and to have Donald Nelson and a small group of Americans visit Greece to survey the needs and possibilities. Roosevelt died a few days later, and this project died with him.

176

There are no rules in this shuffle of mutual accusations and claims, especially as it is played in and about the Balkan states.

Elections in Greece had been held in the spring of 1946, under the supervision of an international group of observers in which the Soviet Union had refused to participate. The Populist Party, led by a monarchist, Constantine Tsaldaris, had won. He was a compulsive talker who shirked the pressing problems of political reorganization and economic reform.[5]

In the referendum that followed in September a majority had voted for the return of the King, George II, who, with his suite, had been living in exile, comfortably supported by Churchill. The return of the royal dynasty and the quick reassembly of their clique, which many Greeks associated with harsh dictatorship of the past, caused dissent to erupt into civil war. The Communists were tightening their grip on the countries bordering Greece to the North—Bulgaria, Yugoslavia, and Albania—and advancing claims to Greek Macedonia and Epirus.

At the Paris Peace Conference in mid-1946, the Greek representative had advanced a counterclaim. He averred that as just reward for its war effort the Greek frontier in Northern Epirus ought to be corrected at the expense of Albania, and its Eastern frontier at the expense of Bulgaria—the former ally of Germany and one of its despoilers.

Molotov was scathing. He orated: "Why not at this moment remember those heroic participants in the National Liberation movement in Greece, the so-called E.A.M. who were the heroes of the glorious struggle in Greece. . . . On the other hand, when the representative of Greece expressed his plans of aggrandizement—cut off this bit of territory from Bulgaria, cut off that bit of territory from Albania . . . why should we not express our criticism?" [6]

A few days later the American naval authorities had announced that the aircraft carrier U.S.S. *Franklin Delano Roosevelt* and the light cruiser *Little Rock,* together with five destroyers, would be sent to Greece for a "courtesy" visit, September 5–9th.[7]

During the Conference of Foreign Ministers in New York City in December 1946, the Greek Prime Minister had urged them to establish the facts and then use their influence to end the rebellion that was being sustained from without. Molotov pretended that he was not familiar with the situation. Later, on December 8th, he opposed any steps which

---

[5] About half of the registered voters, advised by left leadership, had abstained from voting.

[6] Speech, V. M. Molotov, at Paris Peace Conference, August 15, 1946. See also Molotov, *Problems of Foreign Policy,* p. 128.

[7] The news was released from the aircraft carrier *Franklin D. Roosevelt,* then at Naples, not from Washington. Story by Turner Catledge in the *New York Times,* August 28, 1946.

"would stir up passions . . . He felt that the appointment of a commission would not be helpful but would increase the disturbances." [8]

At the end of 1946 the British Government was still retaining 40,000 troops in Greece and providing extensive financial and military aid to its government.

The situation had become even more precarious. The rebels from their sanctuaries in the North were terrorizing the Greek countryside and causing alarm in Athens. The Greek public administration and army had been infiltrated by partisans of the left and were being enfeebled by weariness and corruption.

In these circumstances the Greek Government had called its troubles to the attention of the Security Council. That group listened to the vehement statements by the Greek, Yugoslav, Albanian, and Bulgarian Governments. Thereafter (on Dec. 16th) it had created a Committee of Investigation to ascertain and report on the alleged violations of Greek frontiers. While that Committee was trying to determine the facts, and before it could report to the Council, the American Government—as will be told—felt impelled to accept the expense and risk of relieving the British of the chore of nurturing the Greek Government.

The Encounter over Turkey

The encounter between the West and the Soviet Union over Turkey had been looming since the end of the war.

Until the war was all but won, Turkey had remained a nonbelligerent and had traded with Germany as well as the West. It had held off its declaration of war until February 1945, by which time its aid was not needed either by the Soviet Union or by the Western Allies. This cautious reserve had been regarded by Stalin and his colleagues as proof of indifference about the outcome of Russian struggle against Germany, if not of hostility.

Traditionally Great Britain had been the main opponent of attempts by Russia to extend its hold over Turkey, the Straits of the Dardanelles, the narrow water flue between the Black Sea and the Mediterranean, and to penetrate the Persian Gulf and Eastern Mediterranean regions. But at the Teheran Conference in December 1943, Churchill had been disposed to regard as reasonable, even to favor, the acquisition by the Soviet Union of some controlled egress from the Black Sea to the Medi-

[8] Meeting of Byrnes, Molotov, Bevin and Couve de Murville December 6, 1946, in New York City.

terranean. But as his general view of the intentions of the Soviet Government darkened, he came to think that the Soviets were forfeiting their right to this reward and were giving cause for fear.

When in the spring of 1945 the Turkish Government had proposed a Treaty of Alliance, Molotov informed the Turkish Ambassador in Moscow that as a preliminary, Turkey would have (1) to return two border districts, Kars and Ardahan (which had been within Imperial Russia between 1878 and the Treaty of Brest Litovsk in 1918; (2) to give the Soviet Union land and naval bases on the Dardanelles, and (3) to agree to major changes in the international (Montreux) accord which regulated transit through the Dardanelles. Molotov had justified these clutching revisions by stating that when Soviet Russia had negotiated its previous treaty with Turkey in 1921, it had been weak; but "Now we are strong." The Turkish Government told the American Government that it had refused these terms, and that if the Soviet Union tried to take any of its territory, it would fight.

At Potsdam, in July 1946, on the ground that the Turks were too weak to assure free passage through the Dardanelles, Stalin had proposed that the Montreux Convention should be revised so that only the Soviet Union and Turkey would be the regulators of transit. He asked also that the Soviet Union be accorded the right to maintain a military base in the Straits or in close proximity to them.

Truman and Churchill had both said that it would be preferable to convert the Straits into a free waterway open to all nations and guaranteed by all the great powers as well as Turkey. Stalin had shown no interest in such a convention. In his opinion it would not be a reliable basis for Russian security. Russia was, he said, entitled to the "defensive" arrangements he proposed.

Having failed at Potsdam to get what he wanted, Stalin had, during subsequent months, sought Turkish acceptance of variant proposals of similar import. The American Government had correctly construed them as meaning that they might enable Moscow to compel Turkey to heed Russian orders, and even, perhaps, accept Russian control. The Joint Chiefs of Staff, as well as the Secretaries of War, Army, Navy, and State, had urged Truman to advise the Turkish Government, which had consulted us, to hold out against Soviet terms. So had also the British and French Governments.

The American Government, however, had tried to satisfy the reasonable element in Soviet aspirations—that it be assured of unhindered and secure access through the Dardanelles to the Mediterranean and the seas and lands beyond. In early November 1945, before the scheduled meeting of the Council of Foreign Ministers in Moscow, it had proposed that a conference be convoked to consider what amendments in the

Montreux Convention were desirable to adjust to the changed world situation.

In a note to the Turkish Government, the American Government had set forth three principles to which it thought any revision should conform. (1) The merchant vessels of all nations should be permitted to pass through the Dardanelles at all times. (2) The warships of the Black Sea Powers should be permitted transit at all times; and (3) all other nations would have to secure the consent of the Black Sea Powers to the transit of warships, except for an agreed maximum tonnage in peace time.

The substance of this note had been transmitted to the Russian Government. The British Government had let Ankara and Moscow know that it thought these American proposals fair, and that it was willing to participate in the proposed conference.

The Turkish Government had informed the American Government that although it was somewhat fearful it did not object to the convocation of an international conference to consider a revision of the regime of the Straits. It found the principles proposed by the American Government acceptable.

The Soviet Government had made no reply. It resorted to other measures to secure the advantage it was unable to secure by negotiation. By propaganda and trouble-making maneuvers, it had sponsored claims that the remnant of Armenians that had survived the massacres by the Turks earlier in the century be united with the Armenians living in Russia. The Kurdish tribes in Turkey were aroused to demand unification with Kurds in Iran and the Arab countries. No possibility of causing disunity in Turkey had been overlooked. Soviet military forces in Trans-Caucasia were prominently deployed.

Official complaints had been made in Ankara against demonstrations hostile to the Soviet Union in Istanbul, unmolested by the Turkish police. It could not, the Soviet Government stated, overlook such positive acts. The Turkish Government had asserted that the incidents were of "a purely internal character," a reaction on the part of "unfettered public opinion." The Soviet rejoinder was that the reply was ". . . unsatisfactory, ungrounded and contrary to fact." [9] The American Government had counseled the Turks to avoid any action which Moscow could regard as provocative.

When in mid-December 1945 the Council of Foreign Ministers met in Moscow, Bevin asked Stalin to explain Russian aims and claims. The Marshal said Russian claims were modest, being justified by the need to safeguard the independence of the Soviet Union, and by the historical

[9] *Tass*, December 15, 1945.

fact that these two Turkish provinces had been part of Imperial Russia before 1921 and were mainly inhabited by Georgians and Armenians. However, Stalin had concluded, all talk of war against Turkey was mischievous; the matters at issue should be settled by negotiation.

By negotiation, hurried along by propaganda, subversion, and attempted intimidation. For the tone of the Soviet press was accusatory and bellicose, asserting that the claims for the Turkish provinces were not to be viewed as merely an attempt to secure minor territorial adjustment but as a chapter in the century-old struggle of the Georgian people.[10]

So alarming did rumors of portended Soviet moves become that in March 1946, as related in our account of the contemporaneous crisis over Iran, the American Government had prompted the American press to publish stories that it was going to send and keep a great fleet in the Eastern Mediterranean. It had sent the U.S.S. *Missouri* with a small force to Istanbul in March 1946.

When the newly arrived American Ambassador to the Soviet Union, Smith, had asked Stalin whether Russia was going to continue to require Turkey to satisfy its demands, Stalin said again that Russia's intentions were peaceful, but he stressed the belief that Russia's claims were just and fixed.[11]

The Soviet Union had next tried to overcome Turkish resistance by proposing to Ankara in August 1946, an arrangement whereby the Dardanelles would be under the exclusive control of the Black Sea Powers —Russia and its subservient puppets, Romania, Bulgaria, and Turkey. This was to be supplemented by an accord providing for joint Russia-Turkey defense of the Straits.

The tone of the Soviet press seemed to turn still more menacing. So menacing that Loy Henderson had recommended to Acheson, Acting Secretary of State since Byrnes was in Paris, that he should warn the Russians before they took some steps from which they could not retreat without embarrassment. Acheson asked Forrestal, Undersecretary of War Kenneth Royall, and the Joint Chiefs of Staff to join him in consideration of the situation. He impressed upon these senior colleagues that the note of protest he had in mind was not meant to be a bluff, and that he would not send it unless sure that the American Government would stand behind it if the Soviet Government attacked Turkey.[12]

[10] The press campaign was conducted in the form of extensive leading articles in all three of the main Soviet newspapers, *Izvestia, Pravda,* and *Red Star.*

[11] Walter Bedell Smith, *My Three Years in Moscow* (Philadelphia: Lippincott, 1949), pp. 53–54.

[12] Author's talk with Loy Henderson, May 30, 1966.

181

All thought a warning should be given. They had gone together to the White House on August 15th. Acheson handed the President a copy of the note he proposed to send and began to explain the reasons. We should acknowledge, Acheson said, that some of the Russian complaints against the Montreux Convention were valid but we must "be adamant against any interference with exclusive Turkish defence of the Straits." [13] The President had not waited for him to finish, saying, "I don't need to hear any more. We are going to send it." [14] He remarked that the American Government might just as well find out then as five or ten years later, whether the Russians were bent on world conquest.[15] Alas, that was not definitely to be ascertained then, or in five or ten years therefrom; for Russian diplomacy was patient and persistent, disguised and adapted to temporary retreat as well as advance.[16]

The group had left the White House pleased but grim. Acheson, on handing the note to Henderson for dispatch, remarked: "I hope the President realizes how serious this is. It may mean war." Byrnes readily concurred with the decision and the President approved the immediate transmission of the note. On August 19th it was handed to the Soviet Chargé d'Affaires in Washington, Fedor T. Orekhov.

The American Government had accepted some of the five principles that the Soviet Government had proposed for revision of the Montreux Convention. But it rejected the suggestion that control of the Dardanelles should be confined to the four Black Sea Powers and the connected joint Soviet-Turkish defense arrangement. "It is the view of this Government," the note stated, "that the regime of the Straits is a matter of concern not only to the Black Sea powers but also to other powers, including the United States. This Government cannot, therefore, agree

[13] Acheson, *Present at the Creation*, p. 195.
[14] Talk with Loy Henderson, May 30, 1966.
[15] Walter Millis, ed., *The Forrestal Diaries* (New York: Viking, 1951), entry dated August 15, 1946.
[16] Cabell Phillips in his book *The Truman Presidency* (New York: Macmillan, 1966), pp. 170–1, relates that "Truman agreed so readily with this drastic interpretation that General Eisenhower, sitting in as Army Chief of Staff, hesitantly and anxiously raised the question of whether the President fully understood and appreciated all the implications of his decision . . . Truman took a well-worn map of the region from his desk drawer, and using it as a guide, delivered a ten-minute dissertation on the historical significance of the Dardanelles and the eastern Mediterranean, 'stretching from Tamerlane to the day before yesterday.' "
The history of the area in Biblical times and during the ups and downs of the Assyrian, Jewish, Roman, Frankish, and Byzantine Empires had engrossed Truman's youthful interest.
Phillips continues: "When the President had finished, he looked up with a smile and asked: 'Does that satisfy you, General?' There was good-natured laughter all around as Eisenhower admiringly replied, 'It sure does, Mr. President. Strike my question from the record.' "
Acheson's account of this scene in *Present at the Creation*, pp. 195–6 is in substance the same.

with the Soviet view that the establishment of the regime of the Straits should come under the competence of the Black sea powers to the exclusion of other powers. . . . It is the firm opinion of this Government that Turkey should continue to be primarily responsible for the defense of the Straits. Should the Straits become the object of attack or threat of attack by an aggressor the resulting situation would constitute a threat to international security and would clearly be a matter for action on the part of the Security Council." This American note had been coordinated with those of the British and French Governments.

The Turkish Government was advised that we thought its answer to Moscow should be "reasonable but firm." By Presidential instruction the American Ambassador let the Turkish leaders know orally that our "reply was formulated only after full consideration had been given to the matter at the highest levels." [17]

As the winter of 1946–47 set in, it was feared that what Soviet diplomacy could not achieve, might come about because the condition of the Turkish people, mainly agrarian, was so stagnant and dreary.

The Turkish military forces being maintained in order to convince Moscow that any fight would not be easy were a great burden. Even so, the Turkish army was poorly equipped and clothed, and troops' pay a pittance. The air force was woefully small and most of the planes were obsolete. Tanks were few and mainly older models. Secretary of War Patterson described it as "a 1910 army," formidable in wars between the Balkan States but, no matter how courageous its men and excellent its generalship, not likely to be able to hold back a strong Russian assault.

American and British officals became nervous lest the Turks cave in and accede to Russian demands, or alternatively, that they resist and be quickly beaten unless American and British combat forces intervened, thereby perhaps turning it into another far-flung war. The American Ambassador in Turkey, Edwin Wilson, had advised Washington that Turkey, unless helped more, would not be able to maintain a defiant position against Russia much longer. Discontent was rising. Elements opposed to the Government, some of whom had Communist associations, were becoming stronger.

[17] Truman, *Years of Trial and Hope*, p. 97.

PART SEVEN

The Communist Thrust Confronted

24

Decision Passes to Washington

The crisis of decision came abruptly.

Ever since 1820, when Greece had fought for and won independence from the Ottoman Empire, Great Britain had been its friend and
protector. The enduring admiration for ancient classical Greece in the
hearts of English scholars and statesmen had shed a glow upon the
moves of British strategists and soldiers. But now—in 1947—Britain, itself in a sorry plight, felt compelled to relinquish the role.

The American Government had several warnings that the Greek Government was on the verge of collapsing, and it also had indications that
the British Cabinet was going to ask the U.S. to take over. In a memo to
Acheson, Henderson, then Chief of the Near and Middle Eastern Affairs
Division, had described the predicament. Acheson had sent the memo
on to Marshall. Before leaving on February 21st to talk at the bicen-
tennial celebration of Princeton University, Marshall instructed Acheson
to prepare the measures the American Government might have to take
to save the situation in Greece.

Hardly had the Secretary gone, when the British Ambassador in
Washington, Lord Inverchapel (formerly Archibald Clark-Kerr) sent his
secretary to the State Department with a note stating that the British
Government must end its financial support of Greece and begin to withdraw its troops on April 1st. This had been anxiously discussed by the
British Cabinet. It was inspired in part by the pinch of penury, in part
by purpose.

Some permanent officials of the British Foreign Office had argued that
this appeal could be disastrous. The British Ambassador in Athens had
warned that even a whisper of any intention to "cut and run" would
cause the Greek Government to fall. But the Labor Government was
tired of expending its carefully budgeted funds to sustain the situation
in Greece—only one of many external drains. Dalton, the Chancellor of
the Exchequer, on hearing the decision announced over the air, noted in
his Diary, "I had been for some time trying to put an end to the endless

dribble of British taxpayers' money to the Greeks." [1] Bevin had given in to Dalton's importunities. It may be surmised that he had in mind the possibility of passing the burden and responsibility on to the United States, thereby ensuring that it would be more surely enmeshed in the defense of western Europe.

The reaction in Washington was fast and feverish. Secretary Marshall was out of town. With the stimulus of emergency, Department officials crystalized their views and ideas and brought them before the State-War-Navy Coordinating Committee (SWNCC). The Joint Chiefs of Staff, also in an energetic mood, concurrently discussed the problem. Acheson kept the President and Marshall advised by telephone of the reports and recommendations that were being composed. [2]

The American Ambassador in Greece, Lincoln MacVeagh, in well phrased messages, stressed the urgency of the situation. So did Paul Porter, who was head of the American Mission which had been advising the Greek Government about economic affairs, and Mark Ethridge, who had been sent by Truman to investigate the political turmoil in the Balkans. All three discerned signs of an impending move of the Communists to take over the country. Unless the Greek Government received immediate and enough military and financial aid, they foresaw that it would go down under the effects of surging inflation, strikes, riots, and public panic, giving the Communist guerillas their chance to win control of the country. In the same messages they warned that our aid would not save the situation unless used wisely and honestly. Therefore they recommended that the American Government should stipulate that its aid be administered by an American group large and expert enough, and granted sufficient authority to bring about a thorough reorganization of the Greek economy, public administration, and military direction.

While the American civilian leaders who read these messages from their colleagues in Greece were worrying over the political effect of the downfall of the Greek and Turkish Governments, American military authorities were pondering the strategic consequences. They discerned the possibility that if the Communists secured control of Greece, they might in concert with Bulgaria threaten Turkey and cause it to grant the Soviet Union control of the Dardanelles and a base there. Possibly also the Greek Communists might make Salonika available as a Soviet naval and air base.

Turkey was, our Ambassador in Ankara continued to stress, also vulnerable to Communist agitation and pressure. American assistance was

---

[1] Dalton Diary, entry dated March 14, 1947.

[2] Dean Acheson, in *Present at the Creation,* chap. 24, gives a step-by-step account of the consultations within the American Government during the excited week-end of February 21–24, 1947.

urgently needed for the equipment and enlargement of the army; and beyond that, to shore up the spirit of resistance of the people, and to relieve their poverty.

Marshall was convinced by the reports of our missions in Greece and Turkey, and satisfied with the recommendations of the concerned groups in Washington. Truman agreed that it was vital to American security that the Communists be thwarted in Greece and Turkey. Within hours he approved the proposed program of action.

But he thought with trepidation about what the congressional response might be to the costly hazardous ventures which all those about him were advocating. He therefore asked the two ranking members of the Senate Foreign Relations Committee, Arthur Vandenberg and Tom Connally, and other members of the Congress to meet with Marshall, Acheson, and himself. Admiral Leahy was also present.

Marshall, in his cryptic and dry way, described the situation and explained why he thought it imperative that the United States come to the support of the Greek and Turkish Governments. Incisively, he remarked: "The choice is between acting with energy or losing by default." Most of his auditors were impressed. But some remained unconvinced. They thought the proposed action was not essential to protect American security, being activated rather by Britain's design to salvage its imperial interest. The well-worn question "Aren't we just pulling the British chestnuts out of the fire?" was heard once again.[3]

Acheson took over the presentation.[4] He stretched the panorama of the Communist purpose and saturated it with dread. The Communists, he averred, were trying to get control not only of Greece and Turkey, but of Iran and other Arab countries of the Middle East. They might be on the verge of winning in Italy. They held important places in the French Cabinet; they were extending their area of control in China. If they won in Greece and Turkey, he predicted, it would make it more

---

[3] Some officials and members of Congress—even some who were ready to support the proposal—thought the British had fallen down on their responsibilities. They were of the opinion that Britain had not sent enough troops to Greece and had failed in its efforts to counter Soviet propaganda. Lincoln MacVeagh, in his later testimony, tended to agree with this judgment but excused the British failure on the ground that Britain was no longer strong or capable enough. "British fumbling in the Balkans, fears of what may happen in Palestine, uneasiness as to Syria, doubts regarding Turkey, and alarm over growing Soviet interest in Iran, Saudi Arabia, and Egypt and the whole North African coast . . . all seem to teach the same lesson to their varying degrees." Testimony of Ambassador MacVeagh before the Foreign Affairs Committee of the House of Representatives, March 25, 1947.

[4] In recounting this meeting, Acheson, in *Present at the Creation*, p. 219, writes, "I knew we were met at Armageddon," and recalls he thought his "distinguished chief" had "flubbed his opening statement" and so asked for a chance to speak.

likely they would win elsewhere—and ultimately everywhere.[5] The fall of the dominoes could be heard as he talked along.

Most of the members of Congress present expressed willingness to support the administration's resolve to aid the Greek and Turkish Governments, quickly and in a substantial way. But the Republican Speaker of the House of Representatives, Joseph Martin, remained opposed, and the Republican Chairman of the Foreign Relations Committee, Senator Vandenberg, did not regard himself as committed.[6] Admiral Leahy, who was against acceptance of the risk and responsibility, recounted in his Diary, "The consensus of opinion of the members of Congress present was that such action could obtain the support of the American people only by a frank, open, public announcement that the action was taken for the purpose of preventing an overthrow of the subject governments by the Communists."[7]

[5] The account of this meeting was derived from Acheson, *Present at the Creation,* chap. 25; Joseph Jones, *The Fifteen Weeks: Feb. 21–June 5, 1947* (New York: Viking, 1955), and Eric F. Goldman, *The Crucial Decade: America 1945–1955* (New York: Knopf, 1956).

[6] In his book *The Crucial Decade,* p. 29, Goldman quotes Vandenberg as saying to Truman: "Mr. President, if that's what you want, there's only one way to get it. That is to make a personal appearance before Congress and scare hell out of the country." Acheson's version of Vandenberg's statement after Acheson finished talking is more restrained. "Mr. President, if you will say that to the Congress and the country, I will support you and I believe that most of its members will do the same." Acheson, *Present at the Creation,* p. 219.

[7] Leahy Diary, February 27, 1947.

25

Truman Confronts Communism: March 1947

The Writing of the Message

The President's hesitation gave way before his pugnacious streak. He was aroused by the distending challenge of the Communists. To Clark Clifford he remarked he thought it fortunate that the British Government had placed the Greek and Turkish situation "on our doorstep" for if they had not, our response to Communist expansion would have been "too late and too slow."[1]

As advised, he decided that in order to secure approval of the measures he was going to propose, he would have to encase them within a general appeal to ward off Communism.

Some members of the presidential staff were worried. They urged him to have members of the Cabinet test public opinion by preliminary speeches. State Department officials were also disturbed by the possible impact of what Truman had in mind to say and do upon the meeting of the Council of Foreign Ministers that was soon to assemble again at Moscow to discuss peace treaties with Germany and Austria.

Before acting, therefore, Truman called together his Cabinet again, on March 7th, to consider the statement he had in mind to make. He opened the discussion by saying that he knew the question before them

---

[1] Author's talk with Clifford, June 1, 1966.

James Reston, in a well informed and obviously inspired story he sent from Washington, had explained the turn of official thought clearly. "Through the use of U.S. influence and power in Germany, Austria, Italy and Trieste, naval demonstrations in Greece and in the waters dominating the approach to the Dardanelles; and through the cooperation of the British and some other nations, some kind of balance was achieved . . . but that is threatened by the end of British financial support in Greece." The British and American policy, he observed, was being called in diplomatic circles "stern containment." *New York Times*, March 1, 1946. Reston's use of the term "containment" may have derived from a memorandum by George Kennan, written in February 1946, that was circulating widely and making a strong impression at the time.

was momentous, perhaps as serious as had ever confronted any President. Acheson, in his exposition, admitted that the Greek Government, having many reactionary elements, was not a good government and that the Communist appeals had met response and won followers in Greece because the Greek Government was so corrupt and inefficient. Still, he pressed the point that this small country which had so valiantly resisted Germans and Italians, and was so badly damaged as a consequence, should not be left to succumb to civil war, perhaps Communism. Turkey was regarded as a dependable resistant if encouraged and backed up.

The President was asked by Forrestal (or perhaps by Marx Leva, Forrestal's assistant) whether he really intended to sustain the broad policy being discussed. Were we ready to face the full implications of giving support to free peoples everywhere—in Finland, in China, for example? If not, should not the pertinent sentences be reworded? [2]

All members of the Cabinet agreed that we were engaged in a fundamental struggle and that the Russians would be halted only if stubbornly resisted.

When, three days later (Mar. 10th), the President disclosed his decision and intention to a larger group of influential members of Congress, none spoke in opposition. Vandenberg now said he agreed that, regrettable though it was, it had become necessary to take a public stand against Soviet Communist intrusion into lives of other nations, everywhere. So Truman was assured of Republican approval.

During these same days, with excitement in the air, the work of writing the message which the President was going to send to Congress proceeded. State Department draftsmen consulted constantly with colleagues in the War and Navy Departments, and Averell Harriman, who had succeeded Wallace as Secretary of Commerce, Clark Clifford, and others. Of all the contributors to the drafting, Acheson was the most scintillant and sibilant. His caustic temper, usually well under control, was released by belief that the appeal to the country would have to be spirited and bold. The State Department officer, Joseph Jones, who was the seamstress and custodian of the many drafts, was a crusader, impatient of restraint, and tired of what in his subsequent account he called "The cautious, limited backdoor approach to involvement in world affairs." [3]

Marshall had left on March 5th for the meeting of the Council of For-

---

[2] Clark Clifford does not recall with certainty whether it was Forrestal or Leva who asked the question, nor does he recall the answers.

[3] Joseph Jones in *The Fifteen Weeks: Feb. 21–June 5, 1947*, p. 143. Jones described the drafting process as follows: "The State Department drafted the message. The White House pointed it up and stylized it for presidential delivery. Acheson, using the contributions of many, selected the major lines of argument, phrased a number of parts, and edited the whole closely. In the interest of a homogeneous style a single hand, that of

eign Ministers. It could be foreseen that the message the President was about to send to Congress would offend the Russians. But he had told Acheson and other subordinates to go ahead without regard for the way in which his talks might be affected. While Marshall was en route to Moscow, the text of the Presidential message, which had been given to Clifford by Jones, was sent to him. He answered ". . . questioning the wisdom of this presentation, saying he thought that Truman was over-stating the case a bit." The President replied that only by this strong and dramatic statement of the issues could Congress be moved to take the necessary measures.[4]

Truman Addresses Congress

Truman went to the Capital on March 12th to read the message to the two houses of Congress in joint session. Those sections which gave the reasons why the Greek and Turkish people and governments had to be aided and upheld were forcefully matter-of-fact. He sought to meet criticisms before they were made.

What he specifically asked of Congress was to provide authority for assistance to Greece and Turkey in the amount of four hundred million dollars for the period ending June 30, 1948. The sum allocated to Greece would be expended in part for food, clothing, fuel, and seeds, thereby enabling and encouraging industry and farming to revive; and in part to supply and equip the Greek army so it could restore the authority of the Greek Government throughout the country. In the statement of reasons for assisting Turkey, "The integrity [of Turkey] is essential to the preservation of order in the Middle East" was all he said. Strategic considerations were mentioned but not stressed; the emphasis was on the need to improve economic life and social order.

Truman Enunciates a Global Doctrine

These related requests for Greece and Turkey were framed in a broad affirmation of resolve and intention. The message contained an elaboration of American policy of global scope, and called upon the American people to carry an assignment that could be stretched to the

the writer of this book, held the pen and the master draft until the White House took over for editing." (*Ibid.*, p. 148).

[4] Charles E. Bohlen, *The Transformation of American Foreign Policy* (New York: W. W. Norton & Co., 1969), p. 87. Bohlen was with Marshall when the text of the message was received.

furthermost foreign horizon.

One of the primary objectives of American foreign policy, the President said, was ". . . the creation of conditions in which we and other nations will be able to work out a way of life free from coercion. This was a fundamental issue in the war with Germany and Japan." It was one reason the United States had taken a leading part in establishing the United Nations. But this objective would not be realized ". . . unless we are willing to help free peoples to maintain their free institutions and their national integrity against aggressive movements that seek to impose upon them totalitarian regimes."

In other blunt paragraphs he sharply incised an antithesis between Western democratic political ways and institutions, and Communist ones. Because it was doctrinaire, this statement was to be commonly called a "doctrine."

"At the present moment in world history," Truman continued, "nearly every nation must choose between alternative ways of life. The choice is too often not a free one.

"One way of life is based upon the will of the majority, and is distinguished by free institutions, representative government, free elections, guarantees of individual liberty, freedom of speech and religion, and freedom from political oppression.

"The second way of life is based upon the will of a minority forcibly imposed upon the majority. It relies upon terror and oppression, a controlled press and radio, fixed elections, and the suppression of personal freedoms.

"I believe that it must be the policy of the United States to support free peoples who are resisting attempted subjugation by armed minorities or by outside pressures.

"I believe that we must assist free peoples to work out their own destinies in their own way."

Then came one paragraph that could be construed as intended to lessen the qualms of those who feared the assignment would inevitably involve the United States in war in distant regions.

"I believe that our help should be primarily through economic and financial aid which is essential to economic stability and orderly political processes."

What the American Government would do if this kind of aid did not suffice, the President did not forecast. But he tried to give an answer in advance to any who might argue that he was proposing that the United States step in to prevent change anywhere in social situations or relative power relations. In this he repeated in essence what former Secretary of State Byrnes had said in an address to the Overseas Press Club in New York City in February 1946. The Secretary had then remarked: "Though the *status quo* is not sacred and unchallengeable, we cannot overlook a unilateral gnawing away at the *status quo.* The Charter forbids aggression and we cannot allow aggression to be accomplished by coercion or pressure or subterfuges such as political infiltration." [5] The President's explanation was more affirmative, that in preventing changes achieved by these methods in violation of the U.N. Charter, and by helping free and independent nations to maintain their freedom, the United States would be giving effect to the principles of the Charter.

Truman ended with a clarion call: "The seeds of totalitarian regimes are nurtured by misery and want. They spread and grow in the evil soil of poverty and strife. They reach their full growth when the hope of a people for a better life has died. We must keep that hope alive. The free peoples of the world look to us for support in maintaining their freedoms.

"If we falter in our leadership, we may endanger the peace of the world—and we shall surely endanger the welfare of our own nation.

"Great responsibilities have been placed upon us by the swift movement of events.

"I am confident that the Congress will face these responsibilities squarely." [6]

To interject an historical note: in 1823, after receiving a suggestion from George Canning, the Secreary of State for Foreign Affairs of the United Kingdom, that the United States and Great Britain make a joint declaration that they would not allow foreign interference with the countries of this hemisphere who had won their independence, President Monroe had asked former Presidents James Madison and Thomas Jefferson for their views. Both had advised him to respond positively. Both, moreover, had suggested that the principle he was about to expound might be aimed at the whole world, not merely at the design of the Holy Alliance (as it was then called), led by the Czar of Russia, to reconquer the Spanish colonies in the Western hemisphere.

Madison had answered, "Of course, we must accept the proposal of the British Government, but we ought not to limit the principle of the policy to the Western hemisphere. Let us declare now, in company with Britain, that a weak nation anywhere in the world, threatened by a powerful neighbor, shall receive our support in defense of its right to live." [7] Jefferson had written, "Nor is the occasion to be slighted, which

---

[5] This was one of the passages which the President underlined for emphasis in reading. Curry, *James F. Byrnes,* p. 368, footnote 18.

[6] Text in State Department *Bulletin,* March 23, 1947.

[7] Letter, Madison to Monroe, October 30, 1823. *The Writings of James Madison,* edited by Gaillard Hunt (New York: Putnam, 1900–1910), Vol. IX, pages 157–160.

[Canning's] proposition offers, of declaring our protest against the atrocious violations of the rights of nations by the interference of any one in the internal affairs of another, so flagitiously begun by Bonaparte and now continued by the equally lawless alliance, calling itself Holy." [8]

But John Quincy Adams, then Secretary of State, had opposed a joint and wide-open declaration. He advised Monroe to make a separate declaration, merely expressing our "earnest remonstrance against the interference of the European powers by force with South America, but to disclaim all interference on our part in Europe, to make an American cause and adhere inflexibly to that."

Monroe had taken Adams' advice. He identified the two different political systems with geographical spheres—one of the old world in Europe, one of the new world in this hemisphere. His "doctrine" was pointed toward this hemisphere, and he renounced any intention of taking sides in European divisions.

"In the wars of the European powers, in matters relating to themselves, we have never taken any part, nor does it comport with our policy so to do. . . . With the movements in this hemisphere, we are, of necessity more immediately connected. . . .

"The political system of the allied [European] powers is essentially different, in this respect, from that of America. . . . We should consider any attempt on their part to extend their system to any portion of this hemisphere, as dangerous to our peace and safety. . . . [as for] governments who have declared their independence and maintained it . . . we could not view any interposition for the purpose of oppressing them, or controlling, in any other manner, their destiny, by any European power, in any other light than as the manifestation of an unfriendly disposition toward the United States. . . . It is equally impossible, therefore, that we should behold such interposition, in any form, with indifference."

Thus, in his packet of global spread, Truman seemed to be moving under full sail into regions where President Monroe had feared to luff, and leading the American nation into foreign storms from which Monroe had wanted to keep clear.

It is not possible, until the original file of drafts is opened, to learn just when and by whom the more portentous portions of Truman's message were written, and just what their authors intended to convey. What thus far has been told confuses the inquirer without satisfying him, or giving the historian assurance. According to Jones, "The whole section in the President's message of March 12 beginning with 'One of the primary objectives of the foreign policy of the United States . . .'; including the statement of the choice between two ways of life, and ending

[8] Letter, Jefferson to Monroe, October 24, 1823, in P. L. Ford, ed., *Jefferson Correspondence*, Vol. 10, page 278.

with 'I believe it must be the policy of the United States to support free peoples who are resisting attempted subjugation . . .' was upon Acheson's direction virtually lifted word for word from a SWNCC document and incorporated in the first draft of the President's message," and survived almost intact.[9] But various members of the Office of Near Eastern and European Affairs of the State Department claim, in retrospect, to have been an author of these pages.

Clifford, to whom Truman assigned the final review of the message, recalls that the President himself had felt the time had come to display in clearest fashion our strength and determination. The President has related in his *Memoirs* that he did not find the State Department draft firm and stern enough. According to him, he, himself, demanded changes in its tone and substance. His recorded memory was, "The drafting of the actual message which I would deliver to the Congress had meanwhile been started in the State Department. The first version was not at all to my liking. The writers had filled the speech with all sorts of background data and statistical figures about Greece and made the whole thing sound like an investment prospectus. I returned this draft to Acheson with a note asking for more emphasis on a declaration of general policy.[10] The Department's draftsmen then rewrote the speech to include a general policy statement, but it seemed to me half-hearted. The key sentence, for instance, read 'I believe that it *should* be the policy of the United States . . .' I took my pencil, scratched out *should* and wrote in *must*. In several other places I did the same thing. I wanted no hedging in this speech. This was America's answer to the surge of expansion of Communist tyranny. It had to be clear and free of hesitation and double talk." [11]

The message was a compound of evangelism, as propounded by extreme and excited internationalists, and of spread-eagle bluster. It was puffed up with the assumption that the United States had the power to make its wishes or its will effective anywhere in the world. It was assured of a rousing response from all who feared or hated Communism.

Truman's affirmations marked the fade-out of the vision of a united community of peaceful nations, diverse in social systems and ideals yet all willing to leave others be. Up to then it had still been thought that

[9] Jones, *Fifteen Weeks*, pp. 152–3.

[10] But Acheson implies that the revision was proposed by Clifford—whether after convincing the President or as instructed by the President. "Clark Clifford thought it [the State Department draft] too weak and added some points that I thought unwise. Using General Marshall's great prestige, I got Clark to withdraw his additions and recommend the message as the General had approved it." Acheson does not identify Clifford's suggestions. See Acheson, *Present at the Creation*, p. 221.

[11] Truman, *Years of Trial and Hope*, p. 105.

practitioners of "wars of liberation" would quiet down without being restrained. But now Truman—as flatly and openly as ever Marx and Moscow had spoken out against Capitalist democracies—declared that Communism must be confronted and checked. From then on he seemed to be committing the United States to act in whatever way necessary to foil the wiles and assaults of Communists upon an independent country. In short, President Truman accepted—it might almost be said reached out to grasp—responsibilities which roamed into the hidden future.

Congress gave Truman a standing ovation. Most Americans found temporary relief for their own exasperation and fears in Truman's blunt challenge to Communism and its agents in many lands. Perhaps some did not realize that it would necessitate great increase in our military forces and readiness to use them when other means failed. Some may have been beguiled by the thought that as sole possessor of atomic weapons, our warnings would be like thunderbolts.

Most European diplomats were amazed by the assertiveness of Truman's message. The tenor of most European comment was gratified but grave.

26

The Truman Doctrine Examined

The American mood of exhilaration subsided quickly, and then anxious questioning set in. The day after Truman spoke, James Reston reported from Washington: "It is, on the whole, a grim and resentful Congress that now has begun dealing with the most important foreign policy decision since the end of the war. Like a young man suddenly pushed out on his own and forced to assume responsibilities he always had thought would be comparatively easy, the legislators are finding the reality of world leadership more troublesome than the theory and, for the moment, are blaming others for their plight and looking for a way out. This undoubtedly is a passing phase . . ." [1]

Spokesmen for both conservative right and the radical left opposed Truman's proposals, for different reasons. The conservative right thought them unnecessary for the protection of the United States, as well as meddlesome and dangerous. The excited reaction of the left radicals—who thought Truman's proposals militant and misdirected—was exemplified by the denunciations of Henry Wallace.[2] He wrote and talked with the fury of his conviction: "President Truman confronted the world with a crisis, not of the Greek economy, but of the American spirit. . . . In the name of democracy and humanitarianism, President Truman proposes. . . . in effect that America police Russia's every border. There is no regime too reactionary for us, provided it stands in Russia's path. . . . There is a world crisis. It is not a war crisis; the Soviet Union has made no war-like moves. The real world crisis is the crisis of millions of people left homeless, hungry, disease-ridden, orphaned and ravaged by years of fighting. Of course the crisis demands action. The people of Italy, Poland, Yugoslavia, France, Greece, Hungary, China and other lands urgently need American food supplies. The people of Russia suffered greater losses and contributed more to the defeat of Germany than any other nation. They need American supplies for reconstruction." [3]

[1] The *New York Times*, March 14, 1947.

[2] See, for example, *The New Republic*, March 27, 1947.

[3] In a radio address on the night of March 13th, Wallace denounced Truman's address as bringing the world nearer war. He said: "In proposing this reckless adven-

Other critics argued that the American Government, in concert with the Greek and Turkish Governments, should bring a complaint to the United Nations rather than go it alone. But the Government judged that the United Nations would just expend essential time indulging in long talk about the responsibilities for precarious situations and be prevented from doing anything because of the Soviet veto. It was possible to agree with the former mayor of New York City, Fiorello LaGuardia, and still think his conclusion not serviceable; in his testimony before the Foreign Relations Committee he said that if the United Nations in its present condition was not able to take it on, the United Nations should be strengthened to the point that it could.[4]

When asked whether the United Nations was equipped to provide the necessary means of support, these critics took refuge in their vision of the desirable, as did LaGuardia, "I think it [is] a very opportune time for the United Nations to snap into action and establish their international police force. . . . when we go down there I would like to have a Frenchman and a Briton and a Dane, a Canadian and a Brazilian along with us, and not be left there all alone."[5] So would have the American decision makers. But they feared that the United Nations either could not or would not act in time and with enough vigor to avert what they were warned was an imminent Communist triumph.

What Did the "Doctrine" Mean?

There were many probing questions asked, during the discussions in and out of Congress, about the import of the policy propounded in Truman's message. Some of the hardest to answer were: What did Truman mean by "support"? Was he seeking unconditional authority to use American money and American armed forces as he saw fit? What did he mean by "free peoples"? Would genuine democratic freedom be the real basis of decision or some other criterion? Were we to come to the rescue of any country professing a wish for democratic forms, even if the government were corrupt, inefficient, self-serving and repressive, provided it were anti-Communist and assailed by Communism? Was the policy to be pursued by us in all regions of the world? Had the eventual cost of a "global obligation" been estimated?[6]

ture Truman is betraying the great tradition of America and the leadership of the great American who preceded him." The *New York Times,* March 14, 1947.

[4] Hearings Senate Committee on Foreign Relations on S.938 Assistance to Greece and Turkey, March 24, 1947.

[5] *Ibid.*

[6] These are among the many questions which Arthur Krock had gathered, and to which members of Congress later sought answers from the Administration (The *New*

Then there was the major question whether our resources should be used to bolster armed forces of countries merely because they were holding off the Communists, rather than to improve the economic conditions of all peoples—to relieve the poverty and misery which nurtured Communism?

Some of these questions could not be conclusively answered. They were not then, nor, it may be interjected, have they been to this very day. But the queries asked did secure from members of the Truman Administration interpretations and qualifications which since have been often forgotten or ignored.

Acting Secretary of State Acheson, in his opening statement on March 24th before the Senate Committee on Foreign Relations, tried to reassure supporters and soothe opponents. He discounted Truman's rhetoric and shortened its loop: "There have been various statements in the press that this was an ideological crusade. That is not what the President is talking about. He is talking about the fact that where a free world is being coerced to give up its free institutions, we are interested. . . .

"He did not state, and I think no one would state, that that meant that wherever this situation occurs one must react to it in exactly the same way . . ." [7]

Later Acheson reiterated this interpretation, as in the dialogue with Senator Connally, senior Democratic member of the Foreign Relations Committee:

Senator Connally: "A good many people have propounded the inquiry, Does this mean a complete reversal of our foreign policy, and does it mean that all over the world any country that applies to us will be in such a position that we have to make them a loan or take action similar to that set forth in this bill? Is it not true that those situations will have to be deferred and met when they arise, and that each case must stand on its own bottom in the light of the world situation and in the light of our own situation at the time such application may be made?"

(Acting) Secretary Acheson: "That is very true, Senator Connally. That is exactly the situation."

Senator Connally: "This is not a pattern out of a tailor's shop to fit everybody in the world and every nation in the world, because the conditions in no two nations are identical. Is that not true?"

Secretary Acheson: "Yes, sir; that is true, and whether there are requests, of course, will be left to the future, but whatever they are, they

York Times, March 20, 1947). The State Department wrote replies to more than 100 "very fair and useful questions" from Congress assembled by Senator Vandenberg (The New York Times, April 4, 1947).

[7] Quoted in Jones, *Fifteen Weeks* pp. 192–3.

have to be judged, as you say, according to the circumstances of each specific case." [8]

Perhaps Acheson, even that early, was heeding the admonition which Alexander Pope gave to poets: that they should compose with fury but correct with phlegm. He had earlier confided to his associates in the State Department that he realized—and hoped the President realized—that our interposition might mean war. But by the time he testified in Congress he was less worried over that possibility and more concerned to dispel the fear which might suppress decision. Thus he said: "In recent discussion of these proposals the question has been put to me whether they contain the possibility of friction that might lead to war. I think that quite the opposite is true. These proposals. . . . are not acts which lead to war. They lead in the other direction. They help to maintain the integrity and independence—what the United Nations Charter calls the 'sovereign equality'—of states." [9]

It was left to Senator Vandenberg to smudge the meaning in practice of Truman's declaration more completely, in his remarks in the Senate on April 17th: "I think the President's message defined what is being done in terms of a doctrine, a little more definitely than I interpret the situation. . . . To me it is a plan; it is part of a pattern, and as such is to be distinguished from a policy." [10]

While the debate in Congress was continuing, the American representative in the United Nations (former Senator Warren Austin of Vermont) gave assurance that the President had acted without first seeking the approval of that body only because the situation was so urgent and time was of the essence. He averred that the American Government certainly did not want to bypass the United Nations and would welcome the cooperation of other countries. But could the United Nations take quick effective action, even though it had at this time a Commission of Investigation in Greece?

Other supporters of the President's policy were more forthright, for example Senator Connally. After listening to witnesses who argued that the American Government should look to the United Nations, "To turn this problem over to the United Nations, which is not constituted to handle it, would be a buck-passing arrangement, just a dodging and trimming and flim-flamming around." [11]

[8] Hearings, Senate Committee on Foreign Relations, on S.938 Assistance to Greece and Turkey, March 24, 1947, p. 13.

[9] *Ibid.*, p. 11.

[10] The *New York Times*, April 18, 1947. Webster's *Dictionary* defines "doctrine" as a "speculative truth or working principle" and "policy" as a "settled or definite course or method adopted and followed by a government . . ."

[11] Tom Connally, *My Name Is Tom Connally*, p. 319.

The advocates of the legislation also had to dispute the contention held by many Americans of Greek origin that the United States should not support the existing Greek Government because of its faults and failings. Acheson explained that the American Government was not condoning everything the Greek Government had done or might do. But, he continued, recent fair elections showed that it represented the majority of the Greek people. "In Greece today we do not have a choice between a perfect democracy and an imperfect democracy. The question is whether there shall be any democracy at all. . . . We are planning aid to Greece with the hope and intention that conditions will be created in which the Greek Government can achieve more efficient administration and perfect its democratic processes." [12] How often since have the American people been faced with the same quandary and acted on the same hope!

What About China?

One reason why some members of Congress were grudging in their support of the President's initiative was because the Administration was refusing to provide the National Government of China with more financial and military assistance.

Admiral Leahy noted in his Diary, "I am unable to understand why Marshall is willing to get involved in order to save the Greek and Turkish regimes, but resigned to letting the National Government of China go down the drain." [13] In the Senate, Republican Senator Robert Taft of Ohio and others of like mind opposed the Greek-Turkish bill on the score it was more important to use our means to prevent the Communists from winning in China. Their view was typified by the statement made by Senator Joseph Ball, Republican from Minnesota, that "I do not believe we can take such action in Greece and then stand by and permit armed Communists to seize power in China." [14] Were we not, Representative Walter Judd asked, adopting one policy against totalitarianism in Europe and a hands off policy in China?

Acheson chose to deny the discrepancy rather than admit that the American Government had been letting the struggle in China take its course ever since Marshall, as exasperated at Chiang Kai-shek as at the Communists, had relinquished his effort at conciliation. He implied that in his opinion the danger of Communist victory in China was not as imminent as it was in Greece and Turkey. Taking differences in circum-

[12] Hearings of Senate Committee on Foreign Relations on S.938 Assistance to Greece and Turkey, March 24, 1947, pp. 10–11.
[13] William D. Leahy, Diary, February 27, 1947.
[14] The *New York Times*, March 30, 1947.

stances into account, he vaguely remarked that we had been and were giving similar support to the Chinese Nationalist Government.[15]

Into the real reasons for the difference in our response, he expediently did not enter. But the record makes them evident. The American Government was discouraged by its failure to bring the Chinese Government and its Communist enemies together in a coalition. It had lost faith in the ability of the Chinese Nationalist Government to gain control of China even though we should provide it with immense amounts of economic and military aid. The American military heads were opposed to taking the risk of becoming engaged in a great and interminable land war in China, as Japan had been. Moreover, they feared that if we did, the Soviet leaders would take advantage of our involvement in China to move forward in Europe and the Middle East. At the time it was hoped that even if the Chinese Communists should win we could manage to get along with them.

The Bill, Perhaps the Doctrine, Is Approved

On April 22d the Senate approved the bill that provided help for Greece and Turkey by a preponderant vote. But this vote was of unclear import.

As remarked by Reston, "Few members of the Senate voted specifically today for President Truman's broad doctrine. . . .

"Some of them voted consciously and enthusiastically for a negative anti-Soviet policy, others specifically for blocking Soviet expansion in the critical strategic area of the Eastern Mediterranean . . ." [16]

The bill was passed by the House of Representatives on May 9th. A substantial Republican minority, still yearning for isolation, voted "Nay." Six days later the Senate formally gave its consent to an initial appropriation of four hundred million dollars of economic and military aid for Greece and Turkey. The President signed the act on May 22d.

Before American assistance to Greece could become effective, the situation there became more disturbing. The rebels gained control of a large part of the Pindus and Olympus mountain ranges and nearly all of the northern frontier. The Greek Government fell in dire straits. The following months were tense.

Truman relates that three months later, "On July 16th General Mar-

[15] Acheson's statement in the Committee on Foreign Affairs of the House of Representatives, March 20, 1947, and Judd's query and Acheson's denial, The *New York Times*, March 21, 1947.
[16] The *New York Times*, April 23, 1947.

James F. Byrnes takes the oath of office as Secretary of State.

Ernest Bevin, V. M. Molotov, and James F. Byrnes at the second Moscow conference, December, 1945.

W. Averell Harriman and Joseph Stalin in Moscow.

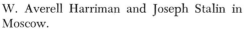

President Truman and Winston Churchill at Westminster College, Fulton, Mo., where Churchill gave his famous "Iron Curtain" speech.

The Truman Cabinet, 1947. Standing, left to right: Postmaster General Robert E. Hannegan, Secretary of Commerce W. Averell Harriman, Secretary of Agriculture Clinton Anderson, Secretary of the Interior Julius A. Krug, Secretary of Labor L. B. Schwellenbach. Seated, left to right: Undersecretary of State Robert A. Lovett, Secretary of Defense James V. Forrestal, President Truman, Secretary of the Treasury John Snyder, Attorney General Tom Clark. Absent from the picture, Secretary of State George C. Marshall.

John Foster Dulles and Senator Arthur H. Vandenberg at the United Nations meeting in San Francisco.

National Archives

Bernard M. Baruch.

Children of London were forced to search through the snow for pieces of coal during the fuel shortage of 1947–48.

Wide World Photos

President Truman addresses a joint session of Congress, March 12, 1947, proposing aid for Greece and Turkey "against aggressive movements that seek to impose upon them totalitarian regimes."

The Committee to study Truman's proposal for aid to Greece and Turkey. Foreground, left to right: Acting Secretary of State Dean Acheson, Secretary of War Robert P. Patterson, Senator Arthur H. Vandenberg, Secretary of the Navy James V. Forrestal, and Senator Tom Connally.

President Truman, Secretary of State George C. Marshall, Paul Hoffman, and W. Averell Harriman.

Secretary of State Marshall at the Harvard University commencement where he delivered the "Marshall Plan Address," June 5, 1947.

Henry A. Wallace.

Czechoslovakian Foreign Minister Jan Masaryk.

Dean Acheson is sworn in as Secretary of State, January 21, 1949, by Chief Justice Fred M. Vinson. President Truman and presidential aide General Harry Vaughan look on.

Cargo planes being unloaded in Berlin during the blockade airlift.

British Ambassador Sir Oliver Franks and Foreign Secretary Ernest Bevin.

General Lucius D. Clay.

J. Robert Oppenheimer.

Dean Acheson signs the North Atlantic Treaty, April 4, 1949, as President Truman and Vice President Alben W. Barkley look on.

President Truman signs the renewal of the Marshall Plan. Behind him, from left to right, are Howard Bruce, Deputy ECA Administrator; Representative John Kee, Chairman of the House Foreign Affairs Committee; William C. Foster, Deputy Special Representative of the ECA; W. Averell Harriman, Special ECA Ambassador to Marshall Plan countries; Paul Hoffman, ECA Administrator; Senator Tom Connally, Chairman of the Senate Foreign Relations Committee; and Secretary of State Acheson. *Acme Photo*

Soviet Foreign Minister Andrei Vishinsky and his aides at the Big Four Council of Foreign Ministers, May 23, 1949.

David Lilienthal, left, Chairman of the Atomic Energy Commission, and Secretary of Defense Louis Johnson.

The Atlantic Pact nations meet, September 1949. Clockwise around the table from the lower lefthand corner are: Belgium's van Zeeland and Silvercruys; United States' George Perkins and Dean Acheson; Great Britain's Bevin and Sir Oliver Franks; Portugal's De Matta and Peereira; Norway's Lange and Morganstierne; Netherlands' Stikker and Van Kleffens; Luxembourg's Bech and LeGallais; Italy's Sforza and Tarchiani; Iceland's Thor Thors and associate; France's Schuman and Bonnet; Denmark's Rasmussen and Kauffman, and Canada's Pearson and Wrong.

Georges Bidault (behind the microphone) after confirmation as France's Premier. President Vincent Auriol stands next to him (center, front) and Robert Schuman is behind Auriol.

U.S. High Commissioner John J. McCloy and West German Chancellor Konrad Adenauer signing an aid agreement in 1949.

President Truman and John J. McCloy confer on Germany.

Dean Acheson, Ernest Bevin, and French Foreign Secretary Robert Schuman confer in London, May 1950.

A defense meeting in New York, September 1950. From left to right are: Ernest Bevin and Emanuel Shinwell of England, Robert Schuman and Jules Moch of France, Dean Acheson and George C. Marshall of the United States.

Marshall and Truman after the President's return from talks with General Douglas MacArthur on Wake Island.

shall sent me a memorandum on the situation in Greece that began with the words, 'The Greek situation has taken a serious turn in the last three days.' Sizable guerrilla units had crossed the frontier from Albania. It appeared that they were aiming at the occupation of some larger communities that could serve as centers for a 'people's republic.'

"I called the Secretary of the Navy," Truman continues, "and asked him how large a part of our Mediterranean fleet he might be able to move to Greek ports. Secretary Forrestal informed me that it would be entirely practicable to have a large part of the Mediterranean squadron shifted on short order. He expressed a belief that such a visit would have some deterrent effect on the activities of the Communist guerrillas but was unwilling to estimate how the American public might react." [17]

During this period of "touch and go" the administrator of the U.S. aid program in Greece, Dwight Griswold, was organizing a staff, arranging for the reception and distribution of aid supplies, and urging the Greek Government to include new elements and seek the widest possible support.

But the Greek Government was most intent on being enabled to enlarge and equip its army. As Truman remarks in his *Memoirs*, ". . . even as we undertook to bolster the economy of Greece to help her combat Communist agitation, we were faced with her desire to use our aid to further partisan political, rather than national, aims." [18] Griswold was neither an effective administrator nor a persuasive advocate for the distressed Greek workers.

In the agreement with Turkey, signed in July, it was explicitly stipulated that most of the funds provided were to be expended upon its military forces. Local plants producing war materials were to be modernized and enlarged, a net of air fields was to be built, and a great naval base to be established on the Mediterranean coast. A substantial residue was to be used to improve roads and port facilities. Turkey, henceforth, was to be one of our pivotal points of resistance to possible Soviet expansion by subversion or force, or a combination of them.

The initial responses of the Soviet authorities were sarcastic but restrained. *Izvestia,* for example, the day after Truman addressed Congress, had remarked: "The pathetic appeal of the Tsaldaris Government to the U.S.A. is clear evidence of the bankruptcy of the political regime in Greece. But the matter does not rest solely with the Greek Monarchists and their friends, now cracked up to American Congressmen as the

[17] *Years of Trial and Hope,* pp. 108–9.
[18] *Ibid.,* p. 109.

direct descendants of the heroes of Thermopylae; it is well known that the real masters of Greece have been and are the British authorities." *Izvestia* went on to observe: "We are now witnessing a fresh intrusion of the U.S.A. into the affairs of other states. American claims to leadership in international affairs grow parallel with the growing appetite of the American quarters concerned." [19]

The editors of the *New Times*, after asserting that our purpose was to obtain strategic positions in the Mediterranean and Middle East as stepping stones, shrugged off the President's denunciation by observing: "Following the example of previous claimants to world hegemony, Truman dragged out the old and tattered banner of anti-Communism." [20]

Ambassador Gromyko's denunciation in the Security Council was vigorous. He, and his chorus in the Soviet press, called the American initiative a continuation of Churchill's attempt to keep reactionary and antidemocratic forces in power in Greece. They deplored our interference in the internal affairs of Greece and Turkey and stated that it was a serious blow to the independence of those nations. They alleged that Truman was using his blasé professions, like Hitler, as a smoke screen for plans of expansion and imperialism. Thereby they indicted his action as a future threat to Russia's territorial integrity and an attempt to encircle that country. Lastly they prophesied that the use of this method of checking what they called "social development" was doomed to fail.

Here, as a postscript, are some brief extracts from the report made by the Balkan Commission of Investigation which the U.N. had sent. In its report to the Security Council, made on May 27, 1947, it found the allegations of the Greek Government and warnings of American and British observers, well founded.

"On the basis of the facts ascertained by the Commission, it is its conclusion that Yugoslavia, and to a lesser extent Albania and Bulgaria, have supported the guerrilla warfare in Greece."

"They trained, recruited and dispatched refugees from Greece for action in guerrilla units there, and supplied them with arms, clothing, supplies, transport, guides and hospitalization and provided place of escape for guerrillas fleeing from the Greek Government forces."

The Commission adjudged that Greece had treated the Slav minority in Greek Macedonia badly, but that this did not justify the efforts of Yugoslavia and Bulgaria to encourage a separatist movement with the aim of detaching the province from Greece and incorporating it in Bulgarian and Yugoslav Macedonia.

The Commission recommended that Yugoslavia, Bulgaria, and Al-

[19] *Izvestia*, March 13, 1947.
[20] The *New Times*, March 21, 1947.

bania desist, and that the Greek Government be instructed to establish neighborly good relations. The Security Council considered a resolution to that effect on July 29, 1947. But the Soviet Government vetoed it. The struggle in Greece was to continue a year longer; there can be little doubt that it was American support that enabled the Government to survive and win.

But by this time much water from many other moving rivers of events was flowing under diplomatic bridges and enlarging the sea of dissension.

27

The Foreign Ministers Meet
Again—March–April 1947

While the sonic boom of Truman's declaration resounded, Marshall was conferring in Moscow with the Foreign Ministers of the Soviet Union, Great Britain, and France—Molotov, Bevin, and Bidault. They came together primarily to discuss policies toward Germany and Austria. In connection with the making of peace with Germany the Conference had to consider many linked questions: boundaries, the form of government, and nature of the constitution; what obligations were to be imposed; and what was to be the relation of Germany to other countries, West and East.

Although the Ministers argued for six long weeks (from March 10th to April 26th in Moscow), there was no agreement on any important element that had to figure in a peace treaty with Germany, or on procedure in preparation of the treaty. Their contentions bounded off the sides of the conference table like billiard balls, before sinking into the pockets of futility. The revealed differences between East and West were left gaping.

About the Form of German Government

Dissension regarding the kind of provisional government which was to be fostered in Germany was crucial.

During this long conference in Moscow both sides maintained that they favored a unified Germany living under one government. But their ideas as to what the nature of this government should be and how it was to be brought about were far apart.

So were those of the German political factions. The Communists favored a centralized government. So did many of the Socialists, in whose spirits the forms of Prussia were still alive. But most members of the

Christian Democratic Party, living or having lived in the southern or the southwestern part of Germany, favored federalism.

The American Government proposed—and the British Government followed its lead—that the provisional German government should be a comparatively weak federation resting primarily on state and provincial organizations. The powers of the central government would be carefully limited.[1]

The reason given by Marshall, when upon his return home he reported to the nation on this conference, was: "Fear [of] a repetition of the seizure of power over the whole of Germany [like that] carried out by the Hitler regime in 1933." [2] The form of government favored was one which would make it very difficult for any extremist group— Communist or Fascist—to gain control of all Germany, by propaganda, penetration, street demonstrations, subversion, and abuse of the police power.[3]

Bidault spoke for the French Government. He had been one of the most notable leaders of the Resistance and had not been timid about putting himself forward both in the public eye and in party politics. On the triumphant re-entry into Paris he had strode beside de Gaulle until the General asked him "please to fall one step behind." Despite the rebuke Bidault had remained a faithful partisan of de Gaulle as long as he was in power and maintained the same views of policy toward Germany until circumstances caused him to make concessions. At Moscow he was unwilling to agree to endow any Central German Government with as much authority as the American and British thought prudent. His reasons for favoring a weak federation were the same as Marshall's. But in mind, also, was the thought thereby to keep open the possibility of obtaining the right to occupy the Rhineland and to bring the Ruhr under international control in which France would have the signaling station.

[1] The proposals of the American Government were most fully stated by General Marshall at the meeting of March 14, 1947. They are printed in the State Department *Bulletin* of March 23, 1947.

On this occasion the Secretary undertook to outline the various stages by which the German Government should be created. There should be, he proposed, three stages: First would be the establishment of a provisional German Government composed of the heads of the existing German states and provinces, including Berlin; this would be empowered to create and operate central administrative agencies. Second, this provisional German Government would arrange for the drafting and acceptance of a constitution that was to be consistent with the democratic principles and the decentralization of authority. Third, the new and permanent government would be created in accordance with this constitution and by the state authorities.

The new Directive issued to the Commander-in-Chief of the U.S. zone on July 11, 1947, superseding that of April 1945, conformed to these ideas.

[2] Radio speech, April 28, 1947. In State Department *Bulletin* May 11, 1947.

[3] The political analysts in the State Department had, in the briefing they had given Marshall, explained why provisions of the German constitution of the Weimar Republic had made it easy for the Nazis to acquire complete control of the country.

The Russians, both in and out of the Conference, carried their suspicious criticisms of the American plan and program of federation to the verge of frenzy. The view of it diffused by the whole Soviet propaganda organization was that it was a scheming combination of capitalist monopolies of the West and the ultrareactionary Catholic Church. These, it was asserted, could be the stronger if Germany was merely a loose confederation of many small states. The editors of the *New Times,* in chorus with all other Soviet publicists, wrote: "The idea is that, with the splitting up of Germany into separate states, areas such as the Rhineland, Westphalia and Bavaria would become instruments of political and economic pressure on the other German states and the countries of Central Europe. As the Vatican conceives it, a clerical bastion in the area between Cologne and Munich must inevitably extend its sphere of influence." [4]

Molotov contended that a federation composed of state governments and provinces (*Länder*), allowing such rights as the Americans desired to have guaranteed by the constitution, would protect Nazis and reactionaries and enable them to consolidate their positions. He accused the supporters of the idea of federation of a wish to preserve intact the German trusts and concerns which had connections with American and British business and financial groups.

The exposition of the positive proposals made by Molotov were enveloped in murk of Communist phraseology. But his auditors interpreted them as another deceptive attempt to convince the German people that the Soviet Government was defending the cause of German unity, and that its primary wish was to institute "true democracy" in Germany. All the organs of power, he contended, must be built on the basis of "democratic" elections, by which the Westerners assumed he meant elections in which only the parties approved by the Communists could take part. The Soviet Commissar for Foreign Affairs was brazen enough to aver that, by the terms of his proposal, "All citizens of Germany, without distinction of race, sex, language and religion are insured democratic rights, including freedom of speech, the press, religion and public meetings . . ." [5]

Western analysts concluded that the Soviet ideas were being shaped not only by the wish to insinuate Communist control over the whole of Germany, but also by the thought that a strong German Government would be the more able and likely to satisfy Russia's sustained demands for reparations.

[4] The *New York Times,* March 1947.
[5] The text of Molotov's proposal "On the form and scope of the Provisional Political Organization of Germany" is in the *New York Times* of March 23, 1947.

Disputes About Reparations and Economic Issues

The Russians had been greatly aggrieved by the tremendous lag in deliveries of industrial equipment from the Western zones as reparations, and fierce in their denunciation of what they regarded as the unjustified unwillingness of the Western Allies to give them what was due. The Americans and British had become most reluctant to dismantle and transfer to Communist claimants industrial plants possibly needed to enable the Germans to become more nearly self-supporting.[6]

The argument roamed from the area of asserted rights and attributed promises into a thicket of contrasting estimates.

Molotov continued to allege that at Yalta the Soviet Government had been promised reparations in the amount of ten billion dollars. Marshall and Bevin denied, and correctly, this allegation. The Soviet Government averred that the Potsdam Accord—since it contained a reference to the previous discussion at Yalta—contemplated that if deliveries in the form of capital equipment not needed for the German peace economy were insufficient, reparations would also be made in the form of "current" annual deliveries of goods produced in Germany. The Soviet Union was procuring substantial amounts of reparations in this way from industries in the Eastern zone and satellite countries which it controlled. Marshall and Bevin, again correctly, denied this interpretation of the Yalta-Potsdam stipulations and refused to promise uncompensated deliveries from current production in their zones.

Their refutations were the more vigorous because, despite their resolve not to finance Germany out of their own treasuries, they were doing so to maintain even the miserable standards of life in their zones, and prevent disease and unrest.

Molotov ignored this assertion, or maintained rather that the Western Allies would not have to support the Germans if they properly organized the economy of the Western zones. He accused them of wanting to preserve Germany's industrial power for the benefit of their own na-

---

[6] Marshall, in statements he circulated on March 17th and 18th enumerated in detail the German industrial plants in the American zone which had been dismantled and delivered as reparations, and those in all three Western zones which had been approved for advance delivery or were awaiting evaluation. The contrast between what conceivably might be delivered and what had been delivered up to then was very great: 2000 plants, more or less, selected for reparations by the Allied Control Authority; 140, more or less, actually dismantled and approved for delivery; 24 thus far delivered.

This is the best interpretation I can make of the several general degrees of status of the program set down in this statement of Marshall, which is in the State Department *Bulletin,* March 30, 1947.

tional business and banking interests, and of aiming to use that power to the detriment or danger of its Communist neighbors in the East and the Soviet Union. His accusations were self-fulfilling.

In the statements made on March 17th and 18th, Marshall emphasized that the provisions of the Potsdam Protocol for the delivery of plants for reparation were dependent on the economic unification of Germany and the observance of an import–export plan for the whole of Germany. In his final and conclusive rejection of Russian proposals about reparations and connected economic proposals, on March 31st, he remarked curtly: "The United States is opposed to policies which will continue Germany as a congested slum or an economic poorhouse in the center of Europe." [7]

He summed up the view he upheld during the Conference in the public report he made on the radio on April 28th: The obligation to pay reparations out of future output, year by year, would mean that a substantial portion of the daily production of German factories would be levied on for reparations payments, which in turn would mean that the recovery of Germany to the point where it could be self-supporting would be long delayed. It would also mean that the plan and hope of our Government, that Germany's economic recovery at the end of three years would permit the termination of American appropriations for the support of the German inhabitants of our zone, could not be realized.[8]

Bevin's view of the Russian claim for reparations out of current production was similar though not as sure of the black and white sides of the subject. As he explained it to his colleagues in the House of Commons after his return from the Conference, "We have not closed our minds to this but we must take first things first. They are as follows: the economic unity of Germany, a balanced economy and the repayment of what we have had to put in to keep the Germans alive. . . . I have no intention of following a policy which allows us once again [as after the First World War] to be placed in a position of making loans on a scale which we know to be quite irrecoverable from Germany." [9]

Molotov replied that the Germans could make reparations out of current production and still live as well as had been contemplated at Potsdam if they were permitted—and if necessary—compelled to increase production, and if, moreover, the Western Allies reduced their self-indulgent and excessive levies for occupation costs. These costs, it may be remarked, were high; the conquerors in Germany, particularly the French, lived well.

---

[7] State Department *Bulletin*, April 13, 1947.
[8] *Ibid.* May 11, 1947.
[9] Parliamentary Debates, House of Commons, May 15, 1947.

I shirk the task of laying bare the economic intricacies that would be required to judge the opposed assertions regarding reparations in a court of equity. This would necessitate an intensive technical tracing of the cat's cradle of provisions in the Yalta and Potsdam Accords and subsequent actions of the occupying authorities in each zone.[10]

Account would also have to be taken of the shrinkage and wastage of value that occurred. The Russians, possibly because of their success in moving Soviet war industries from the Moscow region to the Urals, had been slow to realize that many plants and machines could not be easily transported and recreated. Railways and roads in east-central Europe were still in bad shape. German and Polish Anti-Soviet partisans and saboteurs were active. Thieves were alert. The Germans managed to remove and secrete much equipment and to damage some before delivery. This, to the indignation of the Russians, the Western occupants could not, or did not, prevent.

Moreover, the opposed contentions about equities were supported—or should I write "adorned"—by calculations of reparations already received which were as far apart as those of a convention of maudlin accountants. Due to the objection of the Russian and French authorities to the maintenance of joint and uniform accounts, each occupying authority could produce its own compilation and freely make allegations about the validity of each other's accounts.[11]

The American and British defenders at the Moscow Conference averred that as a matter of fact the Soviet Union had already extracted, by a variety of measures; about seven billion dollars of reparations from the Eastern zone—in part by seizure and transfer of industrial properties, in part by receipts of currently produced industrial, mining, and farm products. This estimate may not have been far wrong, if properties taken were evaluated as operative properties before the war.

But the Soviet officials maintained that much of the property taken by them had been stolen by the Germans, and was merely a replacement of plundered goods; for example, railway cars and locomotives and trucks. Much of the rest should be regarded, by Russian definition, as war

[10] The student will find the pertinent text in Section III of the Protocol of the Potsdam Conference. For a more adequate analysis of this text and of the compromises it represented, and the contradictions it contained, he may, if zealous enough, read Chapter 33 of my book *Between War and Peace: The Potsdam Conference.*

[11] On March 29, 1947, Jacques Rueff, then President of the Interallied Reparations Agency, in answer to requests of Molotov and Bidault, reported to the Conference that in the nine months after the Potsdam Accord 143 German factories (of which 72 were complete installations) had been attributed to the 18 nations which were to receive reparations from the Western zones (*L'Année Politique 1947*, pp. 49–50). But the various records of how many were actually dismantled during the period and up to March 1947, and how many were actually delivered as reparations, are statistically most diverse. I have not tried to assort or compare them.

booty, not reparations.

Molotov, in his turn, accused the Americans and British of securing enormous benefits from their zones. Soviet publicists supplied statistical estimates.[12] According to these, the United States and Great Britain had already procured German assets of a total value of not less than ten billion dollars.[13]

Besides it was charged that the British in particular were securing reparations by paying less than current world prices for German exports of coal and timber and machinery, and reselling some of these to world markets at a great profit.[14]

The American and British representatives dismissed all Soviet estimates as grotesque. In answer, the American Delegation on March 25th circulated a memo which set down the total of reparations from Germany thus far received by the United States as follows: industrial capital equipment, about 75 million dollars; ships, 5 million; German external assets, 150 to 250 million; currently produced goods, none; gold, none; total, less than 275 million dollars. The memo did not contain any estimate of value of patents and processes procured, which probably were of greater ultimate value than all the rest. It then, and later, denied that Americans had acquired ownership or participation in German industrial enterprises.[15]

[12] Numerous estimates of this sort appeared, for example, in the *New Times* and *Izvestia* during March and April 1947; they varied greatly in particulars but almost all were in the same total range.

[13] They calculated that German-owned assets in foreign countries taken over by the Western Allies were worth six to seven billion dollars; German technical formulas, patents, and processes acquired not less than two billion; the German gold and merchant fleet, approximately one billion; German capital equipment taken from the Western zones, one-half billion; and shares of stock in German enterprises as much; in sum, at least ten billion without taking into account items that could not be evaluated. These presumably included mementos from Hitler's Chancery and dugout, guns, cameras, and other souvenirs "liberated" by officials and soldiers.

[14] The Russians continued to make this charge as long as Western Germany remained under Western occupation. The British authorities repeatedly denied that it had any validity. It is notable that Clay believed that it was in a measure true. In a message to Washington in July 1947 he reckoned that the comparatively low export prices the Allies had set for German coal were costing the bizonal area some 50 million dollars annually. Other students put the total higher. See Gimbel, *The American Occupation*, p. 150. To the extent that the German imports were being underpriced, American and British taxpayers had to provide more funds.

[15] Much later, on December 14, 1947, in reply to an inquiry of the Soviet Government, the American Government recalled that it had long since proposed that foreigners not be allowed to acquire German property, but that the Soviet Union had rejected the proposal. It had gone on to state: (1) "There is not a single case of German business property that has been acquired by the United States during the entire occupation" and (2) "All goods shipped from the U.S. and U.K. zones have been sold at world market prices and not a penny of proceeds diverted to the use or advantage of the occupying powers. This includes coal and timber." (This exchange took place during the London meeting of the Council of Foreign Ministers.)

Bevin's denials during the Conference and in his subsequent report to the House of Commons after his return from Moscow were in the same tenor, and no less divergent from Soviet figures.

France was more tenacious in exacting compensation from Germany. French losses during the war were officially estimated at about 40 billion dollars, of which half were goods that were destroyed, and the rest transferred to Germany. The French Military Government scoured its zone for these seized goods; French art experts pursued the quest; French farmers and industrialists sent teams to look for them. But the French Government averred that only a small portion of what had been taken was restored. The French occupation authorities set to work with zeal at dismantling factories in their zone but this slowed up in 1947 by pressure of the bizonal authorities. The French were more permissive than the Americans and British toward the revival of industry, agriculture, coal mining, and forestry, and less heedful of German complaints over the low rations. Consequently the Germans in the French zone paid for imported goods by proceeds of their exports, even though the French purchased German goods at a substantial discount, thereby receiving in effect reparations in kind out of current production.[16]

Attitudes and Economics

Beneath the quarrel over German obligations and the ways of meeting them, there was a deepening difference of attitude. The Western Allies had become worried over the sorry state of the former German enemies and feared that they might in desperation upset capitalist ownership, scorn moderate socialism, and turn to revolutionary Communism.

Progress in the administration of the Bizonia (for the merged U.S.—British zone) program had been disconcertingly slow. The local German governmental authorities were hindering the execution of the directives issued by zonal officials, especially about food and agriculture, because they disagreed with bizonal production estimates and delivery quotas. In April the miners of the Ruhr struck because food rations were too small, despite very large food imports in the first quarter of 1947. Many Germans were unable to pay for even the standard ration of 1550 calories.[17]

[16] This summary account is derived from the fuller and detailed one given by F. Roy Willis in his book *France, Germany and the New Europe; 1945–1947* (New York: Oxford University Press, 1968), pp. 57 ff. of the revised and expanded paperback edition. Willis gives a table of value of imports and exports into the French zone. During the following years, when controls were relaxed, the balance changed, and the zone had a deficit of exports.

[17] A good account of the economic conditions in Bizonia when the Conference met is given by Gimbel in *American Occupation*, pp. 114–6, 127.

215

The Russians were not worried about the possibility of political discontent and disorder or deterred in their demands for reparations for the cruel harm and damage done them by the Germans.

The disdain of occupation officials of German industrialists who had worked with or for the Nazis was waning. Conservative American and British military men were beginning to find some experienced German production executives congenial in outlook and purposes. The Western authorities began to wonder whether, in face of the Russian thrust into the center of Europe, it was wise to continue to debar these elements from German economic life; whether, to the contrary, it had not become advisable to give them a chance. After all, the Russians were using many German plant managers, some of whom were former Nazis or had Nazi associations.

The argument over reparations was connected with the discussion of a revision of the "level of industry" permitted in Germany. This, in the flow of recrimination, was enlivened by charges about the reasons for the elevation of approved German capacity.

Marshall took the lead in advocating the increase of the level that had been fixed by the Control Council, the index of which had first been set at 5.8 million tons of steel production, with capacity retained of 7.5 million tons. But that was proving to be insufficient. As reasons for an upward revision, Marshall called attention to the influx of population from the East into the Western zones, the prospective reduction of German productive resources if the Saar region was given to France, the need of other German industries—such as the electrical power, chemical, and fertilizer—if they were to provide enough to maintain a tolerable standard of living for the German people, and, more and more to the fore, the concurrent needs of other countries of Europe.

Bevin, who had always favored a higher permitted maximum of steel production, recommended that it be raised to eleven million tons—for the whole of Germany. Bidault said that the French Government was still opposed to allowing Germany to increase its industrial capacity in order to be able to provide reparations out of current (future) production; but it wanted to secure greater quantities of coal and raw materials from Germany. His effort was directed by the hopeful wish to build up heavy industries in France—"the industries of transformation."

Molotov, reversing the position previously taken by him, stated that the Soviet Government recognized a need for an upward revision of the level permitted industrial capacity—of 10 to 12 million tons for steel. But he maintained that since this would inevitably curtail the dismantling program, it was another reason why Germany should be required

216

to make reparations out of current production.

The Ministers failed during the Conference to reach an agreement. The question was turned over to the zone commanders; and, to foretell, several months later the Americans and British agreed on an annual permitted steel production of 10.7 million tons for Bizonia alone, with 13 million tons of capacity.

The French Aspirations

Bidault strove to secure assent to claims on Germany of great political as well as economic consequence.

One was that the Saar should be detached from Germany and be fused with the French economy. Marshall and Bevin were willing, and they also agreed that France should receive a larger share of German coal production. But Molotov would not concur. Probably he hoped that withholding his consent would ensure that the French Government would not back away from the plan for the Ruhr industries, then under discussion, whereby Russia would share in their control. But his obduracy had the contrary effect. It caused Bidault to slacken his effort to maintain converging views with the Soviet Union about Germany. The changing attitude of the French Foreign Minister coincided with the sprouting wish of the French Prime Minister, Paul Ramadier, to find a way to eliminate the Communist members of the Cabinet.

Bidault also renewed the French demand that the Rhineland and the Ruhr be detached from Germany.[18] When it became apparent that Marshall and Bevin would not possibly assent to this, Bidault moderated his proposals. Ceasing to insist on the political detachment of the Ruhr from Germany, he began to advocate instead a special international regime of the four powers which would exercise control over the region, particularly over the iron and steel industries. Molotov found such an arrangement acceptable. Had it been effectuated, the Soviet Government would have had veto power, and its concurrence would have been required for current programs, including that for the export of Ruhr products to Western countries badly in need of them—England, France, Belgium, Holland, and others.

Marshall and Bevin were not to be budged. The Americans and British wanted the mines of the Ruhr and its great industrial plants to remain during the period of occupation under supervision of the British

---

[18] For the French position at this Conference and subsequent events, see Ministère des Affaires Étrangères, *Documents français relatifs à l'Allemagne, 1945–1947* (Paris, 1947), pp. 42–64 et seq., *L'Année Politique 1947*, pp. 49–50, 54–58, 79–88, and an article by Léon Blum in *Le Populaire*, April 17, 1947, pp. 694–95.

217

and American zonal commands. Marshall said that the American Government did not regard the Ruhr situation as unique; that of Silesia, now ruled by Poles because of Russian insistence, was similar. German authorities must be in the first instance responsible for the management and operation and sales of the Ruhr industries, as they were elsewhere in Germany. The interests of all could be protected by stipulations for the equitable distribution of essential products in short supply, in order to assure that all countries could buy fair amounts on the same terms, and to prevent any future German attempt to dominate European industry by its control of metallurgical coal.[19]

Bevin's answer to the French proposal was substantially the same. In his exposition to the House of Commons he stressed the point that it would be wrong to put the Ruhr under Four-Power control when other parts of Germany were being managed as closed preserves.[20]

In accepting the rebuff, Bidault resigned himself to the loss of support of the French Communist party. The aggrieved Soviet satellites denounced the exclusion of the Soviet Union from the Ruhr as another sign that the American and British Governments intended to build up the region as a supplier of military equipment, under the combined control of German cartels and American and British "trust and monopolies."

The Prospect of a Peace Treaty Beclouded

Marshall, on April 14th, renewed the proposal for a Four-Power security treaty against German aggression which Byrnes had made a year ago. Its purposes, he explained, as had Byrnes, were to give all assurance against German rearmament and to clear the way toward a peace treaty.

Bidault conditioned his assent on acceptance of French proposals about the Ruhr and the Rhineland. Molotov did not reject the proposal unconditionally. But he declared that it must be accompanied by the creation of a central German Government and acceptance of an obligation to make reparations deliveries out of current production. Marshall, on April 23d, remarked that he regarded the Soviet counterproposal as a rejection, since Molotov wanted to introduce into the treaty nearly every

[19] Marshall statement, April 10, 1947. State Department *Bulletin,* April 20, 1947, pp. 694–5.
The American and British Governments concluded a separate agreement with the French Government in regard to the apportionment of exports of the coal of the Ruhr. This contemplated an increase in Ruhr production and in coal exports to France, and French acceptance was connected with the American and British assent to the incorporation of the Saar in the French economy. The Soviet authorities criticized this accord as improper and dangerous.
[20] Parliamentary Debates, House of Commons, May 15, 1947.

one of the Soviet terms for settlement of the various differences between the four powers.

The policies upheld by the American Delegation at Moscow may have been influenced by the growth of Republican power in Congress and by the thought that it was probable the Republicans would win the next election. Respect for his ability, as well as the wish for Republican support, had induced Marshall to include John Foster Dulles in the delegation. He was the intimate adviser of Governor Thomas E. Dewey, who was to be the Republican candidate for the Presidency. In all probability if Dewey won, Dulles would be the next Secretary of State. During his previous legal career, he had worked for or with German industrial and banking concerns. He had respect for German economic efficiency and power. His views, ably expressed, had been set forth in a speech which had been approved in advance by Senator Vandenberg and Governor Dewey. In this he clearly favored the resuscitation of the German economy and also envisaged that its industrial potential ought to be integrated into Western Europe. The United States, he concluded, should take the leadership for such development.[21]

Dulles' presence may have caused the Soviet authorities to be more hostile to the American proposals than they would have been. For they knew, and in their propaganda recalled, Dulles' record as counsel before the war for American sponsors of large bond issues for German banks and industries and for the Ruhr cartels which had supported Hitler and Nazism.[22]

[21] Speech to the National Publishers' Association, January 17, 1947. Quoted in Jones, *Fifteen Weeks*, p. 220.

[22] Of course, Soviet propaganda, with careless distortion of the facts, exaggerated the connections which the firm of Sullivan and Cromwell, in which Dulles had been a senior partner, had previously had with American financial interests such as the Rockefellers, the Morgans, the Chase Manhattan Bank, and the Schroeders, and the participation of these firms in the Ruhr enterprises. But the association remained lively in the minds of those Communists who construed American policy as being merely an expression of the interests of what they regarded as the dominant groups in American life.

In reality it seems that Dulles, who was adviser to the delegation at this time, favored the setting up of the Ruhr as an independent and neutral state, perhaps after a short period of Four-Power control. His thought was that as such it could best serve the needs of all of Europe. General Clay and Robert Murphy, another adviser of the delegation, opposed Dulles' idea, and Marshall does not seem ever to have considered it seriously.

Clay, in his contribution to the Princeton University Oral History Project, centered on Dulles, describes his impressions of the change in Dulles' judgment; before this Moscow Conference, Clay thought Dulles had believed that France could be a leader in European reconstruction, but soon thereafter he concluded that it could not be, and his hesitation about the regrowth of the German economy was overcome by his fear that unless economic prospects in Germany improved, the Communists might prevail in that country. It is likely that the revision of his judgment was affected by the severe economic and political crisis in France during this spring of 1947, which is covered in chapter 29.

Stalin appeared to discount the failure of this Conference, if we are to regard what he said to Marshall as sincere, not simulated: "These are only the first skirmishes and brushes of reconnaissance forces on this question." [23] Was he counting on trouble in Western Europe to bring the Western Allies and the Germans round to Moscow's inclinations?

American and British official circles also professed to believe it might be possible to agree on a peace treaty for Germany in the autumn of 1947, when the Council of Foreign Ministers was next to meet.

But in the interim under American leadership they took decisive steps to reinvigorate the German economy, to enable countries of Western Europe to pull through the economic crisis which befell them in the early months of 1947, and to ward off a spread of Communism to the West. These measures, as will be seen, so fractured the relations between the West and the Communist East that they never could be set back again into the pattern that had been in the minds of the peacemakers at the end of the war.

[23] Marshall's broadcast address about the Moscow Meeting of the Council of Foreign Ministers, April 28, 1947, printed in State Department *Bulletin* of May 11, 1947, p. 924.

28

Doctrine to Program

Through conduits that cannot be tracked, the way had been prepared for the doctrine which in March 1947 Truman enunciated by the analysis which George Kennan had first impressed upon Washington in February 1946. A rewritten and expanded version of this interpretative warning had been sent in January 1947 by Kennan, who was then lecturing at the National War College, to Secretary of the Navy James Forrestal "for his private and personal edification." Acknowledging it on February 17th, Forrestal had written, "It is extremely well done and I am going to suggest to the Secretary [of State] that he read it." [1] Whether or not Secretary Marshall or Undersecretary Acheson read it has not been ascertained, but they probably did. Nor whether a copy found its way to the White House, via Clark Clifford. However, Kennan had not participated in the composition of Truman's message to Congress of March 17th. On being shown a preliminary draft, he, who had developed in his own verbal productions so astringent a view of Communist intentions, had been disturbed by the ideological tenor and cosmic scope of Truman's statement. He judged the criterion of action insufficient and its galloping language unreined.[2]

This was paradoxical—most paradoxical—because some months later Kennan provided a firmer and sterner rationale for Truman's message. It may also be said that he developed the President's doctrine into a program. This he did in an article which appeared in *Foreign Affairs*.[3] Its authorship was hidden by an anonymous designation X. But since so many officials and auditors of his lectures had heard him make the same statements, or ones of similar import, delivered in similar style, he was

[1] George Kennan, *Memoirs*, p. 355.

[2] These and other reasons why Kennan took exception to the broader passages of the President's message are set forth in his *Memoirs*, pp. 319–322. He contrasts these with the more specific conditions and recommendations in the exposé he was giving at the War College.

[3] "The Sources of Soviet Conduct," *Foreign Affairs*, July 1947. Marshall, in deploring its publication, described it as "a programmatical article." (Kennan, *Memoirs* p. 356).

soon identified as its author.

The reasoning and conclusions of his article had great force and impact. The knowledge that he was its author caused it to be regarded with greater respect. By the time it appeared, he had been designated by General Marshall to head a new staff group called the Policy Planning Staff. That was to be called upon to devise foresighted policies for the conduct of our foreign affairs. The article became "the center of a veritable whirlpool of publicity."

Truman's declaration, connected as it was with the Greek-Turkish situation, might have been regarded as a political grandiloquence. It could be thought to be a sincerely meant but nevertheless transient reaction to circumstances which might change, as they so often did in the flux of diplomacy. The Russians might merely be trying to extend their authority and influence in strategic situations in areas to the south—as they had under the Czarist regime—if and when they thought it could easily be won. They might, if the opposition and risks were too great, compromise and desist. And who knew, they might even some day again value Western cooperation and the prospect of tranquillity above minor gains, and appreciate the necessity of earning the reputation of a power that could be trusted to keep its word.

But Kennan's presentation set a deeper and harder base for active hostile opposition to an extension of Communism. Both because of the essentials of the Marxist-Leninist theory and the nature of the Soviet Communist state, he concluded that the Soviet Union could never voluntarily be quiescent or cooperative; its compulsions confronted all other countries with an inescapable choice between submission and active opposition. Its surge over the world could and would not be stayed by reason, tolerance, sobriety or a wish for peace, but only by tireless vigilance and bold readiness to exert counterforce.

The import of Kennan's analysis may be conveyed by quoting a few sentences:

". . . there can never be on Moscow's side any sincere assumption of a community of aims between the Soviet Union and powers which are regarded as capitalist. . . . If the Soviet Government occasionally sets its signature to documents which would indicate the contrary, this is to be regarded as a tactical manoeuver permissible in dealing with the enemy.

". . . It [Soviet diplomacy] cannot be easily defeated or discouraged by a single victory on the part of its opponents. And the patient persistence by which it is animated means that it can be effectively countered not by sporadic acts which represent the momentary whims of democratic opinion but only by intelligent long-range policies on the part of

Russia's adversaries—policies no less steady in their purpose, and no less variegated and resourceful in their application, than those of the Soviet Union itself.

"In these circumstances it is clear that the main element of any United States policy toward the Soviet Union must be that of a long-term, patient but firm and vigilant *containment* [author's italics] of Russian expansive tendencies. It is important to note, however, that such a policy has nothing to do with outward histrionics: with threats or blustering or superfluous gestures of outward 'toughness.'

". . . Russia, as opposed to the Western world in general, is still by far the weaker party . . . Soviet policy is highly flexible and . . . Soviet society may well contain deficiencies which will eventually weaken its own total potential. This would of itself warrant the United States entering with reasonable confidence upon a policy of firm containment, designed to confront the Russians with unalterable counterforce *at every point* [author's italics] where they show signs of encroaching upon the interests of a peaceful and stable world.[4]

When writing this article, words led Kennan's thoughts by the nose. He may not have appreciated the seemingly plain import of its analysis and recommendations. In his *Memoirs*, written twenty years afterward, he acknowledged that some of his language ". . . was at best ambiguous, and lent itself to misinterpretation."[5] Over and over he deplored the fact that this article (as well as his telegrams and memos) were taken to betoken readiness to use military force when and as it would serve the purpose. His failure to grasp this clear implication of what he wrote is the more perplexing because his original telegram, and the memo on which the article was based, had been taken up particularly by Secretary of the Navy Forrestal and expounded to military men who attended the War College.

Kennan, in reflecting in his *Memoirs* on this "misunderstanding" of the article, observes that perhaps the most serious "deficiency" of the X article ". . . was the failure to make clear that what I was talking about when I mentioned the containment of Soviet power was not the containment by military means of a military threat, but the political containment of a political threat."[6] But this later attempt to confine the applicability of what he wrote is unconvincing. Were not, for example, the threats to Greece and Turkey deemed both political and military, and did not the measures we used to contain these situations employ both political (economic) and military means?

[4] *Foreign Affairs*, July 1947, pp. 575, 581, 672.
[5] Kennan, *Memoirs*, p. 359.
[6] *Ibid.*, p. 358.

It is impossible to tell whether the views propounded in Kennan's article influenced American policy greatly, or whether the article received so much notice because the American Government by mid-1947 had virtually resolved to try to prevent the spread of Communism into Western Europe and the Mediterranean—by any means and measures that might serve.

In one respect Kennan's program was more circumspect that Truman's pronouncement. The President caused his auditors to think that he meant it to be applicable everywhere in the globe. But Kennan, although he did not make it clear in his ringing call for "containment," had Europe in mind.[7]

In a series of newspaper articles Walter Lippmann pointed out the problems lurking in the doctrine which Kennan propounded.[8] Among them were: (1) American military power was not designed for, or well adapted to, a strategy of containing, waiting, countering, blocking; (2) to be effective the United States would have to use and support satellite states and puppet governments, often unreliable; (3) this policy of engagement—in areas not clearly specified—might alienate our natural Allies, the Atlantic community, for they would not want to be constantly in danger of being dragged into a war with the Soviet Union over obscure and distant situations.

Lippmann's analysis was widely and attentively read. It probably had an impact on Kennan's thinking along with others. But during the next three years before the Russians got atomic weapons and the Communists became masters of the Chinese mainland, the doctrine of containment remained uppermost—especially in American military circles.

[7] One snatch of recorded evidence that this is so is in the entry which Admiral Leahy made in his Diary of May 6, 1947: "Attended at Army [sic!] War College a most interesting hour's talk on the European political problem by Mr. Kennan of the State Department.

"He expressed an opinion that Russia is determined to obtain control of the economy of Europe by political manoeuvres, and that Moscow is at the present time counting on an economic crisis in the U.S. which will facilitate Russian assumption of economic and political control of Europe."

[8] They were reprinted in Walter Lippmann, *The Cold War, A Study in U.S. Foreign Policy* (New York: Harper, 1947).

PART EIGHT

To Salvage

Western Europe—

The Marshall Plan

29

To Salvage Western Europe

Western Europe: Cold, Hungry, Depressed

In telling of the development of the general theme of global defense of freedom and independence—to deter and counter Communist expansion—I have passed over the one great American initiative to that end.

One passage in Truman's address to Congress on March 12th had forecast it. "The seeds of totalitarian regimes are nurtured by misery and want. They spread and grow in the evil soil of poverty and strife."

The American Government had not been unmindful of the plight of the millions of those left bereft and in distress by the war. In the autumn of 1943 and in 1944 the United States had taken the lead in forming the United Nations Relief and Rehabilitation Administration. This was created to alleviate the need for food, clothing, shelter, medicines, and other forms of relief to millions of these people left destitute as the German and Italian armies retreated: displaced persons, prisoners of war who were freed, forced laborers who were released, former prisoners of concentration camps, and refugees from war-struck areas. To that work of succor, which kept alive and gave a new start to millions of Europeans, the United States had contributed more supplies than all other members together—about 73 percent of the 3 billion dollars worth from farms, factories, warehouses.[1] Also ours had been the zeal behind the effort to prevent corruption and waste, so that those who needed help were beneficiaries, not middlemen, profiteers, politicians, and bureaucrats. As the endless influx of persons in need and distress swelled, UNRRA funds had run thin, and it was to be closed out June 30, 1947.[2]

---

[1] UNRRA provided supplies in 16 countries; Albania, Austria, China, Czechoslovakia, Dodecanese Islands, Finland, Formosa, Greece, Hungary, Italy, Korea, Philippines, San Marino, Poland, (White) Russia, and Yugoslavia.

[2] The International Bank for Reconstruction and Development had been slow in beginning operations, and its management guided by financial standards. The funds of the U.N. Economic and Social Council were trivial compared to the need.

During the immediate postwar years, American private capitalists had not dared invest their capital in the damaged and disturbed countries. The financial risks seemed great, inflation was rampant, fiscal collapse possible, and the chances of disorder, civil war, and Communism worrisome. In fact during the period immediately after the war new private American investment in western Europe was less than the European capital that was invested, for safety, in the United States. Private enterprise is attracted by profit, not problems.

Truman, believing himself obligated by the terms of the legislation, had terminated Lend-Lease aid as soon as the war in Europe had ended. He was mindful of the fact that when presiding over the Senate he, himself, on the score that it was unnecessary, had to cast the deciding vote against an amendment that would have explicitly prohibited the President from continuing to provide Lend-Lease assistance.

The British had been told to expect no further assignments of supplies except for use in the war against Japan. Orders to end shipments to the Soviet Union were so worded that ships at sea en route to Russia with Lend-Lease supplies had turned about and unloaded.

In his *Memoirs* Truman explains the decision by a belief that there was a fundamental distinction between the powers that he, as President, could properly exercise in wartime and those he should have in peacetime. In his mind a European recovery program appeared quite different from Lend-Lease—to be dealt with in an entirely different way, in year-by-year consultation with Congress.[3] Moreover, he thought the interim could be bridged by extending Export-Import Bank credits for United States exports.[4]

Stalin complained. When Harry Hopkins went to Moscow in May–June 1945, to talk over the urgent questions which interested both countries, Stalin had remarked that he thought the manner in which Lend-Lease had been curtailed was "brutal"; that its abruptness and absence of warning had upset Soviet plans. He also said if our decision no longer to continue such aid was motivated by a wish to bring pressure on the Russians, "in order to soften them up," it was a great mistake and would have exactly the opposite effect.

---

[3] *Year of Decisions*, pp. 46, 232.

An extensive account of American policies in regard to the provision of Lend-Lease after the end of the war against Germany, is given in Herbert Feis, *Between War and Peace: The Potsdam Conference*.

[4] The Export-Import Bank by its statutes could extend only comparatively short period credits, on commercial terms.

But it was Britain that had been left most deeply in trouble when Lend-Lease was ended. For it had used up almost all its foreign resources and reserves to fight the war and had incurred a heavy foreign debt.[5] The British did not have the vast natural resources of the Russians—the fields in which food could be grown and livestock kept and fed, and cotton grown, or the metal mines, or the oil wells. They were vitally dependent on foreign supplies for daily sustenance and the operation of their industries.

Prime Minister Attlee had spoken with restraint when warning the House of Commons not to expect any more Lend-Lease supplies, observing merely that it left Great Britain in "a very serious financial condition." Churchill, who, while Prime Minister, had in May protested because he believed the original American order ignored an agreement he had made with Roosevelt in Quebec, had in August merely remarked that it was "very grave, disquieting news." His pride and belief in the self-reliant powers of the British people were blended with a wish not to hurt the chances of securing a large American postwar loan on favorable terms.

The President had asked Undersecretary William Clayton to go from Potsdam to London and talk with the British about their shortage of dollars and supplies. Clayton was a Texan who had made many millions by trading in cotton and other raw materials and farm products. He had a brilliant, nervously calculating mentality. In his mind a rigid set of precepts and principles about the primal virtues of unfettered private enterprise was deeply nested. He was as fervent a believer as Cordell Hull in the recuperative and peace-producing potentialities of international trade. Yet, even he was becoming aware that some emergency help was essential; some, but not too much; and as it turned out, too little. Moreover, the plight of our former Allies seemed to him to provide a good chance to convert, if not compel, them to "get religion"; and for their own salvation as well as our benefit to reduce tariffs, end trade discriminations (especially British Imperial preferences), and get rid of their restrictions on foreign exchange.

Clayton had told the British officials that American public opinion would probably support a line of credit on three billion dollars on commercially liberal terms if a satisfactory all-over commercial policy agreement could be reached. It was arranged that a Special Mission would go

---

[5] Britain had incurred a foreign exchange deficit of about 40 billion dollars while fighting the war. More than half of this had been provided by Lend-Lease, but the remainder had to be financed by selling its foreign investments (about 4.5 billion), loans by foreign countries which had piled up in "frozen" sterling debt accounts, and dollar loans and gifts by the United States and Canada (about 4.4 from the United States and 1 billion from Canada).

soon thereafter to Washington to negotiate the loan.

Lord Keynes had joined the British Ambassador, the Earl of Halifax, and British Treasury representative, Robert Brand, for the discussions. After listening to Keynes' buoyant talk before his departure, Bevin had remarked, "When I hear Lord Keynes talking, I can hear the coins jingling in my pocket, but I am not sure they are really there." [6] The British sought a grant-in-aid or an interest-free loan of at least five billion to get through the next few years.

Clayton had become inclined to recommend a four billion dollar low-interest-bearing loan. But Secretary of the Treasury Vinson had been obdurate, and he was the senior member of the American negotiating group and closer to Truman than any other member. In this negotiation he was sterner, more ignorant, and more touchy. He suspected that the British were trying to take advantage of us. He resented some of Keynes' remarks and was leery of his economic arguments—because down in Kentucky "folks don't look at things that way." Keynes, the soaring and sinuous analyst of economic affairs, had let his tongue and wit run away with him, in brightest Cambridge manner. The dour Vinson had taken umbrage at some of his repartee and sly digs at the United States.[7]

In the end it had been decided by Truman that Congress should be asked to approve a loan of three and three-quarter billion at 2 percent interest. The British Government dubiously and reluctantly promised to make the pound freely convertible one year after the effective date of the agreement (July 1946).[8] Apropos this and other conditions, the Chancellor of the Exchequer, Dalton, had written in his Diary, "My cynical and secret reflection on the American loan is that we shall be able to make good use of the dollars—though we wish there were more—but it is quite certain that the conditions will have to be 'revised' long before A.D. 2001, and that even in the next year or two it may well be that circumstances will require a considerable variation, which might even be 'unilateral'." [9]

It proved to be far from easy to secure the approval of Congress for even that shrunken amount. Typical of the objections were those of Senator Robert Taft of Ohio. Again, as remembered by Clayton, "The last time I saw him he held up a handful of (legislative) bills and he said

[6] Dalton Diary.

[7] As recalled by Clayton, "Whenever we had a meeting in which Mr. Vinson and Lord Keynes took part, I had to spend a good deal of time keeping them apart. Secretary Vinson did not like Keynes' biting humor and objected to it seriously." Clayton memoir in Oral History Project, Columbia University.

[8] Clayton, the hard bargainer, remarked with satisfaction in a letter to Bernard Baruch: "We loaded the British loan negotiations with all the conditions the traffic would bear" (April 26, 1946). Baruch papers, Princeton University Library.

[9] Dalton Diary, entry dated December 19, 1945.

'You see all these bills? They provide for the appropriation of billions of dollars for domestic projects. I can't vote for them. If I vote for the British loan of three and three-quarters billions of dollars, and vote against these domestic bills, you can see what political effect it would have.' " [10]

In January 1946 President Truman had sent a special message to Congress recommending the necessary legislation. Clayton and Acheson started at opposite ends of the corridors of the Senate and House Office Building, and with doggedness set out to secure support. Those members whom one could not convince, the other took on.

The needed votes were secured after months of delay. Possibly—so Keynes thought and so told Dalton—the vote had been helped by recent Russian attitudes and by the interest of the Pope, who instructed all American cardinals to do nothing that would lessen British will to resist Communism.[11] But there were casualties, personal and political. Not long afterward, the strain which Keynes had endured during the war and in these days of argument told upon him. He had a mortal heart attack.

By the time the loan bill had finally reached Truman's desk (July 1946) and he had signed it, the British had already spent or obligated much of it. Within a year they were in a more critical state of need and deficit than before.

During the same period the American Government had extended substantial loans and credits to the governments of France, Belgium, the Netherlands, and Norway.

Only the imperative need for American aid had reconciled the French Government to seek a loan. For most of the members of the Gouin Cabinet—in office at this time—feared that the American Government would require France to relax its claims against Germany before it provided the money. Bidault, the Foreign Minister, was particularly obstinate in his opposition to any concessions of this sort, and had the vigorous support of the Communist ministers.

Léon Blum, well-known and well-liked in the United States, had been sent to present the request. Was he not that most eminent and moderate of French socialists, the firmest opponent of the Communists? He did well, considering the still active sense in the United States that the French people had defaulted in their duty during the war and could not be counted on to resist Communism. On his return with the pledge of a

[10] William L. Clayton, Memoir in recording for Oral History Project, Columbia University.
[11] Dalton Diary, March 29, 1946.

loan of 1.4 billion dollars he was able to affirm publicly: "The negotiations conducted in Washington [where he had been from March 15th to the end of May 1946] did not involve either explicitly or implicitly, directly or indirectly, any condition of any kind, civil, military, political or diplomatic." [12] But, as was commented on at the time, though the loan had no political conditions, it had political consequences. Blum alerted the American officials to the advantage of a helpful and, especially, a prompt decision before the scheduled French elections. It is safe to surmise that in Washington he was given the impression, which he carried back to the Cabinet, that the loan transaction and other future ones would be facilitated if the Communist members were eliminated from the Cabinet.[13]

During this early postwar period, American Government expenditures for the procurement of essentials to our former enemies—Germany, Italy, and Japan—were large and unchallenged. Congress provided the required funds with less fuss than it made over the loans to our former Allies, for American forces were stationed in these occupied countries, and the relief was judged essential to prevent disease and unrest. The recommendations of military commanders were more readily accepted in Congress than the requests of State Department officials.

But all these measured transfusions of aid—and there were others in the annals—had been insufficient for the circumstances and the purpose.[14]

When in the spring of 1947 the American Government resolved to rush to the support of the Greek and Turkish Governments, and Truman propounded his doctrine of resistance to Communism, the economic plight of most of the countries of western Europe was as bad as it had been at war's end, or worse.[15]

Privation was general, supplies of food and raw materials low, industry stagnant, unemployment high, much of the capital equipment worn down or obsolescent, management discouraged, inflation continuous, and capital nervous. Our former Allies did not know where to secure dollars to buy what they would so badly need, or how to get along with-

[12] *L'Oeuvre de Léon Blum*, pp. 202–3.

[13] G. Elgey, *La République des Illusions*, pp. 140–1, gives the text of a confidential report of Robert Blum, the son and collaborator of his father, about the negotiations.

[14] During the two years after V-J Day, the American Government provided more than 15 billion dollars in grants and loans to our Allies, in supplying essentials to our former enemies, and for the sustenance, relief, and resettlement of war sufferers.

[15] The state of Western Europe at this time has been so fully described in so many reports of agencies of the American Government, by the Organization for European Economic Cooperation (OEEC) and books, that anything more than a short summary would be redundant.

out them. The smell of distress, discontent, and disarray was in the air.

Let it be recalled that during the winter of 1946–47, heavy snowfalls and extreme cold lasted long; it was not merely the traditional "damp that fell over England," (recall Virginia Woolf's wonderful *Orlando*) but a paralyzing freeze. More than a million and a half sheep, England's rural comfort and reliance, perished, and many thousands of cattle. Coal production, so urgently needed for industry, power, and warmth, was hindered. The shortage of coal caused the closing of a hundred mills in Lancashire alone—plants making textiles, clothing, shoes. People shivered and stared at frozen burst pipes. The supply of electricity, light, and power was cut off half of the day. In many offices and shops business was carried on under the dim light of oil lamps and candles. Even Dalton, the bluff Chancellor of the Exchequer, son of a devout Bishop, could be only faintly jocular when he wrote in his Diary, "The frost, snow and fogs—especially fogs—continue unabated, and whoever is trying to be funny in arranging all this is rather overdoing the job. . . . and the most satisfactory place these days is in bed." [16] It could be foreseen that much of the next British crops of wheat, rye, potatoes, and sugar beets would be smaller than usual; and the need for imported food and raw materials would be greater, while the proceeds of American and Canadian loans were being fast expended. At the current rate of use they would be all gone by early 1948. How was Britain to manage thereafter? Could expenditures to maintain occupation forces in Germany and the Far East be cut? What further austerity would the British people have to practice? Would they remain patient and politically calm, even though they once again had to get along without enough food, and less tobacco to console them? Or would their grumblings turn into riots and rebellion? [17]

In France there were ominous indications that if the economic situation was not improved and political leadership was not stabilized, there would be social disorder. By the time May 1947 came around, after a hard and chaotic winter, supplies were so low and rationing so severe that most workers in factories, public utilities, and governments were desperate.

Inflation had resulted in a great increase in the price of all domestic supplies. Causing most grumbling was the shortage of wheat and flour. Freezing had caused the loss of crops; and the farmers were hoarding part of what they grew in order to re-sow and to feed the animals.

---

[16] February 24, 1947.

[17] During this grim February and March 1946 the Conservative Party jibe was "Starve with Strachey [Minister of Food] and shiver with Shinwell [Minister of Fuel and Power]."

Early in April the Cabinet had decided to reduce the bread ration to 250 grammes. All those who know the extent to which French people founded their meals on that best of breads—the long French loaves—will recognize that this measure really hurt. It justifies resort to a colloquialism—this was a blow in the "bread basket."

Making the restriction more unpalatable was the fact that most French people in the cities could not buy butter. The Government, before it received emergency American help (covered in a later section) thought that they would have to order all restaurants to remain closed every other week and all butchers to keep their shops closed three days a week. How heartfelt, for example, was the appeal of Vincent Auriol, the President of the Republic, on May 15th! After stressing the sacrifice of the industrial workers and the suffering of the city people, he said, addressing the nation's farmers: "The appeal is in my name, but also in the name of the children in the cities, that I say to you all—deliver your wheat at once, all your wheat. Respond to the National Bread Committee on which there are represented all the moral, spiritual, economic and political forces of the nation. In each village let the teacher, the priest, the artisan, the mayor and his advisers, the parliamentarians, all together, keep on the job in unity." [18]

The Government, in an effort to end the inflation, had resorted to orders prohibiting any further increase in wages and prices. These caused discontent in the trade unions.

Division in the Cabinet over the maintenance of these controls was the preface to the resignation of the Communist members of the Cabinet. But the event was in line with the weakening of the friendship between France and the Soviet Union. Behind the apparent calm with which the Communist Cabinet members accepted their separation from the Government may have been a lively hope that the time had come when, by agitation, disruption of the economy, and similar means, their party might secure control of the government of France. Conversely, awareness of this Communist aspiration and intention made the more conservative French political parties the readier to try to deal with the problems of the disturbed country without the cooperation of the Communists, even against their intense opposition.

Bidault, the Foreign Minister, had been in Moscow. On his return to Paris he remarked to all and sundry: "It's finished, it's finished. It is impossible to reach an accord with the Russians. There is no longer any alliance or union in the three great powers, or a possibility of understanding with the Communists. A new era is beginning and France must take

[18] Quoted in *L'Année Politique 1947*.

its measure." [19] He reported to the Prime Minister, Ramadier, a Socialist, that he thought a struggle was inevitable and urged him to get rid of the Communist members of the Cabinet at once. It is probable that in fact Ramadier had by this time decided to take the first chance to do so without appearing to force a break.

Following a previous Cabinet discussion of the trade unions' demands for wage increases, the situation came to a climax at the Cabinet meeting on May 4th. Then representatives of the other main parties in the coalition—including the Socialist Ministers—said that they would support the government's policy in regard to wage stabilization. But Maurice Thorez said that the Communists would support the claims of the workers and that their wages could be increased without an increase of prices. Ramadier chose to regard this refusal of assent as tantamount to the resignations of the Communist Ministers and told them that he was going to replace them. These dissenters were taken aback at the abruptness of this action.

Ramadier was steadily thereafter to affirm that the rupture with the Communists was due entirely to internal French politics and was not connected with the development of the international situation. But it may be surmised that in some ways and in some measure the acceptance of this separation was made easier, perhaps desirable, by Truman's direct stand against Communism; tacitly the ruling French groups had come to the conclusion that to preserve traditional France they would have to cooperate with the United States and relinquish any hope of being the arbiter of relations between the West and the Communist nations led by Moscow.

The Cabinet crisis cleared the way for the French Government to stand out firmly in the face of a gyrating strike movement that spread from various industries, including the Renault national automobile factory, to the electrical plants and gasworks, the coal mines, the oil distribution industry, even to the bank clerks and large department stores; then early in June it flared up on various main railway lines. These disruptions, just before the Marshall Plan was announced and before Marshall aid could produce any effect, kept alive the fear that the Communists might be able to create enough trouble so to derange public administration, so to reduce industrial production, and so to ferment disorder on the streets that the French Government might be compelled to give in. The French Communist Party, with Russian encouragement, was ready to take over power.

In short, the American program of aid was developed in the nick of time.

---

[19] Quoted in Elgey, *La République des Illusions*, p. 282.

By the time that the Marshall Program had been developed, there was a great question as to whether an economy so debilitated and upset as was the French could resist the appeals of Communism. The Government showed courageous conviction. The Prime Minister and his colleagues construed the strikes as an assault on democracy and said that the Government must and would assure the function of essential services. "I am here," Ramadier declared, "to defend the authority of the Republic." [20] It may be that if France had been lost to the West at this time, many of the other countries of western Europe would have been lost.

What might happen in Italy was scarcely less alarming. In that country there had been Communists in the Cabinet since 1945; their followers were getting more numerous, and it was possible that after the next election they would be a dominant element in the ruling coalition. Should France or Italy go Communist, the German people would be impressed and perhaps frightened into following them. If this happened, the Western Allies might not be able to control events in that occupied country.

[20] *L'Année Politique 1947.*

30

Marshall Steps Forward

The Awakening of the American Government

During the several talks Acheson had with Secretary of War Patterson and Secretary of the Navy Forrestal about the emergent crises in Greece and Turkey, they agreed these were only a segment of the problems of maintaining stability in Europe. Acting under the stimulus of common concern, on March 5th—the week before Truman announced his "doctrine"—Acheson had asked the State-War-Navy Coordinating Committee (SWNCC) to examine the whole situation in consultation with the Treasury. That group had appointed a Special Committee which was directed to report within two weeks what countries would need United States aid (economic; financial, technical, and/or military equipment).[1] On this same day Clayton, en route to Arizona, wrote an urgent memo stating that he thought prompt and effective help must be given to gravely threatened countries and suggesting that Congress be asked to provide an emergency fund of five billion dollars.[2] The danger had finally gotten the better of his financial prudence.

The task which this SWNCC committee and other quickly formed committees and subcommittees (nothing is as quickly born as a committee) undertook was to consider how much aid was needed; and of what kind; and to explain why such aid should be granted. Their members were junior in their departments, but they were capable and earnest and not in awe of Congress. Seldom has it been remembered how much of the spade work they did on what became known as the Marshall Plan.[3]

[1] The members of this Committee were Colonel William Eddy, Chief of Research and Intelligence in the State Department, Brigadier General George A. Lincoln of the War Department, and Rear Admiral E. T. Wooldridge of the Navy Department. Perhaps because the Secretary of the Treasury was indifferent and skeptical, the Treasury contributed little or nothing to the development of this American program of aid.

[2] Dean Acheson, *Present at the Creation*, p. 226.

[3] Jones wrote in *Fifteen Weeks*, pp. 202–3, 206, that though almost lost to sight, no doubt the studies and recommendations of these committees of officials who worried harder and earlier about the situation than their more eminent seniors were of

They not only instructed and incited their superiors, they impelled them toward action.

The committee adopted the current tag that "Communists can be stopped by bread and ballots rather than by bullets." Their studies were summed up in the preliminary report on April 21st. Their estimates and forecasts were good preliminary appraisals of the plight of a dozen "critical" countries, mostly in Europe; and of how much and what kind of American aid was needed to see them through the emergency; and what the United States could provide without great derangement or shortages at home, or excessive calls on credit and expansion of money and credit. It also contained most of the concepts which remained basic in the Plan that was later adopted.

But action commensurate with the reasons so clearly contrived in the productions of these committees waited on distracting circumstances. Marshall was in Moscow until April 28th, in conference with other Foreign Ministers. Acting Secretary of State Acheson was extremely busy with other matters. John Snyder, who had succeeded Vinson as Secretary of the Treasury, was a nullity. Clayton was in Arizona for several weeks recuperating from illness, and on his return became absorbed in preparation for a conference about trade and tariffs in Geneva—for which tranquil residence of fine purposes he left on April 8th and remained in Europe until after the middle of May.

But the conclusion of the junior technicians and the worried reports from informants in Western Europe together made their impress upon those who could articulate policy and make decisions.[4]

The first signal was given by Acheson. On April 7th President Truman had asked him to go as substitute to Cleveland, Mississippi and speak at the annual meeting of the influential Delta Council. In his ensuing dis-

---

value and influence in producing the decision to offer Europe aid and determine the outlines and dimensions of the Marshall Plan. Norman Ness, a member of Clayton's staff, who participated in the work in all its stages, has recorded the opinion that the memos best remembered—those written by Kennan and Clayton—merely outlined the implications of a situation that by then was plain. "It was written on the wall, yet it was startling when someone said, look at what's on the wall." (Recording of Norman Ness, former Head of the Division of Finance and Development Policy in the State Department, in Oral History Project of Columbia University).

[4] Of the circle of senior decision-makers to whom the problem posed by this situation was at this juncture passed upward, four or five major contributors were: Acheson, Lovett, Clayton, Kennan, Bohlen, and Nitze.

Later on, when the task was to convert Marshall's general proffer into an international political action and a legislative measure, Norman Ness; Ambassadors David Bruce and Lewis Douglas; Lincoln Gordon; Ernest Gross, the Legal Adviser of the State Department; and Averell Harriman—all exceptionally able men—helped to shape the project and carry it through.

cussions with his staff, some of them, members of groups who had been writing gloomy memos and making gloomier forecasts, impressed upon him how bleak was the situation in Europe and besought him to tell the American people that they might be called on to resume great and sustained support of friendly countries, again in deep trouble. In other words, they urged him to "elaborate the economic intent of the Truman Doctrine." [5]

Sometime soon thereafter (April 15–20) Acheson outlined for the President what he might say. Truman told him to go ahead, and said that he would stand behind the presentation and try to deal with the problem resolutely.

While Acheson's speech was being composed by earnest subordinates, another group was busily trying to formulate a general program for the now recognized emergency. Marshall's frustrating experience in Moscow had convinced him of the need to take measures to deal with the situation in Germany. It was becoming apparent to him that the state of many other western European countries was hardly less "desperate" than that of Germany and that drastic action of wider scope must be taken to enable them to get out of the ditch.[6]

On April 29th the Secretary of State instructed George Kennan to apply his talents to this imperative and constructive task. The Secretary wished to have within a fortnight a paper analyzing the problems of European recovery and recommendations. When, as their brief talk was ending, Kennan asked if there were any more instructions, Marshall said merely: "Avoid trivia." [7] Terseness may be an aid to, or substitute for, thought.

Kennan took up the task eagerly. He, who was closely identified with the policy of "containment" of the Soviet Union, had become, he avers in his *Memoirs*, troubled by the tone of Truman's message to Congress; he was disquieted by the flat portrayal of a world divided between two contrasting ways of life.[8] In this assignment he saw a chance not only to sustain western Europe against the menace of Communism, due to misery and discontent, but also to correct the emphasis of American policy, to shift it from militant challenge to a bid for cooperation to restore the economy of the continent, possibly including the Soviet Union. The swish of doctrine in Truman's message was to be washed away by inundations of generosity.

---

[5] Jones, *Fifteen Weeks*, p. 207.
[6] Marshall gave a retrospective account of the progression of his thoughts in June 1949, at an anniversary dinner speech in Washington. *New York Times*, June 6, 1949.
[7] Kennan, *Memoirs*, p. 326.
[8] *Ibid.*, pp. 319–22; see also Jones, *Fifteen Weeks*, p. 155.

Acheson spoke on May 8th. The most reverberant passage in this address was: "The war will not be over until the people of the world can again feed and clothe themselves and face the future with some degree of confidence." After reviewing our past considerable essays with facts and reason, he led his audience toward the conclusion that it had become necessary and urgent that the American Government make greater and more comprehensive efforts than it had ever made before in peacetime. The press featured this presentation, and commentators labored to construe its meaning and significance.

A week after Acheson spoke in Mississippi, Winston Churchill, addressing a large audience in London's Albert Hall, described the woeful plight of almost all Europe and averred that only if its many countries worked together in close unity could they overcome their distress and be secure. With dramatic rhetoric he had asked the question: "What is Europe now?" and his answer was, "It is a rubble heap, a charnel house, a breeding ground of pestilence and hate." [9] He called upon the British and other governments to seek a solution for their problems by means of attitudes and measures that were European, not narrowly national. This speech of Churchill's stirred the gusts of discussion about a coordinated program. By May 23d the report of the Policy Planning Staff was completed, and Kennan gave it to Marshall in the compressed form which the Secretary favored. As succinctly summed up by Eric F. Goldman, it recommended that the American Government should make "a massive offer of American resources, directed toward all of Europe with no ideological overtones, in a positive effort to restore the economy of the continent. There were two important provisions. The Europeans had to take the initiative in working out all details, and the program which the Europeans submitted had to give promise of doing the 'whole job. . . . [of being] the last such program we shall be asked to support in the foreseeable future.' " [10]

The program, Kennan's report to Marshall stressed, should be formulated and developed jointly by the European countries, not by us, and it should contemplate a coordinated effort, not to be merely a combination of separate and perhaps competitive national programs.[11]

[9] At the first rally of the Committee for United Europe, called to organize the appeal that Britain and France take the lead in unifying the rubble heap. May 14, 1947.

[10] Goldman, *The Crucial Decade*, p. 73.

[11] One vital passage in this report which found its way, almost verbatim, in Marshall's address was, "It would be neither fitting nor efficacious for this government to undertake to draw up unilaterally and to promulgate formally on its own initiative a program designed to place Western Europe on its feet economically. That is the business of the Europeans. The formal initiative must come from Europe; and Europeans must bear the basic responsibility for it. The role of this country should con-

Almost at the same time the opinion that such an initiative was neces- sary was jolted forward by a memo written by Clayton on the way home from Geneva. Advised by Jean Monnet,[12] Clayton had realized that his ideal of expansion of free trade areas in Europe could not be achieved at this time. As recalled by him, Monnet had said ". . . that they would not be able to start on such a venture at that time; that they would have to get a little more fat on their bones, and get a little further into peace-time operation, before they could do it." [13]

Clayton, in his memo on May 27th, informed Marshall that he thought it ". . . necessary for the President and the Secretary of State to make a strong spiritual appeal to the American people to draw in their belts just a little in order to save Europe from starvation and chaos and, at the same time, preserve for ourselves and our children the glorious heritage of a free America." He urged that a large three-year grant ($6–7 billion) be made to countries of Europe to enable them to meet their deficit of essentials, of some of which—coal, wheat, cotton, and tobacco—the United States at the time had a surplus. This, he suggested, should be based on an arrangement for European economic federation, starting with a customs union, since if the economy of each country remained enclosed, Europe could not recover and be self-supporting.[14]

The memo was sent by Acheson to Marshall—who had in hand by then Kennan's study, which underlined more clearly the difficulties of bringing the countries of Europe together in a cooperative recovery plan.

The problem and the project were reviewed in a conference with Marshall on (or about) May 28th. The Secretary, impressed by Clayton's sense of urgency, at last really aroused, said, "It would be folly . . . to sit back and do nothing." [15] All agreed there was no time left for hesitation.

The custody of the various expositions of the central idea—a coordinated European recovery plan to be underwritten, after close scrutiny, by the United States—had been left, up to then, to the eager and ardent

---

sist of friendly aid in the drafting of a European program and of the later support of such a program, by financial and other means, at European request." Kennan, *Memoirs*, p. 336.

Actually the American Government found it advisable to take an active part in the formulation of the program, and then to stipulate in bilateral accords and to keep close watch over the use made of Marshall plan aid by the recipients.

[12] One of France's foremost figures of our times, a creative thinker and planner about national and international economics. He subsequently became the central figure and moving spirit in the European integration movement.

[13] Clayton recording in Oral History Project, Columbia University.

[14] See Jones, *Fifteen Weeks*, pp. 246–8.

[15] Acheson, *Present at the Creation*, p. 232.

Joseph Jones. But at this stage the task of culling, merging, and editing the expositions was taken over by Charles Bohlen, who drew on the Kennan and Clayton memos and kept in touch with Acheson as he worked. In the last week in May Marshall brought the inner group together several times to discuss both the project and the text.

The issue hardest to determine was whether our offer should be addressed to the whole of Europe, including the Soviet Union and its satellites, or merely to the more attached and democratic nations of western Europe.

Kennan feared that the Soviet Government would try either to link any proposal made to its own particular aims—such as the exaction of reparations from Germany or the administration of the Ruhr—or if it should accept, seek to make the whole plan fail. Nevertheless, he thought the Soviets should be given the chance to participate, while the American and other governments retained the right to decide whether the conditions of their participation were acceptable.[16]

Eric Goldman has related, probably paraphrasing what he was told, a short dialogue between Marshall and Kennan.

Marshall: "Are we safe in directing such a proposal to all of Europe? What will be the effect if the Soviets decide to come in?"

Kennan: "What better way to emphasize that the program is not mere anti-Sovietism? Why not make the American proposition one which said to Russia, 'You, like ourselves, produce raw materials which Western Europe needs, and we shall be glad to examine together what contributions you as well as we could make.' This would mean that Russia would either have to decline or else agree to make a real contribution, herself, to the revival of the western European economy." [17]

Acheson's and Clayton's thoughts concorded. Their reasoning, as delineated by Jones was: ". . . that it would be a colossal error for the United States to put itself in a position where it could be blamed for the division of Europe. The psychological and political advantage of asking all Europeans to get together would disappear if we should divide Europe by offering to help rebuild only half of it. The problem, however, was a very difficult one. If the Russians came in the whole project would probably be unworkable because the amount of money involved in restoring both Eastern and Western Europe would be so great it could never be got from Congress, especially in view of the strong and growing reaction against the Soviet Union. But there was a strong probability that the U.S.S.R. would never come in on a basis of disclosing

[16] This account of Kennan's reckoning is derived from his *Memoirs*, pp. 339 ff.
[17] Goldman, *The Crucial Decade*, p. 74.

full information about their economic and financial condition, which was necessary if a common recovery plan were to work." [18]

Marshall decided to give the Russians the chance to contribute as well as to benefit, by providing raw materials in exchange for assistance. If they would not, the American Government should go ahead and let them exclude themselves.

The risk would be taken. But it was to be carefully safeguarded by the way in which Marshall's presentation was to be worded. It would call on each and any European participant to disclose its economic and financial situation, to define its needs, to subject its estimates of justified help to discussion, and to abide by the same principles and arrangements for mutual help as others.

The draft of the speech Marshall was going to make at the Harvard commencement exercises was completed during the first days of June. He rewrote the sentences defining the initiative which European countries were to be encouraged to take, and while flying to Cambridge again changed the language slightly.[19]

During the maturation of the proposal the initiative was not, as far as is known, systematically discussed with President Truman. Marshall, after his return from Europe in late April, had reported to him on the worrisome situation left at the end of the abortive conference of the Foreign Ministers; and he and Acheson had told him briefly of the plans which the State Department was developing. The President had permitted Marshall and Acheson to determine their range and content and to decide the way in which they would be put forward publicly. So great was Marshall's assurance that he did not deem it necessary to clear the

---

[18] Jones, *Fifteen Weeks*, pp. 252–3. Acheson's own account of his reasoning and of the discussion of this point is brief and ambiguous. "I (Acheson) pointed out that Russian obstruction in developing a European plan could be overcome by not requiring her agreement; what might be fatal to congressional support would be Russian support and demands. . . . The matter was left inconclusive." Acheson, *Present at the Creation*, p. 232.

[19] A letter that he wrote to Senator Vandenberg on June 4th, the day before he spoke in Cambridge, gives the stamp of his thought. Senator J. William Fulbright was then proposing a Resolution which could be construed as calling upon countries of Europe to accept American conceptions of the form of their cooperation. After expressing agreement with the purpose of the Resolution, he wrote: ". . . But we should make it clear that it is not our purpose to impose upon the peoples of Europe any particular form of political or economic association. The future organization of Europe must be determined by the peoples of Europe." *Documents on American Foreign Relations*, Vol. IX (World Peace Foundation: Boston, 1948), pp. 604–5.

Ernst Van der Beugel in his excellent study of the trend toward closer association in Europe, *From Marshall Aid to Atlantic Partnership: European Integration as a Concern of American Foreign Policy* (Amsterdam: Elsevier Publishing Co., 1966), pp. 103–4, contrasts interestingly Marshall's attitude and the tendency in Congress to attach more definite and fixed conditions to the extension of our aid.

text of his Harvard speech with Truman; and so great was Truman's confidence in Marshall that he did not request him to do so.[20]

On the afternoon of June 5th, Marshall read the speech, dryly, seldom looking up and at his audience. It sounded deceptively simple.[21] "The United States should do whatever it is able to do to assist in the return of normal economic health in the world, without which there can be no political stability and no assured peace. Our policy is directed not against any country or doctrine but against hunger, poverty, desperation, and chaos. Its purpose should be the revival of a working economy in the world so as to permit the emergence of political and social conditions in which free institutions can exist. Such assistance, I am convinced, must not be on a piece-meal basis as various crises develop. Any assistance that this government may render in the future should provide a cure rather than a mere palliative. Any government that is willing to assist in the task of recovery will find full cooperation, I am sure, on the part of the United States Government. Any government which manoeuvers to block the recovery of other countries cannot expect help from us. Furthermore, governments, political parties, or groups which seek to perpetuate human misery in order to profit therefrom politically or otherwise will encounter the opposition of the United States."

Following this exposition of our purpose, phrased so as to be both a bid and a warning to the Soviet Union, he continued: "It is already evident that, before the United States Government can proceed much further in its efforts to alleviate the situation and help start the European world on its way to recovery, there must be some agreement among the countries of Europe as to the requirements of the situation and the part those countries themselves will take in order to give proper effect to whatever action might be undertaken by this government. It would be neither fitting nor efficacious for this government to undertake to draw up unilaterally a program designed to place Europe on its feet economically. That is the business of the Europeans. The initiative, I think, must come from Europe. The role of this country should consist of friendly aid in the drafting of a European program and of later support of such a program so far as it may be practical for us to do so. The program should be a joint one, agreed to by a number, if not all, European nations."

[20] Truman, in *Years of Trial and Hope,* p. 114, the President, paying tribute to Marshall's achievements and character, wrote: "I had referred to the idea as the 'Marshall Plan' when it was discussed in staff meetings, because I wanted General Marshall to get full credit for his brilliant contributions to the measure which he helped formulate." This is a more subtle form of the remark of a leading political figure in Ireland during the struggle for home rule: "we pooled our brains and called it Parnell."

[21] For the text of Marshall's speech see Department of State *Bulletin,* June 15, 1947.

31

Marshall's Proposal: The Response

The Reception

Acheson briefed a few American reporters before Marshall's proposal was released. Moreover, being unsure of the speed in which Marshall's address—being a Commencement address—would be transmitted abroad through official channels, he confided in several British press correspondents. He told them that it would be of unusual importance and major intent, and that it merited urgent attention. They had telephoned the text to their editors with the suggestion that it be passed on at once to Bevin, so on the evening of the same day that Marshall spoke in Cambridge Bevin read the speech in London.

Bevin rejected a suggestion made by Sir William Strang, the Permanent Undersecretary of the Foreign Office, that the Chargé d'Affaires of the British Embassy in Washington be instructed to inquire of Marshall what he had in mind as the nature of the most suitable response. According to Acheson, Bevin answered, "Bill, we know what he *said*. If I ask questions you'll get answers you don't want. Our problem is what we *do*, not what he *meant*." [1] Bevin let Marshall know that the British Government would take the sort of initiative he commended. So did Bidault.

On June 17th Bevin flew to Paris for two days of talk with Bidault. The French Foreign Minister urged that Molotov be asked to join them. The French Government was insecure and worried about the internal situation; it needed the votes of those Socialist Deputies who favored cooperation with Moscow. Bevin was willing to ask the Soviet Government whether it would join in this preliminary consideration of the response to be made to Marshall. After Molotov expressed an interest, he was formally invited to join Bevin and Bidault in Paris for talks to begin

[1] Dean Acheson, *Sketches from Life of Men I Have Known* (New York: Harper, 1961), p. 2. Bevin had, some days before Marshall spoke, sent a message to him saying that in his opinion unless the United States framed a comprehensive policy they would soon find it would be too late. D. Donnelly, *Struggle for the World: The Cold War, 1917–1965* (London: Collins, 1966), p. 242.

on June 27th. Molotov accepted.[2]

In advance of the meeting of these three Foreign Ministers, Clayton went to London. Accompanied by our Ambassador to London, Lewis Douglas, he talked over with Bevin and his colleagues the procedure for developing a program of recovery for Europe and the nature of the program. The Americans reaffirmed that it must be a joint program and visualized a joint effort. Their ideas were not fixed or precise. Clayton's thoughts still strove to keep to the fore his favorite remedies for all ills —the reduction of trade restrictions and the releasing of currencies from control. But the British consultants argued that his analysis of the situation was too simple, that these measures alone could not save Europe then and there and would have to be taken gradually as conditions improved. The Chancellor of the Exchequer was, in particular, not pleased by Clayton's presence or ideas.[3] Dalton was fearful of the consequences of making sterling freely convertible, as Britain was pledged to do under the terms of the American loan.[4] Granting the need for gradualness, the Americans insisted that the program must evidence the interdependence of the participants and call forth the advantages of cooperation. The formulations at this stage did not, could not, deal in detail with the problems of adjustment of the national recipients to a master program.

Russia Rejects the Plan as Framed

The three Foreign Ministers met in Paris at the end of June.[5] Each day the British Foreign Office let the American Government know how their talks were going.

Bidault proposed they be guided by Marshall's statement that the countries of Europe should take the initiative and together reach a joint accord among themselves about the needs and the aims. In this program it would be expected that each would both help itself and the others. Molotov then suggested that the American Government be asked how

[2] When Bevin so informed the House of Commons, the news was cheered. *Parliamentary Debates*, House of Commons, June 23, 1947, cols. 35–36.

[3] In his Diary (June 27, 1947) he referred to Clayton as "Doctrinaire Willie."

[4] Britain, on July 15, 1947, made sterling freely convertible for current transactions. But after a five-week trial it was compelled to reimpose controls.

[5] The most systematic and complete record of their discussions is a publication of the Ministère des Affaires Étrangères of the French Government entitled *Documents de la Conférence des Ministres des Affaires Étrangères de la France, du Royaume Uni et de L'URSS tenue à Paris juin 27 au juillet 3, 1947* (Paris: Imprimerie National).

W. C. Mallalieu had made good use of it in the article he published in the *Political Science Quarterly*, December 1958, entitled "The Origin of the Marshall Plan: A Study in Policy Formation and National Leadership."

much it would give. Bevin demurred. He stubbornly maintained that the context of Marshall's statement made it clear that before answering this question the American Government would want to know what constructive joint plan the European governments themselves were able to conceive. By doing their best to help themselves not only individually but as a group, they could, he stressed, limit to a minimum the amount of aid they must ask of the United States.

At the next session (June 28th) Molotov insinuated that the American Government was activated by a wish to enlarge exports in view of the economic crisis he saw approaching in the United States. Then he strongly objected to the procedure whereby the European countries in conference would draw up a general economic program to which American help would be adjunct. Rather he urged that each country should continue as before to decide for itself the best ways to improve its condition. France and Britain, he said, each had its economic plan as did the Soviet Union, whose successive five-year plans were being realized and would assure constant increase in Soviet prosperity. Let each country, therefore, draw up its own statement of what it needed in the way of American aid. In conference thereafter, the European countries could consider the national statements and draw up a list of their total requirements and ascertain the possibility of getting such help from the United States. The Bidault-Bevin proposals would inevitably, he alleged, bring unwarranted outside interference with their national affairs. Moreover, the needs of those countries that had fought Germany and been occupied should have prior considerations and be the first group invited to take part in the prospective program. He was aggrieved because it was contemplated that Germany would be associated with the program, on the basis of information to be provided by the commanders of the four zones.

To this version of the answer to be made to Marshall, the Soviet officials clung. Russia was proudly maintaining the outward semblance of strength, although its people were in sore need of almost everything—food, clothing, housing, which was appallingly short, tools, transport. Food was so scarce because of the drought in the summer of 1946 that the Soviet Government had been compelled to continue bread rationing and to change its plans so as to give agriculture priority over heavy industry. But a good harvest in 1947 was in prospect, and enough reserve remained to carry over under strict control. Russia was defying its own wants, concealing its own deficiencies, rather than allowing itself to appear dependent on the bounty of capitalist United States. The use of men, materials, and machines for armaments was cramping; the Soviet Government was keeping the fear of war alive, so that its people should work hard, though weary and bewildered.[6]

Molotov grew more open in his accusations. On July 2d—the first day of their talks—he alleged that the British and French Governments were trying to use Marshall's proposal as a pretext to create a new organization which could interfere in the affairs of independent countries and direct their development.[7] The possibility of any country's securing an American credit, he argued, would be dependent on its "docile" conduct toward this organization and its Director.[8] As examples he said the suggested arrangement would enable them to bring pressure on Poland to produce more coal and retard the growth of other industries; on Czechoslovakia to increase its production of food and reduce its production of machines; or on Norway to give up plans to create a steel industry on the grounds that this would better suit certain foreign steel companies. In such ways a combined plan would be an invasion of the sovereignty of all and end their economic independence.

This appraisal ignored the fact that no country would be coerced to agree to features of the combined plan it thought unacceptable, or into joining in it. Each would be free to judge for itself whether the benefits obtained would not outweigh any adaptations required of it.

Behind Molotov's arguments could be detected unwillingness to subject the Russian economic situation and program to discussion.[9] But beyond that the Soviet spokesmen were posing as the defenders—against the American imperialists—of any of Russia's satellites who might be tempted to join in order to get American help (Poland, Czechoslovakia, and Hungary were tempted). He warned Bevin and Bidault that the participants in the combined program being considered would be separated from other European countries. Europe would be divided; one group would be opposed against another. This, he said, might seem advantageous to certain great powers (the United States) who wanted to

---

[6] See Edward Crankshaw's vivid and detailed account of the situation in his article "The U.S.S.R. Revisited," in *International Affairs*, October 1947.

[7] It may be surmised that a similar train of reasoning had caused the Soviet Union to refuse the year before membership in the International Bank for Reconstruction and Development and the International Monetary Fund, though Soviet technicians had been present at the Bretton Woods Conference which created them.

[8] The tenor of the Soviet view, as publicly imparted to and through various Soviet publications, is exemplified by the editorial in the *New Times* of July 4, 1947. This alleged that the British-French proposals would deprive other countries of their economic independence and impair their national sovereignty. "France and Great Britain would be bailiffs of the transatlantic master. This would enable the United States to avoid the crisis looming more and more clearly."

[9] Certainly the Soviet Government would never have been willing to meet the requirements which Congress stipulated, when ultimately it passed the ECA Act, should be in the bilateral aid agreements which the American Government was to enter into with each recipient. For example, the stipulation about the setting aside of "counterpart" funds described later in this chapter.

dominate others.

Milovan Djilas, an emissary of Tito's, was in Paris at the time. In his book *Conversations with Stalin,* he offers an explanation of why Molotov during the previous days had appeared to be considering some kind of compromise procedure. Djilas states that Molotov told him that the Soviet Government was going to refuse to join the conference which was being proposed and that he, Djilas, said Yugoslavia would also do so. But Molotov was turning over another tactic in his mind. He was wondering ". . . whether a conference should not be called in which the Eastern countries would also participate, but only for propaganda reasons, with the aim of exploiting the publicity and then walking out of the conference at a convenient moment. I was not enthusiastic about this variation either, though I would not have opposed it had the Russians insisted. . . . However, Molotov received a message from the Politburo in Moscow that he should not agree even to this." There are corroboratory accounts of the receipt of a message which agitated Molotov and instructed him to cease discussion of Russian participation.[10]

There was in Molotov's demeanor and response, as there had been in so many of the Communist denunciations of the United States, a *jealous* rage. The U.S. could offer what the Soviet Union could not.

The Other European Countries Go Ahead

Despite Molotov's dissent the British and French Governments invited all European governments except Spain, Germany, and the Soviet Union to send delegates to a conference on European cooperation. The governments of Poland, Czechoslovakia, and Hungary, being greatly in need of dollars, manifested a wish to attend that conference,[11] but Moscow pulled the reins and they reared back.

The Communist parties in Western Europe violently denounced, as they distorted, Marshall's proposal. Palmiro Togliatti, the Secretary of the large Italian Communist Party, called upon its members to rise against "enslavement." The French Communists rioted in Paris and industrial centers, and they shut down the railways and many industries by protest strikes. But the police—the blasé Paris police—contained the riots, and the strikers went back to their jobs.

[10] Milovan Djilas, *Conversations with Stalin* (New York: Harcourt, 1962), p. 128. Phillips, in his book *The Truman Presidency,* p. 185, gives a detailed account of the scene without identifying the witness whose description was presumably the source.

[11] The initial decision to participate was taken, I believe, with the approval of the Communist members of the Czechoslovak government—a coalition of four parties. For further details see André Fontaine, *History of the Cold War: From the October Revolution to the Korean War, 1917–1950* (New York: Pantheon, 1968), pp. 329–330.

The State Department hurried Clayton to Paris to discuss with the British and French organizers of the large conference in prospect the sort and substance of a "constructive program" which the American Government could be counted on to support. There and then Clayton cast off one of the principles of international trade which the American Government had hitherto insisted was essential to beneficial and amicable relations between countries—the rule of equality of trade treatment for all countries. Now Clayton let it be known that if the participants in a joint plan should form a regional preferential tariff arrangement, which reduced restrictions on trade between them, the American Government would not object. In fact in the course of his discussions he insisted upon it. Moreover he conveyed word that the American Government thought in order to facilitate trade they would have to form a regional monetary clearing system among themselves. No longer were American officials insisting on the rule of immediate universal currency convertibility.

The way having been lighted, representatives of sixteen European countries which accepted the invitation met on July 12th to formulate the joint response for which Marshall had called (alphabetically: Austria, Belgium, Denmark, France, Greece, Iceland, Ireland, Italy, Luxembourg, the Netherlands, Norway, Portugal, Sweden, Switzerland, Turkey, and the United Kingdom). Sir Oliver Franks was chairman of the Executive Committee of the group.

Each country was asked to submit detailed estimates. What would it undertake to try to produce; what could it export and what would it need to import; what kind and amounts of help could the countries give each other; thus the anticipated deficit of dollars needed to assure European economic revival would be arrived at. Harder still to foretell, what improvement could be achieved during the next few years?

The French were difficult and ambivalent, as they had been time and time again since the end of the war. They wanted help. But they also still wanted to be assured that Germany would be kept weak, that German industrial capacity would be permanently limited, and that the Ruhr region would be put under international control. Still they yielded in some degree to the American and British insistence that German coal and steel production must be increased for the fulfillment of the whole program. Jean Monnet, working along with Sir Oliver Franks, was, as always, constructive and conductive.

During the deliberations of this large group various American officials appeared and met with the Executive Committee. Sir Oliver Franks found the advice of the American Ambassador in London, Lewis Douglas, helpful, the comments of the American Ambassador in Paris, Jefferson Caffery, enigmatic but to the point, and those of Clayton difficult and so persistent that toward the end Franks felt compelled to tell Clayton flatly the group could not discuss his objections further.[12]

The preliminary estimate of the total need for dollars proposed by one of the technical committees shocked the American intermediaries: twenty-nine billion. Clayton insisted that they thoroughly recast their estimate, and contemplate far more definite and extensive mutual aid.

The American consultants stressed the fact that American cooperation was based on the assumption that the participating countries must, at the end of four years, be self-supporting and have balanced their external accounts. Their determined insistence did bring each and all the conferees to set targets for their performance which, if realized, would bring this about. To do so they would have to make good use of American funds to attain monetary and fiscal solvency.

The Americans also urged the creation of a joint permanent organization which should receive, examine, and distribute reports on the current performance of each country, the steps taken by each in the realm of trade, budget, and monetary policies and the use made of American aid received. Sir Oliver Franks was afraid that some of the governments which were ready to participate would refuse to agree to this stipulation, which would mean "each would be looking into its neighbor's back yard." After hesitation, and a pause in the Conference to permit the representatives to consult their governments, all assented. Thus the Organization for European Economic Cooperation (OEEC) was brought into existence; this was to be joined later by the United States and Canada.

The jointly conceived program contained in the Final Report of this Committee was signed at the Quai D'Orsay on September 22, 1947, at a session over which Bevin presided.

The Jointly Conceived Program, Summarily Described

Cool analytical descriptions of its contents are contained in several thorough studies of the Marshall Plan.[13] In brief, the vivid description in

[12] As remembered by Franks and told to the author. Though Franks found Douglas helpful, Bevin was frequently annoyed with him. The Foreign Secretary was displeased with the frequency with which Douglas dined in the House of Commons and the forthrightness of his opinions. In particular he was displeased because Douglas was openly pooh-poohing the idea of nationalizing (socializing) the Ruhr mines and predicting it would result in bankruptcy which the U.S. would have to step in to prevent. Entry Dalton Diary, July 29, 1947.

[13] Three analyses I have found most informative are Ernst Van der Beugel's *From Marshall Aid to Atlantic Partnership;* William Diebold's *Trade and Payments in Western Europe: A Study in Economic Co-operation, 1947–1951* (New York: Harper, 1952); and Harry Bayard Price's *The Marshall Plan and Its Meaning* (Ithaca: Cornell University Press, 1955).

the report made by the Sixteen-member group of the state and prospects of Western Europe confirmed the reports that had been made by American informants. One major paragraph will suffice to convey its import: "One country after another is already being forced by lack of dollars to cut down vital imports of food and raw materials from the American continent. If nothing is done a catastrophe will develop as stocks become exhausted. If too little is done, and if it is done too late, it will be impossible to provide the momentum needed to get the program under way. Life in Europe will become increasingly unstable and uncertain; industries will grind to a gradual halt for lack of materials and fuel, and the food supply of Europe will diminish and begin to disappear." [14]

The remedies suggested were broad rather than detailed. The report did not state or define precisely the end uses of American aid. It expressed the earnest intention of the sponsoring authorities to help one another, but it did not contain any conclusive arrangements for cooperation or plans for allocation of activity between nations.

American officials in subsequent discussions with Franks and some of his colleagues, tried to convince the Committee that the program in mind called for a fuller use of existing European productive capacity; that it should indicate more clearly whether and how national plans would be correlated; and that it should also provide that if necessary participants would allocate food and industrial products in short supply. Also the program should specify that the commitment to reduce trade barriers, form a regional clearing system, and be soberly correct in their public finance should be firmer. The Americans succeeded by their insistence in getting the sixteen European sponsors of the accord to heed these injunctions in some measure.

Very useful in securing congressional assent to the program was the provision insisted on by the American negotiators that the American Government was to retain the right to approve the use of the "counterpart" local funds which were to be set aside by recipient governments who secured income from the sale of products provided by the United States.[15]

[14] The text of this first report of the Sixteen-member group is contained in the *General Report of the Committee of European Economic Cooperation* published by the State Department, 1947, Vol. 1, page 60.

[15] In Section 115(b) of the Foreign Assistance Act of April 1948, Congress set down the principles and provisions to which, in bilateral agreements to be entered into with the American Government, the recipients should subscribe as far as they were applicable. Among these was a provision for deposit in special accounts of local currencies (called "counterpart funds") equivalent to commodities or services furnished as grants. These were to be used, with the concurrence of the American representatives of the Marshall Plan administration, to finance domestic recovery, except for a reserved five percent available to meet American administrative and procurement expenses.

The American Follow-Through

President Truman and all the members of his Cabinet braced themselves for a strenuous effort at persuading Congress and the American people to sponsor and approve the proposed program. Every effort was made to impress them with its soundness and necessity; of its economical nature and political advisability. Committees of respected experts, businessmen, and bankers were formed to examine American ability to provide the needed resources and to explain that in the long run American conditions would be helped, not hurt, by the program's effectuation. Their reports were convincing and influential.

During the autumn of 1947, pending congressional approval of the whole program (which was not given until early 1948), the Chief Executive found it necessary to plead for large allotments of interim aid for France, Italy, and Austria, in order to carry them through the winter.

Legislation for the more comprehensive program was finally put before Congress on December 19th, six months after Marshall first made his proposal. In a special message to Congress, President Truman incised the main purpose gravely. He asked Congress to authorize in support of the European Recovery Program an appropriation of seventeen billion dollars from April 1, 1948, to June 30, 1952. "In providing aid to Europe," he concluded, "we must share more than goods and funds. . . . We must develop a feeling of teamwork in our common cause of combatting the suspicions, prejudices, and fabrications which undermine cooperative effort, both at home and abroad."

On the floor of Congress and on public platforms two groups tried hard to prevent the passage of the bill authorizing the inauguration of the Marshall Plan. One, mainly conservative, led by Senator Taft, condemned the proposal as financially perilous, tainted by welfarism, bringing us into evil association with Socialists, ignoring the greater danger in the Far East—and futile. The other group were of the radical left who denounced it as aggressive and as likely to lead to war. Henry Wallace, who had condemned Truman's statement of policy in the Greek-Turkish crisis as too negative and bellicose, opposed this proposal for peaceful economic aid as provocative and stimulating a dangerous division in Europe—since the Soviet Government and its satellites were not embraced in it.

In overcoming objections the exertions of Senator Vandenberg, Republican Chairman of the Foreign Relations Committee were invaluable. By his enthusiastic endorsement of Marshall's reasons for engaging in these costly programs, he convinced some; by flaunting quotations from *Izvestia* and *Pravda,* he moved others; but most important of all, by his patient reception of proposals for amendment, and by a manifest wish to make sure this was not just another spending program which would not bring a lasting corrective, he persuaded skeptics in the Senate.

Almost all members of Congress were brought to favor the program. In the prevalent mood of crisis they were willing to forego the tax reductions which they had hoped to promise the American people in the coming election campaigns. Still the debate, prolonged as it was, might have gone on still longer, and tactics of delay might have been tolerated longer, if—as will be told—the quarrel about Germany had not become overwrought, and if the Communists had not crushed freedom and democracy in Czechoslovakia.

32

Connectedly: What Was To Be Done About China?

Amid the polemics about aid to Greece and Turkey and the Marshall Plan, the President was dogged by demands that the United States give help of a similar kind and scope to the National Government of China. Some proponents had urged merely that generous loans be granted and that shipments of arms and munitions be hastened and increased. Others had advocated the assignment of large groups of American military advisers. The most excited pleaders wanted American combat troops and planes to take up the fight against the Chinese Communists. Among the advocates of one or the other of these types were some American military men like General Claire Chennault who had fought for Chiang Kai-shek; some diplomats like Ambassador William Bullitt; some commercial interests; and a coterie whom Madame Chiang Kai-shek had entranced. She was not yet aware that her sortilege was being critically judged.[1]

But best able to put the government on the defensive were the Republican party leaders and spokesmen, among them Senators Arthur Vandenberg and Styles Bridges, Chairman of the Appropriations Committee; Governor Thomas E. Dewey of New York, presumptive Republican nominee for the Presidency; and John Foster Dulles, the presumptive Secretary of State if the Republicans won.

These formed a formidable and noisy combination. The logic of President Truman's political rhetoric in his address of March 12th seemed to run with their arguments. If the Greek and Turkish Governments could be regarded as "free" nations, could not the National Government of China, especially since Chiang Kai-shek was promising to yield power to a popularly elected constitutional assembly and government?

But Truman stood out against expansion of our largesse to Chiang

[1] Joseph Alsop, the arrogant columnist, was the foremost advocate in the press of American intervention in China.

Kai-shek and/or the protection to his menaced regime. Marshall and Acheson maintained sturdily and with agility that it would be unwise, and probably futile, to do so. Truman could feel secure in his resistance because the cautionary admonition of the Joint Chiefs of Staff not to become involved in the morass of the Chinese civil war, conjoined with his other reasons.

This resolve not to back our sympathy with great loans, or more arms, or men, was imprinted by recent experience. Marshall, just before his appointment as Secretary of State, had spent a year in China, trying to bring the civil strife to an end by arranging first a truce, then some sort of political coalition between the National Government and the Communists. For the failure of his endeavor he held the National Government as responsible as the Communists. Chiang Kai-shek had been headstrong, and his regime had been shown to be incapable of unifying and ruling the country. Thus, Marshall and Acheson had reached the conclusion that the causes of the plight of the National Government could not be corrected merely by providing American aid. How could it, since Chiang Kai-shek's direction of the war against the Communists was poor and self-serving, and his strategy reckless when it was not stationary?

How could American aid transform his civil administration, which was tottering, corrupt, and unable to achieve betterment of the miserable condition of the Chinese people and armies? To do so, drastic, even revolutionary, reforms were essential. These the elements dominant in the councils of the National Government would not consider. Yet, virtually all American observers agreed that the National Government could only retain the support needed to combat the Communists by correcting the system of land ownership and tenancy, changing the control of banking and finance, reforming from top to bottom the administration of cities, and choosing military commanders by the rule of merit rather than personal loyalty. Even though the United States, when providing the requested military and financial support, might secure promises that these reforms would be made, it was deemed unlikely that the National Government could or would carry them out effectively.

Thus, would it not be foolhardy to engage in a costly campaign in order to sustain Chiang Kai-shek's poorly directed efforts to win? Was it not more sensible to let the struggle in China take its course, while waiting and watching for a possible chance to try again to bring the contestants together by using our resources? Patient detachment might cause the Nationalist Government to become readier to compromise with the Communists, and the wish for American help might induce the Communists to accept a place in a coalition. Such was the political reckoning. Our policy was also somewhat affected by the impression that if worse came to worst, and the Communists became dominant in China, the United States could get along with them, not comfortably or closely but acceptably.

The American decision-makers had still another reason in mind for not linking the American Government too closely with the National Government of China. Both the American and Soviet Governments were still, in 1947, maintaining the pretense that they were pursuing the same policy toward China: to wit, while recognizing formally that the National Government was the government of China, they would refrain from interfering in the internal struggle[2] Was the United States to step forward openly as a supporting partisan, would it not provoke the Russians to uphold and aid the Chinese Communists or at least give them an excellent pretext for doing so? [3] Then, would it not find itself in an outright struggle with the Soviet Union in a contest it did not relish?

Such were the several reasons which the records bespeak why— against the lashing complaints of Chiang Kai-shek's supporters in the United States and the prophets of disaster should the Communists win —Truman and his advisers steadfastly held to the position explained in the statement which the President had issued the previous December, reviewing our past efforts to aid and unify China. After restating his intention of remaining out of the Chinese morass, Truman had said: "China is a sovereign nation. We recognize that fact and we recognize the National Government of China. We continue to hope that the Government will find a peaceful solution. We are pledged not to interfere in the internal affairs of China . . . While avoiding involvement in their civil strife, we will persevere with our policy of helping the Chinese people to bring about peace and economic recovery in their country. As ways and means are presented for constructive aid to China, we will give them careful and sympathetic consideration." [4]

Still, in May 1947, in response to pressure in Congress, the President lifted the embargo on shipments of war materials to China. Then in

[2] For an account of Russian expositions of policy toward the Chinese civil war and its actions, see Herbert Feis, *The China Tangle: The American Effort in China from Pearl Harbor to the Marshall Mission* (Princeton, N.J.: Princeton University Press, 1953).

[3] The Soviet authorities had been noncommittal about Marshall's mission and about its failure. But critical analyses in the Soviet press of the faults and weaknesses of the National Government were by the Spring-Summer of 1947 becoming more frequent and blatant.

[4] Statement, December 18, 1946. State Department *Bulletin,* December 29, 1946. After reviewing Marshall's effort to end the civil war, the President had told reporters that Marshall would stay in China as long as necessary. In fact his return and acceptance of office of Secretary of State had already been arranged. Within two weeks Marshall's nomination had been sent to the Senate.

early July he sent General Albert C. Wedemeyer to China to get a fresh appraisal of the situation. Wedemeyer had been chosen for the task although he was known to be in close touch and accord with opponents of our current policy. His coming aroused hopes in Peking of quick and substantial economic and military help against the Communists. But, in blunter language than ever used by Marshall, he told Chiang Kai-shek that in order to regain the confidence of the Chinese people, the government would have to effect drastic economic and political reforms; that promises would no longer suffice, only performance would count.

Yet, upon his return to Washington in September, Wedemeyer advocated that the American Government should intervene actively in the civil war without waiting for the National Government to take measures that might arrest the revolutionary triumph. He reported to Truman that the advance of the Chinese Communists was gravely menacing the American situation and interests in the Far East; that a China controlled by Communists would be actively hostile to the United States and opposed to principles regarded as vital to peace. Therefore the General proposed that the American Government should give "sufficient and prompt military assistance" to the National Government. This, he advised, should be extended through American military advisers; the scope of their counsel and supervision, he thought, should be extended to include field forces, training centers, and particularly logistical agencies (those resorts of corruption and defection), and to be the contact with tactical forces outside of operational areas. He held back from recommending use of American combat forces in battle.[5]

The idea that these measures could be taken without engaging the United States more deeply if they did not suceed was either naïve or deceiving. In any event, Truman, again counseled by Marshall and Acheson, did not act on the recommendation. As succinctly reaffirmed by Marshall in testimony before the Senate Foreign Relations Committee on November 11th: "An attempt to underwrite the Chinese economy and the Chinese Government's efforts will result in a burden on the United States economy and a military responsibility which I cannot recommend as a course of action for this government."[6]

Largely to appease critics, a relatively small program of relief and rehabilitation of China, separate from that of the Marshall Plan for Eu-

[5] On leaving China on August 24th, Wedemeyer issued a statement criticizing both the Kuomintang and the Communists. He said, after stating that to regain public confidence Chiang Kai-shek would have to eliminate many corrupt and incompetent officials, that force alone would not eliminate Communism in China. *United States Relations With China* (Department of State Publication 3573) pp. 763 ff.

Wedemeyer's report to the President of September 1947, on his mission, was suppressed by the State Department on the score that it contained information the disclosures of which would be harmful to the interest of the countries concerned, including the United States. But it was published later (1949) in *ibid.*, pp. 764 ff.

[6] Hearings, Senate Committee on Foreign Relations, November 11, 1947.

rope, and for the provision of military supplies, was submitted to Congress and approved.[7]

In later years Truman and his advisers were compelled to defend themselves against ferocious accusations that their refusal to give Chiang Kai-shek much greater financial and military support was responsible for his rout. They contested these charges with distended estimates of the monetary value of what the American Government had provided.[8] They stressed the opinion that American military intervention of the scope and magnitude required to try to save a decayed regime and defeat the Communists would have been enormous, that it probably would have failed in its purpose, and that it would have been condemned by the American people.

The defense was succinctly summed up by Acheson in his introduction to the collected documents known as the China White Paper. "Nothing that this country did or could have done within the reasonable limits of its capabilities could have changed that result; nothing that was left undone by this country has contributed to it." [9]

The only real lost diplomatic chance that I can spot in the record was to have insisted in 1945–1946 that Chiang Kai-shek accept a division of China and reform his regime so that it might have been able to retain control of and govern the portion which the National Government could control.

As remarked at the time by Professor John K. Fairbank of Harvard University, "It is not within the power of the American people to bestow the Mandate of Heaven."

To remind, these summary notations have as their purpose to indicate how the American Government in its China policy stopped short in its efforts to apply the Truman Doctrine and the Marshall program. Thereby the United States thought to avoid extension of its clash with the Soviet Union on the Asian mainland. And, such is the ironic twirl of events, that when Chinese Communists triumphed in China, there was rejoicing in Moscow. But Russia soon had as much reason to regret and fear Communist rule in China, as does the United States.

In these incidental notations on the omission of China from the Marshall program, I have sallied past one other main elevation of the contemporary landscape: how the Communists assailed the program in Europe and tried their utmost to cause it to fail.

[7] Truman's message to Congress February 18, 1948, recommending an aid program for China in the amount of 570 million dollars.
[8] See Tang Tsou, *America's Failure in China: 1941–1950* (Chicago: University of Chicago Press, 1963), chap. XII.
[9] *United States Relations with China*, p. XVI.

33

The Communist Assault upon
the Marshall Program

The Soviet authorities and their Communist allies plotted to offset the operation of the Marshall Plan program by denouncing it and by fomenting social disorder. Bevies of propaganda agents strove to convince the workers of western Europe that the program was a cunning way of enslaving them to American imperialists. The comment of the editors of the *New Times* after the publication of the report of the Committee of Sixteen was characteristic: "All the many months of fuss and commotion over the Marshall Plan bids fair to end in a ludicrous farce. . . . to see the rulers of the West European countries lying prostrate before the dollar is a pitiable spectacle." [1]

The Communist parties in France and Italy launched intense campaigns of hindrance and vilification. In France strikes in one branch of industry after another occurred. The workers responded to the calls of their leaders because their conditions of work were bad, their wages too small for decent living, their food poor, and all too often, employment unsteady. Yet withal, the agitators did not dare to tell their followers explicitly that the American aid which might be had should be refused.

The coalition government under Ramadier calmly stood up and held out. It proceeded during the summer and autumn with negotiations first for emergency American assistance (over 300 million dollars) which enabled France to avoid more severe food rationing, to procure essential supplies of oil and coal, and thereafter to go ahead with the national economic plan which had been formulated under the guidance of Jean Monnet.[2] In the wings, ready to try to take over again if the turbulence

---

[1] The *New Times*, October 1, 1947.

[2] Congress did not actually vote funds for this emergency three-country program until December 1947, but the prospect of receiving this help enabled the French Government to dispense with restrictive actions and deal with shortages in the most critical earlier months.

led to impotence, Charles de Gaulle waited, having created his party—the Rassemblement du Peuple Français.

This Communist attempt to keep the French economy down and broken continued far into the autumn of 1947. The Communist trade union and political heads were seen and heard day and night, leading aroused workers in street demonstrations and riots. The government, as a mark of its determination, called up troop reserves for duty, to guard against sabotage and put down street riots. Unreliable police officers were dismissed. The printing plates of Communist newspapers *L'Humanité* and *Ce Soir*, which were going to publish orders for Communist mobilization, were seized. Almost three million workers were idled by work stoppages. The Communist-led General Confederation of Labor ordered a general strike; those trade unions which were not Communist did not participate. Because the railway workers were on strike, the coal reserves of the companies supplying the Paris region were almost used up, and if they were not quickly replenished not only would all households suffer, but many other industries in the area would be compelled to close down. In short, at the end of November, the most critical time since the pinched spring of the year, the economy of industrial France was stricken, and its political structure endangered.

The large contingent of Communist members in the Chamber of Deputies disrupted its sessions abusingly. Finally, the dissenters, including de Gaulle's supporters, succeeded in causing the Ramadier Cabinet to admit it could no longer govern. But, while strikes still raged in Paris and in the provinces, the center political parties reasserted themselves; they elected the superior Robert Schuman as Prime Minister. The Communists gave way; their leaders thought the strikers were "running out of breath" and that if the strikes were not ended, the members of the trade unions would be divided, and the avant-garde of the working class be isolated. Thereafter the efforts of the French Communists to frustrate the Marshall Plan straggled out, or rather took other forms and used other means.

Schuman was to become, during his months as Prime Minister (November 1947 to July 1948) and his almost continuous service as Foreign Minister thereafter, the stabilizing leader in French politics. He was the creative and effective sponsor who abandoned constricting foreign policies shaped by fear and hatred for one guided by a vision of a United Europe in which France and Germany would cooperate. His emergence at this time, along with Alcide de Gasperi's leadership in Italy and Konrad Adenauer's in Germany, is one of the rare wholesome and healing coincidences of history.

Acheson gives a lucid impression of the man and the treacherous crosscurrents amidst which he had to make way. "Schuman, slender, stooped, bald, with long nose, surprised and shy eyes and smile, might have been a painter, musician, or scholar rather than a lawyer, member of parliament, former Premier of France . . . He had grown up and been educated for the law in Metz under German rule, was an intellectual, and broadly read in both French and German literature. His humor was quick, gentle, and ironic . . . The Quai D'Orsay did not give Schuman the support that Bevin got from the Foreign Office. It was deeply divided by strong personalities. . . . This made for delays in negotiation with Schuman, who continually had to watch his flanks and rear and his communications with Paris." [3] What he did, had to be done despite furious opposition of the Communists on the left and Gaullists on the right.

In Italy the Communists, and the trade unions they could control or influence, similarly struck and rioted, but with less turmoil and revolutionary fervor. They wished to keep on working terms with the more moderate Left, in the hope that at the coming elections a coalition dominated by Communists might then win a majority. Then and thus they might secure the power and right to govern Italy. They might lose this chance if they alienated too many of the workers who, despite all Communist propaganda, relished American help to provide jobs, raise wages, and enable them to eat better. Most Italians take a practical view of life and problems of daily existence! They also had to reckon with the possibility that the American Government was not likely to remain passive if a revolution was attempted.

The dilemma of the French and Italian Communist parties during this crucial period in which the alignment of their countries was at issue was made the sharper because they were being incited and harshly reproved for their "timidity" by the spokesmen of the Communists of the Soviet Union, Yugoslavia, and other Communist countries in eastern Europe.

During the week of September 21 to 28, 1947, the Soviet Government called together in the castle of Szklarska Poreba (Goering's hunting lodge) in the former German Lower Silesia, a most secret conference of representatives of nine European Communist parties—the cluster of seven in the East and the French and Italian parties. The purposes of meeting were dual—to rouse all to do their utmost to prevent the recovery of the economy of their countries under capitalism and, by reprimand, to cause the French and Italian Communist parties to act more combatively.[4]

[3] Acheson, *Present at the Creation*, p. 271.

[4] The most enlightening account of the addresses and discussions during the conference is one which Eugenio Reale, then a leading official of the Italian Communist Party but who later left it, gave in his book entitled *Avec Jacques Duclos: au banc des accusés*, trans. Pierre Bonuzzi (Paris: Plon, 1958). Reale, who was at the confer-

The head Soviet representative, Andrei Zhdanov, a member of the Politburo, in his opening address—which was in effect the directing text of the Conference—charged that the imperialist camp led by American monopoly capital wished to dominate all Europe, if not the world, and it was preparing for war to achieve that purpose. He called upon all Communist parties to struggle against these plans of zealous imperialist politicians in the United States and Britain. Against them the Socialist camp led by the Soviet Union, including the champions of peace and democracy everywhere in the world, must struggle harder than ever.

Zhdanov was abetted by the Yugoslavian representatives, Milovan Djilas and Vice-Premier Edvard Kardelj. Yugoslavia was still bitterly at odds with Italy about the control of territory in and around Trieste, and it was aggrieved because the Italian Government was not helping the rebels in Greece. In their discourses the criticisms of the failure of the French and Italian Communist parties to wreck the economies and the political systems of their countries burst forth. By their faltering and erroneous respect for parliamentary institutions, these accusers shouted, capitalism was being permitted to survive in Western Europe, and the American Government was enabled to gather these capitalist countries in a combination hostile to the Soviet Union.

The dominant theme of the Conference's conclusions is conveyed in the Manifesto issued. A few brief extracts will indicate how acrid the separation between the Western democracies and the Soviet Union was becoming.

"In as much as the USSR and the countries of the new democracy become obstacles to the realization of the imperialist plans of struggle for world domination, a crusade was proclaimed against the USSR and the countries of the new democracy, bolstered also by threats of a new war on the part of the most zealous imperialist politicians in the U.S.A. and Britain. . . . The Truman-Marshall plan is only a constituent part, the European sub-section of the general plan for the policy of global expansion pursued by the United States in all parts of the world . . .

"A special place in the imperialists' arsenal of tactical weapons is occupied by the utilization of the treacherous policy of the right wing Socialists like Blum in France, Attlee and Bevin in Britain, Schumacher in Germany, Renner and Schaerf in Austria, Saragat in Italy, etc., who strive to cover up the true rapacious essence of imperialist policy under a mask of democracy and Socialist phraseology, while actually being in all respects faithful accomplices of the imperialists, sowing dissension in the ranks of the working class and poisoning its mind." [5]

ence, kept comprehensive notes and memos of the addresses, and his interpretations are the more illuminating because of his familiarity with the Communist viewpoint and the status of the various Communist parties at the time.

[5] *Pravda*, October 8, 1947.

Thus in the Resolution passed, the participants in the Conference agreed "To charge the Information Bureau [Cominform] with the organization of interchange of experience, and if need be, coordination of the activities of the Communist Parties on the basis of mutual agreement." [6] This was to have its center in Belgrade.

The Communist Party of East Germany had not been invited to participate in this conclave. Whether this was because of a wish to preserve the impression that the Soviet Union might be willing to see this party subordinated in a unified Germany, or because most of the nations represented still did not want to consort with any Germans—even German Communists—or because of mistrust is not to be known.

The anger and anxiety in the Soviet effusions about the Marshall Plan were enhanced by knowledge that the Western occupying powers were going forward with plans to rebuild West German economic strength and to include that country in the concerted surge of the Marshall Plan.

[6] *Ibid.*

PART NINE

The Fateful Spring
of 1947 —
East and West

34

To Resuscitate Germany

The opinion that Germany should be encouraged and, as needed, assisted, to revive its economy and trade, had won its way during the winter of hardship—1946-47.

During the meeting of the Council of Foreign Ministers in March–April, at which the Western and Soviet occupants of Germany foiled each other, Marshall and Bevin had been in favor of relaxing measurably the restraints on the German economy.

This purpose had quickly hardened into a resolve. Truman had almost made up his mind.[1] So had Attlee. Although the British were glum at the prospect of a revival of German industrial activity, they were impelled by the need to lessen the drain on Britain's shrinking supply of dollars. The Foreign Secretary's somber mood is reflected in a remark he made to Hugh Dalton not long before; he "thought the Germans were much more dangerous than the Russians [but] . . . before long everybody would be courting them."[2] After Bevin related to the House of Commons on May 15th what had happened at the Moscow Conference, and after he had explained his dilemma, Eden spoke up for the Conservative Opposition, endorsing Bevin's impressions, saying: "I believe that the hope of success in the future lies . . . in admitting frankly that the Conference was a failure . . . and . . . by taking, immediately, what steps we can to prevent any further deterioration of the situation. . . .

---

[1] President Truman had asked former President Herbert Hoover to study the situation. The conclusion contained in his report which had been released on March 23, 1947, was that " . . . The whole economy of Europe is interlinked with German economy through the exchange of raw materials and manufactured goods. The productivity of Europe cannot be restored without the restoration of Germany as a contributor to that productivity." *The President's Economic Mission to Germany and Austria,* Report No. 3, by Herbert Hoover, March 18, 1947, p. 2. This judgment was generally accepted and approved by the American press, which only two years before had warmly approved the Roosevelt-Truman view that Germany should never again be permitted to recreate its strong economy or its heavy industries which made it so formidable a factor in world trade and sustained its war preparations and effort.

[2] Dalton Diary, January 17, 1947.

The next six months may well be decisive, not only for the economic recovery of this country, but for Europe, and particularly for Germany. . . . It is clear that there is not going to be an agreed Allied solution of Germany's economic problems before this coming winter [1947-48]. . . . Therefore, it is essential that we and our American friends should take the necessary steps to restore the economic life in our two zones, in the closest possible contact with our French Allies."[3] Only Left-wing Laborites were against changing course.

The Dutch were also, by then, wanting German economic activity to thrive; they were unhappy about the great decline in movement into and out of the port of Amsterdam, as were the Belgians over the stagnation of the port of Antwerp. Norwegian shipping interests and sailors wanted German trade to revive, and Swedish iron ore miners and the Swiss lamented because some great power plants that had supplied electricity for Germany were idle.[4]

The formulators of the Marshall program had definitely contemplated that Germany should be included as both a contributor and a beneficiary. Bidault, in his opening statement at the preliminary conference with Bevin and Molotov in June-July, said: "It is indeed evident that it is impossible for us to think of a collective European program which does not include Germany. But, it will be said, the reconstruction of Germany poses all the questions upon which the Council of Foreign Ministers has not yet been able to agree: the level of German industry, reparations, and the regime for the Ruhr. We cannot deny that this is difficult. But I think the first 'rapport European' that we wish to bring about should not prejudice our decision regarding the definitive status of Germany."[5] Even French animosity was beginning to yield to cold and consternation.

The economic fusion of the American and British zones had gone formally into effect (June 10th). The new agreement had provided that the economic affairs of the combined zones should be administered by an Economic Council and an Executive Committee, chosen by the Landtag

[3] *Parliamentary Debates*, House of Commons, May 15, 1947.

[4] William Manchester, in *The Arms of Krupp, 1587–1968* (Boston: Little, Brown, 1968), p. 666, gives a vivid summary of the facts and circumstances that contributed to the decision to encourage German economic revival. He also reflects brightly upon the "economic miracle" in Germany between 1945 and 1950, remarking in summary that 4 billion dollars of American aid was, of course, an important help, but that while the recovery was due to many causes, "One, beyond question, was the powerful Teutonic urge to dominate the Continent. Germans had always been born toilers, and now they drove themselves harder than ever."

[5] Statement made on June 27, 1947. *Documents de la Conférence des Ministres des Affaires Étrangères de la France, du Royaume Uni et de L'URSS, tenue à Paris 27 juin–3 juillet 1947.*

(the legislative body of the two zones). These were to be under the supervision of a U.S.-British Bipartite Board, appointed by the two Commanders-in-Chief, and was not to be subordinate to the Four-Power Control Council in Berlin.

In the first week in June, the Prime Minister of Bavaria, encouraged by American and British authorities, convoked a conference of the Ministers-Presidents of all four zones. At first those of the states in the Soviet zone refused the invitation; then they came and proposed that a central German Government be formed with the cooperation of all "democratic" parties and trade unions. Since the others rejected this proposal they departed, leaving representatives of the states in the Western zones to discuss ways and means to increase productivity and improve living conditions in their states by concerted action. This gave impetus to American and British measures to stimulate production in the Ruhr by increasing imports of food and raw materials, by providing equipment for mines and transport, and promising bonuses for increased output.

By July 10th Washington was able to advise Clay that agreement had been reached in the Committee of Sixteen for the Marshall Plan that Germany would have a vital part in the program for Europe, but cautioned him against letting this appear to have been the result of American initiative. The American Government was willing to increase its contribution toward payment of imports into Germany to enable it to increase exports of essentials such as coal and chemicals to other participants. In the preliminary combined program presented in July to the American Government, this planning group affirmed that Germany was to have a significant place in the collective effort.[6]

When in July 1947 the newly constituted German Economic Council met, it took no position in regard to the nationalization or decartelization of the Ruhr industries, or in regard to the division of landed estates. It discussed measures for restoring the Ruhr industries out of funds which the American Government would provide and arranged to send delegates to participate in the Marshall Plan organization that was to be formed (the OEEC).

The American and British Governments had not waited for the Committee of Sixteen to complete and submit its report. On July 15th a revised Directive [JCS 1779] was issued to the Commander-in-Chief of

[6] In the final *General Report* (submitted in Sept.) of the Committee on European Economic Cooperation. In an attached note on *Problems Relating to Germany*, they stated that incorporation of the three Western zones of Germany into their plan was "essential for practical economic reasons" since "other Western European countries cannot be prosperous as long as the economy of the Western zones is paralyzed." Appendix B, pp. 69–71.

the American Forces of Occupation in Germany, replacing the rigorous JCS 1067 of May 1945. The new instruction made the change in policy manifest. It stated that one of its objectives was "to encourage the German people to rebuild a self-supporting state devoted to peaceful purposes, integrated into the economy of Europe." [7] Therefore the United States Government did not think that the level of industry "eventually" agreed upon for Germany as a basis for reparations removals should permanently limit Germany's industrial capacity; and after a period of reparations the Germans should have the right, consistent with continued disarmament, to achieve a higher standard of living. The Commander of the British zone was similarly instructed and authorized.

The essentials of the emergent view in regard to how and why the German recovery should be encouraged was epitomized in the report prepared in connection with the Marshall program which Averell Harriman (who was to be appointed U.S. representative in Europe under the Economic Cooperation Act) [8] made to the President on August 12th: "We are putting in too little too late. As a result, we have lost a considerable part of the expenditures made so far. The German economy has been living on its reserves, both human and material, and is still on the decline. We will have to increase our current expenditures in order to reduce the total cost over the years. . . . There is inadequate fertilization for agriculture. Industry is using up its spare parts and stocks. Transportation had [been] cannibalized . . . We shall face one crisis after another unless steps are taken promptly to turn the downward trend upward. . . . We cannot revive a self-supporting Western European economy without a healthy Germany playing its part as a producing and consuming unit." [9]

Before the American officials in Washington had received the report of the Committee of Sixteen, the Bizonal Zone Commanders had agreed upon the revision of the level of permissible German production and the regime for the Ruhr.

They had recommended that Germany be allowed to retain sufficient industrial capacity in the bizonal area to produce about as much as it had produced in 1936. The level of permissible steel production would be increased from 5.8 million tons to 10.7 million ingot tons (metric) in the two zones and to 11.5 million tons in all Germany if the other two zones joined. Of that total, exports were to be increased to 2 million

[7] It was released to the press on July 15, and is printed in the State Department *Bulletin*, July 27, 1947, pp. 186–193.

[8] It was passed finally by Congress on April 14, 1949.

[9] Letter from Harriman to the President, dated August 12, 1947.

tons, the proceeds of which would compensate the United States and Britain for the imports they provided. Authorized heavy machine production was increased to 80 percent of the 1936 level; retained production capacity in the chemical industry was to equal that of 1936; the machine tool allowance was to be more than doubled; and the production of precision optics and photo equipment was to be sufficient for greatly increased exports.

These recommendations were, in general, approved by the American and British Governments in talks which went on in London from August 22d to 27th. They were announced in a joint U.S.-British statement. In summarizing the revised plan, it was stated: "The old plan provided for very sharp cuts in production capacities in the metals, machinery and chemical industries, from which the bulk of reparations were to be obtained. It is impossible to provide a self-sustaining economy in the bi-zonal area without materially increasing the levels in these industries." [10]

The French Government protested against the agreement to allow this great increase in German industrial production in the recently merged zones. It objected particularly to the enlargement of permitted production capacity for machine tools and basic chemicals. But by then its complaints, so frequent and self-centered, were not being permitted to hinder actions deemed imperative.

Bidault sought guarantees that France would get all the Ruhr coke and coal French industries might need. But he had to be content with assurances of a general character: that German recovery would not be given priority over needs of France and other countries and that the American and British Governments were still determined that Germany should be demilitarized.

Spokesmen for the German political parties were indignant, on the other hand, because the Western occupants appeared to continue to contemplate some further dismantling of industrial capacity, for example, in the heavy machine tool industry and the removal for reparations.[11]

Actually, by this time the American authorities had ceased to dismantle plants, except those that had manufactured weapons, and the British were lagging and pausing. Some further shipments of equipment and machinery from plants previously broken down, however, were still being made. In the French zone dismantling continued, though reduced in scope, even after the inclusion of Western Germany in the Marshall Plan.

[10] State Department *Bulletin*, September 7, 1947, pp. 468–72.
[11] Adenauer, *Memoirs*, pp. 98–99.

To anticipate, when in October 1947 the American and British military governments released a dismantling list, it contained much less than half the number of plants on the original list, including those previously allocated as war plants or advance deliveries. Even so, the Germans angrily protested. And the Foreign Affairs Committee of the House of Representatives insisted that the State and Army Departments secure the approval of the Economic Cooperation Administration (ECA) before permitting any other plants to be dismantled. As succinctly observed by Gimbel ". . . While Washington studied, restudied, and delayed the dismantling and reparations program, Germans continued to try to save individual plants, to stop the program entirely, and to halt operations and deliveries that were the result of prior allocations and commitments." [12]

As the intentions of the West became more definite, Soviet protests and allegations of bad faith had become even more shrill. The Soviet press asserted that the new course, as set out in the recent Directives to the American and British commanders, meant that in order to establish themselves in the rest of Europe they were ". . . prepared once more to raise up in the very heart of Europe the virulent pest of German imperialism, ever a menace to its neighbors." Noting that the mines and industries of the Ruhr were not to be nationalized, but merely to be subjected to supervision by a U.S.-British Control Board, and noting that important German executives of enterprises which had served Hitler were being employed in the restoration of industries of the Ruhr, the Communist press remarked with rage that the new policy was shaped by American monopolists and bankers who were ". . . making the former patrons of Hitler in the Ruhr industries their vassals." Thus, they averred, the Western Allies were in actuality nullifying the joint decision of the Allies to disarm Germany militarily and economically.[13]

Soviet protestations were officially voiced by Marshal Vasili D. Sokolovsky in the meeting of the Control Council on August 30th. He charged: "The very appearance of this document [the communiqué about the revised level of industry in Bizonia] is witness to the fact that U.S. and British military administrations have taken the road of a complete breaking away from the decisions of the Potsdam Conference. . . . The agreement can only lead to a situation in which, to the detriment of the German people's interest . . . wealth will be wrested from her and will be used for . . . foreign monopolies." Clay had replied: "For two and a half years the American delegation has tried desperately to get

[12] Gimbel, *The American Occupation of Germany*, pp. 177–82, 184.
[13] See for example the articles and editorial comment in *New Times* and *Izvestia* for July–August.

economic unity. The record speaks for itself. We do not propose to let continued and indecisive discussions draw the U.S. Zone into a state of economic chaos which would retard recovery of Europe as a whole. Our invitation to our colleagues to join still stands." [14]

The Soviet Government had also protested directly to Washington and London on August 18th, declaring that the two questions of the level of industry and the regime of the Ruhr ". . . concern Germany as a whole and consequently decisions on them can be taken only with the agreement of the Four Powers occupying Germany." [15]

The American rejoinder was made on August 29th by Robert Lovett, who had succeeded Acheson as Undersecretary of State. His interpretation of past occurrences and the drift of his arguments should be now as familiar to readers as the Soviet accusations, and need not be repeated. In conclusion, he asserted that the American Government was unwilling to accept the judgment that nothing could be done to lessen the expense being incurred to relieve the situation in Germany or to increase the contribution of the Western zones to the economic revival of Europe "until the consent of the Soviet Government has been obtained." [16]

In this cross volley of explanations and allegations neither admitted that it had concluded that the provisions of the Potsdam Agreement were untenable. The Soviet Government denied that it had been seeking to bring all Germany under Communist control; the Western governments denied that they wanted to have Western Germany strong enough to restrain Russia and perhaps shake Communist control of Eastern Germany and the Soviet satellites. Both were hiding such thoughts, on which the program of each was borne along.

The Russians were all the more troubled by Western initiatives to promote German recovery because during this autumn of 1947 those countries of Western Europe which only a few months before seemed vulnerable to Communist control were slipping away and placing themselves under the tutelage of the United States.

The French Government, though not ready to fuse its zone with the two Western zones, had agreed that Western Germany should come within the scope of the Marshall program. This it did over the enraged protest of the French Communists. Their abuse of those assenting to the resuscitation of Germany rose to its highest pitch at the end of November 1947, shortly after Schuman succeeded Ramadier as Prime Minister. When Schuman entered the Chamber, René Duclos shouted "Voilà la

[14] Clay, *Decision in Germany,* pp. 156–7.
[15] S. Tsarapkin (Russian Chargé d'Affaires in Washington), in a note to Acting Secretary of State (Lovett), dated August 18, 1947.
[16] Lovett to Tsarapkin, August 29, 1947.

Boche!" As the Socialist Minister of the Interior, Jules Moch, who had fought against Germany in two wars, walked to his seat, Communist members shouted "Heil Hitler" and "Valet." When in debate he tried to defend the measures to maintain order, he was called "Assassin" and "Bloody polichinelle" (Jack in the Box). Together the Ministers were called "chiens couchants" and "salauds" (skunks). The clamor of the Communist Left was so loud that the Assembly was stunned; its somnolent President let the storm rage while sheltering himself from time to time "sous le Règlement." [17] And as told in the preceding chapter, widespread strikes and disorders prolonged the distress in France, especially among the workers. But as the government defied the Communist assault and went forward with its plans to participate in the Marshall Plan, with German participation, the opposition gradually lost power.

When in November 1947, after protracted further consultations with the European beneficiaries, Marshall submitted a revised four-year program to Congress, it included a substantial allocation for the economic betterment of West Germany. The American authorities had come to fear and dislike Soviet Communism more than Germany.

[17] Jacques Fauvet, *La Quatrième République*, (Paris: Arthème Fayard, 1959), p. 136.

35

Germany: The Rift
Becomes a Rupture

The Doomed Conference

Despite the clatter of their arguments, the Western Allies and the Soviet Union had kept open the possibility of coming to terms about Germany. This was the main purpose of the Conference of Foreign Ministers which met in London in late November 1947.

A fortnight before that conference opened, the editors of the *New York Times*, with foresight, had remarked: "With the Deputies to the Foreign Ministers assembled in London to prepare for the meeting of their chiefs later this month, the curtain has gone up on what may be the last act of the Grand Alliance that won the Second World War." [1] The diplomatic correspondent of the *Times* of London, in his anticipatory comment, had given that paper's readers to understand that it would be a miracle if agreement was reached. "Amid all the wider forces the four Foreign Ministers might seem to be like men trying to play water polo in an Atlantic swell. . . . Yet, in spite of all, each of the Ministers acknowledges that the splitting of Germany would be a dangerous second best. So the conferences go on. The wider suspicions of the other's motives are in each side's mind; every proposal is given the worst gloss; but. . . . the order of the day is still to devise a unified scheme." [2]

Before leaving for the Conference Marshall had made it clear that he had concluded the resuscitation of the German economy, still dragging along midst uncleared ruins, was essential to any plan for revitalizing western Europe. Testifying before the Foreign Relations Committee of the Senate on November 11th, he said he was fully cognizant of the fears "of people who have suffered greatly" that a rehabilitated and strong

[1] The *New York Times*, November 8, 1947.
[2] The *Times* (London), November 22, 1947.

Germany might again imperil Europe; and of the opinion that we were about to rebuild Germany against the interests of France and Italy, and, implicitly, against the Soviet Union, which was stimulating such fears by its propaganda. But that was a perversion of the facts that was to be fought. ". . . The economy of Germany must be rebuilt to the point of where they [sic] can support themselves, and make a vital contribution, an essential contribution, to the general economy of Europe." [3]

The Deputies had made no progress toward agreement on either an agenda or the terms of agreement. Then on November 21st, four days before the Conference opened, Marshal Sokolovsky, the Russian representative on the Four-Power Control Council, had railed at the Western members. He dressed them down like a sergeant before a squad of misbehaving privates, accusing their governments of having broken every rule in the book. Collectors of specimens of abusive accusation should include his statement in their folders.

They were permitting the Germans, Sokolovsky declared, to rebuild their military organizations under various guises; they were letting stand German military installations, especially naval bases, which they were pledged to destroy; they were leaving intact most important industrial plants—which he named—that had produced planes and tanks and munitions for Hitler, on the pretext that they were indispensable for the production of such peacetime articles as kitchen utensils and milk cans, and, presumably, spoons for the soup kitchens. For not all the capital equipment being retained, he maintained, was essential even for the increased level of productivity in Germany.

These actions, Sokolovsky stated, could have no other purpose than to convert the American and British zones into an imperialist military base in the heart of Europe.

An adequate review of the facts pertinent to these charges would require a stout and detailed monograph for which there is no room here. True, the Americans and British had suspended the dismantling of plants, even of some which had formerly produced war materials. But they had not done so because of any military reckoning or purpose.

True—also in a measure—had the bizonal authorities had the will to do so, the volume of capital equipment that might have been delivered to the Soviet Union as reparations without hindering the recovery, current and future, of German industry was greater than that actually sent East. But, as has been mentioned, the Germans were sulking against any more transfers, and the Western occupants wanted German cooperation in the political program they were going to advance.

[3] *Interim Aid For Europe*, Hearing, Senate Committee on Foreign Relations, 80th Congress, 1st session, November 11, 1947, p. 48.

The Western Allies, Sokolovsky had continued, had also failed to carry out their obligation to break up the excessive concentration of industrial power and control. They were deliberately falsifying what they were doing, because in the execution of orders given for the dispersal of such huge concerns as the I. G. Farben Industry and Vereinigte Stahlwerke (steel trust) they were permitting some former owners, among them Nazis, to control the new companies that were formed.[4] In a measure this was becoming true, but these Germans were acting as advisers or managers, under controlling authority.

To make the offense worse, Sokolovsky had gone on, the Americans and British were taking a vast amount of invisible reparations by paying too low a price for products they exported from Germany and selling them again on the world market at higher prices. This accusation Molotov was soon to repeat, and he elicited definite factual disproofs, of which we will shortly take note.

In the political sphere Sokolovsky, ignoring what was being done in the Soviet zone, argued that the Western countries were disregarding the provision in the Potsdam Agreement that stipulated all "democratic" parties should be licensed and encouraged, by refusing to permit the Socialist Unity Party, which was the Communist front in Eastern Germany, to operate in the British and American zones.

Becoming still more rampant, he had reviewed those many actions which the Americans and British had taken during the past year in regard to their zones "behind the back of the [Four-Power] Control Council." Among them he singled out particularly the U.S.-British agreement for the joint control of the Ruhr coal mines and heavy industries. As for the Marshall Plan, he again averred that it " . . . aims at subjugating of the economy of the American, British and French occupation zones in Germany to American and British monopolies and at converting these regions of Germany, and primarily the Ruhr, into a war industry base of Anglo-American imperialism in Europe with a view to utilizing it as a means of pressure to bear upon European states which refuse to be enslaved by American and British monopolies."

Sokolovsky's galled and galling declaration forecast what Molotov was going to say over and over again in the course of the Conference of the Foreign Ministers.

What makes the available incomplete record of the Conference more difficult to decipher is that both the Western Allies and the Soviet Union, each in its own verbal usage and form of thought, professed

---

[4] Sokolovsky's statements were a sequel to similar denunciations that had been made by Molotov on March 27th in the previous meeting of the Council of Foreign Ministers.

identical desires.[5] They both posed as being in pursuit of the same ends; a Germany unified; a peace treaty with that Germany; a Germany "democratic"; a Germany independent; a Germany thriving and peaceful. But the two had basically different models of what they wanted Germany to be, and different preferences in regard to the political procedure for bringing that Germany into existence.

The discussions about a peace treaty, about the formation of a German Government, and about reparations became as intersecting as the traces animals leave in shrub country, and as misted over by the spume of accusation.

A literal rundown, session by session, of the trail of twisted arguments at this chaotic Conference would be misleading as well as tedious. All that may be usefully attempted is to trace a few main elements in the continuously boiling mess of rhetorical porridge called a "conference."

Some Main Elements of the Controversy

Molotov, in his first statement on November 26th, attempted to define the basic differences between the Western Allies and the Soviet Union and the "democratic" countries friendly to it. This litany of scorn for the base and bellicose practices of the West and praise of the noble and "peaceful" ideals of the Soviet Union was standard.

He then outlined the principles on which the peace treaty with Germany must be based. Centralization of governmental authority; "demilitarization"; socialization of basic industries; more thorough de-Nazification. His most immediate purpose, it could easily be deduced, was to bring about a dissolution of the merger of the American and British zones. Then Molotov had gone on to voice his suspicious fear of what the Western Allies were really seeking to do in Germany, saying: "There is evidently another plan for Germany, one designed to prevent her economic recovery, for fear that Germany might become a rival in the European and World Market. Hand in hand with this plan goes a policy of weakening Germany economically and destroying her as a united state . . . In that event endeavours to utilize Germany will be made by those Powers which need one or other piece of German territory as a base for

---

[5] The official minutes of the Conference remain closed. The historian is therefore compelled, discontentedly, to compose his account as best he can from newspaper reports (I have turned primarily to the current issues of the *New York Times*, the *Times* (London), *New Times*, *L'Année Politique*, and *Izvestia*, the public statements issued by the Foreign Ministers (the most important of which are contained in the collection of documents published by the Royal Institute for International Affairs, Chatham House), and the addresses which each of the four Foreign Ministers gave after his return from the Conference.

the development of a war industry, and Germany's reactionary forces as a support for a policy of dominating over the democratic countries of Europe and opposing the development of the democratic movement in the European countries liberated from fascism." [6]

In his response, on December 5th, Marshall agreed on the necessity of proceeding toward the formulation of a "democratic" government for the whole of Germany. But, he added, "The United States wants a real government and not a facade. . . ." Before the Council decided on the kind of government to be set up for Germany, Marshall thought it must agree on the common principles which enable the government to function effectively. These should include, he declared, "The basic freedoms for the individual. . . . [and] no hindrance to the free flow of persons, ideas and goods throughout the whole of Germany; and a clear determination of the economic burdens the German people are to bear."

Bevin tried to turn this exchange of opposed affirmations into a discussion of a workable step-by-step procedure, leading to the creation of a *federal* constitution with a bicameral system.[7] Since his most sensible proposal was soon lost in the maelstrom of argument, we will not now dive into the records to salvage its details.

Marshall, in consultation with Washington, concluded that before needed steps could be taken there should be definite agreement as follows: (1) that there would be no obstacles to the free movement of persons, goods, and ideas throughout all Germany; (2) that each of the four occupying powers would have to relinquish any German properties they had seized as reparations without the sanction of the Control Council; (3) that the determination of the burdens Germany should be called upon to bear in the future must take account not only of reparations but also of the sums that had been advanced by the occupying powers; and (4) that there must be one all-over export-import plan for the whole country. These conditions, in summation, would have required the transformation of the economic system of East Germany to fit into that of the greater Germany.

Thenceforth progress toward any kind of constructive agreement ended. The discussions degenerated into a repetitive exchange of assertions, contradictions, and accusations. Diplomats have to endure the ordeal of listening to them; historians have to plod through the dense, depressing documentary records. But readers need not, for all the important elements of the argument figured in those which we have previously traversed.

The American and British authorities were still giving the impression

[6] Molotov, *Problems of Foreign Polity*, p. 507.
[7] See Konrad Adenauer, *Memoirs*, pp. 104 ff.

that they intended to proceed with dismantling of many German industrial establishments. On October 17th they had published a list of 682 factories in Bizonia to be dismantled in the next two years—those not needed for German reconstruction. But their hearts were not in the program, and the head of the Federation of German Trade Unions declared that the German workers would refuse to dismantle them. By this time the Soviet Union had come to the conclusion it could secure little more reparation of this nature from west Germany. Thus it became more insistent upon payment out of current (future) production.

Molotov insisted that any peace treaty must obligate Germany to compensate these countries which had suffered from Hitler's aggression. This should be done, he averred, by requiring Germany to deliver a portion of current production of designated manufactures. In order that the total amount be sufficient for the Germans and for reparations, he proposed that the approved limit of German industrial production be raised to 70 per cent of what it had been in 1938, before the war. Marshall and Bevin rejected this method of securing reparations on the score that it was imperative that Germany become self-supporting as soon as possible.

The ensuing argument led into mazes not only of economics but of hypothetical suppositions about the effect on German economy under diverse systems of operation. In consequence, the question of reparations was made more difficult than it need have been by this mixture of free-flying facts and fixed theories. With reason on both sides and impartial judgment, a safe and satisfactory compromise could have been conceived by the negotiators. But no compromise of this nature was ever considered. And the Germans by then felt sure enough of themselves to protest and perhaps to resist all future reparations.

On December 12th Molotov repeated all his complaints and accusations in another long and insulting attack. Thereupon all three Western Foreign Secretaries—Marshall, Bevin, and Bidault—answered him sternly, rebutting his statements in almost contemptuous terms. One of the milder of the reciprocal accusations was that the other was concealing and lying about what it had taken from Germany.[8]

[8] On December 17th, after the Conference had adjourned, Bevin gave out detailed estimates of British reparation receipts in rebuttal of Molotov's allegations—to wit, capital and ships, approximately 25 million dollars; German external assets, 80 million dollars; substantial benefit from knowledge gained of German industrial products and processes, "but the British and American Governments have freely made public the results of their investigations . . . and the Soviet Union has been among the best customers for copies of these reports." He averred that no German industry or plant had been taken over either by the British Government or British private interests. While acknowledging that German coal and timber had been bought at German internal prices and sold at world market prices, Bevin declared no profit had been made, since all foreign exchange earned from these exports were used to buy

On one point the Western retorts were misleading. Molotov had charged that there was a secret plan afoot to merge the French zone with Bizonia. Marshall denied that there was any such plan, even a tentative one. Bidault said: "We know, as Mr. Marshall does, that there is not only no plan for fusion of the French zone with the zones of the U.S. and the U.K., but there is not even any preparation for such a plan. Any information to that effect I can only regard as false information." [9] However, in fact, as the Conference was about to end, Bidault, Marshall, and Bevin discussed methods and terms for Trizonia. And shortly thereafter Bidault revealed his intention of supporting fusion, without formally committing the Government.[10]

Bidault, it may be noted at this point, had in the course of the Conference definitely indicated that although the French Government still favored a special regime for the Ruhr, in which France would have primary place, it was ceasing to advocate the political detachment of the Ruhr and Rhineland from Germany. This change in its diplomacy made it much easier for the three Western Foreign Ministers to reach agreement on all other matters.

The Failure of Diplomacy

December 12 and 13, 1947, were black days in the calendar of Soviet-Western relations. The rift over Germany became an irreparable rupture.

Molotov's rejoinders and recriminations had convinced the three Western Foreign Ministers that there was no possibility of an agreement. They thereupon agreed that Marshall should, at the next session, "Blast Molotov and then on Bevin's motion adjourn the Conference."

Marshall, in the final statement he issued, enumerated what he thought the chief subjects of disagreement were, as seen by the American Government.[11] His official formulation indicated that Western views were not pliable, that the Western negotiators would not give in on any truly essential point in the hope of inducing a retraction of Soviet demands or Soviet acceptance of Western formulas for the future of

and pay for imports into Germany of raw materials and other products needed by German industry and agriculture. The *Times* (London), December 17, 1947.

[9] The *New York Times*, December 13, 1947.

[10] *L'Année Politique*, December 1947; and Fontaine, *History of the Cold War*, p. 338.

[11] Marshall's statement, December 15, 1947, on *Fundamental Principles for Germany*.

I abstain from repeating the long and rather straggling summary, since they have appeared so frequently in other expositions of American policy previously set forth in this narrative.

Germany. To the contrary, Marshall reintroduced issues lately dormant, in particular his suggestion that the existing German-Polish frontier be revised.

This exposition was a preface for his undeniable statement that "A German Government of any type established to function in present conditions and under the supervision of the Control Council reflecting these basic disagreements would be powerless." [12]

Marshall then moved sternly to his dismissive conclusion, "In view of these facts, it seems impossible at this time to make practical progress. Therefore, I reluctantly conclude that no useful purpose would be served by a debate on the other points on our agenda, and I suggest that the Council of Foreign Ministers might now consider adjournment of this session."

Molotov's rejoinder was, for him, weak and aimed to cast the blame for the failure of the Conference on Marshall and Bevin. They decided, he declared, to act upon a plan rather than enter into discussions, and so refused to consider the reasonable Soviet proposals. He again rehearsed all the allegations he had made in previous sessions. Distorted as his mode of expression was, his discernment of Western purpose was correct. "Mr. Marshall's proposal for the adjournment cannot be considered as anything else but a desire to untie his hands so that he can continue to act as unilaterally as he has done in the past."

The addresses of each of the Foreign Ministers after his return from the London Conference were, as was habitual, justifying expositions of the positions they had maintained and of the differences which had caused the Conference to be so fruitless. Conjoined, they left a jagged landscape, a field trampled over and rent by the hooves of national diplomatic buffaloes.

Marshall's radio and television address, given on December 19th, stressed his opinion, ". . . Until the division of Germany had been healed and conditions created for German political and economic unity, any central government would be a sham and not a reality." The tone of his concluding paragraphs was grim, "We cannot look forward to a unified Germany at this time. We must do the best we can in the area where our influence can be felt."

In his concluding remarks Marshall portrayed Germany as being merely one sector of the field of struggle. The basic issue, he said, was "really clear-cut and I fear there can be no settlement until the coming months demonstrate whether or not the civilization of Western Europe will prove vigorous enough to rise above the destructive effects of the

[12] The text of the statements made by Marshall and Molotov on December 15th are in the *New York Times,* December 16, 1947.

war, and restore a healthy society. Officials of the Soviet Union and leaders of the Communist Parties openly predict that this restoration will not take place. We, on the other hand, are confident in the rehabilitation of Western European civilization with its freedoms." [13]

Bevin's account of the Conference was first given in a speech he made in the House of Commons on December 18th. He, too, attributed the failure to reach an agreement in part to Soviet resentment of the Marshall Plan and its wish to disrupt the program for the recovery of Western Europe. The main matters over which the Conference had gone afoul he identified in the same way as had Marshall. After summarizing the difference of opinion in regard to the way of establishing a central German Government, he said: "An attempt was made to make us appear as the opponents of German unity, and the opponents of a German Government. Nothing can be further from the facts. The essential unity of the German people is something which we recognize, and, sooner or later—and I hope, for the sake of all of us, sooner—this unity will be achieved. . . . I would prefer that it came democratically, on an organized basis, and on the foundation of a proper Constitution." His conclusion, though not as dark as Marshall's, was akin to it in meaning. "We cannot go on as we have been going on. We have hoped against hope that Four-Power collaboration would work. . . . We shall close no doors. We shall maintain all the contacts we can and we shall do our best to try to find a way out of all these difficult situations. . . ." [14]

The Soviet rendition of what had occurred added nothing to Molotov's accusations during the Conference. The whole official Soviet press accused the West, especially the United States, of vicious purposes in contrast to those of the Soviet Government. In sum, the Soviet propagandists sustained the theme that the Western occupants of Germany preferred a divided Germany which could be turned into an American colony, to one which could be unified, democratic, and peace-loving.[15]

A "heart-to-heart" talk between Bevin and Molotov at Bevin's flat in London, retold by Harold Nicolson, has the ring of authenticity:

> Bevin: ". . . . Tell me what you are after. . . . What do you want?
> Molotov: I want a unified Germany.
> Bevin: Why do you want that? Do you really believe a unified Germany would go Communist? They might pretend to. They would say all the right things and repeat all the correct formulas. But in their hearts they would be

[13] State Department *Bulletin*, December 28, 1947.
[14] Parliamentary Debates, House of Commons, December 18, 1947.
[15] See, for example, the special article in *Pravda*, December 18, written by B. Izakov and Y. Zhukov, special correspondents for *Pravda*, reproduced in *Soviet Press Translations* (United States and Great Britain) January 15, 1948.

longing for the day when they could revenge their defeat at Stalingrad. You know that as well as I do.

Molotov: Yes, I know that. But I want a unified Germany." [16]

During the next few months, the Winter of 1947–1948 and early Spring of 1948, the Western Allies proceeded to go forward toward the creation of a separate Western Germany; and the Soviet Government continued to rage at this progression and to try to impede it. But before we pursue the course of this crucial conflict over Germany we must, in order that the whole drift of relationship between the Western democracies and the Soviet Union be borne in mind, consider what occurred during this period in other situations, where, also, proponents of the West and proponents of Communism were contesting.

[16] Harold Nicolson, *The Later Years: 1945–1962, Vol. III of Diaries and Letters,* entry December 3, 1947, p. 116.

36

Western Initiatives:
January into February 1948

A Mutual Defense Pact for Western Europe

Following the rupture over Germany, the Western democracies and the Soviet Union both moved to strengthen their opposed situations. The actions of each impacted on the other. So jostling, so nearly coincidental were the occurrences, so self-enclosed the explanations of their sponsors, that one cannot be sure just how Western measures affected what Russia did, or how Russian measures affected what the West did. Efforts to trace the reciprocal flux must reckon with the fact that each had advance intimations of the other's intentions and plans. But I cannot tell what credence they were given, or judge the extent to which the decision-makers acted on surmise and suspicion.

The first new step was initiated in January 1948 by the British Government, which set out to create a western European defense pact.

Bevin and Bidault had discussed the project of a defense pact as long ago as the previous June (1947), when they were in Paris discussing their joint response to Marshall's offer. Molotov had been cognizant that the refusal of the Communist group to participate in the Marshall Plan program might quicken the impulse of the Western participants to draw together. Bevin thought that the Russians had risked that eventuality because at the time they believed they could wreck or intimidate Western Europe by political upsets, economic chaos, and even revolutionary measures. On the last day of those talks in Paris, Molotov warned Bevin and Bidault that if they proceeded with their plans, ". . . It would be bad for both of us, particularly for France." Bevin had answered that Great Britain was accustomed to threats, that it would face them, and it would not be deterred from doing what it thought was right.[1]

---

[1] Bevin gave an account of this conversation with Molotov in his address to the House of Commons on January 22, 1948. (*Parliamentary Debates.*)

When he was in London in December 1947, Marshall, while dining with Bevin at his flat in Carlton Terrace, had talked over the problems of military defense of Europe. The Secretary had suggested that the several General Staffs consider them. In a fort near New York, General Pierre Billotte, who had been de Gaulle's Chief of Staff and was then representing France in the United Nations, met with General Matthew Ridgway, representing the United States, and General Sir Frederick Morgan, representing Great Britain. They agreed on the need for a common policy and global strategy. Ridgway, even then, said that in his opinion no defense would be effective without German participation.[2]

Bevin had, on January 13, 1948, notified Marshall that the British Government was about to discuss with France and the Benelux countries the possibilities of common defense. He inquired what the attitude of the American Government would be and solicited its views. In acknowledging this inquiry Marshall, after consulting Truman, told Bevin that the American Government thought there was an urgent need for such an accord and would do anything it properly could to assist in its realization.[3]

During a comprehensive debate in the House of Commons on January 21st and 22d, leaders of both political parties showed how exasperated they were by Russian actions and criticisms. Hector McNeil, Minister of State, speaking for the Labor Government, was most vehement in his attack on what he called Russian unreliability and duplicity. What was most wanted, he said, was a clarification of Soviet policy and Soviet intentions outside their own borders. "No study of speeches, no study of Communist doctrine, no private conversations, apparently, can be taken at their face value when we are up against this problem. None of them give us any indication of Soviet policy." After citing recent statements that Stalin had made, he said: "What worries everyone is the inconsistencies between Generalissimo Stalin and Generalissimo Stalin . . . Probably there will be an outcry, another blare of propaganda following . . . [this] statement, and this Debate. But the outcome of this Debate, this association upon which we are entering, has not been built up by anyone else except Generalissimo Stalin. He is the architect of any coali-

[2] Elgey, *La République des Illusions*, p. 381.
[3] Kennan, in his *Memoirs*, p. 398, states that this answer must have gone out between January 15 and January 20, 1948. And he adds his belief that "Its tenor was influenced, I strongly suspect, by the views of Mr. John Foster Dulles," who had been in Paris in December 1947 just as the strikes and riots, by which the Communists had sought either to compel the French Government to withdraw from the Marshall program or bring about such economic collapse that the program could not succeed in France, were ending. Theodore H. White, *Fire in the Ashes: Europe in Mid-Century*, p. 288, recounts that Marshall talked over Bevin's project with Dulles on the boat trip returning to New York and that Dulles favored it. A detailed account of their talk is given by Theodore Achilles in his reminiscences for the Dulles Oral History Project of Princeton University.

tion which forms against him; . . . ." [4]

Bevin's comments were more moderate; one section of them seemed an echo of what Churchill had declaimed at Fulton, Missouri, two years previously. "It has been quite clear, I think, that the Communist process goes ruthlessly on in each country. We have seen the game played out in Poland, Bulgaria, Hungary, more recently in Rumania, and, from information in our possession, other attempts may be made elsewhere. Thus, the issue is not simply the organization of Poland or any other country, but the control of Eastern Europe by Soviet Russia, whose frontiers have, in effect, been advanced to Stettin, Trieste and the Elbe. One has only to look at the map to see how since the war, Soviet Russia has expanded and now stretches from the middle of Europe to the Kurile Islands and Sakhalin. Yet all the evidence is that she is not satisfied with this tremendous expansion. In Trieste we have difficulties. . . . Then we have the great issue in Greece, which is similar to the others I have mentioned." [5]

After surveying the international scene as he had come to view it, the Foreign Secretary revealed to the House of Commons that talks about a mutual defense treaty or a connected series of mutual defense treaties were beginning. He remarked: "I hope that treaties will thus be signed with our near neighbours, the Benelux countries, making with our treaty with France an important nucleus in Western Europe. We have then to go beyond the circle of our immediate neighbours. We shall have to consider the question of associating other historic members of the European civilization, including the new Italy, in this great conception. . . . We are thinking now of Western Europe as a unit." [6]

Attlee had added that he believed the support for this policy was coupled with recognition that western Europe could not live by itself as an economic unit. "Hence the desire for wider integration with Africa and other overseas territories, and with the great Western democracies and with our own Dominions. Union of Europe is a fruitful idea. . . . While I think that the idea of a united Europe is one which is most fruitful, we must be careful not to think that it is something exclusive, and something which precludes the rest of the world." [7]

Toward the Creation of a West German Government

Before the negotiations about a mutual defense pact resulted in a definite accord, other vibrating measures and countermeasures were taken

---

[4] *Parliamentary Debates,* House of Commons, January 21, 1948.
[5] *Ibid.,* January 22, 1948.
[6] *Ibid.*
[7] *Ibid.,* January 23, 1948.

by the Western Allies and the Soviet Union to consolidate their situations.

Despite the discordant Conference of Foreign Ministers, the Soviet Government strove to keep alive nominal Four-Power control over the whole of Germany. Apparently it thought it still might be possible to hinder Western initiatives in Germany by use of the veto in the Control Council, while carrying out its own policies in the zone occupied by its troops. Conversely, the working premise of the Western Allies was that it was not possible to agree upon or carry out a four-power policy. They were determined to disengage themselves from the deadlock.

Early in January 1948 Generals Clay and Robertson had conferred at Frankfurt with German officials of the recently created bizonal reorganization, with the prime ministers of the provincial governments within Bizonia, and with members of the Economic Council, in regard to the creation of more centralized governmental bodies and the assignment of some political functions to existing administrative agencies.[8]

Some of the German officials had been rather upset. They feared that this move would divide Germany. The French Government had opposed the move and recorded their criticisms in a memo on January 24th. But the American and British Governments went ahead and on February 9th they signed the proclamation creating a transitional German government in the bizonal area.

The Russian press alleged that the projected plans were proof of a design to subject Germany to the control of reactionary officials and dummies. How else, it queried, could the refusal to heed the protests of groups which the Russians deemed "democratic" be construed? The comment in New Times was typical: "The structure of the new bodies leaves no doubt that a separate puppet government is being created in West Germany . . . and that another major step is being taken toward the dismemberment of Germany.

"Not even the semblance of a democratic system in forming them [the new government bodies] is being maintained . . . Both the decision to create these bodies and the modus of forming them are bereft of all vestige of democratic procedure." [9]

The Soviet criticisms did not deter the American and British authorities. They were intent on satisfying the dominant German leaders and by so doing to spur them on to greater efforts to restore German productive capacity. They also reckoned that by stimulating the hope that occupation controls in the Western zones would soon be lightened, the re-

[8] See Gimbel, *The American Occupation of Germany*, pp. 195–6, and Clay, *Decision in Germany*, p. 180.
[9] *New Times*, January 21, 1948.

sistance of the Germans to Russian promises and threats would be firmer.

Bevin took the lead in the next step. He announced in the House of Commons on January 22d that he had sent invitations to the other Western occupying powers of Germany and to the Benelux countries to meet in London on the 23d of February to disucss the next measures to be taken in and for Germany.

"We cannot," he said, "accept the Russian view that Germany should be kept strictly in hand under an over-centralized government, nor can we let continued poverty and disease continue to cause havoc in Germany and weaken all of Europe." Therefore, he concluded, the only practical course that Britain could then take was to abandon for the time being the futile striving for Four-Power all-German arrangement and, instead, work constructively within the framework of bizonal—and hopefully, in time—trizonal cooperation. The Conservative members of the House showed that they were even more out of patience with Russia than was Bevin. Former Secretary of State for Foreign Affairs Eden warmly agreed with Bevin's reasoning and intention, concluding his comments by saying: "I am sure that is the course the government ought to pursue." [10]

But the Soviet authorities had complaints and they were bitter. When the Control Council for Germany met on February 11th, by which time more details had been published regarding both the reorganization of German administration in Bizonia and the inclusion of Western Germany in the Marshall program, the Soviet representative, Marshal Sokolovsky again displayed his talents for denunciation.

"In these documents," he said, "there is not one word of the rights of the German people, nor of the democratization of the political order. . . . We have now a deformed anti-democratic German constitution enforced . . . through the intermediary of a small group of Germans. There is being prepared the inclusion of Western Germany in a military and political Western bloc. This is a dangerous course." [11]

The Soviet Government also sent formal notes of protest to the British and French Governments on February 13th, as did also the Polish Government. The American comment, made on February 21st, sought deeply to incise lines of responsibility for what had happened and was about to happen. Its charge was unqualified. "The fact that it [the Soviet Government] now protests against the endeavors which will be made to develop constructive measures to deal with the present situation in Germany can only be construed as an effort to shift the responsibility

[10] Parliamentary Debates, House of Commons, January 23, 1948.
[11] Clay, *Decision in Germany*, pp. 350–1.

incurred by the Soviet Government itself for the present division of Germany, with all the unfortunate consequences which this division entails, not only with respect to Germany, but for the recovery of Europe as a whole."

Even as the Soviet Government was declaiming and protesting against the Western separated action in Germany, or perhaps in some measure as a counterpoise, it was plotting to stifle Czechoslovakia's independence and drag it into the Communist camp.

37

The Coup in Czechoslovakia

Czechoslovakia, having survived Munich and the savage German incision, was regarded with admiration in the West. Perhaps because of a sense of guilt at having advised its beleaguered government to yield to Hitler the West sought relief, or redemption, in restoring Czechoslovakia after the war as an independent country. The merits of its people gleamed brightly in the central European setting. They were thought to be managing well in the precarious position into which they were placed by history and geography. The government was a coalition (National Front) in which a Communist, Klement Gottwald, was Prime Minister. Eight other Communists were members of the Cabinet—including the Minister of the Interior, Vaclav Nosek, who controlled the public and secret police, and the Minister of Information, who controlled the national radio. But it seemed to be maintaining a safe equilibrium between opposed political groups. Capitalism was constrained but personal freedoms were alive. Though the Government cultivated connections with the Soviet Union, most of the officials and people were receptive to the West.

Eduard Beneš, the veteran President, and Jan Masaryk, Foreign Minister, son of the founding head of the republic, had striven by deed and words to assure the acceptance of this policy of balance, particularly to have Russia accept it, if not condone it.

To illustrate the note they struck in public and private utterances, two short excerpts may be summoned from the records. One: Masaryk talking at the Peace Conference in Paris in August 1946. "Czechoslovakia, loyal to her allies, is very proud to be a Slav country, proud that her sons fought in the Ukraine and entered Prague with the victorious liberating Red Army, that her boys took part in the battle of Britain and fought at Tobruk, that her brigade besieged and delivered Dunkirk, proud to have fought alongside the great armies of the great United States of America and alongside the armies of the other Allies who are assembled in this hall, and remembering the Slovak uprising behind the lines of the German army, the barricades of Prague and the wonderful, magnificent behaviour of her population during seven endless years of Hitler's inferno.

"Czechoslovakia is looking forward with reasonable, realistic optimism to the ultimate result of this and the following peace meetings. . . . Imagine, fellow delegates, a long, long peace, maybe even permanent peace—wouldn't that be wonderful!"

At a reunion of resistance organizations on the anniversary of the Prague uprising, May 6, 1947, President Beneš had said: "Faced with danger from Germany and a threat to our security we march with the Soviet Union and will continue to do so in the future."

Hopefully Beneš had thought this affirmation would satisfy Russia and reconcile the Communist elements in the country. But he had gone on to say: "Culturally we are Europeans. We will never range ourselves with the East alone, or with the West alone, but always with the East and West simultaneously."

These statements had not evoked any reprimand from Moscow, or caused the Communist members of Czechoslovakia's government openly to rebel. But by February 1948, perceiving that western Germany was to be included in an association opposed to Communism, these officials who did the bidding of Moscow decided that the government and people of Czechoslovakia should no longer be able to traffic with both sides.

Either as pretext for their rebellion or because of fear that the Czech people might be attracted by the Western combination, the Communists set out to oust the government.

A Cabinet majority had decided on measures intended to prevent the Communist Minister of the Interior from influencing coming elections by dismissing non-Communist police officers in Prague and replacing them with Communists. When the Communist Ministers, concerned as well over their personal political future, refused to abide by this Cabinet decision, the representatives of the Populist (Catholic), Czech Socialist, and Slovak Democratic parties presented their resignation to President Beneš.

Thereupon the Communists raised the hue and cry that this was an attempt to change the nature of the Government and a plot against the Republic. Home and foreign reaction, they alleged, had joined forces to sabotage all measures of public welfare. They aroused factory councils and trade unions to demonstrate. Nosek, abetted by Zdenek Fierlinger, the sinister former Czech Ambassador to Moscow, on the night of the 22d brought Communist-controlled police units into Prague. Opponents were dragged out of bed, hustled into "Black Marias," flung into prison, and charged with conspiring to convert the country into a vassal of the United States. Soviet agents were active in giving directions to the Communist agitation; Valerian Zorin, a Deputy Foreign Minister of the Soviet Union, arrived and stayed in Prague on a paltry excuse.[1] He kept in close touch with local Communist leaders and with the Commander of the Red Army units near the Czechoslovak frontier. On the 24th a general strike was ordered by Gottwald, and armed Communist groups camped in the woods near the city, ready, the word spread, to enter.

The representatives in the Cabinet of the Social Democratic Party—a workers' party—did not resign, but its numerous members did nothing to defend the government. So Beneš, feeling beaten and fearful lest Russian armed forces enter the country, did not dare test the loyalty and courage of the Czechoslovak army. He caved in, accepted the resignation of the non-Communist Ministers, and on February 29th accepted a Government dominated by the Communists. He was then a sick man, dispirited by disproof of his belief that he could manage to get along with Moscow. A fortnight later (Mar. 10th) the smashed body of Jan Masaryk was found on the cement courtyard of the Foreign Office—tossed out of the window, most Westerners thought; a suicide, the Communists alleged.[2]

As postscript, it is of note that all independent political parties, having been by that time put in or under bonds, elections were held for a new National Assembly; 237 of the 300 new members chosen were candidates of the Communist Party. With haste and push the new government took over important industries. The Communists gloated, and justified their action. Gottwald was named President after Beneš went out. Talking to the Central Committee of the Czechoslovakian Communist Party months afterward, he declared proudly: "Until February there was still a possibility of capitalist and pre-Munich conditions being restored in our country by the internal forces of reaction. . . . The most important result of the February events was that they eliminated the possibil-

[1] For example, *New Times* several months thereafter (May 12, 1948) explained the Communist take-over by charging that a "handful of reactionary political adventurers" supported by the American Ambassador, Laurence Steinhardt, sought to liquidate the republic and convert the country into a vassal state.
   The charge apparently has not yet become wholly stale. In July 1968, the followers of Moscow in and out of Czechoslovakia alleged that its recent attempt to reintroduce some margin of freedom into the Communist regime was being inspired and supported by the United States; that American arms, secretly hidden and suddenly found, were intended for an armed uprising against the government.
[2] Masaryk had been of the opinion that the United States had made a serious mistake in refusing to provide Czechoslovakia with help except in connection with the Marshall Plan. This policy made it easier, he believed, for the Communists to convince their co-nationals that the Soviet Union could be their only real friend. As related by Trygvie Lie in his book *The Cause of Peace* (New York: Macmillan, 1954), p. 233.

ity of capitalism being restored by the internal forces of reaction, political and economic. Today the reactionaries are not in a position to carry out a *coup d'état* by their own efforts." [3]

The tragic death of Masaryk, coming after Beneš' sad submission, gave an emotional tone to the Western reaction to this Communist coup. Sympathy for these two victims of Communist percussion, esteemed for their good will and lofty natures, was fused with indignation at the methods used, and anger over the upset of the last remaining democratic and friendly government in Central Europe.

This coursing emotion gave impetus to strong and bold measures of the Western governments cohesively to deter or offset any further Communist attempts by whatever means—conventional, subversive, or forcible—to extend their power into Western Europe or the Mediterranean. These measures, animated by the same purpose, and conjoined with the Marshall Plan program, created a connected Western common front. In a rapid sequence of actions, this front proved to be both strong and flexible.

Each measure had its own history, but each was affected by the others in some way or degree. Since it is impossible to know just how and when, it is best, I think, to let chronology convey the tale, as history relentlessly unrolled its script of this drama of antagonism.

[3] *New Times*, November 25, 1948.

38

The Tides and Ides of March—1948

March 4, 1948

Czechoslovakia had been France's ally before the war; and many if not most Frenchmen had a sense of regret, if not shame, at the way the country had been left to the mercy of Hitler. Now it was being brought to heel again by a dictatorship which also menaced freedom in France.

"Anything is possible, but nothing is inevitable. Watch and pray," the Prime Minister had said on hearing the news. Soon thereafter, on March 4th, the Foreign Minister, Bidault, sent a message to Marshall saying: "The moment has come to weld in the political field, and, as soon as it can be done, in the military field, the collaboration of the old and the new world, so much at one in their devotion to the only civilization which avails." He proposed that consultation be begun quickly ". . . on the problems posed by common defense against a danger which may be close at hand." [1]

This marked the end of the lingering hesitation about challenging both Russia and the strong French Communist element in France. Thereafter the French Government ceased to insist on acceptance of its claims before agreeing that the program for the future of Germany be discussed at a Six-Power Conference about German affairs.

March 5, 1948

In all centers where Western and Russian diplomacy was clashing, there was, after the coup in Czechoslovakia, apprehension over other possible Russian moves. But the point at which the eruption was deemed most likely to occur was in and over Berlin, within the Eastern zone. The meetings there of the Four Power Control Council had turned into brawls.

[1] Quoted in Fauvet, *La Quatrième République* pp. 141–2.

295

General Clay had the impression that anything might happen at any time. In a message relayed to the Chief of Staff, General Omar Bradley, who had succeeded Eisenhower, Clay said that although he had previously thought the Soviet Union was unlikely to want war for at least ten years, he had recently changed this view. For "Within the last few weeks, I have felt a subtle change in Soviet attitude which I cannot define but which now gives me a feeling that it may come with dramatic suddenness." [2]

In Clay's book, written later, about his experience in Germany, he explained why he sent this alarming report. "Somehow I felt instinctively that a definite change in the attitude of the Russians in Berlin had occurred and that something was about to happen. From Sokolovsky down there was a new attitude, faintly contemptuous, slightly arrogant, and certainly assured. . . . I pointed out that I had no confirming intelligence of a positive nature, but that I did sense a change in the Soviet position which I was certain portended some Soviet action in Germany." [3]

Clay was a Southern soldier (son of the Confederacy), quick to take offense, quick to sense indifference or hostility. The event was to show that the Russians had no thought of sending troops into Germany, and were not ready to risk war. But they had decided to cease to consort with the Western Allies in the Control Council, to go it alone, and to expel them from Western Berlin.

Clay's message set off alarm and excited conjecture not only around the Pentagon and the White House but in congressional committees. The Central Intelligence Agency hurried to make a special estimate of the situation for the President, saying that war ". . . . was not probable within sixty days." President Truman thought Clay was more alarmed than circumstances indicated, but he heeded the foreboding report. It was one of the stimulants of the somber address which he sent to Congress some days later. And it conduced the first whole-hearted attempt to end the harmful rivalries between the several branches of our armed services.

The Six-Nation Conference on Germany, which was to lead to the formation of the West German Government, had recessed on March 5th, since the head American representative, Ambassador Lewis Douglas, had to return to Washington to testify on the legislation for the European Recovery Program.

Before the brief adjournment the six participants were in agreement

[2] Millis, ed., *The Forrestal Diaries*, entry dated March 5, 1948, p. 387.
[3] Clay, *Decision in Germany*, p. 354.

on essentials, but there were points of difference about which the representatives wished to consult their governments. All favored a Federal structure for the government of Germany, but the British group, headed by Sir William Strang, Undersecretary of State in the Foreign Office, wanted the Federal government to have somewhat greater powers than did the American group, while the French group, headed by the French Ambassador in London, René Massigli, conceived only of a loosely knit confederation of German states with stiffly restricted authority. All were agreed also that there should be closer coordination in economic affairs between Bizonia and the French zone but that complete economic fusion should await political fusion.

Also, as phrased in the communiqué issued, "Since it had not proved possible to achieve economic unity in Germany, and since the eastern zone has been prevented from playing its part in the European Recovery Programme, the three western powers have agreed that close cooperation should be established among themselves and among the occupation authorities in western Germany in all matters arising out of the European Recovery Programme in relation to western Germany." [4]

In the preliminary design of the system of international supervision to be formed for the Ruhr all agreed that Germany was to be represented. The French Government was urged to resign itself to be on a par with the United States and Britain in the control. France grimaced and complained because its hold upon the Ruhr was much weaker than it had wished. But since the Ruhr was in Bizonia it could not get its way, or even superior rights. All had concluded that the Soviet Government should have no part in the supervisory arrangements. It was to have no chance to interfere with the regime or development of the Ruhr, even as it was rejecting all suggestions that the Western Allies be consulted about the development and export of the resources of Silesia.

March 6, 1948

Having learned that the London Conference on German affairs was about to recess, and perhaps having prevision of what would be said in the public communiqué, the Soviet Government delivered another protest in which it declared that it deemed any Three-Power agreement about Germany would be illegal and without international authority.[5]

[4] This communiqué, dated March 6th, was included in the final report of the London Six-Power Conference, February 23 to June 2, 1948.
[5] The first Russian note protesting the Six-Power Conference had been delivered on February 13, 1948; see chap. 34.

March 10, 1948

The arguments in the meeting of the Four-Power Control Council for Germany were even more caustic than before. Why, Sokolovsky rhetorically asked, did the American and British Commanders refuse to permit the Socialist Unity Party (SED) to function in their zones; was it not because they were intolerant and afraid of genuine democratic working-class parties? Clay and Robertson said their exclusion was due to the fact that the SED was an amalgam forced on the Social Democratic Party by the Communists of the Eastern zone.

Once again Sokolovsky denounced the Marshall Plan. After Robertson spoke of it as the Star of Bethlehem for Germany, the Soviet general said it was the Star of Bethlehem for the American monopolists only, not for the German working class. *They* know perfectly well, he continued, that its purpose is to keep them enslaved, being under the rule of the large landowners and capitalist monopolists.

So on the slanging harangue went, to its ominous end, until Sokolovsky declared: "From the statements made . . . it is *quite* evident that it is absolutely useless to continue the discussion . . . since they [Clay and Robertson] have very clearly expressed themselves as being against the creation of democratic working parties in their zones." [6]

Sokolovsky's rudeness as well as his contentions impressed Clay as storm signals. He connected the angry and dismissive note with the interferences with transportation between West Germany and Berlin. The Russians were claiming the right to have their inspectors enter military trains coming from the West and check the identity of the passengers. The train commanders had been ordered not to allow them aboard.

March 10–12, 1948

Marshall informed Forrestal that the British Government was worried by reports that the Soviet Government was pressing Norway to enter into a pact with it similar to the one it was requiring Finland to sign. [7]

March 17, 1948

The five Foreign Ministers formally signed the 50-year Treaty of Brussels (also called the "Western Union"), a defensive alliance of Great Britain, France, Holland, Belgium, and Luxembourg.

[6] Clay, *Decision in Germany*, p. 352.
[7] Millis, ed., *The Forrestal Diaries*, entry dated March 12, 1948, p. 392.

298

At first they had in mind merely a broadening of the French-British treaty of Dunkirk—which was specifically a defensive alliance against Germany. But Marshall had sent them word that in his opinion this did not offer sufficient guarantee of mutual support, and he suggested that the treaty which the United States had entered into with Latin American countries at Rio de Janeiro be taken as example. The suggestion was quickly accepted.

The core of the Treaty signed at Brussels was in article 4, which stipulated: "if any of the high contracting parties should be the subject of an armed attack in Europe, the other high contracting parties will . . . offer the party so attacked all military and other aid and assistance in their power." To that end the military policies and the armed forces of the upholders were to be coordinated.

This treaty was the clearest mark of the trend in the conduct of the Western Allies and the proximity of their policies. This Brussels Accord was clearly directed at the Soviet Union. For some of its signatories it was a great change in past attitudes. The Netherlands, Belgium, and Luxembourg relinquished the posture of neutrality to which they had clung before the war. Britain linked itself more closely with a group of continental powers than it had since the Napoleonic Wars.

On this same day, St. Patrick's Day, Truman delivered a most important address to a joint session of Congress. His condemnation of the actions of the Soviet Union and its agents was more salient even than in the message he had sent to Congress one year before, enunciating the "Truman Doctrine."

He charged that the world's troubles were "Chiefly due to the fact that one nation has not only refused to cooperate in the establishment of a just and honorable peace, but—even worse—has actively sought to prevent it. . . . faced with this growing menace, there have been encouraging signs that the free nations of Europe are drawing closer together for their economic well-being and for the common defense of their liberties. . . ." He continued, "At the very moment, I am addressing you, five nations of the European community, in Brussels, are signing a 50-year agreement for economic cooperation and common defense against aggression. . . . This development deserves our full support. I am confident that the United States will, by appropriate means, extend to the free nations the support which the situation requires. I am sure that the determination of the free countries of Europe to protect themselves will be matched by an equal determination on our part to help them to protect themselves." [8]

[8] The *New York Times*, March 18, 1948.

The President's utterance was given weight by his accompanying requests that Congress hasten to pass pending legislation for the fulfillment of the Marshall Program, and to provide for universal military training and a temporary Selective Service Act.

The reckoning which dictated this address is recorded in the *Diaries* of the Secretary of Defense, Forrestal, "It is inconceivable that even the gang who run Russia would be willing to take on war, but one always has to remember that there seemed to be no reason in 1939 for Hitler to start war, and yet he did, and he started it with a world practically unprepared. Our effort now is to try to make the Russians see the folly of continuing an aggression which will lead to war, or, if it is impossible to restore them to sanity, that we at least have a start which will enable us to prevent our being caught flat-footed as we were in 1941." [9]

Did the Secretary of Defense, in his zeal, forget about the atomic bombs?

March 20, 1948

This was the day on which the Four-Power Control Council, the pivot of the Potsdam plans for the occupied country, broke up, never to come together again.[10]

The Soviet authorities had probably foreseen that this was likely to happen, for they could have hardly expected that the Western members would respond differently than they did to a proposal that Marshal Sokolovsky made. He insisted that the Council discuss a resolution that had been passed by a conference of Foreign Ministers of Czechoslovakia, Poland, and Yugoslavia, which was an attack on the policies of the Western Powers in Germany. Clay said that the American Government could see no useful purpose in considering resolutions based on misstatements and distortions of fact. Sokolovsky remarked that Clay's answer proved once again that the Western representatives did not consider the Control Council as an agency for Four-Power administration of occupied Germany. "They regard the Control Council merely as a suitable screen behind which they can hide the unilateral actions taken in western Germany and which are directed both against the interests of the peaceful countries and peace loving Germans . . ." Clay, in his turn, retorted that if there was a screen, it was not on the Western side of the border between the American and Soviet zones, but on the Eastern side.

[9] Millis, ed., *The Forrestal Diaries*, entry dated March 16, 1948, p. 395.

[10] The main available source of information regarding this fateful meeting is that given by General Clay in his book *Decision in Germany*, pp. 355–6. He based it on the unagreed minutes of the Council. The State Department still refuses to allow students to study the original files of Clay's papers.

Thereupon, and revealingly, Sokolovsky asked to be told of all agreements regarding Western Germany that had thus far been reached at the London Conference. Clay put him off by saying that the governments concerned had not yet approved the report of the Conference. Later he commented: "We considered his request to be reasonable but we could not provide him with the information he desired until we had heard from our governments." [11] Sokolovsky, it may be interjected, knew that Generals Clay and Robertson had been present during some of the sessions of the London Conference and were informed of its recommendations.

As remembered by Clay, Sokolovsky barely waited for the translation of the answer before reading a long statement in which he repeated the accumulated Russian charges against the Western Powers in aggravating language. As Robertson began to reply, Sokolovsky, who was the Chairman, interrupted and said: "I see no sense in continuing this meeting and I declare it adjourned." With that, the whole Russian delegation arose, and without a backward glance, walked out of the conference room.

At the moment no one was certain as to whether the Soviet Government intended once and for all to forsake the Control Council. No date had been set for the next meeting. The three Western military governors waited for Sokolovsky to call another one but they heard nothing more. When Clay, at the start of April, succeeded Sokolovsky as chairman of the Council, the French member, General Pierre Koenig, urged him to summon the Council again. But Clay, probably in accord with advice from Washington, did not want to take the initiative. His account ends, "No request [for another meeting] was made and it soon became apparent that further meetings would not take place." [12]

This Soviet fling showed how strong was its frustration at not being able to deter the Western Powers from organizing a West German Government of the sort they favored. In their effusions the Soviet official press enumerated all the protests and proposals of the Soviet statesmen which had been neglected or ignored, including the way in which the Western Members of the Council had "spurned" the declaration of the Foreign Ministers of the three satellite states, and their refusal to divulge the recommendations of the London Conference on Germany. Marshal Sokolovsky, the Communist publicists averred, had "Unmasked their double game." [13]

By these fulminations the Soviet authorities were working up their

[11] *Ibid.*, p. 356.
[12] *Ibid.*, p. 357.
[13] See for example the editorial in *New Times*, March 31, 1948.

case for blockading Berlin. But it should be noted that when first they imposed the blockade they denied that they were seeking to undo or off-set the plans for Western Germany that were in the course of consummation in London.

March 30–31, 1948

General Dratvin, the Deputy Military Governor of the Soviet zone, notified the military authorities in Berlin that the movement of persons to and from Berlin through the Soviet zone would be subject to inspection by Russian officials, and would have to be authorized by them. At once confirming orders and regulations were issued.

Dratvin asserted that these measures were necessary because the right of freedom of transit was being abused by both Western military personnel and Germans. No doubt, in this era of helter-skelter and deranged currencies, black marketeers, money smugglers, crooks, and sharp operators of all sorts took advantage of the chance to trip back and forth. But in the Soviet explanations, all rogues were in the West, and all the harm was done in the East. Many, the Communist press charged, were illegally crossing from the Western zones into the Soviet zone in search of work, food, and shelter, some of them criminals and saboteurs who were disturbing law and order in the Soviet sector of Berlin and the Soviet zone. The order regarding inspection of trains leaving Berlin, the Russian officials explained, was made necessary because grain and cattle as well as industrial equipment were being shipped from the Eastern zone westward through Berlin. How much or how little truth there was in these charges was never investigated or established—as far as I know.

Clay submitted to the Department of the Army the protest which he wished to make to Dratvin. He suggested that the Western authorities should not comply with these Soviet orders affecting transit to and from Berlin, but they might agree that the train commanders would certify passenger lists and documentation to Soviet inspectors. He proposed that he be authorized to issue orders to American personnel not to allow the Russians to enter the trains operated by our military organizations, shooting if necessary.

The problem of decision drew together in conference at once all the senior officials of the military and the State Departments. When the text of Dratvin's letter was received, it was not as truculent as had been inferred from Clay's report. Drastic moves were considered, among them a direct protest by the President to Stalin, and consultation with congressional leaders about countermeasures. But it was decided for the time being merely to confirm Clay's authorization to prevent the Russians from entering trains headed for Berlin. The British Government had already sent similar instructions to General Robertson.[14]

Clay sent a test train with a few armed guards on board to see whether the Russians would stop it by force or sidetrack it. After traveling some way into the Soviet zone, it was shunted to a siding. For a few days some rail routes were closed down and Allied trucks carrying manufactured goods from Berlin on the autobahns were detained.

At this juncture Washington grew nervous lest a firm stand bring incidents which would lead to fighting. Clay did not think so. He advised his military colleagues in Washington, "I do not believe this means war. . . . Please understand we are not carrying a chip on our shoulder and will shoot only for self protection. I do not believe we will have to do so." [15]

In a telecon conference on April 2d, the Department of the Army informed Clay that anxiety was growing in the United States and asking whether American dependents in Berlin should be evacuated. Clay's answer was, "Evacuation in face of the Italian elections and European situation is to me almost unthinkable. Our women and children can take it, and they appreciate import. There are few here who have any thought of leaving unless required to do so." [16]

The Western Governments refused to budge, and, to get ahead of the story, the Russians at this time avoided a showdown. (I will not infringe on the monopoly academic rebels have on the word "confrontation.") The Russians, however, did resort to a variety of frequently changing methods of harassment.

These interferences were troubling and even menacing, but they did not seriously affect the traffic between the West and Berlin. Yet, in Washington and London they were taken to be ominous portents rather than mere gestures intended to test German and Western reactions. This judgment did not cause the Western Allies to hesitate in their formulation of plans for Western Germany. On the contrary, it gave faster impetus to the search for measures of resistance.

During the coming spring the protagonists nerved themselves for an impending challenge.

[14] Millis, ed., *The Forrestal Diaries,* entry dated March 31, 1948, pp. 407–8.
[15] Clay, *Decision in Germany,* p. 359.
[16] *Ibid.,* p. 360.

39

Toward Western Coalition:
The Spring of 1948

Three actions in the spring of 1948 drew the Western Allies toward close coalition:

One was the passage of the European Recovery Act, which provided the means and methods for the sixteen-nation Marshall Plan program.

Another was the consequential discussions for transforming the Brussels Pact into a transatlantic military alliance in which the United States and Canada were to be embraced.

The third, and most affronting to the Soviet authorities and their Communist associates, was the comprehensive prospectus for West Germany, which, at the end of their conference in London, the six conferring delegations agreed to recommend to their governments.

The European Recovery Act

The legislation to give effect to the Marshall Plan program by providing the necessary means had been long and strenuously debated in the American Congress. The advocates of the legislation, both Republican and Democratic, were stirred by the belief that if the program was not activated, Communists might become dominant even in Western Europe; and if that occurred, as John Foster Dulles expressed it, "The Congress is going to be pressed with demands for an increased military establishment which will make this plan look like a bag of peanuts." [1]

True, there was an attempt to dispel the idea that the program was animated primarily by fear of the spread of Communism. The positive aims rather than the negative ones were emphasized. But the sustaining purpose was plainly discernible, for example, in the minstrel-like ques-

[1] Testimony at Hearing on European Recovery Program before the Foreign Relations Committee of the Senate, January 20, 1948, p. 606.

tion and answer between Senator Tom Connally and William J. Donovan:

> *Senator Connally:* "I want to ask you one other question. A lot of people talk about this being a move against Russia. It seems to me—and I want to ask you if you agree with it—that it is highly important in this whole program for us to maintain this on a level of high principles and stress the principles that we have in mind—the rebuilding of Europe, the making of these countries independent, to stand on their own feet, their own legs—rather than creating the impression that we are just aiming this at one single nation, to wit, Russia.
>
> *Mr. Donovan:* "I think that is right, Senator. But we do not want to err on the other side and show that we still want to genuflect to appeasement. I think it is a very important thing in dealing with Russia . . . that they must have your respect.
>
> *Senator Connally:* "I want to ask you the further question. If it collides with Russia, it will be because Russia is violating and challenging these principles that we are standing for?
>
> *Mr. Donovan:* "That is right." [2]

As already observed, the reluctance to devote so large a sum asked might have caused Congress to try to do the job for less, had it not been for the alarming and angering effect of the Communist coup in Czechoslovakia.

On April 3, 1948, President Truman signed the European Recovery Act, which made the Marshall program effective. This was almost a year after Acheson had, in his address in Mississippi, informed the Americans how miserable most nations of Western Europe were, how bleak their prospects, and how real the possibility of revolution, unless some restorative action was taken.

The Transatlantic Clasp

When, the previous January, Bevin had first set about forming a mutual defense treaty with France and the Benelux countries, he had hopefully conceived that the original bounds of that treaty (the Brussels Pact) could be expanded into a transatlantic system. As already mentioned, Marshall, after consulting with President Truman, had let Bevin know that the American Government was amenable. But before deciding, Marshall explained, evidence was wanted that the western European countries were really determined to defend themselves.

[2] *Ibid.,* January 22, 1948, pp. 720–1.

Soon after the Brussels Pact was signed—on March 17th—Bevin began to find out from the other members whether this extension of the mutual defense system was acceptable. Gathering that it was, he thereupon encouraged the Canadian Government to make known that it favored the project.[3] And he had hurried a special emissary to Washington, Gladwyn Jebb, the United Kingdom representative on the Brussels Treaty Permanent Commission. Out of his probing talks with members of the State Department and the Canadian Government there came ". . . a tentative draft treaty" which, according to his later account, "was very similar to the treaty actually signed a year later." [4]

Secretary Marshall and Undersecretary of State Lovett, on April 11th, began exploratory talks with Senators Vandenberg and Connally.

The President carefully watched each step along the route. As he recalled in his *Memoirs*, ". . . I always kept in mind the lesson of Wilson's failure in 1920. I meant to have legislative cooperation. Our European friends apparently remembered the League of Nations, too; they were most anxious to have not only a Presidential declaration of policy but also a Congressional expression confirming it." [5] During the first three weeks of April Lovett and Vandenberg continued to try to phrase a declaration of policy which was to put the Senate on record as favoring regional arrangements "based on continuous and effective self-help and mutual aid." [6]

State Department draftsmen rewrote the text of a mutual defense pact so that it would conform more nearly to the language of a resolution which Vandenberg and Lovett were drafting.

On April 22d the project was considered by the National Security Council. Uncertainty centered on the nature and extent of the mutual obligation to be incurred by the members of the pact and the procedure for bringing about collective action. When, on the day after this meeting, Forrestal, who had become the Secretary of Defense, asked Lovett how far in his talks with the representatives of the foreign governments we were committed to military actions, Lovett's answer—if the entry in Forrestal's diary is reliable—implied that he anticipated our assistance would be, chiefly, the provision of combat equipment, rather than participation in combined military action.[7]

---

[3] Donnelly, *Struggle for the World*, p. 208.

[4] Gladwyn Jebb (now Lord Gladwyn), *Halfway to 1984* (New York: Columbia University Press, 1966), pp. 17–18.

[5] Truman, *Years of Trial and Hope*, pp. 243–4.

[6] *Ibid.*, p. 244.

[7] Millis, ed., *The Forrestal Diaries*, entry dated April 23, 1948, p. 425. The entry reads: "This morning I asked him [Lovett] how far we were getting committed to such countries on a military basis. He said the whole point of the conversation was that we wanted to make it clear that we were not willing to become bound to an

But the conception of the European negotiating powers went beyond that. On the 23d Lovett brought to the President a special message from Bevin. This said that he had discussed the risks involved in a formal treaty association with Prime Minister Attlee and a few of his closest associates; that all agreed that if the United States Government summoned a conference to discuss defense arrangements for the North Atlantic area, the action would be more likely to guarantee peace than to provoke Russia into rash measures. In his opinion, only by devising a reliable Atlantic security system could the French be brought to agree to the program for Germany which was evolving at the Six-Power London Conference.

The primary point of Bevin's message was that to be effective the security arrangements "must carry real assurance for the nations of free Europe." [8] Unless it provided for collective resistance, Bevin said, it would be very difficult for Great Britain and the other western European countries to stand up to any new acts of aggression.

Late in April Lovett and Vandenberg met with Marshall, Dulles, and several congressional leaders and senior military officials at a consequential meeting at Blair House. Vandenberg produced from his pocket the most recent draft, over which he had been sweating many late afternoons with Lovett, of the resolution to be presented to the Senate. It had been reduced to a single page. All present thought well of it.[9] Dulles' enthusiasm seemed to have soared higher than those of the others; Hitler had not completely converted the Republican isolationists, but Stalin did.

At this juncture, on April 28th, the Canadian Government stepped to the fore. The Prime Minister, Louis Stephen St. Laurent, speaking in the Canadian Parliament, proposed formally that there should be a united transatlantic mutual defense system which would include and supersede the Brussels Pact.

One week later (May 4th) Bevin told the House of Commons, "The organization of all the Western European democracies, excellent and necessary though it is, in present circumstances can hardly be accomplished save within the framework of some even larger entity. I am not content to confine either propaganda or speeches or action to the assumption that Western Europe alone can save itself." [10] For months Sir

---

unequivocal contract to come to their assistance unless and until they manifested a desire to help themselves. Such assistance by us, he said, would of course have to take the form of some kind of lend-lease. I asked him what he would guess the total of arms procurement might be, and he replied 'Not less than $3 billion.' "

[8] Truman, *Years of Trial and Hope*, p. 245.

[9] Arthur H. Vandenberg, Jr., ed., *The Private Papers of Senator Vandenberg*, p. 406.

[10] *Parliamentary Debates*, House of Commons, May 4, 1948.

Stafford Cripps, the Chancellor of the Exchequer, had been complaining that the demands on the British financial resources were unbearable, certainly insufficient to support a European alliance; means and ends could only be equated in a broader combination, one that would have a transatlantic reach.

Onward from the Vandenberg Resolution

After it had been considered by the Foreign Relations Committee, Vandenberg introduced his Resolution May 19th.[11] The text was to remain almost unchanged in its transit through the Senate.

What was the next step to be? Bevin and most European Foreign Ministers were looking to the American Government to take over the initiative.

Truman and his advisers, although they preferred the procedure by which the Marshall program had been developed, were not unwilling. They still had not resolved in their own minds the nature and range of the obligations to be accepted in the contemplated mutual defense pact or the military arrangements for making it effective.[12] These questions had been thrashed out again at a meeting of the National Security Council on May 20th, the day after the Vandenberg Resolution was introduced on the Senate floor. Lovett pointed out the advantage of having the obligation mutual and reciprocal. He said: "We did not want any automatic, unlimited engagements under our constitutional system. We could not agree upon anything amounting to a guarantee. But we had to give assurances sufficient enough to inspire the confidence and bolster the faith of the countries of Europe who felt themselves under constant and heavy Soviet pressure." [13]

And how clear and conclusive ought, or must, our military arrangements be in evidence and support of the political pact? The Secretary of the Army, Kenneth Royall, reported to the President that the Joint Chiefs of Staff thought we should reserve decision until we found out

[11] According to the senior Democratic member of that Committee, Connally, "The resolutions were so ineptly redrafted that the entire committee worked them over, changed them and agreed on a draft of its own. Vandenberg's name was appendaged [sic] on the committee draft which became known as Senate Resolution 239." *My Name is Tom Connally*, p. 328.

[12] Lovett at this time thought " . . . the Western Union nations must display energy and competence in the perfection of their own plans—standardization of equipment, reactivation of their military organizations, etc.—before we give any indication of the scope or degree of our support." He had, he told Forrestal, advised the Western Union nations to be mindful of the history of the ERP. Millis, ed., *The Forrestal Diaries*, entry dated May 11, 1948, p. 434.

[13] Truman, *Years of Trial and Hope*, p. 245.

what the European countries had in mind. The Defense Ministers of the Brussels Pact powers had held their first meeting in April and had agreed on the organization of a permanent Military Committee. Concerted projects were being concocted by them. They were scheduled to meet again in July in London to continue their discussions of the coordination of national military plans and of weapons, the construction of bases to be used by all, and perhaps the formation of a combined staff. Royall reported that the Joint Chiefs thought we need send only observers to the military talks between the members of the Brussels Pact.

One question perplexed those conceiving the alliance. What nations should be asked to join, and be included in its protective mantle? It was agreed that Italy, Denmark, Iceland, and Portugal (mother country of the Azores) should join the seven countries whose representatives were conferring in Washington. Decision about Italy was hesitant. It did not border on the Atlantic. It could be expected to contribute little to joint defense, more probably to require support in a crisis. On the other hand, were Italy left out of the pact, it would be exposed to Russian threats and blandishments, and its large Communist party would use the grievance to convince their fellow countrymen that safety lay by taking up with Russia. The American representatives persuaded the reluctant British and French authorities that it was advisable to include Italy, since the American Government would supply it with arms to strengthen its powers of resistance.

On June 11th Senator Vandenberg, acting for the Foreign Relations Committee, called up the resolution for a vote in the Senate. Vandenberg's presentation speech is such a prime example of the grandiloquence not uncommon in Congress, that I am tempted to quote the whole of it, for the enjoyment of connoisseurs of the flourishes with which simple ideas may be adorned. But I refrain, and limit myself to remarking that the whole purport of his speech was to assure the world that our aim in entering the Pact and increasing our armed forces was " . . . to stimulate more effective relationships in pursuit of dependable peace for free men in a free world." [14]

The mantle of words within which the inner purpose was wrapped softened the main lines of the action recommended and made them seem deferential to the United Nations. The impacting purpose of the resolution was in those three paragraphs advising the President that it was the sense of the Senate that the American Government should favor:

"(2) Progressive development of regional and other collective arrangements for individual and collective self-defense in accordance with the purpose,

[14] Congressional Record, Senate, June 11, 1948, p. 7791.

principles, and provisions of the Charter.

(3) Association of the United States, by constitutional process, with such regional and other collective arrangements as are based on continuous and effective self-help and mutual aid, and as affects its national security.

(4) Contributing to the maintenance of peace by making clear its determination to exercise the right of individual or collective self-defense under Article 51 should any armed attack occur affecting its national security." [15]

The Senate was at the time in a hurry to end what had been a long and tiring session, and many members were engrossed in completing assignments of their committees. Thus the debate on the resolution was short and desultory. It was approved by a vote of 64 to 4.

The passage of the Resolution, as could have been predicted, was regarded in Moscow as another proof of hostility to the Soviet Union. The official Russian press, apparently well informed of the preliminary talks about concerted military arrangements, had tried to stimulate popular resistance in the Brussels Pact countries by bemoaning the fact that the burden of military expenditure they would incur would use up aid promised under the Marshall program. Thus the *New Times*, on June 2d, had concluded that "The Brussels treaty leads to a frenzy of armament building which will strike first and foremost at the living standards of the people of Western Europe."

Only two or three days after the newspapers in the West printed the text of the Vandenberg Resolution, they gave prominent place to excited reports of Soviet measures of obstruction and blockade of Berlin.

These almost simultaneous occurrences—the passage of the Vandenberg Resolution and the inauguration of the blockade of Berlin—quickened the impetus toward the completion of the Atlantic Pact envisaged in the Resolution. Soon thereafter the President authorized the State Department to complete the negotiations for a comprehensive defense pact.

In still another important way the policies of the countries in the Atlantic region were converging—in the formulation of plans for the reconstitution of Western Germany, and its inclusion in the economic, political, and military combinations of the West.

But the rough and challenging attempt of the Soviet Government to counter that impinging move is more explicable, I think, if account is taken of the frustrations and defections which, during these months of spring in the year 1948, upset the Communist realm. To these briefly, then, we will advert before relating Western plans for Germany.

[15] *Ibid.*

40

Frustrations and Fractures
in the Communist Realm

Italy Remains out of Communist Grasp

The American Government exerted itself strenuously to influence the outcome of the election in Italy in April. It was deemed crucial, since a Communist victory might confront the Brussels Pact countries and the United States with grave decisions. What was to be done, the diplomats had anxiously wondered, if the Communists won, and then, their main strength being in the industrial North, seized the power, set up a People's Government, and asked Tito to help them?

President Truman, experienced in Missouri politics, had been "very practical and approved use of every means to influence the election." [1] The Embassy in Rome had openly espoused the side of the Government, and it dispersed small sums among its supporters. The Pope, Pius XII, had reminded Italian Catholics of their duty to oppose atheistic Communism. Tens of thousands of Americans of Italian origin appealed to their relatives and friends to cast their vote for parties which would co-operate with American democracy and so assure Italy of continued aid within the Marshall Plan program.

The outcome had been gratifying to the West. The moderate government of Prime Minister Alcide de Gasperi secured a sufficient majority to enable it to govern effectively, even though the Communist vote was large.

The Communists denounced the elections as neither free nor democratic, as having been determined by pressure from within and without Italy. They made much in their public comment of the showing of the People's Democratic Front (Communist), for that reason acclaiming the elections as a victory rather than a defeat.

But Italy remained an active partner in the Western grouping.

[1] Conversation with Clark Clifford, June 1, 1966.

The Greek Rebellion Weakens

At cocktail parties it had been hinted that Tito was about to lessen his support of the rebels in Greece, perhaps had already begun to do so. Since, it has been learned that as long before as January (1948) Stalin had told Edvard Kardelj, an emissary of Tito's, "The uprising in Greece will have to fold up. . . . it had no prospect of success at all. What, do you think that Great Britain and the United States, the most powerful state in the world, will allow you to break their line of communication in the Mediterranean? Nonsense. And we have no navy. The uprising in Greece must be stopped, and as quickly as possible." [2]

In April, Gromyko, Deputy Foreign Minister, talked several times with Dean Rusk, Assitant Secretary of State for U.N. Affairs, and Hector McNeil, Britain's Minister of State, about ways and conditions of ending the civil war in Greece. But by then the American and British authorities were so confident that Tito was withdrawing his support from the Greek rebels that they were unwilling to consider the proposals for a settlement which the Soviet diplomat suggested—probably without much enthusiasm. [3]

I have no conclusive explanation of Stalin's reckoning. A good surmise is that he hoped that as a consequence of the termination of Yugoslav support, the control of the rebel movement in Greece would pass back from the adherents of Tito to those Communists who looked to Moscow.

Whatever the reasoning, the Communist effort to keep Greece in a revolutionary turmoil began to subside so much that the Chief of the Mission to Greece, Dwight Griswold, was able to report on May 25th that conditions in Greece were "substantially improved." [4]

Anxiety faded about what might happen in the Mediterranean region as the United States and its associates went forward with its program for restoring German economy and a German state; more confidently so because it was known by then that Tito and Stalin were quarreling, as we shall next tell. By the spring of 1949 Greek Government forces were clearly winning, and the rebel contingents made known their willingness to make peace.

To indulge in a leap into the present (1970)—when Greece is ruled by a military dictatorship constantly challenged by anti-American elements—an observation of Truman's has not lost pertinence. On learn-

[2] Djilas, *Conversations with Stalin*, p. 141.
[3] See Marshall Shulman's *Stalin's Foreign Policy Reappraised* (Cambridge, Mass.: Harvard University Press, 1963), pp. 71–2.
[4] Millis, ed., *The Forrestal Diaries*, entry dated May 25, 1948, p. 445.

ing that the Greek Government in power at the time was going to erect a statue of him commemorating American aid to Greece, Truman remarked: "I have never been in favor of erecting statues of people who are still alive. You never know when you have to turn around and tear it down."

Tito Quarrels with Moscow

As the coursing tide of events was coalescing the adversaries of Communism, another tide was eroding the connections between the Soviet Union and one of the most stalwart members of the Communist group, Yugoslavia. In their depths the movement of each of these tides affected the force and momentum of the other.

Russia had been tightening its control over the other East-Central European allies during 1947 and the early months of 1948. The potential enemy looming up was a mighty Western coalition including a resurgent Western Germany. In their frustration and suspicion the Russian political leaders became more exacting in their attempts to assure the complete subservient support of the nearby Communist associates. The better to prepare for the imminent contest with the West, the Russians were seeking to create, under their direction, a more thoroughly integrated Communist bloc; to enclose the political, economic, military, and intellectual life of these other countries safely within the mesh of Russia's making.

But the Yugoslavs had won their own independence. The elements which had secure control of the country had founded their own government, without deferring to the Russians. Tito, the partisan leader, was self-willed and hardened by many hazards. The Western Allies had bidden for his friendship. But he had chosen to be a staunch ally of Russia. Staunch and given to put himself to the front in some political situations —as when Yugoslav spokesmen took the lead in the formative meeting of the Cominform to reprove French and Italian Communists for their caution (see chap. 31); and bold, as in his support of Greek Communists; and stubborn, as in his claims for a segment of northeast Italy and the Carinthian province of Austria. Thus Tito was not disposed to subordinate his own leadership to Stalin when the Russians set about consolidating their hold over the whole of east-central Europe.

The first rift had occurred over economic relations. The current Russian plan contemplated that industrialization would be centered in Russia, and all other parts of its empire, except Czechoslovakia, should apply themselves mainly to the production of farm products and food supplies for Russian industrial workers. But Tito had other plans. He had already, without consulting Moscow, negotiated economic agreements with countries that were non-Communist, whereunder he could acquire machines and other equipment for basic industries. Russia had shown its displeasure by reducing its trade with and loans to Yugoslavia.

Tito had probably attributed Stalin's advice to desist from aiding the Greek rebels to a wish to deprive Yugoslavia of credit—and possibly territory—if the rebels won. Stalin was at the time discouraging Tito's project of a Balkan Federation.

In March 1948, during the same weeks that Marshal Sokolovsky was disrupting the Control Council for Germany by his accusations, the Russian Government made plain its displeasure at Tito's behavior. Early in the month a Yugoslav mission to Moscow had tried to induce the Russians to remove the trade restrictions between the two countries which were setting back Yugoslavia's industrial plan. The Russians resented the complaint. Characteristically they tried to smother it by their own.

On March 18th, Belgrade was notified that all Russian military advisers then in Yugoslavia would be brought home because of the unfriendly way they were being treated. This hid the real reason for Moscow's dissatisfaction: its inability to bring the stalwart Yugoslav army and well-organized secret police under the control of Russian officers, as they were in other satellite countries. Two days later all Russian civilian missions had also been ordered home.

Tito, saying he was surprised and hurt, asked for an explanation. It had been given not by Stalin but by the Russian Communist Party. In many, many ways, Tito was told, his regime had given offense; hostility to and harassment of Russian Missions; slander, deviation from Marxist-Leninist doctrines; and worst of all, a wish to win the favor of imperialist states and subject Yugoslavia to their influence. Western historians who have carefully studied the course of the Russian-Yugoslav break have concluded that Stalin's deepest grievance was due to the fact that Tito was dismissing Communist officials whose assignment had been to weaken his regime, and ejecting the most ardent supporters of the Soviet Union in the Central Committee of the Yugoslav Communist Party.[5]

This catalogue of Yugoslav offenses—called "errors"—had been also brought to the attention of the other members of the Cominform by a special letter. Stalin was bent on browbeating the Yugoslavs, calling other members of the Communist fraternity to join in doing so, and thereby cause Yugoslav Communist elements to cast Tito off. But Tito and the group about him did not scare. They had denied Moscow's allegations as unjust fabrications. They had stood fast, and even discharged

[5] Read, for example, Adam B. Ulam's interpretation in his book *Titoism and the Cominform* (Cambridge, Mass.): Harvard University Press, 1952).

from high office two officials who were defenders of Moscow. That happened in April. The resistant four—Tito, Djilas, Kardelj, and Rankovic —retained their control of the Yugoslav Communist Party and the government; perhaps they hoped that, nevertheless, the Soviet authorities would recognize their basic loyalty to Communism and cease to regard them as enemies.

The Russians were soon to risk war by blockading Berlin. Just before doing so, they made a daring play to bring Tito to heel. In June, the headquarters of the Cominform was moved from Belgrade to Bucharest. The Communist parties of all the Russian-led combination summoned the Yugoslav leaders to appear and be judged at a special meeting of the Cominform. They stayed home. So on June 28th, as the West was being shut out of Berlin, the other members of the Cominform resolved to expel Yugoslavia. In doing so, they expressed the conviction that enough "healthy" elements remained in the Yugoslav Communist party to cause Tito to recant or replace him. The vehemence of the Russian attacks proved how wrong was their judgment. Tito and his supporters maintained their defiant attitude and retained their power.

Whether Tito's defiance, along with the acceptance of the Italian Communists of the result of the elections, and the check of the Greek rebels, caused the Russians to become more determined to exclude any penetrating Western contact with East Germany and its other satellites is not known. Probably so.

The West Excluded from the Danube River

One step, besides the blockade of Berlin, that Russia took toward that end was to foreclose the possibility that had been cultivated in the West that the regulation of traffic on the Danube River—as an international waterway—would be again entrusted to international commissions, as it had been before the war. Then, by treaty, free and equal opportunity had been ensured to the shipping of all nations.

Truman at Potsdam had particularly shown his wish to secure an agreement that all the European waterways which ran through several countries into the seas and oceans, including the Danube, should be turned into genuine international thoroughfares. For he thought neighboring and nearby nations thus brought into friendly association would not be as likely to quarrel, and rivalries between larger powers would be averted. His pleas for this policy had a glow brighter and more personal than any he made at Potsdam for any other cause. Stalin had not been responsive, and his proposal had been subsequently submerged in the current of events.

315

The peace treaties signed with the Soviet satellites contained Danubian clauses which the Western negotiators believed meant acceptance of the general idea of accessibility and equality.[6] Both Byrnes and Bevin had regarded them as diplomatic achievements. But they had been disregarded as the Soviet Union and the satellites entered into their economic and political contracts.

At the meeting of the Council of Foreign Ministers in December 1946, during the brief spell of euphoria, it had been agreed to convene a conference of the four powers and the riparian countries to work out a new Danube regime. The conference had been scheduled to take place within six months after the Balkan peace treaties came into force. This having occurred in September 1947, the United States had immediately pressed for a conference. The Americans wanted Austria to participate, but they had to give up on this point, as no peace treaty had been signed with her.

When the conference opened in Belgrade on July 30th, it had become clear that Russia's position was impregnable. The riparian states along the greater part of the river were her satellites, and all (including Yugoslavia) unfailingly supported the Russian position vis-à-vis the Western states. Vishinsky, who presented Russia's draft of a new Danube convention, made it clear that the Soviet Union, which had been effectively excluded (by the London Six-Power recommendations about Germany) from the affairs of the Ruhr and other Western-held German territories, meant to exclude the Western powers from that part of the Danube which flowed through Communist-controlled area, that is, from Linz, in Austria, to the Black Sea. Russia, with the support of her satellites, had no intention of having Western shipping compete on the Danube and compile their observations; or, as expressed in their propaganda, they intended to make it impossible for the Western powers to use the Danube as a "thoroughfare for their own economic and political expansionist proclivities." [7]

The Yugoslav representative was as vehement as his other Communist colleagues in denouncing the previous presence of Britain, Italy, and France on the Danube commissions as imperialist exploitation.

In the interest of a common anti-Russian coalition, the United States supported the Franco-British claim that the 1921 Danube convention (to which America had not been a party) was still valid. But only these three representatives upheld this view; the other seven voted for the

[6] The pertinent provision in the peace treaties with Bulgaria, Hungary, and Romania read: "Navigation on the Danube shall be free and open for the nationals, vessels of commerce, and goods of all states in regard to port and navigation charges and conditions of merchant shipping."
[7] *New Times*, August 11, 1948.

passage, by a vote of 7 to 3, of the Russian proposal. Thereby the mouth of the Danube and the Iron Gates were to be placed under a joint Russian-Romanian administration; and membership in the new Danube Commission was to be restricted to riparian states exclusively (Russia had become riparian by annexing Bessarabia).

The new Danubian convention was signed by the seven Soviet bloc countries on August 18th. By then the blockade of Berlin was in full effect and the Western airlift into Berlin inaugurated.

41

Plans for Creating
a German Government

During the year-long fracas that followed the breakup in March 1948 of the Allied Control Council for Germany, the Western Allies had proceeded with their plans for regenerating the German economy and enclosing Western Germany within their general program for Western Europe.

The Six-Power discussions in London traveled fast along a route which was startlingly different from the one marked out three years before at Potsdam. The ruling attitude of the conferring governments was most plainly expressed by Bevin in the House of Commons on May 4, 1948, when he said in part: " . . . I can assure the House that we shall do all that is within our power to restore the Germans to a reasonable and healthy standard of life, politically and economically. There has been some speculation about the results of these talks, in particular on the question of the future constitution of Western Germany. . . . All I want to do now is to stress our recognition of the fact that there must be a development in the political life of Germany and that the Germans themselves must play a most important role. . . . We are satisfied that keeping Germany in a state of uncertainty is holding back its recovery and prejudicing all its neighbors as well. If a military government has to enter into every detail of the peoples' life, that government cannot be as efficient or as satisfactory as a government created with its roots in the people themselves. It is towards the latter objective that we are now striving and endeavoring to find a solution." [1]

Not all members of Parliament thought the program in mind for Germany complete, since it did not contemplate German rearmament as part of Western Union. It was argued in the debate most ably by a re-

[1] *Parliamentary Debates,* House of Commons, May 4, 1948.

tired military officer—Brigadier Head—that even if the Western Allies succeeded in producing an economic recovery, it would have been in vain if they neglected to build up their military forces—including German forces. "If they do not do so," this militant member of the House remarked, "we shall in all probability have a cardboard front of alliances, unions and a tough foreign policy. The right honorable Gentleman [Bevin] is very good at being tough, but I am sure that no one would want him to have to repeat the humiliating role of my right honorable Friend, the Member for Warwick and Leamington [Eden] of protesting against continued aggression by brandishing a revolver in the face of the aggressor—a revolver which everybody knew contained a rather damp blank cartridge." [2]

The French propensity to act as mediator between the "Anglo-Saxons" and the Soviet Union had slackened. On April 6th, Couve de Murville (then head official in the French Foreign Office) had flown to Berlin to see whether the differences of opinion among the Western Allies about the nature of the government-to-be of Germany could be adjusted. During his brief visit there, Clay had composed a memorandum on guide lines. De Murville and General Koenig agreed it might be acceptable to all. So the three Commanders-in-Chief had sent it on for consideration at the Conference in London, which was about to reconvene. [3] The Conference was impressed, and in essentials adopted the suggested procedure and principles.

The French Government had continued to pause before subjecting its zone to trizonal control before a West German Government was established. The consultations about Trizonia had been the subject of special denunciation in Soviet press and propaganda. The French Cabinet, though on the route to separation from the Soviet Government, was still reluctant to have the break sharp and final. But it had agreed that in the interim further steps should be taken to insure full coordination of the three zones in economic, trade, banking, and currency policies and measures.

On adjourning (June 2d) the London Conference issued a statement of the recommendations made to the governments concerned. [4] They were in accord with previous indications. Three were of primary importance.

(1) That German economic redevelopment should be assisted. As explained in the accompanying comment, "Not only would a chronically depressed Germany be unable to contribute sorely needed goods and

[2] *Ibid.*

[3] This memo is printed in full in Clay, *Decision in Germany*, pp. 398–400.

[4] The text of this communiqué, with its Annex on the international control of the Ruhr, was published on June 2d; a letter of explanation justifying the recommendation was issued June 7, 1948.

materials to the participating countries of the ERP, but it would contribute a positive menace to the prosperity and security of these countries. It has now been fully agreed that the bizonal area, including the
critical Ruhr industrial complex, and the French zone should participate
in the recovery program. . . . In these plans there is no intent that German recovery shall have priority over the needs of other participating
countries, but only the intent that Germany shall share in the common
effort and the common welfare."

(2) That it was desirable that the German people should quickly form
political organizations and institutions which should enable them to assume responsibility for government, compatible with the minimum requirements of the occupation as long as it lasted, and thereafter independence.

Thus, the Military Governors approving, the Ministers-Presidents of
the states in the three zones should be authorized to convene a Constituent Assembly in order to prepare a constitution for the approval of the
participating states. Delegates to the Assembly were to be chosen in
each of the states in accordance with procedure determined by the legislative bodies of each.

The constitution, it was stipulated, should bring into existence a Federal form of government; one which would adequately protect the rights
of the respective states, while providing sufficient central authority, and
which would guarantee individual rights.

(3) That there should be established for the control of the Ruhr an international authority in which the six conferring countries and Germany
would participate. This arrangement would not require the political separation of the Ruhr from Germany. It was contemplated that the authority would " . . . control the *distribution* [not the production] of coal,
coke and steel of the Ruhr in order that, on one hand, industrial concentration in that area shall not become an instrument of aggression, and
on the other, will be able to make its contribution to all countries participating in a European cooperative economic program, including, of
course, Germany itself." (author's italics)

No recommendation more clearly marked the breakaway of the West
from the Soviet Union than this one concerning the Ruhr. In the supervision of the Ruhr industries—regarded by Moscow as the real creating
and upholding force behind Hitler—Russia was to have no part, while
Germany, as owner, would sooner or later dominate.

The sponsors of these recommendations tried hard to allay fears that
after gaining strength, Germany might again become an aggressive menace. The peoples who were sufferers and survivors of German efforts to
be masters were being asked to release this nation again.

But not yet entirely on trust. Various "security" provisions were to be retained. One of these signified how deeply the United States had become mired in Germany. This was the recommendation that each government which shared in the occupation should be pledged not to withdraw its forces without prior consultation with the others. The authors of the report of the Conference also adjured the occupying powers to make sure that Germany remained disarmed and demilitarized. The question of how and how long this rule was to be enforced was left in suspense.

One statement in the Conference's report could hardly have carried conviction even in the West. This averred that the recommendations did not preclude eventual Four-Power agreement, that on the contrary, they should facilitate it. For concurrently it was asserted that any Four-Power agreement must be in line with the policies recommended in the report, since these were the only sound terms for the entry of a democratic Germany in a community of free peoples.

The Response to the Recommendations

Even before the London Conference evolved the program whereunder the past would be put aside and Western Germany would be invited to be a partner in the program for European revival and in the anti-Soviet coalition, the American authorities in March had revised their rules about de-Nazification. They urged the German officials to bring the program to a rapid close. The Germans at first hesitated, then eased and constricted the program. Some of those spared were Nazi criminals.[5]

Bevin promptly (June 8th) praised the recommendations of the Conference. Marshall on the next day made known that the American Government also approved them. In doing so, he said, reassuringly: " . . . the U.S. Government believes that the London recommendations, which at the outset will apply to the larger part of Germany, represent a major step toward a comprehensive solution of German problems." Also that "the United States believes that the London program will stand the test of experience and that if conditions can be developed for its application to Germany as a whole, it would resolve the issues which have thus far divided Germany under the occupation powers and would thereby remove the principal obstacle to the development of a peaceful Europe." [6]

The historians and all who may read these observations are left to wonder how and why the Secretary conjured up the belief that the poli-

[5] Gimbel, *The American Occupation of Germany*, pp. 172–3.
[6] State Department *Bulletin*, June 20, 1948, pp. 810–11.

cies propounded at the London Conference could become, with Russian assent, the basis of the social, economic and political life for the whole of Germany.

The French Government, which had stipulated that the recommendations of the Conference must be submitted to its Parliament for approval, found that very hard to secure. Despite the stipulation that the emergent Western German Government must be a federation with limited powers, many members of the Cabinet as well as the Assembly feared that Germany could become so powerful that France might again become subject to its will. Other members deplored the fact that the Ruhr, and its industries, would remain in German possession. In the Assembly the large Communist contingent railed against acceptance. So did the supporters of General de Gaulle, who predicted that the agreement would have tragic consequences. They urged that the French Government should insist on its revision, and if rebuffed, manage the French zone of occupation in the same way as the Saar. Even the Socialists were upset because there was no definite provision for control of the Ruhr *production* (author's italics), and because Germany might be able to cast a deciding vote in the Ruhr authority. Moreover, many of them were unhappy about the widening separation between East and West. At the end of an impassioned debate, even while insurrectional strikes were taking place, the Assembly recorded its approval on June 16th by a close vote: 297-289.

Prime Minister Robert Schuman had stood fast behind the Foreign Minister, Bidault, who had approved the London recommendations. But already unsettled by a decree (known as the Poinso-Chapuis Decree) which touched on the sensitive question of government support for religious education, the Ministry was condemned. Within a few days Schuman was voted out of office.

The Soviet Government had repeatedly complained and protested at the course being marked out by the Western Allies in the London Conference.

The opposition and anxieties of the Soviet authorities were not dissipated by the affirmation that a unified Western Germany would be subject to rules and constraints. With vision still darkened by memories of blood and death, they remained mistrustful of the eventual intentions of the Western Allies and their former enemy, Germany. The scarred spirits of the Russians still ached with the thought that the Germans, alone or in combination, would seek to revise Germany's eastern boundaries, threatening Poland and the Soviet Union.

Their distrust and dislike was too self-enclosed to allow room for the thought that the future conduct of the Soviet Union and its subservient associates might largely determine whether lifting the ban on the rearming of Western Germany would be hastened.

The tenor of Soviet official judgment was similar to those in the *New Times* of June 9th after the recommendations were made public: that the state to be formed would be a puppet state, an industrially developed colony of American monopolies, a breeding ground of reaction and Fascism, a strategical bridgehead, a supplier of cheap common fodder. "Hence, the day of the separation of Western Germany is announced as the day of the revival of the policy of Kaiser Wilhelm and Hitler, the Drang nach Osten."

Just as the West tended to consider that only a regime opposed to Communism would be a reliable ally, so the Soviet Government probably felt that only if Germany were under Communist regime could Russia and its neighbors really be secure against German pressure and hostility.

Although, when it imposed a blockade of Berlin, the Soviet Government chose at first to explain this action as a countermeasure against the long-postponed currency reform in Germany which the Western powers were effectuating, there is ample evidence that the real object of its wrath was the London program for Germany.

Its final attempt to use diplomacy and propaganda to induce the Western Allies to abstain from going forward with the London program was the convocation by the Russian and Polish Governments of a conference of the Foreign Ministers of the whole Communist bloc—of their two countries, and of Albania, Bulgaria, Czechoslovakia, Hungary, Romania, and Yugoslavia. Its communiqué published June 25th, after denouncing the London program, advocated (1) the resumption of four-power control of Germany, including the Ruhr; (2) the establishment of a provisional government for the whole of Germany; (3) the conclusion of a peace treaty with that government, to be followed by rapid departure of all occupation forces; and assured reparations.[7]

But by then the blockade of Berlin was on. Thereby the Russian authorities hoped to shake the Western combination and cause it to suspend its program for Germany; or alternatively so to isolate and smother Berlin that it could be absorbed into East Germany and subjected to Communist control.

[7] See *L'Année Politique*, June 1948, for fuller description of this proposal.

PART TEN

The Dangerous Crunch over Berlin

42

To Remind, The Unwritten
Accords About Access

Was access to the Western zones through the Soviet zone to and from Berlin a right or a privilege? And if a right, what was its scope? The verbal barrages, while the Russians blockaded the city, formed a pattern around these eristic questions. In reality the brisk exchange of notes was merely a supporting exercise of the opponents. The arguments about the meaning of the pertinent accords gave countenance to their actions but did not determine them. Nevertheless, a brief reminder of these accords, and of the conjuncture in which they had been made, may assist judgment.

The joint, but divided, occupation of Berlin, like the zonal arrangements, had been shaped by political rather than military prevision; and how wrong it was! It was encased by the then prevalent supposition that allies in the war, West and East, would continue to cooperate, and have common—or at least compatible—interests in the occupation and control of Germany.

A local German Administration (the Magistrat) was entrusted with the task of governing all four sectors of the city. But it was to have limited powers and be subject to the orders of a Four-Power allied authority, the Kommandatura.

The American military authorities had taken the initiative as early as February 27, 1945, when the United States Chiefs of Staff had sent a memorandum to the British Chiefs of Staff and the Soviet General Staff, which stated: "The United States Chiefs of Staff propose that the general principle of freedom of transit across zones of occupation and zones of tripartite occupation be accepted. Details of transit shall be worked out between the local commanders. The foregoing is proposed as an interim military measure pending general agreements as to transit which may be expected from the European Advisory Commission." [1]

[1] *Foreign Relations of the United States,* 1945. Vol. 3, p. 189.

The British Chiefs of Staff concurred. The Soviet General Staff did not reply. The question of access to Berlin did not find its way to the European Advisory Commission. This was due, I believe, to the wish of the American military authorities that the arrangements for access be left to military commanders and postponed until it was clear what routes were desirable and serviceable.

Subsequent haste did not compensate for the delay and slip-out of the subject between the American military and civilian authorities. The understandings that were tardily reached by zone commanders were unwritten, incomplete, and in one respect inconclusive.

Having consulted Churchill, who sadly shelved his previous strong objections and said: ". . . we are obliged to conform to your decision," Truman, on June 14, 1945, proposed to Stalin a withdrawal of their armies into respective zones of occupation in Germany and Austria on June 21st. "As to Germany, I am ready to have instructions issued to all American troops to begin withdrawal into their own zone on 21 June in accordance with arrangements between the respective commanders, including in these arrangements simultaneous movement of national garrisons into Greater Berlin and provision of free access by air, road, and rail from Frankfurt and Bremen to Berlin for U.S. forces." General Marshall (or his staff), who in 1948 as Secretary of State was going to have to worry over the blockade of Berlin, drafted this message.[2]

Stalin had agreed to the entry of U.S. troops into Berlin, but he had *not* mentioned any arrangements for permanent access from the Western zones to Berlin.

In the first directive which Marshall had sent to Eisenhower regarding the redeployment, access had not been mentioned. But on June 25, 1945, he wrote the Supreme Commander: ". . . of our thinking about access rights to Berlin. . . . It will be noted that the proposed . . . directive . . . contains no action to obtain transit rights to Berlin and Vienna on a combined basis. In accordance with the President's message to Stalin . . . these should be arranged with Russian commanders concerned simultaneously with arrangements for other adjustments, by Eisenhower for Berlin and [General Mark] Clark for Vienna. It is assumed that appropriate Russian commanders have been instructed accordingly . . . and it is desired that Deane [General John Deane, head of the U.S. Military Mission to Moscow] confirm this with the Soviet staff." [3]

Deane had advised Marshall and Eisenhower on June 25th that he had asked General Alexei Antonov, the Soviet Chief of Staff, to confirm by

[2] Truman, *Year of Decisions*, p. 303.
[3] *Ibid.*, p. 306.

328

letter that Soviet commanders had been authorized to agree with American commanders on freedom of access by road, rail, and air to Berlin and Vienna. Two days later he reported that Marshall Georgi Zhukov, Commander-in-Chief of the Red armies in the West, had been empowered to *negotiate* for the Russians with General Clay, Deputy in Berlin to General Eisenhower, and General Sir Ronald Weeks (for Britain). Deane had followed up this report by informing Marshall: "it is my opinion that when our representatives meet with Zhukov there will be little difficulty in arranging for free access for our troops in Berlin, and that, if I am correct in this, the same principle will apply to Vienna . . ." [4]

In three talks, the first on June 29th, all at Zhukov's headquarters in Berlin, agreement was reached on the arrangements for Four-Power control of Germany. But the question of access to Berlin was not resolved. As recalled by Clay, "We [he and Weeks] had explained our intent to move into Berlin utilizing three rail lines and two highways and such air space as we needed. Zhukov would not recognize that these routes were essential and pointed out that the demobilization of Soviet forces was taxing existing facilities. [5] I countered that we were not demanding exclusive use of these routes but merely access over them without restrictions other than the normal traffic control and regulations which the Soviet administration would establish for its own use. General Weeks supported my contention strongly. . . . We did not wish to accept specific routes which might be interpreted as a denial of our right of access over all routes, but there was merit to the Soviet contention that existing routes were needed for demobilization purposes. We had already found transport a bottleneck for our own re-deployment. Therefore Weeks and I accepted as a temporary arrangement the allocation of a main highway and rail line and two air corridors, reserving the right to reopen the question in the Allied Control Council. . . . While no record was kept at this meeting, I dictated my notes that evening and they include the following: '*It was agreed that all traffic—air, road and rail, . . . would be free from border search or control by customs or military authorities.*'" [6]

[4] *Ibid.*, p. 307.

[5] The assumption behind this discussion was that the problem which the military commanders had in mind in discussing access at this time was that of travel and supply of the garrisons. This is indicated by Zhukov's statement that " . . . one railway and one highway should be enough to feed and supply a small garrison of 50,000 troops, the overall combined figure of British and American occupying forces." The question of supply for people of Berlin was not mentioned. Memo by General Parks; see fn. 6.

[6] Clay, *Decision in Germany*, pp. 25–26.

Robert Murphy, Political Adviser to Eisenhower, who was present at the meeting, sent a summary report the next day, June 30th, to the State Department, which stated that the Russians agreed that "with respect to roads, Autobahn Hanau-Magdeburg-Berlin will be used by U.S. and British troops without restrictions"; and with respect to rail transport they agreed to "exclusive use by U.S. of standard gauge line

The agreement reached with Zhukov on June 29, 1945, about Western access to Berlin, had been made more precise in subsequent sessions of the Control Council for Germany.

At the meeting of the European Advisory Commission on July 9th it was agreed that "the Allied [Control] Council will make necessary arrangements for transit in Austria by road, rail, air and water for goods and supplies required by the forces of occupation in Austria, including those forces allotted for the occupation of the city of Vienna and personnel of Allied Commission, and likewise for common use of transport and communication facilities and public utility services in city of Vienna." Russia's Ambassador F. T. Gusev had said that these principles applied to Berlin as well as Vienna.[7] This was properly regarded as formal recognition of the right of access to Berlin.

On September 10th the Four-Power Control Council had agreed that 16 trains a day could travel from Western zones to Berlin; on October 3d this was increased to thirty-one trains, seven passenger and twenty-four freight trains. On November 30th the Council had agreed that the three Western occupying Powers should have free and unhindered use of the three air corridors. Subsequently detailed agreements were also reached in the Control Council about traffic on rivers and canals to and from Western zones through the Soviet zone to Berlin. The Soviet authorities had wished to reserve the right to regulate the movements of trains and passengers through the Soviet zone, but they agreed to arrangements to assure prompt Soviet disposition of the formalities; these did not include the right to inspect.

Each occupying power, it was understood, was to provide food, power, and other supplies needed to maintain its garrison in Berlin. But who was to assure a supply of essentials for the Germans living in that city? The Western Allies had wished Russia, as occupant of the adjacent zone, to assume that task. But on July 7th, at the second of the three preparatory

---

Greine-Göttingen-Belra and unrestricted use by the allies of the line Goslar-Magdeburg-Berlin," and "It was agreed that all road, rail and air traffic on authorized routes would be free from border search or control by customs or military authorities; but traffic to conform to Russian police control in the normal way." State Department Publication, Potsdam Papers, Document 112.

General Parks, Commander designate of the American garrison in Berlin, who was present at this conference, made rather complete notes of the discussion, but these were not sent back to Washington until April 7, 1948, by a letter from Robert Murphy to the Assistant Secretary of State for Occupied Areas, Charles Saltzman. In a memorandum of April 1, 1948, to Major General Alfred M. Gruenther, then Director of Joint Staff of the Joint Chiefs of Staff, General Parks transmitted a copy of these notes and identified them as his own.

The notes are printed in *Foreign Relations of the United States, 1945*, Vol. III, pp. 358 ff. They in general corroborate Clay's account.

[7] *Ibid.*, pp. 158–9.

talks between Clay, Zhukov, and Weeks, Zhukov had refused to accept any responsibility for providing supplies for Germans in the Western sectors.[8] Thus the American and British Governments had been compelled to do so. But how could they deliver what was needed and ship out what the people of Berlin might provide in return unless they had adequate and unhindered right to traverse the Soviet zone?

However, the strongest basis for the opinion of the Western Allies that access to Berlin was a right, not a privilege, not only for the occupation forces but for the Germans in the Western zones, was the stipulation in the Potsdam Agreement that all Germany "shall be treated as a single economic unit." The inference that Germans should be allowed to move anywhere in Germany as needed to carry on their business was natural and justified.

---

[8] He said that Poland controlled the coal of Silesia and all food grown in the Eastern zone was needed by the inhabitants or for its Eastern neighbors. Clay, *Decision in Germany*, pp. 27–8.

Had the Soviet Union provided these supplies, it would have made the whole of Berlin dependent on the East, and probably would have brought about the economic amalgam of Berlin with the Eastern zone.

43

The Dissolution of the
Four-Power Administration

The first postwar elections in Berlin had been held in October 1946. Despite the effort of the Soviet Government to legitimatize Communist rule in East Germany by forcing the Social Democratic Party to merge with the Communist Party to form the Socialist Unity Party —dominated by the Communists—the outcome of the elections in the whole of Berlin was: (in percent)

SPD (Social Democratic Party)	48.7
CDU (Christian Democratic Party)	22.2
LDP (Liberal Democratic Party)	9.3
	80.2
SED (Socialist Unity Party—Communist)	19.8

With prevision *The Economist* had asked: "Will the Russians swallow the affront? Or will they draw the conclusion that wooing Germany does not pay them, and resort to retaliation? If the Russians decided on retaliation they will not be lacking means to carry it out." [1]

When first the city (Berlin) Assembly had met, only one-fifth of the members were Communist. Ernst Reuter, former Communist who had left that group and returned to the Social Democratic Party, had been elected Mayor (Oberbuergermeister) of Berlin. But the Soviet representative on the Berlin Four-Power Kommandatura had objected to him and prevented his assumption of office. Thus the city government had to stumble along under an Acting Mayor, Frau Louise Schroeder, who was also a stalwart resistant against the Communists.

By the fall of 1947 the Western and Soviet members of both the Control Council and the Kommandatura had fallen out about almost all

[1] *The Economist*, October 26, 1946.

features of the conduct of the occupation in Berlin. The antagonisms were the more constant and abrasive because in Berlin the antagonists were forced to deal daily with one another. The Kommandatura, conceived as a cooperative council of concordant Allies, had become a cradle for their contentions.[2]

Precursory to the Blockade

There had been ominous warnings before Russia lunged. For instance, as early as December 19, 1947, after the breakup of the Conference of Foreign Ministers in London, the *Tägliche Rundschau,* the newspaper of the Red Army in Berlin, had stated, "It was decided at Yalta that Berlin must remain the German capital. . . . This means that as long as there is a quadripartite administration of Germany and the Control Council functions, Berlin will have a quadripartite administration. The situation changes if quadripartite administration becomes fictional. . . . if a West German Government were set up it would affect Berlin." [3]

By April 1948, Russian interference with the movement of personnel and goods in and out of Berlin had become so deranging that the American and British occupation authorities had, in the course of the spring, begun to air-lift members of their garrisons and supplies for them into Berlin. The Russians buzzed the planes. As Clay remarked at the time, "Berlin is no place for a nervous person."

Then, a few days after the report of the London Conference on Germany was made public the Russians made their main move. On June 11th Soviet military officers halted all rail traffic between Berlin and West Germany for one day, saying, however, that the arrest was temporary. Then they closed the main automobile road from Helmstedt on the pretext that repairs were needed for a bridge over the Elbe.

While these barriers were being set, the Soviet member quit a meeting of the Berlin Kommandatura, almost with a curse. He notified the Western members that the Four-Power joint administration of Berlin was at an

[2] Some of the more intense quarrels within the Kommandatura had been over trade union election procedures; wage policy; the distribution of imported goods, especially coal, electricity, and gas; between inhabitants of the several sectors; and the trade between Berlin and Western zones.

The Soviet Government wanted to require permits for transit of goods from Berlin westward through the Soviet zone. This might have been induced partly by a wish to prevent the circuitous flight of assets originating in Eastern zones via Berlin—often in connection with plans to emigrate to the West. But it was also a form of political pressure.

[3] Quoted in Donnelly, *Struggle for the World,* p. 254.

end. The Russian publicists blamed the Western Allies for their obstinacy in rejecting all Communist proposals for improving the lot of the people, their reactionary outlook, and their rudeness. One of the typical Russian versions of the occurrence read: "When the . . . [Soviet Representative] proposed that concrete measures to be taken to improve the condition of Berlin workers be considered, Colonel Frank Howley, the American representative on the Kommandatura, got up and left the room, remarking casually on the way out that he had no desire to take further part in the discussion and was going to get some sleep. Marshall Sokolovsky's protest concerning Colonel Howley's unseemly behavior . . . remained unanswered. General Clay's tacit approval of the scandalous behavior of his subordinate made it quite clear that Colonel Howley's deliberate rudeness was intended to provoke the termination of the activities of the Allied Commandants." [4]

In truth, Howley and Clay were fed up by the Russian practice of putting forward proposals for the record, with the foreknowledge that they were unacceptable. They decided not to put up any longer with the Communist use of the Kommandatura as a funnel for their stream of abusive agitation.

[4] Article by L. Ilyin, "The Truth About the Berlin Situation," in *New Times,* July 14, 1948.

44

The Igniting Monetary Reform

Undaunted, though still undecided how to deal with the Russian pinch on traffic to and from Berlin, the Western Powers in mid-June went ahead with another measure over which they had been wrangling with the Soviet Government. They enacted a comprehensive monetary reform in their zones. Berlin was specifically left outside its range.

The Western occupants had long before come to the conclusion that a thorough monetary, banking and fiscal reform program was essential. There were imperative reasons for putting it into effect. A new currency in which the Germans would have confidence was needed so that investment, production, and trade would revive. The German banking system was still weak and disorganized; a more adequate and unified system was badly wanted. Then, to satisfy a prevalent sense of injustice and imbalance, it was deemed necessary to bring about a fairer allocation of war burdens and losses, by a reformed system of taxation and a capital levy.

A program to these ends had been carefully worked out by three American economic and financial specialists. It had been approved by the War and State Departments as long ago as August 1946 and had been laid before the Control Council in September 1946. At first all four members had seemed to favor the principles of the drastic measures contemplated, but then a serious hitch had occurred because the proposed reforms raised the issue of the nature and control of the German monetary and banking system.

By June 1948 the immediate effectuation of one segment of this program of reform was judged crucial for the revival of the German economy envisaged by the London Conference and the Marshall Plan projections. The Western Powers had grown impatient over the prolonged parleys and postponements, and felt justified in acting without Russian assent.

A most summary review of the history of the monetary situation and problem will indicate clearly why they decided to delay no longer.

335

The prewar reichsmark had continued to circulate in all Germany. The Allies had also introduced a military currency which the Germans had been required to accept. It was exchangeable for the old German mark at a ratio of one to one. The American Government had given a set of printing plates for this military currency to the Soviet authorities. These had circulated substantial sums of this currency, without informing the Control Council of the amount.

This addition to the quantity of military currency had shaken confidence in the value of the mark. It was, moreover, costly for the United States and Britain. For while the Soviet officials in Germany refused to give rubles in exchange for military currency, the American and British finance officers in Germany gave dollars and pounds, not only for the military currency they had expended but for some of the Russian issue which had percolated into the Western zones. Thus it had come about that many more dollars and pounds were being paid out in exchange for military marks than had been reckoned.

Therefore, the American and British Governments, as well as the Germans, wished for a new currency, the quantity of which could be controlled. Their proposal had been that an identical (new) currency would circulate in the whole of Germany, as did the reichsmark. The Western Allies had thought the facilities in Washington, Paris, and London were best qualified to print the new currency. The Soviet Government had wanted to have it printed in Leipzig (in the Russian zone) and in Berlin. The British and French Governments had been willing to agree to the Soviet proposal provided the printing, and presumably issuance, were under "identical quadripartite control" in both cities. But the American Government had insisted that it be printed and issued in Berlin alone, since it was only there that a Four-Power administration was operative.

That question had been discussed by the Foreign Ministers at their alienating meeting in Moscow in March 1947. But the quarrel over other elements of German policy had scraped away the chance of agreement about the whole comprehensive program of reform, including the currency change-over. The negotiations had foundered time and time again.[1]

The Americans and British had become convinced that they had to go

[1] In January 1948 when General Clay offered a compromise proposal in the Control Council, the Soviet member agreed that the new currency should be printed only in Berlin, under quadripartite control. The financial experts advising the Council seemed to be near agreement even as regards the allocation of the currency among the occupied powers. But the negotiators had differed about the extent of economic unity needed to conform to the monetary reform. The Soviet representative urged that there be a joint German central bank under joint Four-Power control and a joint central finance department. The Western representative did not see, in light of past differences, how this could operate effectively with a Soviet veto. So

forward at once. They had planned that the monetary reform should be made effective in the bizonal area on June 1st, despite Russian objections. But when, at the last session of the Six-Power Conference in London, the French Government had agreed to have its zone included in the currency reform because their occupation troops were partly paid in German currency, its provisions had to be considered anew. The French asked for a better quotient of the new currency than the others were ready to concede. This and other differences were so stubborn that the Americans and British finally informed the French that they would have to proceed in the bizonal area. At the last moment, in the small hours of the morning, after the National Assembly had approved the London Six-Power agreement about Germany, the French Government had accepted a compromise offer and the delayed reform measures were made trizonal.

On June 18th the currency measures were proclaimed by the commanders of the Western zones.[2] These provided for the substitution of one new Deutsche mark for every ten of the old reichsmarks, and for an equivalent reduction in the nominal amount of all indebtedness.[3] The currency reform law did not foreclose the question of area of circulation of the new mark. The American and British Governments were willing to consider a separate currency for Berlin. When Robertson informed Sokolovsky of the intention to introduce the new mark into the British zone, he explicitly stated that the British sector of Berlin would not be affected, and that all appropriate measures would be taken to maintain trade between the British zone and Berlin and also between the British and Russian zones.[4] General Clay's notification also excluded Berlin.

But the introduction of the New Deutsche mark in the Western zone was deemed troublesome by the Soviet Government. It asserted that demoted old reichsmarks would seep into East Germany and invigorate

---

they demurred. The talks had thereafter remained stalled as the quarrel over German policy went from bad to worse to worst.

See Manuel Gottlieb's analytical narrative *The German Peace Settlement and the Berlin Crisis* (New York: Paine-Whitman, 1960), p. 186.

[2] The original intention had been to introduce the financial tax and social reform measures, including the capital levy, at the same time. But at the last moment these were postponed. For all the technicians were busy with the complexities of the currency reform, and the occupying powers concluded they did not have the administrative capacity to carry out the other measures at the same time.

[3] The terms of the four reform measures promulgated were complex. Since all holders of reichsmarks were required to deposit them, and except for a minimal amount, 35 percent of all bank accounts were extinguished, the other 65 percent to be converted at a 10 to 1 rate, and five percent had to be invested in government securities, it might be more correct to say that, in effect, owners of the reichsmarks got only 6 new Deutsche marks in exchange.

[4] His Majesty's Government Publication (1948). *Germany: An Account of the Events Leading up to a Reference of the Berlin Question to the United Nations* (CMD 7534) p. 17.

the black market and interfere with Soviet currency control. The East Germans might think the new marks worth more than their official value and seek to procure them, thus causing the value of old reichsmarks still in circulation in the Eastern zone to fall.

On June 19th, Sokolovsky issued a statement accusing the West of disrupting German economic unity, and he announced that Russia would prevent the new Deutsche mark (which quickly became known as the westmark) from circulating in Berlin. He also wrote letters to his three associates in the now defunct Control Council, protesting any attempt to introduce it into any part of Berlin.

A meeting of the financial and economic advisers of all *four* occupying powers was immediately arranged. The Western representatives stated they were willing to have Soviet zone currency used in *all* Berlin, provided that its issuance was controlled by the four-power Kommandatura.

Refusing this bid, on June 23d the Soviet authorities affixed stickers to Eastern currency notes, devalued them in the same ratio as had the West, and declared them to be valid for *all* Berlin.[5] Concurrently they ruled that the new westmark must *not* circulate in Berlin. Sokolovsky informed the Mayor of Berlin that these measures were justified because "Berlin is located in the Soviet zone of occupation and economically forms a part of that zone." At the same time he claimed the right to exercise authority over the Magistrat in matters which concerned all parts of the city.

The Crisis Within Berlin

Thereupon, the three governors of the Western zone, the French reluctantly, made known that the westmark would be introduced into their sectors of Berlin.[6] On informing Sokolovsky of their intention, the

[5] The Russian currency reform law provided in Article 14 that "The putting into circulation in the Soviet occupation zone or in greater Berlin of currency notes other than those provided in . . . this order will be regarded as an act designed to undermine the economy, and persons guilty of such will be punished accordingly."

[6] In an effort to avert Soviet rejoinders, the Western military governors issued an order stipulating that 75 percent of all salaries and wages in the Western sectors of Berlin should be paid in Soviet zone currency and 25 percent in the new westmark. In effect this meant a lingering willingness to end the dispute over currency by having both currencies circulating freely in all Berlin. There they could compete for acceptance. The Germans living in West Berlin could save and trade in the new westmarks if they chose. The Germans in East Berlin could do whatever the Soviet authorities permitted them to do and they decided to do.
The Soviet authorities took this to be testimony of the failure of the attempts to include the Western sector of Berlin in the economy of Bizonia rather than an effort to be accommodating. See, for example, *New Times*, July 14, 1948.

Western representatives stressed the opinion that no one Power could make enactments valid for the whole city, that any orders for the whole of Berlin must be endorsed by all four occupants.

What happened next has been so vividly described by Desmond Donnelly it will be quoted in full: "Clearly the next forty-eight hours were to be critical and most confusing for the Berliners, who found themselves confronted with the choice of changing their money into two rival currencies. A special meeting of the City Assembly was called for four o'clock in the afternoon [June 23d] in the City Hall, which stood in the Soviet sector. Long before the meeting was due to take place a large crowd had begun to gather, nearly all of them Communists. The crowd then broke into the building, displaying almost military precision, and it forcibly took possession of the gallery in the Assembly and the upper floors of the building. The uproar and hooliganism became so bad that the Assembly's meeting was held up for two hours. When it was possible to begin the meeting, a resolution was put before the Assembly agreeing that the Soviet currency would operate in the Soviet sector and the Western currency in the other three sectors.

"This was opposed strongly by the Communists but—despite threats to confiscate the savings and social insurance funds of West Berliners that were held in the Soviet sector and the hostile mob in and around the building—the Assembly refused to be intimidated and voted strongly to accept this proposition. There followed one of the most ugly scenes in Berlin since the early days of Nazism. Communist thugs, some of them well known as former Nazis, assaulted the non-Communist members of the City Assembly as they emerged from the building. Their especial targets were the members of the Social Democratic Party. One Social Democrat Assembly woman, Jeannette Wolff, was singled out to be beaten up; and the fact that she had been in a Nazi concentration camp and had suffered a similar fate only pointed out the parallels. The Soviet Zone police stood blandly by, often aiding the Communist gangs of hooligans. 'That's the car of that criminal Neumann', one was heard to say, indicating the chairman of the Berlin Social Democrats. Another gang of Communists struggled to overturn the cars of some Liberal Democrats. The mob surged back and forth for several hours before all the non-Communist Assembly members got away in the deplorable event." [7]

Lucius D. Clay informed Washington on June 25th, while the rioting in Berlin was going on and the blockade was becoming effective, that the "principal danger is from Russian-planned German Communist groups. . . . Conditions are tense. . . . Our troops and British are in

[7] Donnelly, *Struggle for the World*, p. 257–8.

hand and can be trusted. . . . Every German leader, except SED (Socialist Unity Party) leaders, and thousands of Germans have courageously expressed their opposition to Communism. We must not destroy their confidence by any indication of departure from Berlin." [8]

[8] Clay, *Decision in Germany,* p. 366.

45

The Blockade and Airlift
Under Way

The Russians extended the blockade of the city. By troops and road blocks they prevented *all* movement by rail and road and water between Berlin and the Western zones. They also cut off the flow of electric power from the Soviet sector of Berlin to the Western sectors.

In the United States, after a week of conventional uproar, the Republicans nominated Thomas E. Dewey for the Presidency. Was it coincidence, or did the Russians think that in the ruction of the campaign the American Government could not take a firm stand on Berlin?

The Western Allies faced critical choices; whether to allow Berlin to be isolated and be gradually compelled to abandon their sectors of the city; or to use land forces to break the blockade; or to see whether they could supply their garrisons and the people in their sectors by air.

Clay, as already noted, in pulsating messages to Washington, said the West must resist. Retreat would, he said, represent defeat, appeasement, and greatly lessen the confidence of the Germans in the Allies. The people of West Germany might waver about the plan for the construction of a West German Government and for close economic associations of Germany with the West. Moreover, all other European countries would lose confidence in the will or ability of the American people to withstand the Russian-Communist threat.

The British Cabinet held an emergency meeting. Bevin, cruising in the Solent, was fetched back by a torpedo boat.

Interim counteractions were approved and coordinated between Washington and London. Orders were given to suspend all trading between the Western zones and East Berlin and the whole Soviet Zone. This had importance because East German industry needed coal from the Ruhr. The American and British military air transport organizations were instructed to continue to operate to and from Berlin, and to carry essential supplies into the city.

On June 26th Wilhelm Pieck, Chairman of the Russian favored Socialist Unity Party, declared: "The Berlin crisis can be settled only when the Western Allies leave Berlin."

In Washington on the afternoon of the 27th, a Sunday, the top men of the Pentagon and of the State Department again thrashed over the pros and cons of doing this, or that, or nothing. On the next day they submitted their dilemma to the President. It was one of those occasions on which Truman saw a situation in plain white and black. He was unhesitating in his decision. After the meeting the Secretary of Defense, Forrestal, recorded in his diary, "When the specific question was discussed as to what our future policy in Germany was to be—namely, were we to stay in Berlin or not?—the President interrupted to say that there was no discussion on that point, we were going to stay, period." [1] When Secretary of the Army, Royall, queried whether the risk was clearly recognized, since "we might have to fight our way into Berlin," the President said that "we would have to deal with the situation as it developed," but that the essential decision was "we were in Berlin by terms of an agreement and that the Russians had no right to get us out by either direct or indirect pressure." [2]

But how could the West keep their sectors of Berlin fed and supplied? General Hoyt Vandenberg, Chief of Staff of the Air Force, was disquieted by the proposal that the United States try to do so by an airlift. He doubted its effectiveness and was worried about exposing so much of the Air Force to danger. But the President and Cabinet concluded that this venture would be harder for the Russians to counter than an attempt to push trains or convoys through to Berlin, and be less likely to lead to war. Lovett's belief in the potentialities of the airlift was based on his experience; during the war as an Assistant Secretary of War, he had directed the airlift over the Himalayas into China. Those valiant flying crews had managed to carry substantial tonnage over the most rugged terrain—the most dangerous for planes and hardest for the pilots and crews—but then there had been no hostile planes sent to intercept or down those flown by Americans.

The President, having so firmly favored the attempt, orders were issued at once greatly to expand the improvised airlift. Every plane that could be made available to our European Air Command was to be put on the route. Planes were brought in from as far away as Alaska and Hawaii. Some B-29s (bomber planes capable of carrying atomic bombs)

[1] Millis, ed., *The Forrestal Diaries*, entry dated June 28, 1948, p. 454.
[2] *Ibid.*, p. 455.

were stationed in West Germany. The British, who were also augment-ing their flights between their zone and Berlin, were asked whether they would like to have two B-29 groups proceed to Britain. Bevin said they would. But the American Government hesitated before sending them. Marshall was unsure as to how the Russians would react to what they might regard as a provocative step—as might also some members of Congress. But they were flown over and based in England (July 17th).

On June 30th Bevin, in a somber speech in the House of Commons, after reviewing the development of the crisis, said to cheering members: "We recognize that as a result of these decisions a grave situation might arise. Should such a situation arise, we shall have to ask the House to face it. His Majesty's Government and our Western Allies can see no al-ternative between that and surrender, and none of us can accept surrender." [3] He was the Foreign Secretary in a Labor Government speaking for the nation.

Attempts To Negotiate a Settlement

On July 3d the three Western Powers tried again to find out whether the issues in dispute could not be adjusted. The three Western zonal commanders (Generals Clay, Robertson, and Noiret, Koenig's Deputy) called on Marshal Sokolovsky at his headquarters near Potsdam. Robert-son, who spoke for the group, said they wished it were possible to reach an agreement on the currency issue which had disturbed the coopera-tion in Berlin. "Sokolovsky interrupted to state blandly that the techni-cal difficulties would continue until we had abandoned our plans for West German Government." [4]

The Western Powers followed up their inquiries in Moscow. On July 6th each of the three gave similar notes to the Russian Ambassadors in

---

[3] *Parliamentary Debates*, House of Commons, June 30, 1948.

[4] Clay, *Decision in Germany*, p. 367.

The version of Sokolovsky's answer, as given in the British official publication, is less definite than Clay's. But I think its essential import is the same. It read: "Mar-shal Sokolovsky replied that the question raised by General Robertson (about the technical difficulties obstructing transportation to Berlin) was important to the West-ern Allies and that they wished to treat it alone, whereas there were other questions important to him. . . . He declared at length that the Western Allies as a result of their London Conference had created economic disorders in the Soviet zone, which made it impossible to provide alternative routes. He reiterated that the present stop-page was for technical reasons, although he would not guarantee that when these technical difficulties had been cleared, others might not occur elsewhere." His Maj-esty's Government Publication (1948). *Germany: An Account of the Events Leading up to a Reference of the Berlin Question to the United Nations.* (CMD 7534), p. 19.

Washington, London, and Paris.[5] The language of the American protest had been stiffened, as Lovett listened to Vandenberg. "I drew the final form [of the note] on my own Corona one midnight," the Senator recorded proudly in his Diary.[6]

These notes stated that the Western Governments would not renounce their right of access to or presence in Berlin, won by arms and confirmed by agreement. They were willing to discuss the causes of the clash if the blockade was lifted; they would not do so, however, under duress of the Russian blockade.

The Soviet answers (made on July 14th) to the American and British Governments were identical; that to the French Government slightly softer. After averring that the offensive currency reform, because of its impact on Berlin and the Eastern zone, was the reason for introducing the blockade, the note went on to enumerate the many acts of misconduct of which it thought the West guilty, the "systematic" violating of the Potsdam Accord. All had figured in previous altercations.

The answers ended in a vitriolic denial of the right of the Western Allies to stay any longer in Berlin or to share in the direction of its affairs. The pertinent paragraph in the note to the American Government, so averring, read: "With reference to the statement of the Government of the United States that it will not be compelled by threats, pressure or other actions to renounce its right to participation in the occupation of Berlin, the Soviet Government does not intend to enter into discussion of this statement since it has no need for a policy of pressure, since by violation of the agreed decisions concerning the administration of Berlin the above-mentioned Governments themselves *are reducing to naught their right to participation in the occupation of Berlin.*" [7] (author's italics)

Thus the pretext first given for the blockade—"technical troubles"—was abandoned. The exchange of notes revealed how deep and furious were the differences over Germany which had found vent in the Soviet sideswipe at Berlin—the vulnerable center in the heart of the Eastern zone. Here was exposed the astigmatism of those who conceived the lines of zonal occupation of Germany. Berlin was a bruise that would not heal.

As though to mark their defiance, Russian combat planes began to frequent the three air corridors through which supplies and persons were being transported into Berlin. The correspondent of the *New York*

---

[5] The French note was milder than the other two, scolding rather than challenging.

[6] Arthur H. Vandenberg, Jr., ed., *The Private Papers of Senator Vandenberg*, p. 453.

[7] The text of the notes sent July 14, 1948, to the American, British and French Governments are in *Germany: An Account*, pp. 50–52.

Times reported from Berlin a growing impression that the Russians were ready to go to war if the United States attempted to break the blockade by force.[8]

In his book of reminiscences about Truman, William Hillman prints a private memo of the President, dated July 19, 1948, which reads, in part, "A meeting with General Marshall and Jim Forrestal on Berlin and the Russian situation. . . . I made the decision ten days ago to *stay in Berlin*. Jim wants to hedge. . . . I insist we will stay in Berlin—come what may.

"Royall, [William] Draper and Jim Forrestal come in later. I have to listen to a rehash of what I know already and reiterate my 'Stay in Berlin' decision. I do not pass the buck, nor do I alibi out of any decision I make." [9] Attlee and Bevin shared his determination.

But had all chances for diplomacy been used up? Marshall, on July 21st, reiterated publicly that the Western governments were willing to resume talks if the Soviets recognized their right to be in Berlin and suspended the blockade. The publicists in Moscow took heed, to mock.

On the next day, Clay and Murphy, summoned from Berlin by Truman, attended a meeting of the N.S.C. at the White House. Clay said he believed the West could manage by enlarging the airlift from the current 2400–2500 tons a day of cargo to almost double that total, mainly food and coal; that was the minimum needed in winter. At the time approximately fifty-two C-54s and eighty C-47s were making about 250 deliveries a day in Berlin. Seventy-five more C-47s, Clay said, would enable the United States to bring in 3500 tons daily. The British could be counted on to supplement the American effort substantially, but the French Government had indicated it would not contribute any aircraft.

General Vandenberg reported that in order to gather enough planes to double the inflow into Berlin, the United States would have to use planes and aircraft personnel then on other prime assignments; and that at least one more major airfield in Berlin and one more maintenance depot would be needed. Beyond these operational problems, he explained, were serious military contingencies. If the Russians interfered with the airlift, the West would be compelled to choose between submission and an air fight. Should this occur, and war ensue, these planes and air force personnel would be lost, leaving the West weakened in the event of a greater emergency. Was it worth while to take these risks in order to sustain the Western sectors of Berlin by an airlift?

[8] *New York Times*, July 18, 1948.
[9] William Hillman, ed., *Mr. President: The First Publication from the Personal Diaries, Private Letters, Papers and Revealing Interviews of Harry S Truman* (New York: Farrar, 1952), p. 140.

When Lovett asked Clay if the Russians would try to block our planes by fighter patrols or other methods, Clay answered that he thought that unless the Russians were ready to go to war they would not attack our planes even if the airlift were greatly increased. He did not think they would gamble on the chance that the U.S.—if threatened—would suspend or end the airlift.

No one mentioned atomic weapons. But by this time, as already mentioned, sixty B-29s, capable of carrying atomic bombs, had arrived in Britain—as well as those in West Germany. No attempt was made to conceal knowledge of their presence.

Truman asked Clay what then if we tried to supply Berlin with armed convoys. Clay thought the Russians would set up road blocks, destroy bridges, and pull up railway tracks. If an effort was made to clear away such obstacles, the Russians might well interpose their tanks and guns.

Truman thereupon confirmed his decision. As recalled in his *Memoirs*, "The airlift involved less risks than armed road convoys. Therefore, I directed the Air Force to furnish the fullest support possible to the problem of supplying Berlin." [10]

Then and afterward Truman kept in touch with Governor Dewey, through John Foster Dulles. Dewey steadfastly supported the airlift.

[10] Truman, *Years of Trial and Hope*, pp. 125–6.

46

Diplomacy Falters

While preparations for the extension of the airlift were being energetically carried forward, the diplomatic effort continued. Appeals were made to Molotov and Stalin to reconsider. On reading in full the reports of the ensuing talks, in particular the roles of Stalin and Molotov, a passage in one of Honoré de Balzac's greatest tales flashes back into memory: "The two brothers had each selected his appropriate part. Upstairs, François, the brilliant man of the world and of politics, assumed a regal air, bestowed courtesies and promises, and made himself agreeable to all. His manners were easy and complying; he looked at business from a lofty standpoint; he intoxicated new recruits and fledgling speculators with the wine of his favor and his fervid speech, and he made plain to them their own ideas. Downstairs, Adolphe unsaid his brother's words, excused him on the ground of political preoccupation, and cleverly slipped the rake along the cloth. He played the part of the responsible partner, the careful business man. Two words, two speeches, two interviews, were required before an understanding could be reached with this perfidious house. Often the gracious 'yes' of the sumptuous upper floor became a dry 'no' in Adolphe's region. This obstructive manoeuvre gained time for reflection, and often served to fool unskilful applicants." [1]

Summarily, on July 30th, the U.S. Ambassador, Walter Bedell Smith, together with the British and French envoys, asked the Soviet Foreign Office for a chance to talk with Molotov and Stalin. He was told that Molotov was on vacation and he would have to wait. But—whether due to reports of the enlargement of the airlift or for other reasons—the next day Molotov sent word to Smith that he would see him and his diplomatic consorts. When they met Molotov said that any discussions should deal with all German questions, not merely Berlin.

---

[1] Honoré de Balzac, *La Comédie Humaine: Histoire de la grandeur et de la décadence de César Birotteau.*

Stalin accorded the three Western Ambassadors an interview on August 2, 1948. He was affable—almost avuncular. Smith read a résumé of the views of the governments of the Western Allies. This averred that their right to be in Berlin was unquestionable and absolute, and that they would not be coerced into giving it up. And then, "If in any way related to the currency problem . . . [the blockade is] obviously uncalled-for, since this problem could have been, and can now be, adjusted by representatives of the four powers in Berlin. If, on the other hand, these measures are designed to bring about negotiations among the four occupying powers, they are equally unnecessary. . . . However, if the purpose of these measures is to attempt to compel the three governments to abandon their rights as occupying powers of Berlin . . . such an attempt could not be allowed to succeed." [2]

Stalin denied that the Soviet Government was trying to force the Western governments out of Berlin. But, repeating the allegation in the previous Soviet note, he argued that they had forfeited that right juridically, by the decision to set up a West German Government—which the zone commanders were urging the Minister-Presidents to do—and by introducing new Western currency into Berlin. Soviet measures in Berlin were, he averred, with righteous sobriety, in self defense. He wished for some changes in the policies that the Western Allies were developing for West Germany, particularly a share in the control of the Ruhr. Pending discussions about such changes, he suggested that the formation of a separate West German state be deferred. But he did not, to the relief of the Western representatives, definitely insist that there would have to be a conference about these German problems *before* discussion regarding the situation in Berlin could go on. (author's italics)

Toward the end of the talk Stalin abruptly asked whether the Western representatives wanted to settle the matter that night. If so, he could meet them with the following proposals: First, "there should be a simultaneous introduction in [all of] Berlin of the Soviet Zone Deutsche Mark in place of the Western B (Berlin) Mark, together with the removal of all transport restrictions. Second, while the Soviet Government will no longer ask as a condition the deferment of the implementation of the London decisions for setting up a separate government in West Germany, this should be recorded as the insistent wish of the Soviet Government." [3]

This proposal was deemed in Washington to be a hopeful clearance. But when the negotiators met with Molotov to work out the way in which it was to be carried into effect, they found themselves going

[2] Smith, *My Three Years in Moscow*, pp. 243–4.
[3] *Ibid.*, p. 245. This is in essentials the same as given in *Germany, An Account*, published by the Foreign Office of the United Kingdom, p. 23.

around the same circle as before. Molotov again challenged the right of Western Powers to be in Berlin; his proposals were thought implicitly to require them to recognize that they were in Berlin by sufferance of the Soviet Government. And though Stalin had seemed to be willing to accept a mere acknowledgment that the West was cognizant of Russian views about the recommendations of the London Conference about Germany, Molotov sought a definite promise that the West would suspend the program pending the outcome of a Four-Power conference. Moreover, in the bargaining, he would agree to lift only these restrictions that had been imposed *after* June 18th, the date of the currency reform, leaving transit to and from Berlin still subject to Russian control and vulnerable to future Russian obstructions or hindrances (author's italics).

Overgrown in the tangle of talk was the matter of regulation of the issue and distribution of the Soviet marks in all Berlin. The Soviet Government wanted this to be exercised by the German Bank of Emission in the Soviet zone, which was controlled by the Soviet Government. Western negotiators feared that the Soviet Union would use that power to "strangle" trade with West Berlin, just as they were now trying to starve it out. They wanted Four-Power regulation.

Ambassador Smith thought this a dubious bargain. Washington and London agreed with him. Again Stalin appeared inclined to give up the unacceptable conditions for ending the blockade.[4] He was understood to say he would be satisfied if the West would assent to having the currency for all Berlin printed and issued by the Soviet Zone bank, it being agreed that the flow of currency into Berlin would be regulated through banks in all parts of Berlin, and that in issuing currency and providing banking and credit facilities, all sectors would be treated alike. Moreover, he was willing to have the arrangements for the introduction of a single currency supervised by a commission of representatives of the four Berlin Commanders.[5]

As for the basic aspects of German policy out of which the dispute over Berlin currency had spurted, Stalin said merely that he thought it would be desirable to have some indication in the Four-Power communiqué which would be issued, that the question of the establishment of a West German Government had been discussed. He suggested a text: "The question of the London decision was also discussed, including the formation of a Western German government. This discussion took place

---

[4] The Soviet draft presented by Stalin provided for the removal of " . . . all restrictions which have been recently imposed on the transport of persons and goods in either direction between the three Western Zones and Germany and Berlin . . . " *Germany, An Account*, p. 34.
[5] *Ibid.*, pp. 34–35.

in an atmosphere of mutual understanding." [6]

Stalin was up to his old tricks—those he had used to deceive Harry Hopkins and Truman before the conference at Potsdam. For his meaning, disguised by his phrases, was revealed as he talked on. In essence, if the West gave up its plans to form a West German Government, and if Four-Power control over all Germany was restored, Russia would not object to the presence of the Powers in Berlin, but otherwise Berlin would lose its standing as the capital of Germany. Even in this case, he added, however, he would not wish to oust the Western Occupation forces from Berlin.

How would the Germans and our Allies understand any such vague public statement as Stalin suggested? Would it not be construed as hesitation on the part of the Western Powers? Would not quarrels swiftly occur about its meaning?

The representatives of the German States in the Western zones were about to meet at Bonn to start drafting a constitution for West Germany. The American and British Governments suspected that Stalin's proposal was a subtle way of shaking the faith of the Germans; and, perhaps, also of causing the French to waver.

So Washington and London agreed that Stalin's suggestion was not acceptable. Yet, in order to clarify the Soviet position and make it more explicit, the Western diplomats again engaged in tedious talks with Molotov and Vishinsky. These only thickened the murk, and in the end it was agreed to leave to the *four* Military Governors the task of condensing an acceptable accord on measures for a détente out of Stalin's cloudy and clouded statements to the ambassadors.

Lovett wondered, as negotiations were passed down to the military commanders, whether Clay would be able to preserve his calm and poise, as he seemed at the time to be drawn as tight as a steel spring.[7]

The military commanders were requested to report results by September 7th. They met daily during the allotted week. At the end the differences were accentuated rather than lessened. Impressions shared by Robertson and Clay are succinctly summed up in the official British record: "It soon became apparent that Marshal Sokolovsky was not ready to honor the understandings reached in Moscow. During the course of the meetings it was evident that he was seeking to increase, rather than to decrease, the restrictions on transport, and also to exclude any measure of quadripartite control over the German Bank of Emission for the Soviet Zone with respect to Berlin and to assert for the Soviet Military Authority sole jurisdiction over the trade between Berlin and the Western zones of Germany as well as third countries." [8]

[6] Smith, *My Three Years in Moscow*, pp. 249–50.
[7] Millis, ed., *The Forrestal Diaries*, entry dated August 27, 1948, p. 480.
[8] *Germany, An Account*, p. 41.

Diplomacy was in the shoals, with shifting winds, and rocks on the lee side.

At this juncture in September, the Communists in Berlin went amok again. By assaults and intimidation they chased all the non-Communist members of the Assembly and reporters out of the meeting hall. Once in possession, they voted Communist measures.

The Germans in the Western sectors of the city showed their stamina in crowded meetings in memory of those victims of the Nazis who had given their lives in opposition to Hitler. In his address, Franz Neumann, Chairman of the Social Democratic Party, boldly declared: "These people gave their lives in the cause of freedom. The concentration camps are still the same, but now the hammer and sickle flies over them instead of the swastika." [9]

The Soviet commentary was exemplified by an article in the *Neues Deutschland,* accusing the protestors of seeking to provoke another war: "These criminal fools," it said, "are now trying belatedly to win Adolf Hitler's war against the Soviet Union. . . ." [10]

The Soviet authorities still seemed confident that under their privations the people of Berlin would falter, and the Western Allies would have to give in. In contrast, the Western Powers were becoming assured that they would be able to supply the people of West Berlin with essentials throughout the winter. Unwavering, they kept on their course, although Sokolovsky had announced that beginning September 6th air maneuvers would be held in the area of Eastern Germany traversed by our planes. Here was a threat to endanger the airlift. It seemed as though the crisis was at hand. September is the month of wars in Europe.

Lovett, on Labor Day, September 6th, went to the office of Forrestal to review the situation. According to the notation of their talk which Forrestal made, it was the Undersecretary of State's "hunch" that the Soviet authorities did not want an agreement, that they would just as soon have a break now unless they could get the Western Allies to accept their terms.[11] The "hunch" was wrong.

The American authorities not only maintained the airlift, but resolved to engage still more planes in it, and they ordered Clay to plan protective measures against interference by the Russians. How Washington tensely waited for their next move is indicated by Marshall's statement at the meeting of the National Security Council called on September 9th to consider emergency plans. " . . . the situation was so dangerous that

---

[9] Quoted in Donnelly, *Struggle for the World,* p. 265.
[10] September 10, 1948. Quoted in W. Phillips Davison, *The Berlin Blockade: A Study in Cold War Politics* (Princeton, N.J.:Princeton University Press, 1958), p. 190.
[11] Millis, ed., *The Forrestal Diaries,* entry dated September 6, 1948, pp. 482–3.

the slightest element added might be the fuse to spark a general conflagration." [12]

On September 10th Forrestal talked to Marshall in search of an answer to a question which he, Forrestal, had pressed—whether or not to use the atomic bomb in war. Then, at a meeting with Forrestal, Royall, and Bradley, a few days later, the President said "he prayed that he would never have to make such a decision, but that if it became necessary, no one need have a misgiving, but what he would do so. . . ." [13]

In a private memo Truman made on September 13th, he referred to that meeting: "Forrestal, Bradley, [Hoyt] Vandenberg, Symington brief me on bases, bombs, Moscow, Leningrad, etc. I have a terrible feeling afterward that we are very close to war. I hope not. Discuss situation with Marshall at lunch. Berlin is a mess." [14]

With some hope that the Soviet Government might be impressed by a stern statement, the three Western Allies on September 22d again sent identical notes to the Soviet Government. Bevin agreed, with qualms. He was not sure he could count on the support of the war-weary British people, and reminded Marshall the British "were in the frontline."

These notes to Moscow reaffirmed the essential points of the position maintained by the Western Allies; however, seeking another channel for negotiations, they asked whether the Soviet Government would not end the blockade in order to create a favorable atmosphere for further discussion of the situation; the three Western Foreign Ministers, who were soon to meet, would be pleased to have the Soviet response as soon as possible. It was negative, adding to the heap of accusations. And ominously it stated that it regarded Soviet control of the transport *by air* of commercial freight and passengers to be as necessary as the control of transport by rail, water, and highway.

By this time the argument back and forth about actions, rights, and previous understandings was so knotty and variable that it is doubtful whether the negotiators themselves knew clearly what the other side was really proposing. This is not infrequent in negotiation with the Russians. [15]

[12] Truman, *Years of Trial and Hope*, p. 128. Forrestal's *Diaries* date this NSC meeting September 7th.
[13] Millis, ed., *The Forrestal Diaries*, entries dated September 10, 13, 1948, pages 486–7. This, of course, is Forrestal's language, which did not always convey the remarks of others quite correctly.
[14] In Hillman, ed., *Mr. President*, entry dated September 13, 1948, p. 141.
[15] The text of the notes presented by the Western Ambassadors to the Soviet Government on September 22d and the Soviet reply of September 25th are in *Germany, An Account*, pp. 61–63. Even after careful study I am not sure of the points in regard to currency questions and Soviet control of access to Berlin on which the contestants agreed and those on which they differed. In this answer the Soviet Government appeared to introduce new conditions and perhaps made new concessions.

The Foreign Ministers of the United States, Great Britain, and France, meeting in Paris, notified the Russian Government of their intention of asking the U.N. Security Council to take cognizance of the dangerous quarrel over Berlin (September 26–27, 1948).

Warren Austin, the American envoy to the U.N., was instructed to present an official charge to the Secretary General, Trygve Lie: that the Soviet blockade of Berlin was illegal, coercive, a threat to the peace, and an effort to use brutal pressure to serve a political aim, in transgression of the Charter. It accused the Soviet Government of seeking complete domination over Berlin and its incorporation in the Soviet zone. The Soviet member of the Security Council, Vishinsky, with impudent logic, denied that the situation was a threat to the peace. Hence he refused to discuss it.

Balked in their attempt to pass a resolution favoring the West, and a compromise proposal having been killed by a Russian veto, assent was given to a proposal of the Argentinian President of the U.N. Security Council, Juan Bramuglia, that the issues be referred to a committee of experts nominated by the Council's neutral members. That committee's consultations ended futilely.

47

The Soviet Peripeteia

During the American campaign and the months thereafter the contest over Berlin remained deadlocked. Despite bleak Berlin winter weather, with heavy fog and rain, the airlift carried on with growing dimensions.

An election in the Western sectors of Berlin—which was then divided —went preponderantly in favor of the West. The Germans in the Western zones, stimulated by association with the Marshall Plan and provided with a stable currency and banking system, improved their economic conditions. They became more united and resolved to uphold the Western resistance to the blockade.

The belief and interest of the American officials in the restoration of a Four-Power administration for the whole of Berlin, the Russians retaining a veto power, was waning. The only alternative solution was thought to be the permanent political division of the city—with the autobahn from the West separate from West Berlin. But that did not seem, at this time, negotiable.

Regrettably, in my opinion, no thought was given either in the West or the East to a different conception that was in the air. As outlined, for example, by F. S. Cocks, Member for Broxtowe, in the House of Commons on December 9th, ". . . the suggestion could be put to Russia that the Four Powers withdraw from Berlin simultaneously, and that Berlin be made temporarily a free city under the protection of the U.N.O. with a governor appointed by some neutral state." The municipal government, he added, would be continued under an elected Assembly.

For so sensible a settlement, mutual trust was essential. The Russian Communists never had it. Whatever measure of it the Western statesmen once had, had been rubbed away. The grim and dangerous contest went on in and over Berlin until the Russians concluded that this round, this bout, they could not win.

354

The Ending

The historian, ruffling through the records, can exhume from them various Communist declarations which indicated the seepage of the opinion that the blockade was failing. Italian and French Communist leaders were openly intimating that they believed the damage it was doing their cause exceeded any possible benefit even if Western Berlin was brought under Communist control—which was becoming less and less likely.

The denouement came abruptly. There occurred a peripeteia, sudden as these reversals in policy in reaction to changes in circumstance which the Soviet Government not infrequently makes, to the bewilderment of foreign diplomats. On January 30, 1949, Stalin, in a matter-of-fact way, let it be known through an American journalist, Kingsbury Smith, that the Soviet Government might end the blockade if the Western Powers postponed the establishment of a separate West German government pending a meeting of the Council of Foreign Ministers and simultaneously ended the restrictions on transactions with East Germany and East Berlin. Acheson, who had just succeeded Marshall as Secretary of State, noted that Stalin had not linked this measure to others—particularly to the currency question, which had been so long and hotly argued.

What did Stalin mean? Acheson, in a press conference staged on February 2d, referred to Stalin's answers to Kingsbury Smith, indicating in circumambient language that the American Government would welcome a "serious" proposal to discuss terms of ending the blockade—including an agreement on Germany as a whole.[1]

On January 13th President Truman in a press conference, remarked that he was ready to welcome Stalin in Washington at any time. Stalin, responding on February 2d, had made known that he wanted very much to go to Washington but that his doctor advised him strongly against taking the medical risk; he suggested they could meet in Moscow or Odessa, in Poland or in Czechoslovakia.[2] But Truman had resolved never again to venture into the heart of Europe; and moreover, at this juncture he was inclined to believe Stalin's statement was merely a propaganda pose.

But Philip C. Jessup, the intelligent and subtle acting American member of the Security Council, was instructed to inquire of Jacob Malik whether the omission of reference to other matters was "not accidental." This he

[1] Acheson, *Present at the Creation*, p. 268.
[2] *L'Année Politique*, February 1949.

355

did on February 15th. After a month during which the question was ignored, Malik informed Jessup that the fact that Stalin had not referred to the currency question in his answer to Kingsbury Smith was not accidental. The Soviet Government, he added, regarded the currency question as important, but it could be discussed by the Council of Foreign Ministers if a meeting of that body could be arranged to review the whole German problem. In response to Jessup's further inquiries, Malik replied that if a definite date should be set for the meeting of the Council, the blockade could be lifted in advance. Malik then asked whether the Western Allies would suspend preparations for the formation of a West German Government until after the Council meeting. Jessup, as instructed, replied (Mar. 21st) that the American Government expected preparations to continue, but they would not be completed for some time. And so, "they would be of no moment." [3] To this question we shall revert.

Surprisingly, this time the Soviet negotiators did not try to amend this understanding in the course of subsequent discussions pursued to give it needed precision. Thus on May 5th, a communiqué subscribed to by all four Powers, announced merely that they had agreed that the blockade and counterblockade of Berlin would end on May 12th, and that the Council of Foreign Ministers would convene eleven days thereafter.

All restrictions imposed since March 1948 by all four Powers on transport, communication, and trade between the respective zones of Germany and sectors of Berlin were to be "lifted."

The accord, though not conclusive, ended the crisis. There was lively rejoicing in West Berlin—the natives and airmen mingling.

Why did the Soviet authorities decide to yield when and as they did? Lacking confidential records, the historian must resort to surmises: (1) By February 1949, 7000 to 8000 tons daily were being air-lifted into Berlin, almost as much food and fuel as before the blockade. One plane was landing every two minutes. It was evident that the blockade would not succeed in stifling or starving Berlin unless the Russians knocked the transport planes out of the sky. (2) Western countermeasures were harming the economic life in East Germany and the Soviet satellites. (3) Many of the East Germans were becoming restless under the blockade, while in West Germany the parties that favored closer association with the West were gaining strength. (4) Most important, probably, resistance to the blockade was drawing the Western Powers together under American leadership for common defense. As will be discussed later, the formation of NATO was being stimulated by the crisis over Berlin, as were the plans for the formulation of a constitution for West Germany, as preface to the

[3] As recounted in Acheson, *Present at the Creation*, p. 270.

356

formation of a West German Government.

Within the Soviet counsels, consideration of recourse to force to break the airlift may have been affected by reports, purveyed by Russian intelligence agents in Germany, that in the event that the provisioning planes were attacked, the Western Allies would fight rather than submit, using, if necessary, atomic weapons. The presence of B-29s—always kept fueled and manned—in Germany and Britain, and concurrent British official statements that Great Britain would rely mainly on air power in any future combat, may have lent credence to such reports.

When shortly before the termination of the blockade in May 1949 the Parliamentary Council of German states consulted the Western representatives about the text of the constitution they intended to adopt; it wished to include Greater Berlin in Western Germany as a state (Land). But the Western authorities objected. They informed Konrad Adenauer, as President of the Parliamentary Council (May 12th) " . . . that while Berlin may not be accorded voting membership in the Bundestag or Bundesrat, nor be governed by the Federation, she may, nevertheless, designate a small number of representatives to attend the meetings of those legislative bodies." [4]

Two days later the Western Berlin Commandants notified Berlin city officials that, subject to such limits as exceptional circumstances might necessitate, they would pursue the same course in Berlin as in Western Germany and allow the local Berlin government full legislative, executive, and judicial powers—within the Constitution.

Among realms reserved to the Berlin Kommandatura (now without Soviet representation) were: disarmament and demilitarization, relations with authorities abroad, control of foreign trade and exchange, and banking credit and currency policy—so that these could be coordinated with West Germany.

The settlement of the crisis over Berlin dulled fear that the Soviet Government might resort to war over secondary matters. Yet the people of Western Europe remained afraid of its hostile temper. As observed by Gottlieb: "The spirit of the anti-fascist front was burned out and a highly militant anti-Russian . . . mood was inspired." [5]

It transfixed the American notion that it was imperative for American security and the integrity of NATO to preserve the existing situation in Berlin indefinitely.

It left the city sundered physically, economically, and politically. The SED faded away as a political party in the West and all remnants of

[4] Letter from the Military Governors to Konrad Adenauer, May 12, 1949.
[5] Gottlieb, *The German Peace Settlement* p. 201.

Western political parties were expelled from the East. Western Berlin became more capitalistic. East Berlin was more extensively socialized, and its Communist authorities became more antagonistic. The chance of reunifying the city was consumed in the pushful conduct of Berlin affairs by both the Soviet Government and the Western ones (in behalf of West Germany).

I may be permitted to stretch my reflections far beyond the period of this narrative—to make a point that I think as important now as it was in 1948 and again in 1961.

The subsequent dangerous legacy of the original arrangement became starkly clear when in 1961 the control of the city again became a dangerous cause of dissension and dispute. While the West Germans were trying to tie Western Berlin more closely to West Germany, the Soviet Government rejoined by constructing a virtually impassable wall shutting off East Germans and East Berliners from the West.

The height of emotion to which many Americans worked themselves up is marked in my memory by President John Kennedy's statement as he spoke to a Berlin throng, in sight of the wall, "Ich bin ein Berliner." [6]

I do not think most victims of past German cruelty and force shared his aroused indignation. I know I did not. I thought, and still think, an opportunity has been neglected ever since the end of the war, to end the turbulent flow of accusations by a positive, creative plan for making Berlin a neutral, international center under the U.N. with free access to all; as such it might become a liaison between the two Germanys.

While the outcome of the blockade crisis was a setback for Russia, it was not a satisfactory victory for its opponents. For it left the Western Allies and Western Germany still in the embrace of the need to protect and nurture this Western enclave, not only against the Communists but against the slow course of attrition. In 1948, in the face of the bullying and hate-spewing ways of Moscow, the West wisely upheld Berlin as a symbol of its determination to retreat no further before Communist surge, and to confront it fearlessly. But while it was essential to remain in Berlin as a temporary measure, its status should have been changed at the first auspicious moment.[7] However, the Western Allies, having felt ever since they must not seriously strain the alliance with West Germany, have failed to find any time auspicious and have dismissed all proposals for another kind of agreement with the Soviet Union—one which might eliminate Berlin permanently from the area they contest.

[6] The *New York Times,* June 27, 1963.
[7] Ambassador Smith inclined to the same opinion, as recalled in Lucius D. Clay, *Decision in Germany,* p. 376.

The problem of Berlin has been at times stagnant, at times near erup-tion. The assumption has prevailed that the present situation can con-tinue forever. Or until by flow of international change, not at present perceptible, the Western Allies and the Soviet Union agree on the unifi-cation of Germany.

I have allowed myself to roam far ahead, though not afield. Returning to our historical trail, let me next note the progress toward self-govern-ment of Germany, and of the other issues and events that were affecting relations with the Soviet Union, while Berlin was being blockaded in 1948-1949.

PART ELEVEN

While Berlin
Was Blockaded:
Western Initiatives

48

The American Elections

It must not be forgotten that while the crisis over Berlin was most tense a campaign for the election of an American President was in spate.

Early in October 1948 President Truman had the impulse to send a special envoy to Stalin—to allay the mistrust, convince him that our intentions were peaceful and friendly, and persuade him to cease the blockade of Berlin. For reasons hard to discover, Truman thought that Justice Fred Vinson was a sagacious and persuasive negotiator. But Secretary Marshall was not enthusiastic. He was afraid that the Russians on the one hand, the Germans on the other, would construe the initiative as a sign that the United States was caving in. He hastened back from Paris to Washington. But even before his arrival on October 9th Truman had second thoughts and dropped the project.

Our European Allies and the Soviet Union were pondering how American policy might be affected if Truman was superseded by the candidate of the more conservative and prudent Republican Party. Our Allies wondered whether, if Dewey won, the American Government might be slower and more guarded in its participation in the transatlantic alliance being formed. On the other hand, the Soviet authorities may have thought a Republican victory would mean an even more exigent and combative spirit of anti-Communism, since John Foster Dulles would replace the stern, yet levelheaded Marshall. Or, on the contrary, they might have anticipated that American resistance in Europe would wane because a Republican victory would bring on a serious internal depression.

But probably, most of the observing foreign statesmen thought that whatever the outcome of the election, the posture and main elements of American policies would be much the same. For people of both parties thought well of them, or were willing to measure up to their demands.

The spokesmen for the two main political parties were professing much the same views and intentions. The policy-makers of the two parties were in close touch with one another. The Republicans Vandenberg and Dulles had been active and cooperative consultants of the Democratic Administration and members of American delegations to international conferences which bespoke Truman's instructions. These liaisons were portents that, although there might well be some strain, there would not be any significant change in policy if Truman were voted out of office.

Henry Wallace was earnestly challenging our course. He was seeking the votes of elements traditionally Democratic on the ground that American foreign policy was inflexible, aggressive, and perilous. But his contentions and interpretations were convincing only to a staunch but small minority; some of the admirers that clustered about him hurt his personal standing and his cause.

Still there was well-founded malaise lest the American Government be unable to make any leading decisions during the interim between the election and the inauguration—since personal and party responsibility for decisions might be in question (as it was in 1933 after Roosevelt defeated Hoover). Awareness that the barbed wire of party division might slow down decision is illustrated, for example, in a letter which his brother Allen sent to John Foster Dulles on October 22d. "I assume," he wrote, "that your position, once Tom [Dewey] is elected, will be extremely difficult and that you should come back for consultations almost immediately after elections. I rather surmise that after November 2nd it will be the tendency of both Truman and Marshall to drop the difficult and contentious questions into the Governor's [Dewey's] lap and more or less take the position that they cannot speak authoritatively unless they know what the Governor's views are. . . . It is quite a puzzle—what ought to be done if that happens, and I think it important that you and possibly General Marshall be back in the United States when important policy decisions are made." [1]

Possibly alerted by this letter, John Foster Dulles a few days later sent on from Paris to Governor Dewey in Albany a memo telling him of a talk with Marshall in which the Secretary explained his ideas of how current foreign policy questions should be handled after Dewey was elected. Dulles told Dewey he was worried by signs that the French and British were anxious lest negotiations about NATO be suspended during the interim. Dulles suggested that Dewey make publicly known his wish that the current discussion in the U.N. Assembly should continue, no matter what the outcome of the election. Dewey answered that he was disposed to do so. But, he added, he was not yet ready to decide in what degree to share responsibility with Truman for measures that

[1] This correspondence is in the collection of the papers of John Foster Dulles in the Library of Princeton University.

might be considered or taken in this interim.[2]

Needless to recall, Truman, to the sorrow of his opponents and to the chagrin of most forecasters, was kept in office by the American people. The same men, with the same opinions and intentions, were left in control of American foreign policy.

[2] *Ibid.*

49

Toward a Self-Governing Germany

While the Russians were choking Berlin, conditions in Western Germany improved rapidly and future prospects greatly brightened. The effects of the currency reform were quick and substantial: the distribution of goods, much of which had been diverted to the black market, returned to regular channels; the tonnage of the coal mines rose; the farmers carried on their work with better will and sent more supplies to the cities; though unemployment remained large and demoralizing, more and more men and women were at work; and there was a rapid increase in bank deposits. These were proofs of German trust in Western protective measures.

Advances were made toward the constitution for Germany—the formation of a provisional German Government—and toward a Statute whereby a large measure of authority would be accorded this government, superseding the discarded provisions of the Potsdam Accord. In sum, the relations between the people of West Germany and the occupying Powers evolved toward equality and stability. As analogue, the separation between West and East Germany became deeper and more fixed.

As foreseen in the Six-Power London Agreement, early in July 1948 the three military governors had given the Ministers-Presidents of the West German States documents to guide the course of the prospective Constituent Assembly. The Ministers-Presidents had balked and hesitated; they were disquieted by some of the instructions given by their mentors. While accepting the project for a trizonal German Government as the only feasible arrangement, they were worried lest *they* be reproached for dividing Germany. Some opposed the suggestion that the constitution adopted by the Assembly should be subjected to a popular referendum. They were angry over the concessions made to secure French acquiescence in the London agreements which they were expected to accept. Some complained that under the Occupation Statute, as forecast in the London program and in the preliminary proposals regarding its observance in the Basic Law, Germany would be under constraints, as though it was to be still treated as a "conquered country."[1]

Clay, at a meeting with the Ministers-Presidents in the American zones on July 14th, had warned them that by their objections and delay they were putting their fate in General Koenig's (the French Military Governor) hands. As for their concern about East Germany, Clay said they would be charged with splitting Germany, no matter what they did; so they would be well advised to create a strong West Germany to permit "genuine and full economic recovery." And when, on the 20th, the three Governors met with the Ministers-Presidents again to answer objections, as Clay has recounted, "We told them that the London decisions were governmental and that marked deviations might require further governmental consideration, which would delay the whole program, and that they would have to accept responsibility for failure to return government to German hands promptly."[2]

After the Allied Governments changed the terminology, the Ministers-Presidents agreed to select and convoke representatives to prepare the constitution. In deference to their wishes, the gathering was called a "Parliamentary Council," not a "Constituent Assembly," and the constitution they were to write was called a "Basic Law (Provisional Constitution)."

The delegates to the Parliamentary Council had been selected by the state parliaments in August. It had 65 members, of which 27 were associated with each of the two main political parties—the Christian Democratic Union and the Social Democratic Party. Berlin was represented by a delegation of five, without any voting rights.

This Council met on September 1st. Adenauer, leader of the Christian Democratic Union, was elected President of the Council, and he carried more weight with the Military Governors than any other German official. The deliberations of the Council had continued throughout the Autumn of 1948. During the following months while the Basic Law was being drafted, the Western Allies were discussing among themselves: (1) the terms for the Ruhr and (2) the terms of an Occupation Statute which would define the realms over which they would retain authority. This work was done—whether in the Occupation headquarters in West Germany or Washington or London—to the grim cadence of the planes going back and forth in the Berlin air shuttle, but in the sustaining warmth of the knowledge that a pact of joint defense against any Soviet attack upon their territories (NATO) was being conceived.

---

[1] See Gimbel, *The American Occupation of Germany*, chap. 12, for an account of the vigorous dissension between the Western military governors and the German political leaders, especially some of the Ministers-Presidents.

[2] Clay, *Decision in Germany*, p. 410.

The Russians construed these developments as hostile, but they were at a loss as to how to check them. Their accusations were defensive justifications for maintaining the blockade of Berlin. In tenor they resembled an editorial in the *New Times*: "However jesuitically the American and British diplomats assert that they are eager for agreement on the Berlin issue, the facts point the other way. While the talk is going on in the Security Council and at press conferences in the Western zones of Germany, an occupation statute is being drafted, preparations are being made to set up a puppet government and the future of the arsenal of war, the Ruhr, is being decided arbitrarily. Feverish preparations are being made to turn the Western Union into an Atlantic bloc. In order that the Western part of Germany be made the core of an aggressive bloc and an American bridgehead in Europe, all negotiations for the framing of a peace treaty with Germany are frustrated. The democratic development of the Western zones of Germany is hampered. The forces of reaction, aggression and militarism are being revived there." [3]

The Ruhr Industries and the Ruhr Statute

The drafting of a Statute for an International Ruhr Authority had been begun when representatives of the Six Powers again convened in London early in November 1948.

In reality the primary determinants of the future of the Ruhr industries had already been decided. They were to remain in private ownership and were to be managed by the Germans. Clay, in accord with Washington, was intent on these principles.[4] The British Labour Government had, after much hesitation, subscribed to them. Bevin had defended the decision in the House of Commons on December 9th, with the assertion that ". . . any attempt to impose international ownership on the Ruhr industries would lead to friction, depress production, and hinder German cooperation in Europe."

Adenauer and other German leaders, rapidly gaining confidence, had opposed any transfer of ownership or the installation of foreign management. The Germans by then had the mines and factories and were prepared to thwart any effort to loosen their grasp.

On the day before the Conference which was to write the Statute for a

[3] *New Times*, December 1, 1948.
[4] In October 1947, Clay had corresponded with General William Draper, Undersecretary of the Army, and Secretaries Royall and Forrestal about the question of socialization. He had then advised them: "If we can thus defer the issue while free enterprise continues to operate and economic improvement results, it may never become an issue before the German people." Gimbel, *American Occupation of Germany*, p. 170.

Ruhr Authority met, Generals Clay and Robertson had promulgated a law (No. 75) whereby German management of the Ruhr industries was recognized and ownership vested *temporarily* in German trustees, until the ultimate disposition could be decided by a German Government.[5] The trustees were to be nominated by the Allied Military Commanders in consultation with German political representatives. Thus died the prospect for international ownership of the Ruhr resources and effective international control of production.

But French opposition still had to be reckoned with, although Bidault had been succeeded as Foreign Minister by Robert Schuman, who was attracted by the possibility of combining the Ruhr industries with those of France and Belgium.[6]

The French authorities were upset by the promulgation of Law No. 75 and the trend of discussions in the Conference about the Ruhr Statute, and they feared that the International Authority, which was to have only supervisory duties, would not be able to prevent a resurgence of German war industries. The vehemence and universality of the feeling in France is indicated by the fact that even Léon Blum, the international Socialist, wrote, "London and Washington have struck a severe, perhaps irreparable, blow at the French system of security." [7] Not unexpected was de Gaulle's denunciation.

Bevin also faced opposition in the Cabinet and remarked impatiently at one of their meetings that the British Government ". . . had to make up its mind whether it regarded Germany as still a danger or as an ally of Western Europe." He was, he said, trying to steer a middle course.[8]

But the French Government could not hold out inflexibly. It was aligned in the Berlin crisis, dependent on American economic aid, and eager to have the United States join an Atlantic Pact. Thus, after some modifications to appease the French—especially by stipulating that France would share as an equal with the United States and Britain in the control agencies—a provisional agreement on a statute for the Ruhr was reached on December 28, 1948. Law No. 75 was left unaffected. Due to French reservations the Statute was not signed until remaining differences were adjusted by the Foreign Ministers in April 1949.

It envisaged that the International Authority for the Ruhr would be composed of representatives of the six Western signatory powers and

[5] Military Government Law No. 75, November 10, 1948. See Clay, *Decision in Germany*, pp. 327–9 ff.

[6] When the French Parliament had approved the London Agreement about Germany in June 1948 by a very slim margin, it had also passed a recommendation that the Government demand international control of the mines and industries of the Ruhr, continuance of reparations, and an extended occupation of Germany.

[7] *Le Populaire*, November 19, 1948.

[8] After this discussion in the Cabinet meeting, Dalton in his Diary under the date of December 21, jotted "a bad presage for the future."

Germany, but that during the period of occupation the German vote would be cast by the zonal officials. The Soviet Union was not to be granted the participation it had sought. Its recent actions had generated so much antagonism and fear of how it would use any chance to exercise influence over the Ruhr, that all thought of allowing it to have that chance had died away.

The Authority was instructed to maintain a supervisory watch over the Ruhr industries to see that their conduct and allocation of its production (especially coal, coke, and steel) were consonant with the Marshall Plan program. It was also to see that these industries should show "due regard" for the requirements of international security.

Other provisions of the Statute were aimed at preventing excessive concentration of ownership and control of the Ruhr industries.

The Acceptance of Former Nazi Industrialists

Still other provisions debarred persons who had served the Nazi regime from positions of influence in these industries. But these were bypassed before and after the Ruhr Statute was enacted.

Most German conservative political leaders had not been zealous in punishing former government officials and industrialists with a Nazi record—unless their deeds were black and notorious; they had been loath to condemn them. For several years they had been urging the zonal authorities to ease the denazification orders, circumscribe their scope, and end them soon.[9] Clay had lectured, reprimanded, and threatened. At a session of the Landerrat, as early as November 1946, he had said: "How can you demonstrate your ability for self-government or your will for democracy if you are going to evade or shirk the first unpleasant and difficult task that falls upon you?"[10] And in a trying session with the Ministers-Presidents in August 1947 he had opposed changes in the Denazification Law and said that if the German political leaders were not willing to do the job, the military government would.

As one feature of the change in American policy vis-à-vis Germany that occurred, Secretary of the Army Royall had brought to Germany in August 1947 instructions to end denazification proceedings by April 1948.

The American sponsors of the rule of exclusion in the Ruhr Statute were by then no more inclined to insist upon its observance than the

[9] A more consecutive account of the German pressure on American and British occupation authorities to be less thorough and stern, is to be found in Gimbel, *American Occupation of Germany*, pp. 101–110, 158–162.
[10] *Ibid.*, p. 106.

Russians in the Eastern zone. The test of usefulness was gradually to prevail over the taint of having been a Nazi or having served the Nazis. Some former Nazis regained entry and influence in the West if they had great wealth, or local political pull, or good connections with American administrators, bankers, businessmen, and/or if they had prized experience and knowledge. And in the East, Nazi offenders were pardoned and assigned to important posts if they were capable and thought to be obedient servants of Communism because of fear.

The first list of trustees for the Ruhr steel industry submitted by the German authorities contained names of men closely connected with the ownership and management during Hitler's rule, and none of trade union representatives. After prodding by Military Governors, some of these were dropped, and three persons who had been previously declared unacceptable to the German authorities were added to the list. In Washington, Paris, and Bonn alike, critics were fobbed off by statements such as Secretary Marshall's at a press conference on November 24th. "The final determination of the security problem of Europe in relation to the future of the Ruhr must await the terms of the peace treaty which will be conclusive in the matter." [11]

The Russian commentators had predicted that Law No. 75 and intimations of the conclusions of the Conference would mean that the control of the Ruhr industries would be turned back to executives of those great German concerns such as Krupps and Thyssen, "notorious criminals."

After the Statute was published, they denounced it as confirmation of their suspicions. The Communist condemnation was summarily: "As a result of the Ruhr Statute the entire economy of West, North and South Germany falls under the iron hand of international monopoly." [12]

No sector of political opinion in Germany was wholly pleased by the Ruhr Statute. The leaders of the conservative groups protested that Allied authority was given so much power that it meant that the Ruhr would remain indefinitely in a state of "servitude" for the benefit of France. The Socialists were alienated because the Statute made it impossible for the German Government to take over the ownership and control of the Ruhr industries.

---

[11] Department of State *Bulletin* December 5, 1948.

[12] Manifesto issued by the Presidium, February 1, 1949. Printed in Documents on International Affairs (Royal Institute of International Affairs, 1947), pp. 378–9. (The Presidium's full title is The Presidium of the Supreme Soviet, the Supreme Soviet being the Russian legislature. The Presidium exercises the supreme legislative powers in the intervals between plenary sessions.

The Military Security Board

The Germans were still forbidden to produce war materials, radioactive materials, certain machine tools, synthetic oil products, magnesium, and beryllium; and the output of some basic industries was not to exceed designated levels. (Steel at 10.7 million tons annually). The Americans would have ended these restrictions. They tried to convince their French colleagues that they were not genuine guarantees against possible future German aggression; that a Germany held back would be more likely to develop an aggressive temper than one free to exert itself to the full.

The American and British Governments for a while longer avowed their intention of maintaining a watch to insure that Germany remained unarmed. Thus, after discussion with the French Government, they established a Three-Power Military Security Board, the duty of which would be to see that the controls over the prohibited and restricted industries were not evaded, and to enforce the ban on armaments and any measures of militarization in the Western zones.[13] This Board was to be authorized to carry out any necessary inspection and to recommend to the Military Governors any measures that might be required to prevent a revival of German military effort or organization.

The Communist press alleged that the real function of this Board, well disguised, was to prepare for German rearmament. The Soviet commentators scented what was in the wind to which they had given velocity by blockading Berlin.

A Constitution for West Germany

The work of the German Parliamentary Council on the Basic Law—the Constitution—lagged into the Spring of 1949. The Federalists (Christian Democrat Party) stood up against the Centralists (the Social Democrats and the Free Democrats). The Military Governors had let it be known that they would disapprove any undue trend toward centralization such as marked, they thought, the provisional draft of the Constitution drawn up by the Council. When they objected to the election law favored by the majority of the Council, even the usually cooperative Adenauer pleaded with the Military Governors not to continue to demand "an exaggerated federation." The Council, moreover, wanted to in-

[13] This took place at the same London Conference which produced the Ruhr Statute.

clude Berlin as the twelfth state of West Germany. However, it accepted the ruling of the Governors that Berlin was to be outside the jurisdiction of the Constitution.

At long last, the stiffest differences between the Allies were un-starched by the three Western Foreign Ministers (Acheson, Bevin, and Schuman) when they met in April for the signing of the North Atlantic Pact. Thereafter, on May 12, 1949, the Military Governors approved the Basic Law—the same day that the blockade of Berlin was lifted. The final compromises reached may have been induced by the prospect that since, as a sequel to the end of the blockade, the Foreign Ministers of the West were to meet almost at once with the Foreign Minister of the Soviet Union, the accord on the Basic Law would rule out any possibil-ity that the Western Allies would agree to the dissolution of the em-bryonic state of West Germany.

American and British officialdom was fairly content with the Constitu-tion (Basic Law) that had emerged, since it might end the confusing, though still disciplined diversity among the German states. But the French Government was displeased and did not conceal its anxiety. It regarded the concessions made to satisfy the desire of the German So-cialists for centralization as a victory for German Nationalism.

The Occupation Statute

Under the Statute the occupying powers reserved the right to pass judgment on German actions affecting disarmament, demilitarization, controls over the Ruhr, reparations, decentralization, foreign trade, and foreign policy. And, if they so wished, to decide policies and acts affect-ing relations with East Germany and the Communist countries.

The Germans at once began to try to rid themselves of these restraints on their right to govern themselves.

These several connected measures (and the belated fusion of the French zone with Bizonia), conceived to guide the government of West Germany until the occupation ended, were completed as the blockade of Berlin was being called off.

The impassioned push of the Communists had induced the recreation of the German State they hated and feared. Probably I should say: "in-duced sooner rather than later." For it only released and gave quicker impetus to tendencies which, prevailing over memories and active fears, could, within, let us say, a decade, have freed Germany from the plastic strapping of the occupation.

But one query still craves an answer: Need the restored Germany have been a divided Germany? What if the Russians in 1946–47 had not rejected the proffer of a long-term treaty obligating all four of the war allies to stand by one another to assure that a unified Germany would long be unarmed, peaceful, *unaligned?* History, indifferent to those who peer into its mysterious caves, leaves them to search for an answer.

50

The NATO Alliance Is Formed

The Gestation

During the same fateful months in which a West German state was being constituted, the great Western Alliance came into being. I could not possibly follow closely and definitively the course of the negotiations in which the pact was given its final form,[1] for the clamps of "national security" have kept many of the records closed and tongues sealed to this day. But perhaps it is now possible for historians of diligence to be as well informed as the Soviet authorities in Moscow presumably were at the time.[2]

The Vandenberg Resolution, assuring bipartisan support, had emboldened the American negotiators to go ahead with the discussions about an Atlantic Defense Pact. The imposition of the Berlin blockade had given impetus to them.

As has been told in a different context, in July 1948 the permanent

---

[1] A useful and comprehensive collection of the pertinent documents is North Atlantic Treaty: Documents Relating to the North Atlantic Treaty (81st Congress, 1st session, Washington, 1949), prepared by the Staff of the Senate Foreign Relations Committee. The most informative account of the negotiations as viewed in Washington—as well as of the consultations between the State Department and congressional committees—is traced in Acheson's book *Present at the Creation:*

[2] This supposition is based primarily on the fact that during the crucial periods of negotiation, Guy Burgess was an assistant private secretary to the British Minister of State, Hector McNeil, who was Bevin's chief spokesman in Parliament and in his confidence, and Donald McLean was first Secretary of the British Embassy in Washington. Both were proven Communist agents, now known to have been in steady secret communication with Soviet diplomats. The supposition is in general corroborated by evidence in current Soviet official comment that the Russian Government was au courant with the Western talks.

The defection of Burgess and McLean was an unbearable shock to Hector McNeil, the able and hopeful professional who had shown much promise as a stalwart opponent of Communism. As Rebecca West wrote in *The Meaning of Treason,* "It is really hardly bearable to think of their relationship. It is as if one had discovered a new novel of André Gide, and read of a horrible little Parisian schoolboy advancing on some earnest provincial as the poor greenhorn carries his suitcase out of the Gare de Lyon . . ." (p. 261 in the 1965 Penguin edition).

Military Committee of the Brussels Pact members had met in London. American and Canadian military representatives had joined as observers in their discussion of combined plans. On receiving the report of these emissaries, Truman authorized the State Department to continue consideration of the form and terms of a defense pact of greater scope.

It may be that at this time, when there was no certainty as to whether Berlin could be sustained by the airlift, some American, British, and French officials thought that by creating a close security system the Western Allies might quit Berlin with less damage and danger than if they could only remain by bringing about a great war. Dulles was believed to be influenced by this thought.[3]

An American group, of which Undersecretary Lovett was in charge, and Ambassador Lewis Douglas and General Lauris Norstad and General Alfred Gruenther were members, had held secret intense talks in Washington with similar foreign groups. Lovett reported to the President, bringing the minutes of each meeting with him. Eelco Van Kleffens, the Netherlands Ambassador to the United States, was outstandingly helpful. He had a keen grasp of essentials and the gift of finding the right formula at the right time. The British Ambassador, Oliver Franks, as always, contributed much to the search for acceptable terms and language. Modest Hume Wrong of Canada was another donor of useful ideas.[4]

Three crucial problems demanded skill and good will of all.[5]

One was to determine the language in which the mutual obligation should be expressed. Draft after draft was discussed and discarded.

Another was whether the pact should be merely a pact of mutual defense or one that drew together the life of its members in other ways—political, economic, and social. Lester Pearson, the Minister for External Affairs of Canada, was a convinced advocate of this wider vision of cooperation and mutual aid. He and his Canadian colleagues thought that the pact should, at least, obligate members to collaborate economically. They wanted it to confirm the basic tenet of the Marshall Plan: that the primary way to combat Communism was to improve conditions of work and life.[6] This wish corresponded also to major Canadian interest in enlarging international purchasing power and trade.

The third problem was the determination of the geographical area over which this protective roof was to extend. Should it, for example, include French North Africa or Greenland?

[3] As reported in memo by James Reston, September 28, 1948, in papers of Arthur Krock, Princeton University Library.

[4] Author's conversation with John D. Hickerson, former head of the State Department Division of European Affairs, July 1, 1967.

[5] Author's conversations with Lord (Oliver) Franks.

[6] Conversation with the Honorable Lester Pearson.

By September 9th the representatives of all seven conferring governments had agreed on the report to be submitted to their mentors at home.[7] Their report reposed on the opinion that the Soviet Union would continue to take advantage of weakness at any point to extend its domain. Each and every one of the Western European combination were fearful of this constant threat aganist their stability and independence, and afraid that the Soviet armies might overrun one or other, or several of them, before effective help arrived. The only way perceived of dispelling these fears, and thereby creating the sense of safety needed to secure the progress envisaged in the Marshall Program, was to form a combined security system. The U.N. could not be counted on because of Communist obstruction.

The pact ought to be, the negotiators had recommended, wide in geographic scope, since enemy occupation of any country adjacent to the main powers—Norway, Denmark, Iceland, Eire, Portugal, and Italy— would endanger all and be a threat to the security of the larger Atlantic countries.[8] The question of whether western Germany and Spain should also be included was left for time to determine; none was yet ready to countenance German rearmament.

The group attached to their report a draft of the provisions of the North Atlantic security arrangement they had in mind. The Permanent Commission of the Brussels Pact (Western Union), by December 10, 1948, had transmuted the report into a draft treaty. That had been reexamined by the ambassadors of the Western powers in Washington in consultation with the State Department, and thereafter amended texts had been remitted to all governments for consideration. It was already conceived, and the Defense Ministers of the Brussels Pact Powers had agreed, that the members should have a common defense policy, under a top command, and a permanent group to deal with questions of equipment and supply.

By early January 1949 the American Government thought agreement enough assured to expound the aims and principles of the proposed treaty in a press release; and the President, in his inaugural address on January 20th, spoke briefly of it.

But Congress had to be taped in. By early February 1949 members of the Senate Foreign Relations Committee had become impatient with the State Department for leaving them so much in the dark about the negotiations. Thus Acheson began a series of four meetings with the Senators, and he also met once with the House Committee of Foreign Affairs. At the same time that he was prodding and pushing the reluctant Sena-

---

[7] They kept the other five governments who were prospective members of the pact informed in some measure of the course of their talks.

[8] Sweden was sounded out about possible participation but refused.

tors he also had to hold in check the coterie of eager foreign ambassadors whose governments had to assent to any changes in the text previously proffered. As remembered by him, "In general, the ambassadors wished to push further than the senators were prepared to follow. . . . I was like a circus performer riding two horses—for one to move ahead of the other would mean a nasty fall. Safety required use of the ambassadors to urge on the senators, and the senators to hold back the ambassadors." [9]

Let anyone who thinks that dual task is easy try it—or better, leave it to someone as exact in thought, apt in words, and as adroit in tactics as Acheson.

The Pact, borne along by a common political sentiment was primarily a military alliance. The determining provision was Article 5. *"The Parties agree that an armed attack against one or more of them in Europe or North America shall be considered an attack against them all; and consequently they agree that, if such an armed attack occurs, each of them, in exercise of the right of individual or collective self-defense recognized by Article 51 of the Charter of the United Nations, will assist the Party or Parties so attacked by taking forthwith, individually and in concert with the other Parties, such action as it deems necessary, including the use of armed force, to restore and maintain the security of the North Atlantic area."*

The clutch of this engagement had been loosened to secure acquiescence. The Brussels Pact Members had wanted the pact to contain a more conclusive obligation of each and all members of NATO to supply all military aid in their power to any one that was attacked. But this would have been an obligation to go to war, which could not be assumed under the American constitution. Hence the language had been amplified to allow each country to provide support to others through *"such action as it deems necessary, including the use of armed forces."* Moreover, in a related provision (in Article 11) it was stipulated that *"This Treaty shall be ratified and its provisions carried out by the Parties in accordance with their respective constitutional processes."*

The Canadians were the finders of this mode of expressing the mutual obligation in language which satisfied the Foreign Relations Committee and yet did not appear to other members to make the pact unreliable and too dependent on American judgment. But every American President since—before and during every crisis—has been compelled to state that the United States would stand with any attacked member of NATO even if it meant that war—even atomic war—would come to America.

---

[9] Acheson, *Present at the Creation*, p. 277.

The Atlantic Pact was signed in Washington on April 4th. President Truman, speaking at the ceremony, said that the American Government had hoped to establish an international peace force under the U.N., but that purpose had been frustrated by the Soviet Union, and consequently the members of the alliance had been compelled to band together. Surely, he observed, if a pact of this kind had existed in 1914 and 1939, the two great world wars would not have happened.

When transmitting the Treaty to the Senate on April 12th, in accordance with the standard avowal of all governments that all acts of foreign policy are intended to serve peaceful ends, the President said: "The North Atlantic Treaty is further evidence of our determination to work for a peaceful world." [10]

The congressional hearings were thorough and repetitive. Acheson, in his appearance before the Committee on Foreign Relations on April 27th, expounded his views at length. As regards Article 5, he construed the obligation which the American Government was accepting as follows: "Under the treaty we would be bound to make an honest judgment as to what action was necessary to attain that end [to restore and maintain the security of the North Atlantic area] and consequently to take such action. That action might or might not include the use of armed force. If we should be confronted again with an all-out armed attack such as has twice occurred in this century and caused world wars, I do not believe that any action other than the use of armed force could be effective. The decision, however, would naturally rest where the Constitution has placed it." [11]

The Democratic Chairman of the Senate Committee on Foreign Relations, Tom Connally, in his defense of the pact in the subsequent Senate debate, muffled the whole issue by saying: "How far each state will go and what action it will take to fulfill its obligation will be determined by each state in the light of existing circumstances." [12]

Acheson also made known that in connection with the pact the United States was going to provide much more military aid to the other members, remarking: "As you know, the President will shortly recommend to the Congress the enactment of legislation authorizing the transfer of military equipment and assistance to other nations . . . the proposed program will request authorization and appropriation of $1,130,000,000 for Atlantic pact countries and approximately $320,-000,000 for other countries including Greece and Turkey, making a total

[10] Department of State *Bulletin,* May 8, 1949.
[11] *Ibid.*
[12] *Congressional Record,* Senate, 81st Congress, 1st session, July 5, 1949, p. 8984 ff.

of $1,450,000,000 for the fiscal year 1950." [13]

However, in regard to a more vital and continuing element of the obligation that has fallen upon the United States, Acheson was a poor and misleading prophet. When asked during the hearings of the Senate Committee on Foreign Relations whether under the pact this country was "expected to send substantial numbers of troops over there as a more or less permanent contribution to the development of these [the other Atlantic Pact] countries' capacity to resist," he answered with a "clear and absolute 'No.' " [14]

On July 21st the Senate approved the treaty by a vote of 83 to 13. In an impressive ceremony a few days later, Truman affixed his signature to the treaty ratification. "We are not arming ourselves and our friends," he averred in a major address while some protests against the pact—as a step along the route to war—were in the air, "to start a fight with anybody. We are building defenses so that we don't have to fight." [15] So speak all nations: arms the deterrent of enemies; arms for peace!

To the United States (and its allies) the military forces were "the shield of the Republic," a shield which was to grow and grow, as the Republic embraced many, many foreign countries within the corpus to be protected. But these Western countries, while maintaining their military organizations had in the past regretted the grim necessity to do so. In the Soviet Union, however, before and after NATO, all the press and periodicals were given over not merely to praise, but to adoration of the Red Army and its feats of valor, and to tributes to the renown and ability of its Marshals, led by Stalin. The Red Army was not only the glory of the country, but its liberator and the protector of the Soviet peoples and frontiers. This was the accompanying music for the great conferences and petitions for peace which in 1949–50 the Communist organizers arranged.

After he had signed, Bevin remarked to an associate: "[This is] one of the greatest moments of my life." In repeating these words, Francis Williams, in his book about his chief, added, "He [Bevin] was no more unaware than his critics of the dangers inherent in the pattern of Western power he had helped to establish. He recognized the risks that went with the immense preponderance of American force over that of all other members of the Atlantic Community. He knew that by its very na-

[13] Statement made before the Senate Committee on Foreign Relations, April 27, 1949, and released to the press on the same day. The necessary legislation which authorized the Military Assistance Program was sent by the President to Congress on July 25, 1949. For details, see *The Military Assistance Program*, Department of State Publication 3563.

[14] Acheson, *Present at the Creation*, p. 285, recalls this statement and calls his answer "deplorably wrong. . . . but . . . not intended to deceive." But he maintains that this is a matter within our discretion and not an obligation.

[15] Speech at Miami, Florida, August 22, 1949.

ture the existence of this force might compel him to some unpalatable concessions to American conceptions." [16]

To remind: how far had been the American traverse around the arc of policy in twenty years, we may recall the statements of President Franklin D. Roosevelt at a press conference on February 3, 1939, seven months before war broke out in Europe.

"The [foreign] policy has not changed and it is not going to change. If you want a comparatively simple statement of the policy, I will give it to you. . . .
    No. 1: We are against any entangling alliances, obviously.
    No. 2: We are in favor of the maintenance of world trade for everybody—all nations—including ourselves.
    No. 3: We are in complete sympathy with any and every effort made to reduce or limit armaments.
    No. 4: As a nation—as American people—we are sympathetic with the peaceful maintenance of political, economic and social independence of all nations in the world."

Hitler had propelled the American people along the first long swing of this arc of change, and Stalin had hurtled them to its end. One terminal of the arc rested in North America, the other along the boundaries of the Communist realm dominated by Russia.

While the pact was being conceived, the Soviet Government had tried hard to dissuade the Scandinavian countries—Norway, Denmark, and Sweden— from joining. The Norwegians, attached to the West by their brave fellowship in the war, and believing that only the United States could enable them to build up their military forces, had decided to risk Soviet resentment and join the pact. Thus, when at the end of January 1949 Moscow asked the Norwegian Government menacingly whether it meant to defer to the "aggressive Western aims" by joining the Atlantic Alliance, the answer was that it had the matter under consideration, but the Soviet Government could be sure that Norway would not be a party to any aggressive act or grant either naval or air bases in its territory. The Foreign Minister of Norway had hurried over to Washington. There Acheson had told him that unless Norway joined, the Americans could not promise wanted military equipment. Thus, bluntly faced with a choice, the Norwegian Parliament had authorized Norwegian participation.

Denmark, rather than be alone, followed, as had Iceland.

Moscow had also protested against the adherence of Italy to the pact

[16] Francis Williams, *Ernest Bevin: Portrait of a Great Englishman* (London: Hutchinson, 1952), p. 270.

on the score that it violated the obligations assumed by Italy in the Peace Treaty. With his customary legal skill, Acheson argued that the terms of the Peace Treaty left Italy free to join in a collective defense arrangement, and no obligation assumed by Italy under the NATO pact violated the restrictive military provisions of the Peace Treaty. Stalin, temporarily subdued by the stride of events elsewhere—in Germany and in Yugoslavia—accepted the alignment.

The Communist Denunciation

While Stalin measured the ground, the Soviet commentators and officials denounced the pact, shrilly and tirelessly, as an extension of the aggressive foreign policy of avaricious capitalists. Communist parties throughout the world agitated against it. Great "Peace Congresses," organized with most strident fanfare, in the West and in the East, condemned it.

As expected, the debate in the French Assembly about ratification was acrimonious and noisy. Schuman, in his answer to Communist critics, made the point that the Soviet system of alliances was anterior and that it was more compacting. He challenged them by asking: "Can we remain inert before that cold war directed from one center, sustained by military forces much more powerful than our own and an organization formed even in Paris? It is treason to let it happen."

The sustained opposition of the French and Italian Communist parties did not languish. The wish of the American Government to have these two countries join in NATO was not restrained by doubts about the reliability and value of their contribution—especially that of Italy—to mutual defense in face of a Russian attack. Even now some uncertainty lingers lest, should a dangerous crisis arise, local Communist supporters might demoralize and shake their resistance. This suspected weakness has fostered the willingness of the other members to transfer the weight of strategic and operational responsibility to the Germans. It gives ground for the surmise that if ever NATO is seriously threatened, recourse would almost certainly, and quickly, be had to tactical atomic weapons. Were this a military assessment, note would certainly be taken of the probability that the Soviet Union could not count on the loyalty and steadfastness of the people and armies of its satellites—except perhaps those of East Germany. In the divided Europe, the two parts of Germany are pivots of force—a quarter of a century after the end of the war.

To look ahead briefly: with amazing speed arrangements were worked out for an integrated NATO military force. Dwight Eisenhower, the

American who had commanded the Western forces in the invasion of Germany, was named Commander. Despite the laments and warnings of cautioning political figures such as Ex-President Herbert Hoover and Senator Robert Taft, President Truman maintained that he had the constitutional right to send American troops abroad in time of peace without the approval of Congress, and he did so. American troops who had first been placed in Europe to fight Hitler were going to remain there to deter or fight Soviet Communism. In words used by de Gaulle in 1966: "An American protectorate was set up in Western Europe under cover of NATO."

PART TWELVE

The Schism:

Atom-Haunted

51

The Last Meeting of the Council
of Foreign Ministers

No Retreat in the Program for West Germany

The agreement ending the blockade of Berlin had been given the face and form of reciprocity; as soon as the barriers were lifted, diplomacy was to flow once more. Foreign Ministers of the United States, Britain, and France were to confer with the Soviet Foreign Minister about the possibility of devising a mutually acceptable program for Germany, and perhaps, a peace treaty.

Despite a previous American attempt at clarification, Malik again in early April had expressed, in his talk with Jessup about ending the blockade, the wish of the Soviet Government that a West German Government would not be formed *before* or *during* the session of the Council of Foreign Ministers (see chap. 47). Acheson had agreed with Bevin and Schuman that the Western position should be put in writing—that Jessup should be given a short statement to read to Malik, to the effect that the three Western Foreign Ministers understood that only two points were under discussion. These were the simultaneous lifting of the blockade and counterblockade and the setting of the time for the meeting of the Council of Foreign Ministers. On April 5th Jessup had read this statement to Malik; it said that the Western negotiators wanted it clearly recorded that agreement on the two designated points would not be qualified or made subject to any other understanding.[1] Despite this notification, five days later Malik told Jessup that Vishinsky had been given to understand—how or by whom was not specified—that the formation of the German Government would be posponed until after the Council of Foreign Ministers had met.

From Acheson's public statements, the Soviet authorities may have inferred that the Western Allies would be willing to review with the So-

---

[1] Acheson, *Present at the Creation*, pp. 269–70.

viet Government, through the Council of Foreign Ministers, the whole German situation and the program for the creation of Western Germany.[2] Willing to *review* the situation, they were; but they were firmly indisposed to renounce or modify the program for West Germany. General Clay and his staff in the American Military Government, who had weathered the blockade, made it plain to Washington that they thought any return to a four-power control of the whole of Germany would not be feasible and, even if it were feasible, would not be desirable. Needlessly Clay feared that the American Government, in order to improve relations with the Soviet Union, might agree at the coming Conference to arrest the creation of a separate West Germany and restore a four-power regime of occupation. Indeed, as he recalled in his retrospective account of his experience in Germany, "I was apprehensive that Soviet representatives would [at the coming Conference] accept the establishment of an all-German government on our terms so that they could work from within to destroy it, and I was glad that this did not take place." [3]

Advised by Acheson, President Truman had made up his mind that there could be no return to these policies for Germany which had formed the Potsdam Agreement. In accord with its Allies the American Government did not intend to restore Russia's chance to intervene in the affairs of West Germany.

During the preceding months, as previously related, the American authorities, under Acheson's direction, had been composing drafts of the following: (1) an Occupation Statute—to be discussed with the Germans and (2) an Agreement between the Occupying Powers about the exercise of the powers to be retained by them. These Acheson had reviewed with Schuman and Bevin in April, when they were in Washington for the formal signing of the Atlantic Pact. Agreement had been quickly completed, not only about these arrangements, but about the administration of the Ruhr, the future of reparations, and "the closest integration of the German people under a democratic federal state within the framework of a European association." [4] All the tripartite accords had been made public within a month, before the scheduled meeting with the Soviet Foreign Minister in Paris.[5]

[2] Particularly Acheson's speech in New York City, before the American Society of Newspaper Publishers, April 28, 1949. State Department *Bulletin*, May 8, 1949, pp. 585–8.

[3] Clay, *Decision in Germany*, p. 439.

[4] Acheson, *Present at the Creation*, pp. 289–290.

[5] The three Western Foreign Ministers agreed on eight texts concerning Germany: (1) an aide-mémoire on main principles of policy toward Germany; (2) an agreement about tripartite control; (3) a procès-verbal concerning Berlin; (4) a message to the German Parliamentary Council at Bonn; (5) a Statute of Occupation; (6) a message from the Foreign Ministers to the Commanders-in-Chief of the three occupying pow-

In a blunt statement Acheson issued before leaving for that Conference, he observed that it was not likely that the convocation would remove the burr of Germany in the relations between the West and the Soviet Union.[6] So much had happened, he had gone on to say, since the last meeting of the Council. Consequently, he explained, "It is not our intention, no matter how much we may desire agreement, to accept anything which would tend to undo what has been accomplished or impede future progress along the course we have charted toward revival of health and strength for the free nations of the world." The Western Allies, he went on to emphasize, would not waver. "We cannot allow it [U.S. foreign policy] to become subject to the fluctuations produced by a raising and lowering of international temperature. To accept these fluctuations as a guide for our policy would be to put in foreign hands a large measure of control over the conduct of our foreign relations. . . . We shall not barter away successes achieved for the sake of promises which might again prove to be illusory, as they too often have been in the past." [7]

Bevin and Schuman were no more inclined than Acheson to compromise. Immediately upon their arrival in Paris, on May 21st, the three Foreign Ministers agreed to turn down any Soviet proposal for German economic unity unless it was based on Western conceptions, and was not subject to the veto, and went our way on reparations and currency.[8] Could they have thought there was any chance that Russia would jettison its whole policy? It is most improbable, though Acheson in his Memoirs opines that he regarded the requirements to be "severe but not impossible." [9]

The Last of the Conferences About Germany

The Conference opened on May 23d in the Palais Rose. This pink marble palace was the former residence of the American-born Duchesse

ers; (7) an agreement about the port and city of Kiel; and (8) a procès-verbal regarding a plebiscite in Baden-Wurtemberg about boundaries. *L'Année Politique 1949*, pp. 69, 378. The texts of those various agreements are in the issues of the State Department *Bulletin:* April 17, 1949, pp. 499–501; April 24, 1949, pp. 524–531; May 8, 1949, pp. 589–590.

[6] May 19, 1949. State Department *Bulletin*, May 29, 1949.

[7] *Ibid.*

[8] *New York Times*, May 22, 1949.

[9] Acheson defines the requirements, chief among them: "The creation of an all-German Government should be based on the reception of the eastern zone into the trizonal government already in process of creation. . . . and that industrial enterprises partly or wholly owned by Soviet Government agencies be returned to private German interests. We did not propose to have Marshall Plan aid given to West Germany siphoned into Russia via East Germany." *Present at the Creation*, p. 292.

de Talleyrand. From its spacious rooms, General Otto von Stuelpnagel, the Nazi Commandant, had ruled over occupied Paris. The Council of Foreign Ministers met in its Grand Salon, "upon the frescoed ceiling of which," Acheson was to remember, "satyrs pursued nymphs through clouds without gaining on them even through the double translation of Vishinsky's longest speeches." [10] Neither did the diplomats, during their long romp, draw nearer to the heavenly peak of reconciliation.

The Conference lasted a month. The Western pariticpants found Vishinsky as voluble—as uninterruptable—as usual. But as long as there seemed a chance of compromise he did not engage in tirades and seldom in polemics. He was calm, politic, almost affable.

Moreover, although the Soviet official press did not desist in its campaign against the West, its reports of the Conference were relatively uncensored. The journalists noted, however, that while Vishinsky was being polite in Paris, no less than fifteen of the dramas being played in the Moscow theaters were openly anti-American. Of one, written by Anatoli Surov, one of the leading Soviet ideologists, the White House did not ask for a translation. It was called "The Mad Haberdasher." The main character was an unsuccessful haberdasher with a strong facial resemblance to Hitler.[11]

The tactics arranged by the experienced conferees in Washington have been recalled by Acheson. "We obviously wanted Vishinsky to disclose his hand as fully as possible as early as possible. This could best be done by Schuman opening the session with . . . a review of the unhappy past, and a plea for a brighter future. Bevin could then follow by goading the Russian. The Soviet Union had broken up four-power control of Germany, brought us perilously close to trouble of major proportions, and now insisted upon this meeting. Where did Vishinsky propose that we go from here?" [12]

At the second session Vishinsky presented the Russian plan for Germany: he proposed that the Four-Power Control Council for Germany be recreated and Four-Power control—dependent on unanimity—of all Germany be resumed. Measures were to be agreed on for the economic and political unification of the whole country. The Germans could be allowed, he suggested, somewhat more freedom in managing their affairs —through a Government Council. The Soviet Union was to be granted a share in the direction of the Ruhr. The Four-Power Berlin Kommandatura and the all-Berlin Magistrat, responsible to the Kommandatura, were also to be reconstituted. In sum, the Russians tried to retract pol-

[10] *Ibid.*, p. 295.
[11] Dispatch of Cyrus Sulzberger, *New York Times,* May 25, 1949.
[12] Acheson, *Present at the Creation,* p. 293.

icy toward Germany into the same groove—though somewhat enlarged —in which it had been mired since Potsdam.

The Western representatives regarded these proposals as "setting the clock back." The Potsdam Agreement, they contended, was obsolete in view of the political and economic progress which had since been made in West Germany. Thus Acheson, in his comments, said the American Government would not consider this regressive plan and that the East Germans should rather adopt the progressive democratic institutions of West Germany for their own zone. The unification of Germany and Four-Power cooperation, he and his colleagues stressed, would have to be on the basis of the Bonn Constitution; and elections throughout Germany for a national federal government should be under Four-Power supervision, with all political parties, except those associated with the Nazis, permitted to participate in them. If the Four-Power supervision were revived, no member should have a veto power.[13] Moreover, with both natural and cultivated talent, he scornfully rejected the Soviet Union's demand for ten billion dollars in reparations.

Vishinsky was stumped. On May 30th, when formally rejecting the Western proposals, he for the first time reverted to recrimination.

By then, as recalled elsewhere, the Parliamentary Council of West Germany had (May 8th) adopted a Constitution. The Communists in East Germany had conducted elections for a new People's Congress (May 15–16). But this body did not assemble in Berlin for a fortnight— while Vishinsky in Paris was trying to persuade the Western powers to abandon their plans for a separate West Germany. Then, after Vishinsky recognized failure, on May 30th the People's Congress adopted a Constitution for a German Democratic Republic—as a compensatory measure. It was designed to be a centralized authoritarian government modeled on those of the other "people's democracies" under Russian tutelage, and it was destined to be the rival of the Bonn Government. Thus, even as the Foreign Ministers talked about unity, the conception was abandoned; the division of Germany was being formalized.

The Council of Foreign Ministers also considered the future of Berlin. The commendable object was to revive the Four-Power Kommandatura and to have it control all segments of the city as a unit. The Russians wished it to have such extensive authority that it would be able to control everything the Berliners might do except die.[14] The Soviet Govern-

---

[13] The course of the discussion can be followed well from the reports in the *New York Times* of May 25th and the following days. Evidently the Western newspapermen were being well briefed.

[14] As remarked by Dean Acheson. *The New York Times,* June 8, 1949.

ment wanted to be absolutely sure that a German administration in Berlin could not be unfriendly to it or to East Germany.

Acheson urged that the local German administration should be allowed more freedom. Moreover, he and his Western colleagues did not want the future status of the city to rest solely on any agreement that might be reached in this Conference. They thought it must be defined in a treaty, a treaty which would confirm in indisputable and legal form the right of the Western zones to maintain air and land communications with Berlin. As implacably as ever, the three Western members and Vishinsky quarreled over whether the Kommandatura would have to be unanimous in its decisions (the old veto question). In the end the four Foreign Ministers arranged for further consultations about joint administration of Berlin in order to normalize the life of the city.

While the Conference of Foreign Ministers at Paris was, in the first week of June 1949, rotating around these differences, the Foreign Relations Committee of the Senate unanimously recommended that the NATO treaty be approved. Its report could be read either as an attempt to reassure Russia or as a warning. "In both intent and language, it [the Pact] is purely defensive in nature. It comes into operation only against a nation which, by its own action, has proved itself an international criminal by violating the [U.N.] Charter." [15]

Germany was not to be asked to be an original signatory of NATO. During the debate in the National Assembly about NATO, Schuman had assured that body that western Germany was not to be a signatory of the Pact and as such be rearmed. "The question," he had asserted, "does not arise. There is no German peace treaty. Germany has no arms and cannot have any." [16] But the armies of occupation of the three largest Western members were to remain in western Germany and that country was by way of entering into more and more extensive association with them.

The Russian official publicists, who up to then had kept alive the hope that agreement about Germany would be reached, changed their tune and began to accuse the West of dictatorial ways. Vishinsky, however, had one other ploy by which he may have thought still to win over German opinion and discredit the Western program. On June 10th he proposed (1) that a four-power peace treaty with Germany should be speedily concluded; (2) that all occupation forces be withdrawn within a year after its signature; and (3) that the Council of Foreign Ministers proceed to determine at once the procedure for preparing the peace treaty.

[15] State Department *Bulletin*, June 19, 1949, p. 792.
[16] Assemblée nationale, *Débats*, July 25, 1949, pp. 5227–31.

Acheson and his colleagues asked: How could a peace treaty be concluded with a Germany that was divided? The downward swoop of mutual regard was reflected in the language with which Bevin and Acheson rejected the proposal. Bevin called Vishinsky's statement a "tragic farce." [17]

Truman was not disturbed by the bleak result of the Conference. He praised Acheson for his stalwart stand and skill. In a public statement he attributed the failure of the Conference to the refusal of the Russians to accept democratic principles and conditions. The Western countries, he stressed, were determined "not to jeopardize the basic freedoms as they now exist in Western Germany merely to obtain a nominal political unity." [18] Progress toward unity would be impossible as long as the Russians insisted on a reversion to the policies of the Potsdam Agreement, which they had so long traduced. To the Russian authorities this was effrontery. *Pravda*, for example, called Truman's statement "a mixture of immodest boasting and tendentious imterpretation . . . as far from the truth as the sky is from the earth." [19]

The sense that it was no longer incumbent upon the United States to court Soviet cooperation, animated, for example, Acheson's expositions to Committees of the Senate and House of Representatives on June 22d and 23d, after his return to Washington, in behalf of the NATO treaty and of the Military Assistance Program. They bristled with pride; they glistened with satisfaction over the result of the initiatives which he more constantly and constructively than anyone else (save perhaps Robert Schuman) had sustained. He recalled how hard the Russians had tried to obstruct the economic recovery and political convergence of Western Europe. And how they had failed. But, he warned, the West must go forward with its cooperative measures "with renewed determination."

In contrast, for the time being, the Russians continued to try to maintain the illusion that the conference of the Foreign Ministers had revived the idea and practice of Four-Power cooperation. Their publicists even tried to convince themselves and others that this Conference had been a vindication of Soviet foreign policy and a defeat of the West's attempt to include all Germany under the Bonn Constitution.

At this time, this Soviet appraisal of the outcome of the Conference

[17] Acheson, in the course of continuous discussions with Vishinksy during this period, took up Vishinsky's practice of adorning his statements with Russian proverbs, and remarked à propos of one of Vishinsky's ". . . to use an old Indian expression [it was] as full of propaganda as a dog is of fleas, though in this case it was all fleas and no dog" (*Present at the Creation*, p. 300).

[18] June 21, 1949. State Department *Bulletin*, July 4, 1949.

[19] *Pravda*, June 27, 1949.

which it had sought, and the relinquishment of some of its claims on Austria—of which we shall soon tell—puzzled the West. The State Department took this attitude to be the result of the great improvement of the position of the countries of Western Europe, and an attempt to show that Russia was not perturbed. So it was in one respect, but I believe this turn of Russian policy also had a deeper and darker meaning.

Henceforth, the Politburo had resolved, East Germany must be kept under even closer Communist control and joined more firmly with the other subordinate Communist states. It would no longer try to prevent the creation of a West German Government. In the East it would strive to make the Communist connection stronger and more exclusive and confront the world from its enclosed plane—and plains—of power.

On the very day the Conference ended, June 20th, Acheson, Bevin, and Schuman in Paris signed the Charter of the Allied High Commission in Germany to watch over the conduct of the new German government in accordance with the provisions and powers of the Occupation Statute. General Clay left for home. He and his British and French colleagues were gratified by the fact that the Communists had been kept out of Western Germany; resigned to the definite division of Germany; and expectant of even more rapid economic improvement in Western Germany. Their worries were over; but those of the world through which the frontier between the two Germanys ran like a wartime trench, were not.

The three High Commissioners who were soon to assume their duties were named: John J. McCloy for the United States, General Brian Robertson for Great Britain, and Ambassador André François-Poncet for France. They kept close watch over German affairs from their perches over or near the Rhine.

Before continuing with the further course of the separation between West and East we must turn back briefly to Austria, which, at this May-June Conference of Foreign Ministers, was released from the four-ply apron of foreign control.

The Release of Austria

The Potsdam Agreement for the Four-Power control of that country and of its capital, Vienna, was similar to those agreements for the control of Germany and Berlin. However, the subsequent experience had been more quiescent. A moderate and modest Provisional government had operated in all four zones during the intervening years.

The meetings of the Control Council for Austria had been relatively calm. At the sessions of the Council of Foreign Ministers, at Moscow in the spring of 1947, and at London late in 1947, some progress had been made toward agreement on the terms of a peace treaty with Austria, but that progress had been obstructed by stubborn differences on two important questions.

One was what reparations should Austria be required to make to the Soviet Union? To recall briefly the previous history of the controversy, the Russians, after their entrance into the country, had hastened, without asking anybody's permission, to carry off and out many kinds of equipment and reserve stocks, on the score that they belonged to the Germans—including much formerly Austrian-owned that had been taken over by the Nazis. Then at Potsdam the Russians had asked for 250 million of reparations in the form of industrial products. Churchill and Truman had refused to agree to fix any definite obligation, without denying Molotov's contention that the Austrians ought to be made to pay substantially, since they had caused great damage and suffering to the Russian people. All that Truman and Attlee (who by then had succeeded Churchill) had been willing to deed to the Soviet Union as reparations were the German assets in the Soviet zone of Austria.

The Russians had subsequently construed this to mean almost all the industry in that zone. The Western powers had continued with reason to refuse to approve the larger scope of Soviet claims, judging them to mean that Russia would be able for a long time to control the economic life in all Austria. The Russians had construed Western resistance to indicate the wish to enable American monopolies, especially the big oil companies, to acquire a dominant position in the Austrian economy.[20]

The Foreign Minister of Austria, Karl Gruber, had, in May 1949, traveled to Paris to confer with all four members of the Council of Foreign Ministers. In his presentation he combined pleasing persuasion with courage. He appealed for a settlement of the reparations question that would not prevent Austria from becoming self-supporting and regaining a tolerable standard of life. Already, before leaving Vienna for Paris, he had declared that if the great Powers found themselves unable once more to settle their differences, they should at once withdraw their armies of occupation; and he stated that the Austrian Government would

[20] Interpretation of the Potsdam Agreement, of what could reasonably be judged to have been German assets, and hence subject to a reparations lien, exhausted the talents and time of the negotiators. So involved were the threads in the tissue and history of ownership that in the end they were compelled to give up the effort and resort to a simple broad formula.

The Russians claimed the right of possession of the oil fields and oil refineries which, before the war, had been in part American and British properties. Over this the American Government later made a fuss.

denounce as an aggressor before the United Nations any one of the occupying Powers who refused to do so. The purport of his statement was that if no settlement was reached, the Austrian Government would seek Western support for a declaration of independence—support of the kind that was being given to Western Germany.[21]

Molotov had indicated that the Soviet Union's primary interest was in the procurement of reparations and of economic advantages; it was not activated by a design to bring all Austria under Communist control. This, and the willingness of Austria to pay heavily to regain its independence, made it possible to find a way past this obstruction to a treaty of peace.

The four Powers had agreed that it should provide that the Soviet Union would receive from Austria $150,000,000 in freely convertible currency to be paid over six years, a substantial but quite bearable liability. It should also provide that in return for relinquishing all other claims on German assets in Austria, the Soviet Union would secure 60 percent of the controlling rights to extract oil in the Austrian oil fields and acquire the assets of the Danube Shipping Company, not only in Eastern Austria but in Bulgaria, Hungary, and Romania. This meant that the Soviet Union would continue to have a rein on Austrian economic life, especially on transactions with western countries. By this ransom the Austrian people would be rid of their occupiers, and the Western Allies be freed to depart.

The second obstruction to a peace treaty had been the Yugoslav claim for the Austrian province of Carinthia. An earlier understanding that "Austria's frontiers shall be those of January 1, 1938" was ratified at this session of the Council of Foreign Ministers. Ignoring Tito's angry recrimination, Stalin ceased to insist on the Yugoslav claim. As reparations, Yugoslavia was granted only the right to take over all Austrian property within its own frontiers.

It seemed as though the way had been cleared for the rapid conclusion of the peace treaty with Austria and an end to its division.[22] But after the Conference the Russians became most evasive and dilatory about concluding the treaty. And, to look beyond the span of this narrative, it was not until May 1955 that the peace treaty was signed and foreign troops withdrawn.

The prospect for that despoiled and divided country—Austria—had seemed almost hopeless, but its people did finally regain the chance to live independently after the travail which it had gone through since the

[21] The *New York Times* for March 25, 1949, contained an informative account of the views and intentions of the Austrian Government and of the Foreign Ministers.

[22] This Agreement was published in the Communiqué of the Council of Foreign Ministers at the end of their meeting in Paris, June 20, 1949. State Department *Bulletin,* July 4, 1949.

Nazis had seized control of their country and led them into a war which left them so poor and miserable.

The Austrians then and since have wanted only to live at peace with both the West and the Soviet Union. To do that they have had to be constantly careful to remain unaligned and on good terms with both. That they have managed to do so is evidence of their gifts. If only the Russians and Germans could learn from them!

But again I have strayed from the narrative of the muddy tide of separation between the West and the Soviet Union in order to indulge in remembrance of one of the few healthy events during the period when the quarrel between the Soviet Union and the West was unabated, and about to extend to more distant parts of the world.

52

Atomic Energy: The Default
of the Nations

To look back—as we should and must—during this
same period of bisection of Europe, the talks about control of atomic energy came to an abominable end. The paltering within the United Nations did not end; the ritual went on; and the talks limped along, becoming more and more shrouded in suspicion as disputes over other
situations—recalled in the preceding sections—between the two opponents became stonier.

Since neither of the protagonists essentially changed views or tactics,
it would be unrewarding to tell of their jousting, speech by speech,
thrust by thrust. Little would be learned by a review of their dishearten-
ing trudge. Specialists and lawyers might find a little genuine significance hidden in the crevices of the mutations of the Soviet responses
and statements of policy, but the mistrustful American analysts did not.[1]

We shall traverse only briefly and in summary, then, the course of the
argument between the submission of the divided report of the U.N.
Commission to the Security Council and the end of the impulse to lock
up atomic weapons in a vault built and guarded by all nations.

The Soviet view, as argued by Gromyko in the Security Council on
March 5, 1947, was: "The U.S. proposals on control proceed from the erroneous premise that the interests of other states should be removed to
the background during the exercise by the control organ of its control

---

[1] Extensive excerpts from the various mutable and viscous proposals of the Soviet
representatives on the Atomic Energy Commission of the U.N. (Gromyko and Malik)
and in the General Assembly and Security Council (Molotov and Vishinsky) and the
American responses as well, are to be found in State Department publications and
The International Control of Atomic Energy: Policy at the Crossroads (1948); *Atomic Impasse: 1948; A Collection of Speeches by Frederick Osborn* (1948).

A systematic, though sometimes careless, account of Soviet diplomacy in regard to
the control of atomic energy is, *Soviet Policy Towards International Control of
Atomic Energy*, by J. L. Nogee (Notre Dame: University of Notre Dame Press, 1961.

and inspectional functions. Only by proceeding from such fundamentally vicious premises, was it possible to come to the conclusion . . . on the necessity of transferring atomic enterprises to the possession and owner-ship of the international organ which is to be charged with the responsi-bility for the realization of control." The Soviet authorities defended their dissent—as did Gromyko in this same speech. "The Soviet Govern-ment has stood and is standing for strict and effective international con-trol of atomic energy. . . . Effective inspection is a necessary component part of the system of international control. . . . At the same time this . . . should not develop into interference with those branches of indus-try which are not connected with the production of atomic energy. . . . Interference in the internal affairs of States is not required by the inter-ests of effective control." [2]

This fenced-in acceptance of right of inspection had not satisfied the Americans and their associates. They feared evasion and deception. Moreover they thought that nations would be more likely to resent the continuous roving and probing of foreign inspectors over their whole economy and industry more than the presence of an operating agency.

In June 1947 the Soviet Government had submitted its own plan for a system of control—supplementary to the ban. But that had not brought the adversaries nearer to an accord.

In October, Vishinsky, speaking before a Committee of the U.N. As-sembly, had for the first time seemed to abandon the demand that prohi-bition precede control. He had suggested that there be two conventions, one providing for destruction of stocks and atomic weapons and a ban upon their production, and the other establishing a control system "both . . . to be signed and brought into operation simultaneously." [3] But by then the American authorities were convinced that Moscow would not accept a thorough and trustworthy system of control, and that the suggestion had no value unless the Soviet Government accepted all the essentials of the plan approved by the majority. But Secretary Marshall had been worried enough about its effect on other members of the U.N. to recommend the advisability of conducting a counterpropaganda cam-paign, and to urge Baruch to issue a keynote statement.[4]

To the end, three central differences peered through the curtains of words: The majority members of the U.N. Commission, grouped around the United States, continued to maintain that it would be foolhardy to

[2] *Policy at the Crossroads*, pp. 78–80.
[3] Quoted in Nogee and Spanier, *Soviet Policy*, p. 140.
[4] Messages to Bernard Baruch from American representatives in U.N. Atomic En-ergy Commission, Frederick Osborn, and Robert Lovett's message to the American delegation at the U.N., October 5 and 6, The Baruch papers, Princeton University Library.

introduce a ban on, and elimination of, atomic weapons *before* an effective and reliable system of control had been brought into operation, or even to impart what was deemed significant information that might be helpful in the production of the bombs. Their position on this question was from start to finish almost static. The small minority grouped around Russia had maintained that an agreement outlawing atomic weapons and providing for the destruction of stockpiles of these weapons should be the first step, or, as belatedly proposed by Vishinsky, at least concurrent with the signature of an agreement about control.

Another irrepressible difference was in regard to the nature of the control system. The majority upheld the American opinion that it was essential that the international agency own or control the materials for atomic explosives and the facilities which produced the atomic materials. The Russians insisted that each country should have its own stock of atomic materials and operate its own atomic facilities—subject to "periodic" and "special" inspections, by an International Control Commission.

The third unresolved difference concerned the veto. The utmost concession that the Russians offered was to agree that it would not apply to the day-by-day operations of the Control authority. They continued to insist that it must be retained in reference to any allegations of violations brought before the Security Council.

All the talk of all the King's men in the scores of committee meetings, in the Security Council and the Assembly had not turned up solutions for these differences. By the spring of 1948 the U.N. Commission on Atomic Energy at long last had been compelled to admit failure.[5]

The Deplorable Conclusion of the Discussions

Thereafter the discussions in the U.N. became even more a divided silhouette. Each of the two antagonistic sides spoke just to its own audience. Thus in July 1949 the Commission adopted a resolution which concluded: "Further discussion would tend to harden these differences, and would serve no practicable or useful purpose." [6]

The American Government and people accepted this conclusion with

---

[5] In submitting the Third (and last) Report of the United Nations Atomic Energy Commission to the Security Council, May 17, 1948. See State Department Publication, *International Organization and Conferences.* Series III, 7 (1948).

[6] I have been told that when the atoms heard this verdict, a few of the rougher and delinquent ones cheered because they were not to be constrained, and jeered at those who had sought to control them; but that most of the atoms grieved, because they did not want to be enslaved to human folly. See Cyclotron News for Day of Atonement, any and all years.

regret, but they saw no warrant for reconsidering the program proposed. The Soviet Government may have regarded the outcome as the triumph of diplomacy. Had it not managed to inhibit any American impulse to enforce its diplomacy or views about control by threat of use (or actual use) of atomic weapons? Had it not assured itself enough time to learn to produce atomic weapons, being on the verge of the achievement for which it had been intensely striving?

In August 1949 an atom bomb was successfully exploded in the presence of the Commander-in-Chief of the Soviet armed forces and other high government officials. The biographer of the physicist Kurchatov, who had directed the Russian effort, in recounting this triumph, blended piety and satisfaction: "The Soviet scientists knew that they had made a weapon for their own country to protect the peace of the world. . . . They had knocked the trump card out of the hands of the American atomic politicians." [7]

[7] Igor Golovin, *Kurchatov: The Man and His Work* (mimeographed English translation).

53

Divided Germany; Divided Europe; Divided World

The Autumn of 1949

While the dream of an accord among the nations to banish atomic weapons was dying, their division was deepening.

After the pantomine of Paris—the Conference of Foreign Ministers—Germany had been split by a deep trench. Others have described well the laborious—yet swift—transition of western Germany from a segment of a defeated nation under military occupation to a country with a government of its own, under temporary tutelage, and of its subsequent passage to independence and its adoption as a valued, almost courted, ally of the West.

Swayed by their wish to rid themselves of foreign military control, and encouraged by Western triumph in the contest over Berlin, the State Parliaments quickly ratified the Basic Law. On September 7, 1949, the elected delegates had constituted themselves as a Federal legislature and within the next week had chosen a President and a Chancellor, Konrad Adenauer. On September 21st the three Allied High Commissioners met with the newly formed Cabinet and recognized its authority under the Occupation Statute. The West German Government was thus inaugurated. Concurrently, the three Western Allies had erected a trisectoral city government in Berlin.

All along this course, Secretary of State Dean Acheson and John J. McCloy, the American High Commissioner for Germany, were the prime movers. The British Government was a willing confederate, despite its very live memories of what the Nazi Germans had shown themselves to be, and of their cruel threat to Britain's survival. The French Government went along in spite of its uneasy suspicion that the American Government was going to cultivate German friendship assiduously. Would not the Americans, who had not been invaded and maltreated by the

Germans and who were so intent on "containing" Communism, be inclined to subsidize the Germans as stalwart and obedient soldiers?

Western Germany at this time was rapidly rebuilding and regaining vitality. But no one was as yet certain that it could be self-supporting since its people now were 47 million, while only 40 million had lived there before the war, and substantial food-and coal-producing areas in the East were frozen by the ice of diplomacy or ideology. Uncleared ruins everywhere were grim reminders of war, defeat, and suffering.

The Russian publicists mocked at the Adenauer Government. They professed to see it as a shelter for former Nazi industrialists and their monopolist associates. The regime, they averred, was akin to that of Franz von Papen's, which had paved the way for Hitler. These fanatical comparisons stung the Western posteriors. Which country, after all, had made a deal with Hitler; which had fought Germany while Russia was bending its knee? So they regarded the Russian reprise—the turnover by the Soviet Military Administration of almost all its powers to the Peoples' Democratic Republic of East Germany, set up in October—with angry scorn rather than with regret.

The arrangement between the Allies and the West German Government, as defined in the Occupation Statute, was disliked because of the extent of the powers reserved to the Commissioners. It was soon worn down by German grumbling and supplemented by an agreement reached between the Chancellor and the High Commissioners on November 23d, known as the Petersberg Protocol (named after the hilltop mansion overlooking Bonn where the High Commissioners conducted their business).[1] This Petersberg Protocol contemplated not only that Western Germany would be accorded membership on the Ruhr authority, but that it would be a formal participant in the Marshall program. It forecast the end, once and for all, of the dismantling of German industrial plants and reparations.[2] And it contained an understanding that the German Government could start to reestablish its consular and commercial offices in foreign countries. Little wonder, then, that in the

[1] It was to the Petersberg Hof that Prime Minister Neville Chamberlain and Premier Édouard Daladier had gone to see Hitler and to edge toward the appeasement that eventuated in Munich in 1938.

[2] Some dismantling was still going on in the English and French zones. In August 1949 Adenauer had written Schuman, offering to turn over the Thyssen Steel Works at Duisburg-Hamborn, one of the largest and most modern in Europe, as reparations, if dismantling of all other plants in the French zone were ended. He had gone on to remark that he thought this arrangement could constitute the beginning of international cooperation in coal and steel industries, which would promote international understanding. The text of this letter is in A. Grosser *Die Bonner Demokratie*, pp. 524–6.

French National Assembly the Protocol was vehemently criticized—by the Communists as putting German reactionaries and monopolistic interests again in control of the country, and by the Gaullists as dangerous, and certain to foster the revival of the structure of heavy industries which enabled Germany to make war on Europe.

The fear of Germany was still active though the Petersberg Protocol definitely reaffirmed that it would remain "demilitarized," and that the German Federal Government would prevent the reconstitution of any and all armed forces. But incredulity about the maintenance of that ban soon prevailed. For the members of the Western coalition, especially the United States, were showing signs of eagerness to have German participation in their military arrangements.

Acheson and the Joint Chiefs of Staff, rather than Adenauer, were beginning to want a rearmed German component in the integrated NATO force that was to be maintained to deter any further thrust. A reason for the initiation of training and the formation of a West German army was found in the creation in East Germany of a supersize police force (Volkspolizei), estimated within the following months to have been enlarged to 100,000 men, half of whom were, in effect, a strongly armed force. The all-too-familiar process of action and reaction, of belief that force that opponents had, or were supposed to have, must be matched and overmatched, was soon to stimulate remilitarization of both parts of Germany.

As NATO's strategic plans were developed, the conclusion was reached that Germany, being "the very core of Europe," was consequently the key to the defense of the West.[3]

But the tale of why, how, and when western German rearmament was accomplished and Western Germany brought into NATO is for the author of the next segment of the history of divided, atom-shadowed Europe.

By the time the leaves fell in the Autumn of 1949, the lines of separation in continental Europe were set. But the alignment in the Far East was fluid and on the verge of a major change. There, the American Government, as leader of those countries who had been at war with Japan, was hurrying to arrange a peace treaty with that nation. Despite all Russian objections and maneuvering, it had been—in consultation with other members of the Far Eastern Advisory Commission— discussing the terms of a treaty with the Japanese political leaders.[4]

[3] Truman, *Years of Trial and Hope*, p. 253.
[4] An account in historical perspective of the determined bent of American policy toward and in Japan is to be found in Feis, *Contest Over Japan*. A thorough and consecutive account of the reasoning and steps leading to the peace treaty is in Acheson, *Present at the Creation*.

Clearly in mind was the intention of adopting Japan as main associate in the Pacific and a main military base.

The ominous downdrift in China caused all to hasten. For Nationalist China, the ally which since the 1930's we had held against Japan, was stumbling and stricken. It was succumbing to the more competent and compelling Chinese Communist movement. Thus even as the United States was managing to stabilize the balance of power in Europe, it was about to suffer a severe shock in the Far East.

Despite the old ties of friendship and its anxiety, the American Government, disappointed by the poor use the Kuomintang Government had made of our aid and support, had remained aloof in the latter stages of the Chinese civil war. It had concluded that it would be futile and exhausting to engage in a land war on that vast continent of China, and that it would be wasteful and cruel to enable the Chinese Nationalist Government to continue the fighting that could end only in defeat. Several months before (March 1949), in commenting on legislation intended to provide much more financial assistance to the National Government, Acheson wrote to Senator Connally: "The National Government does not have the military capability of maintaining a foothold in South China against a determined Communist advance. . . . There is no evidence that the furnishing of additional military material would alter the pattern of current developments in China. There is, however, ample evidence that the Chinese people are weary of hostilities and that there is an overwhelming desire for peace at any price. To furnish solely military material and advice would only prolong hostilities and the suffering of the Chinese people would arouse in them deep resentment against the United States." [5]

By September 1949, Canton and all South China were imperiled, and soldiers under the Red flag were striding across the land, meeting little resistance from Chiang Kai-shek's demoralized and deserting armies.

The American civil and military authorities were aware that the contest against Communism had become global. But they decided to leave Chiang Kai-shek's regime—on the mainland or in Formosa to which he was soon (December 1949) to flee—to stand or fall by its own efforts. The Joint Chiefs of Staff had informed the President and State Department on August 17th that they did not regard Formosa of sufficient military importance to the United States, under current circumstances (as long as the divergence between American military strength and American global responsibilities existed), to warrant the commitment of American forces to the occupation of Formosa under conditions short of war. Neither did the State Department believe Formosa of sufficient political or strategic importance to do so. Moreover—and this was an important

[5] March 15, 1949. *United States Relations with China* (State Department Publication 3573) p. 1053.

streak in State Department thinking at the time—it was believed that if Americans joined battle in Formosa, the Communists might concede Soviet claims in Manchuria, Mongolia, and the great border province of Sinkiang.

It was not comprehended that the Chinese Communists were rampant ideologists, with fury in their spirits against the West. The Secretary of State and his advisers on Far Eastern affairs at the time did not think it inevitable, perhaps, or even probable, that Communist China would be a subordinate or even obedient partner of the Soviet Union. Might not Communist China turn out to be another and more formidable Yugoslavia on the Asian borders of the Russian empire, opposing Soviet expansion toward the East? [6]

During the summer of 1949 American diplomatic representatives had discussed with the governments of its main European allies and of Canada the question of whether and when to recognize the Communist regime as the Government of China. An informal agreement to act in concert was made. But, because of emergent evidence that the Chinese Communists were going to treat the West with insult and hostility, perhaps implacable, and because of the smoldering opposition in Congress to recognition, the American Government had deferred decision. Truman and Acheson preferred to wait until the dust settled. They remained aloof until there was more conclusive evidence of the attitude, intentions, and temper of the new rulers of China. Thus, even though Britain and France were disposed to accord recognition, in September Acheson informed Bevin and Schuman that under the circumstances the American Government would not do so. As the American Government waited to see whether the upset situation in Asia could be righted, the balance in Europe became transfixed, and Russia emerged as an atomic power.

The world was about to enter one of its most perverse eras. The canopy of circumstances under which the nations cavort, was to be set luridly alight by fearful bursts of atomic power. The contest between the Western capitalist (and Socialist) democracies and the Communist dictatorships was going to continue, though all knew it might end in extinction.

[6] Cyrus Sulzberger, in a special article in the *New York Times*, as early as February 15, 1949, wrote an interesting and impressively detailed, though speculative, exposition of this possibility as a probability.

54

Not Mutual Trust, but Mutual
Terror—It Was To Be

On September 17, 1949, the Council of the North Atlantic Treaty Organization (consisting of the NATO Foreign Ministers) had its first meeting. It created the committees and groups through which joint policies and plans were to be set, and a coordinated—but not integrated—military force was to be formed. The plans contemplated the appointment of a Supreme Commander for NATO forces and the inclusion, at some time in the near future, of a German military component. Concurrently the Soviet Government was compacting its coalition of controlled Communist dependents, under its heavy fist, holding the Red flag.

And even as the Council met, Russian success in producing atomic weapons became known. Science, spreading, was playing fast and loose with national diplomacy—trifling with it, challenging it, taunting it, frightening it, as it is even unto this day.

The Russian political and military leaders had often presaged publicly that they would soon have atomic weapons. When first commenting on the American rejection of Soviet proposals (Sept. 17, 1946) Stalin, in reply to a British newspaper correspondent, had said: "Monopolist possession of the atomic bomb cannot last long." [1] Later, in the following month, Molotov, in an address to the U.N. General Assembly, had remarked in a similar context, "It should not be forgotten that atomic bombs used by one side may be opposed by atomic bombs and something else from the other side, and then the utter collapse of all present-day calculations of certain conceited but short-witted people will become all too apparent." [2]

[1] Quoted in the *Information Bulletin* of the Russian Embassy in Washington, October 2, 1946.
[2] October 29, 1946. Plenary Meetings of the General Assembly: Verbatim Record 23 October-16 December 1946. pp. 842–3.

The Soviet authorities, while secretly gloating over their achievement, did not announce it. They let it be discovered by the Americans, who were sniffing the air and finding it decidedly radioactive. The President took upon himself, on September 23, 1949, to announce that momentous finding.[3] He implied that it was no surprise to him or to his advisers and that it would not make any difference in our strategy or diplomacy. The first paragraphs of the self-soothing announcement may be recalled: "I believe the American people, to the fullest extent consistent with national security, are entitled to be informed of all developments in the field of atomic energy. That is my reason for making public the following information. We have evidence that within recent weeks an atomic explosion occurred in the USSR. Ever since atomic energy was first released by man, the eventual development of this new force by other nations was to be expected. This probability has always been taken into account by us." [4] (Author's query: Why then did Truman attach so much importance to secrecy?)

On this same day, September 23, 1949, Vishinsky, the vicious prosecutor of Stalin's purges, who had succeeded Molotov as Foreign Minister, introduced into the U.N. a proposal for a *Four-Power Pact for Strengthening the Peace.* His statements were hypercritical and his language nauseatingly smug. The Russian publicists, in paraphrasing the speech, used even stronger language. "Every proposal of the Soviet Union aimed at preserving peace and averting the threat of war is met with hostility in the camp of the imperialists and their servitors. But it becomes harder and harder for foes of peace to weave their sinister intrigues. . . . The Soviet policy of promoting peace has the ardent support of all peoples.

"The enemies of peace reposed their main hope in the atomic bomb. They calculated on implementing their maniacal schemes of world supremacy with the help of threats and intimidation. That is why they are so stubbornly resisting prohibition of the atomic weapon and stirring up war hysteria. It is generally known that no one is preparing to attack the United States. Although it possesses the atomic weapon, the Soviet Government adheres and intends to adhere in the future to its old posi-

---

[3] Truman, *Years of Trial and Hope* p. 306, states detection of radioactive pollution first occurred on September 3d. Available records do not make it possible to judge various statements that have come to my attention that there were earlier atomic test explosions in the Soviet Union. For example, Roger Massip, the head of the foreign news service of the newspaper *Figaro,* wrote in December 1949 that the White House received a report of a Russian atomic explosion as early as July 14, 1949, and that Truman immediately discussed this with Acheson, the Secretary of Defense Louis Johnson, and General Eisenhower, but he delayed the announcement while hurrying on the rearmament of Western Europe. *Politique Étrangère,* December 1949, pp. 566–7.

[4] Department of State *Bulletin,* October 3, 1949.

tion and insist on the unqualified prohibition of the use of this weapon." [5]

The press and radio throughout the world diffused the news that the Russians had the atomic bomb, with fanfare as assailant to the senses as a saxophone. Yet Jacques Dumaine, the sensitive French diplomat, truly noted in his diary: "But our ears are deaf and our spirits inert. . . . I call the epoch in which we live, the 'back of the duck.' Clothed with an impermeable skin, we let everything rub off. What happens to us hardly touches us. . . . You explain to me that the atomic bomb is henceforth directed against me; so much the worse, for I doubt whether my life will be reduced by it. . . . All reality runs off us like water from the back of a duck." [6]

Though the Soviet atomic bomb explosion did not immediately affect Western diplomacy, it gave a quick thrust to the program for providing American military aid to the other members of NATO. The portended mutual defense assistance program was expensive.

The Senate had been resistant to the request which Truman had made a few hours after signing the ratified North Atlantic Treaty—for an authorization of about one billion four hundred million dollars to be expended by the Chief Executive according to his best judgment. The news propelled the Congress into acceptance of the bill, and it provided funds which roughly satisfied the administration, though they were far less than the military (American and foreign) thought necessary for successful mutual defense against an attack from the East. The bill was enacted on September 28th and signed by the President on October 6, 1949. It was hoped that it would be a convincing sign that newly aroused fear would not shiver Western diplomacy or shake the pact into which the Atlantic powers had entered.

On October 25, 1949, about one month after Truman's announcement about Russia's bomb, the American, British, French, Canadian, and Chinese members of the U.N. Atomic Energy Commission sent to the Secretary General an integral report about the outcome of the expired negotiations. It was well written and correct; but seldom was a requiem more prosy. "The Soviet representative insisted that two separate conventions, one on prohibition and the other on control, should be put into effect simultaneously. The other representatives maintained that the important point to be resolved was what constitutes effective control, and

[5] *New Times*, September 28, 1949.
[6] Jacques Dumaine, *Quai D'Orsay, 1945–1951*, entry dated September 25, 1949, p. 424.

that this control had to embrace all uses of atomic materials in danger-ous quantities. In their view the Soviet proposals would not only fail to provide the security required but they would be so inadequate as to be dangerous. They would delude the peoples of the world into thinking that atomic energy was being controlled when in fact it was not. On the other hand, under the [majority] approved plan, the prohibition of the use of atomic weapons would rest not only on the pledge of each nation, but no nation would be permitted to possess the materials with which weapons could be made. Furthermore, the Soviet Government took an impracticable stand as regards the question of timing or stages by which prohibition and control would be brought into effect." [7]

Although both Truman and Stalin stated that the Russian acquisition of atomic weapons made it even more imperative that agreement be reached to ban their use and control their production, the nations did not change the cant of their policies or statements.

The hostility of the Soviet Government became less restrained in its denunciations. Re-read a few paragraphs of the speech given by Georgi Malenkov—who was to be, briefly, Stalin's successor—on the 32d anni-versary of the October Revolution in Russia.

"The programme of the main enemies of peace becomes more nakedly revealed every day. This programme envisages the creation by means of violence and new wars of an American world empire, which is to surpass any of the world empires built by conquerors in the past. The idea is nothing more nor less than to turn the whole world into a colony of the American imperialists, to reduce the sovereign peoples to the status of slaves.

"In what do these insensate designs of 'Americanizing' all countries and continents differ from the maniacal plan of Hitler and Goering for the 'Germanisation' first of Europe and then of the whole world? In what way do these designs differ from the no less maniacal plans of Tanaka and Tojo for the subjugation of all Asia and the Pacific to the Japanese imperialists?. . . ."

"The purpose of the North Atlantic Military Pact signed in 1949 is perfectly obvious. It is an instrument for direct and outright preparation of a new imperialist war.

"One of the most important component elements of the aggressive line of the warmongers is what is known as atomic diplomacy, the adventur-ist character of which has now become fully revealed. For, indeed, this diplomacy was based upon the absolutely false initial assumption that the United States possesses a monopoly of the atomic weapon. Actually,

[7] State Department *Bulletin*, November 7, 1949, p. 687.

as we know, the Soviet Government made no secret of the fact that it possessed the atomic weapon. In 1947 the Soviet Government made it known to the world that the secret of the atomic bomb no longer existed. Nevertheless the overweening warmongers, devoid of all sense of reality, are still not desisting from their notorious atomic diplomacy." [8]

In the United States and Russia, scientific laboratories and atomic plants hastened their efforts to produce hydrogen bombs. Within the next year both governments became busily engaged in the task of perfecting them.

To revert—at the end of the period to which we have devoted our attention, Russia, though held back politically in western Europe, had acquired by science and by stealth the power to forefend any Western atomic assault upon it. But no more than the West was it able to escape the scathing whim of History.

Stalin may not have anticipated the completeness—perhaps only the rapidity—of the victory of the Chinese Communists.[9] It may be also that Stalin and his colleagues were not wholly pleased at the power the Chinese Communists had displayed, at the energies Mao Tse-tung had displayed, as signals of their independence. But within a few months the Soviet authorities decided that it was wiser to make Communist China a companion than to treat it fearfully as a rival. Thus in February 1950 a Sino-Soviet Treaty was to be signed, whereby both were pledged to ". . . consult each other in regard to all important international problems affecting the common interests of the Soviet Union and China and . . . to render each other every possible economic assistance." [10]

In partial fulfillment of this comradely obligation, the Soviet Government, which had so zealously guarded the secret of its atomic energy project, passed on to Communist China knowledge of how to produce atomic weapons. The Chinese scientists and engineers who were engaged in the work received training, it is true, not only in Moscow, but in the universities and laboratories of the United States, England, and France.[11] But it was the Russians who gave the Chinese the blueprints

[8] Text in *Soviet News*, November 7, 1949. Translation in Royal Institute of International Affairs publication *Documents on International Affairs, 1949*, pp. 132–3.

[9] Although Vishinsky's proposal at the last meeting of the Council of Foreign Ministers (in May–June 1949) that the Council of Foreign Ministers *including China* prepare a treaty with Japan may be construed as preparing the record for the admission of the Communist Chinese Government to the Council and to permanent membership of the Security Council. See dispatch of Cyrus Sulzberger from Paris in the *New York Times*, June 11, 1949.

[10] *Soviet News*, February 15, 1950. Reprinted in *Documents on International Affairs*, 1950, pp. 541–3.

[11] The Director of China's Institute of Atomic Energy (1966), Chien San-chiang, had secured his advanced degree in physics at the University of Paris. His two prin-

of the fabricating plants, the samples of devices, and it was the Soviet technicians and advisers who greatly helped the Chinese to build up plants that produced uranium and the reactors.

Thus—and here History blinked at the Russians as it had been blinking at the West—their refusal to subscribe to a thoroughgoing system of international control and their antagonism to the West led them to conjure up what may turn out to be a more reckless and rival possessor of atomic weapons in the Far East.

Down this tunnel, then, all the negotiations about the banishment and control of atomic weapons vanished into the polluted air and never since have they emerged into the light. The separation between the Western democracies and the Communist countries as grouped under the Soviet Union has been flecked but not illuminated by atomic particles. The peace for which the leaders of both have so constantly said they longed, was to be, then, a peace resting not on mutual trust but on mutual terror. Dread was henceforth—and up to the present—to sway and often to determine the demeanor of the Powers.

At this dark grove of history, having tried to trace the trails of separation that were trodden in the five years since the Allies had defeated the Axis, we must turn over the tale to the philosophers, and the future to the since-born. Will they merely resign themselves? Or will East as well as West rebel against that past, and reform?

---

cipal deputies had studied first in California and then in the Institute of Nuclear Research in the Soviet Union. Still other important contributors of the scientific and engineering staff studied at Cambridge University, England, and California Institute of Technology, in the United States. See Hal D. Steward, "West-Trained Experts Build China's Bombs," a syndicated article in the *Boston Globe,* May 21, 1966.

Printed Sources Cited

Acheson, Dean. *Sketches from Life of Men I Have Known* (New York: Harper & Row, 1961).
——. *Present at the Creation: My Years in the State Department* (New York: W. W. Norton, 1969).
Acikalin, Cevat. "Turkey's International Relations," *International Affairs* (October 1947).
Adenauer, Konrad. *Memoirs 1945–1953*, trans. Beate Ruhm von Oppen (Chicago: Regnery, 1966).
Ambrose, Stephen E. *Eisenhower and Berlin, 1945: The Decision to Halt at the Elbe* (New York: W. W. Norton, 1967).
Anderson, Oscar E., Jr., and Richard G. Hewlett. *A History of the United States Atomic Energy Commission.* Vol. I: *The New World, 1939–1946* (University Park, Pa.: Pennsylvania State University Press, 1962).
Armstrong, Hamilton Fish. *Tito and Goliath* (New York: Macmillan, 1951).
Arnal, Pierre. "Konrad Adenauer sous l'occupation britannique, 1945–1947," *Revue d'histoire diplomatique* (January–March 1967).
Bader, William B. *Austria Between East and West, 1945–1948* (Stanford, Calif.: Stanford University Press, 1966).
Baruch, Bernard. *Baruch: My Own Story.* Vol. II: *The Public Years* (New York: Holt, Rinehart & Winston, 1960).
Blackett, P. M. S. *Fear, War and the Bomb: Military and Political Consequences* (New York: Whittlesey House, 1949).
Blum, Léon. *L'Oeuvre De Léon Blum*, 6 vols. (Paris: A. Michel, 1954–1965).
Bohlen, Charles E. *The Transformation of American Foreign Policy* (New York: W. W. Norton, 1969).
Bundy, McGeorge, and Henry L. Stimson. *On Active Service in Peace and War* (New York: Harper, 1948).
Byrnes, James F. *Speaking Frankly* (New York: Harper, 1947).
——. "Byrnes Answers Truman," *Colliers* (April 26, 1952).
——. *All in One Life Time* (New York: Harper, 1958).
Campbell, John C. *The United States in World Affairs, 1945–47, 1947–48, 1948–49* (New York: Council on Foreign Relations–Harper, Annual).
Carpenter, F. B. *Six Months in the White House with Abraham Lincoln* (Boston: Hurd and Houghton, 1866).
Churchill, Winston S. *The Second World War.* Vol. VI: *Triumph and Tragedy* (Boston: Houghton Mifflin, 1953).
——. *Sinews of Peace: Post-War Speeches* (Boston: Houghton Mifflin, 1949).
Clay, Lucius. *Decision in Germany* (New York: Doubleday, 1950).
Connally, Tom. *My Name is Tom Connally* (New York: Thomas Y. Crowell, 1954).
Cooper, Alfred Duff (Viscount Norwich). *Old Men Forget* (New York: Dutton, 1954).
Crankshaw, E. "The U.S.S.R. Revisited," *International Affairs* (October 1947).
Crossman, Richard. *Palestine Mission: A Personal Record* (New York: Harper, 1947).
Curry, George, and Richard L. Walker. *Edward R. Stettinius, Jr., 1944–1945 and*

James F. Byrnes, 1945–1947. Vol. 14 of American Secretaries of State Series, ed. Samuel Flagg Bemis and Robert H. Ferrell (New York: Cooper Square, 1963).

Dalton, Hugh. *High Tide and After: Memoirs, 1945–1960* (London: Mullex, 1962).

Davis, Franklin M., Jr. *Come as a Conqueror: The U.S. Army's Occupation of Germany, 1945–1949* (New York: Macmillan, 1967).

Davison, W. Phillips. *The Berlin Blockade: A Study in Cold War Politics* (Princeton, N.J.: Princeton University Press, 1958).

Deane, John R. *The Strange Alliance: The Story of Our Efforts at Wartime Cooperation with Russia* (New York: Viking, 1947).

De Gaulle, Charles. *War Memoirs,* trans. Jonathan Griffin et al. (New York: Simon and Schuster, 1960), III.

Diebold, William. *Trade and Payments in Western Europe: A Study in Economic Cooperation, 1947–1951* (New York: Harper, 1952).

Dennett, Raymond, and Robert K. Turner, eds. *Documents on American Foreign Relations,* vol. VIII, June 1945–December 1946 (Princeton, N.J.: World Peace Foundation–Princeton University Press, 1948).

Dixon, Pierson. *Double Diploma: The Life of Sir Pierson Dixon, Don and Diplomat* (London: Hutchinson, 1968).

Djilas, Milovan. *Conversations with Stalin,* trans. Michael V. Petrovich (New York: Harcourt, Brace & World, 1962).

Donnelly, Desmond. *Struggle for the World: The Cold War, 1917–1965* (New York: St. Martin's, 1965).

Druks, Herbert. *Harry S. Truman and the Russians, 1945–1953* (New York: Robert Speller, 1966).

Dulles, John Foster. *War and Peace* (New York: Macmillan, 1950).

Dumaine, Jacques. *Quai D'Orsay (1945–1951)* (Paris: R. Juillard, 1955).

Duroselle, J. B. "The Turning Point in French Politics," *Review of Politics* (July 1951).

Eisenhower, Dwight D. *Crusade in Europe* (New York: Doubleday, 1948).

Elgey, Georgette. *La République des Illusions 1945–1951; ou, La Vie Secrète de la IVe République,* vol. I (Paris: Fayard, 1965).

Fauvet, Jacques. *La IVe République* (Paris: Fayard, 1959).

Feis, Herbert. *The China Tangle: The American Effort in China from Pearl Harbor to the Marshall Mission* (Princeton, N.J.: Princeton University Press, 1953).

——. *Churchill, Roosevelt, Stalin: The War They Waged and the Peace They Sought* (Princeton, N.J.: Princeton University Press, 1957).

——. *Between War and Peace: The Potsdam Conference* (Princeton, N.J.: Princeton University Press, 1960).

——. *The Atomic Bomb and the End of World War Two,* rev. (Princeton, N.J.: Princeton University Press, 1966).

——. *Contest Over Japan* (New York: W. W. Norton, 1967).

Fontaine, André. *History of the Cold War: From the October Revolution to the Korean War, 1917–1950,* trans. D. D. Paige (New York: Pantheon, 1968).

Forrestal, James J. *The Forrestal Diaries,* ed. Walter Millis (New York: Viking, 1951).

Franklin, William L. "Zonal Boundaries and Access to Berlin," *World Politics* (October 1963).

Gimbel, John. *The American Occupation of Germany: Politics and the Military, 1945–1949* (Stanford, Calif.: Stanford University Press, 1968).

Goldman, Eric. *The Crucial Decade: America 1945–1955* (New York: Knopf, 1956).

Golovin, Igor. *I. V. Kurchatov: Biography of the Soviet Nuclear Scientist,* trans. William H. Dougherty (Bloomington, Ind.: Selbstverlag Press, 1968).

Gottlieb, Manuel. *The German Peace Settlement and the Berlin Crisis* (Racine: Chicago: Paine-Whitman, 1960).

Gowing, Margaret. *Britain and Atomic Energy 1939–1945* (London: Macmillan, 1964).

Grosser, Alfred. *Die Bonner Demokratie: Deutschland von draussen gesehen* (Dusseldorf: K. Rauch, 1960).

Hewlett, Richard G., and Oscar E. Anderson, Jr. *A History of the United States*

Atomic Energy Commission. Vol. I: *The New World, 1939–1946* (University Park, Pa.: Pennsylvania State University Press, 1962).

Hillman, William, ed. *Mr. President: The First Publication from the Personal Diaries, Private Letters, Papers, and Revealing Interviews of Harry S. Truman* (New York: Farrar, Straus & Young, 1952).

Hoover, Herbert. *The President's Economic Mission to Germany and Austria.* Report No. 3 (Washington, D.C.: Government Printing Office, 1947).

Ilyin, L. "The Truth About the Berlin Situation," *New Times* (July 14, 1948).

Izakov, B., and Y. Zhukov, "U.S. and Great Britain," *Soviet Press Translations* (January 15, 1948).

Jebb, H. M. Gladwyn. *Halfway to 1984* (New York: Columbia University Press, 1966).

Jefferson, Thomas. *Jefferson Correspondence,* ed. P. L. Ford (New York: Putnam, 1892–1899), X.

Jones, Joseph M. *The Fifteen Weeks: Feb. 21–June 5, 1947* (New York: Viking, 1955).

Kennan, George F. "The Sources of Soviet Conduct," *Foreign Affairs* (July 1947).

———. *Memoirs, 1925–1950* (Boston: Little, Brown, 1967).

Kennedy, Robert F. *Thirteen Days: A Memoir of the Cuban Missile Crisis* (New York: W. W. Norton, 1969).

Keynes, John Maynard. *The General Theory of Employment, Interest and Money* (New York: Harcourt, 1936).

Kramish, Arnold, and Melville J. Ruggles. *The Soviet Union and the Atom: The Early Years* (Santa Monica, Cal.: The Rand Corporation, 1956).

Krock, Arthur. *Memoirs: Sixty Years on the Firing Line* (New York: Funk & Wagnalls, 1968).

Lie, Trygve. *In the Cause of Peace: Seven Years with the United Nations* (New York: Macmillan, 1954).

Lippmann, Walter. *The Cold War: A Study in U.S. Foreign Policy* (New York: Harper, 1947).

Lukacs, John A. *A New History of the Cold War,* 3rd edition, expanded (New York: Anchor, 1966).

MacArthur, Douglas. *Reminiscences* (New York: McGraw-Hill, 1965).

Madison, James. *The Writings of James Madison,* ed. Gaillard Hunt, 9 vols. (New York: Putnam, 1900–1910).

Mallalieu, W. C. "The Origin of the Marshall Plan: A Study in Policy Formation and National Leadership," *Political Science Quarterly* (December 1958).

Manchester, William. *The Arms of Krupp, 1597–1968* (Boston: Little, Brown, 1968).

Marjolin, Robert. *Europe and the United States in the World Economy* (Durham, N.C.: Duke University Press, 1953).

Matloff, Maurice. *Strategic Planning for Coalition Warfare 1943–1944* (Washington, D.C.: Historical Division of the War Department, 1953).

Molotov, V. M. *Problems of Foreign Policy* (Moscow: Foreign Languages Publishing House, 1949).

Monroe, Elizabeth. "Mr. Bevin's Arab Policy," *St. Anthony's Papers,* No. XI (London: Chatto & Windus, 1961).

Mosely, Philip E. "Soviet Exploitation of National Conflicts in Eastern Europe," *The Soviet Union: Background, Ideology, Reality,* ed. Waldemar Gurian (Notre Dame, Ind.: University of Notre Dame Press, 1951).

———. "Hopes and Failures: American Policy Toward East Central Europe, 1941–1947," in *The Fate of East Central Europe: Hopes and Failures of American Foreign Policy,* ed. Stephen D. Kertesz (Notre Dame, Ind.: University of Notre Dame Press, 1956).

Murphy, Robert O. *Diplomat Among Warriors* (New York: Doubleday, 1964).

Nicolson, Harold. *Diaries and Letters of Harold Nicolson.* Vol. III: *The Later Years, 1945–1962* (New York: Atheneum, 1968).

Nogee, Joseph L. *Soviet Policy Toward the International Control of Atomic Energy* (Notre Dame, Ind.: University of Notre Dame Press, 1961).

Phillips, Cabell. *The Truman Presidency* (New York: Macmillan, 1966).

Price, Byron. *Report to President Truman on the Relations Between the American Forces of Occupation and the German People* (Washington, D.C.: Government Printing Office, 1947).

Price, Harry Bayard. *The Marshall Plan and Its Meaning* (Ithaca, N.Y.: Cornell University Press, 1955).

Reale, Eugenio. *Avec Jacques Duclos: au banc des accusés à la Réunion Constitutive du Kominform a Szklarska Poreba (22–27 Septembre 1947)*, traduit de l'Italien par Pierre Bonuzzi (Paris: Plon, 1958).

Roosevelt, Elliott. "A Personal Interview with Stalin," *Look* (February 4, 1947).

Ruggles, Melville J., and Arnold Kramish. *The Soviet Union and the Atom: The Early Years* (Santa Monica, Calif.: The Rand Corporation, 1956).

Ryan, Cornelius. *The Last Battle* (New York: Simon and Schuster, 1966).

Shulman, Marshall. *Stalin's Foreign Policy Reappraised* (Cambridge, Mass.: Harvard University Press, 1963).

Smith, W. Bedell. *My Three Years in Moscow* (Philadelphia: Lippincott, 1949).

Smyth, Henry deWolfe. *Atomic Energy for Military Purposes: The Official Report on the Development of the Atom Bomb Under the Auspices of the United States Government, 1940–1945* (Princeton, N.J.: Princeton University Press, 1945).

Taigin, I. "Development of Democracy in the East European Countries," *New Times* (May 15, 1946).

Tang, Tsou. *America's Failure in China, 1941–1950* (Chicago: University of Chicago Press, 1963).

Truman, Harry S. *Memoirs.* Vol. I: *Year of Decisions* (New York: Doubleday, 1955).

——. *Memoirs.* Vol. II: *Years of Trial and Hope* (New York: Doubleday, 1956).

Turner, Robert K., and Raymond Dennett, eds. *Documents on American Foreign Relations,* Vol. VIII, July 1945–December 1946 (Princeton, N.J.: World Peace Foundation–Princeton University Press, 1948).

Ulam, Adam. *Titoism and the Cominform* (Cambridge, Mass.: Harvard University Press, 1952).

Vandenberg, Arthur H., Jr. *The Private Papers of Senator Vandenberg* (Boston: Houghton Mifflin, 1952).

Van der Beugel, Ernst Hans. *From Marshall Aid to Atlantic Partnership: European Integration as a Concern of American Foreign Policy* (Amsterdam: Elsevier, 1966).

West, Rebecca. *The Meaning of Treason* (Baltimore: Penguin, 1965).

White, Theodore H. *Fire in the Ashes: Europe in Mid-Century* (New York: Sloane, 1953).

Whyte, Anne. "Quadripartite Rule in Berlin," *International Affairs* (January 1947).

Williams, Francis. *Ernest Bevin: Portrait of a Great Englishman* (London: Hutchinson, 1952).

——. *A Prime Minister Remembers: The War and Post-War Memoirs of the Rt. Hon. Earl Attlee* (London: Heinemann, 1961).

Willis, F. Roy. *France, Germany and the New Europe,* rev. paperback edition (New York: Oxford University Press, 1968).

Yindrich, Jan. *Tito vs. Stalin: The Battle of the Marshals* (London: Ernest Benn, 1950).

Zhukov, Y., and B. Izakov. "U.S. and Great Britain," *Soviet Press Translations* (January 15, 1948).

Official Publications

U.S. Government

STATE DEPARTMENT:
Atomic Impasse: A Collection of Speeches by Frederick Osborn (1948).
The Bulletin (weekly periodical).

Foreign Relations of the United States, annual volumes.
    Foreign Relations of the United States:
        The Conferences at Cairo and Teheran, 1943 (1961).
        The Conferences at Malta and Yalta, 1945 (1955)
        The Conference of Berlin (The Potsdam Conference), 1945, 2 vols. (1960).
The International Control of Atomic Energy: Growth of a Policy (1946).
The International Control of Atomic Energy: Policy at the Crossroads (1948).
United States Relations with China (1949).
General Report of the Committee of European Economic Cooperation (Committee of
    Sixteen for the Marshall Plan) (1947).

CONGRESS:
Congressional Record, Senate speech June 11, 1948, Introduction of Vandenberg
    Resolution.

SENATE:
Committee on Foreign Relations:
    Documents Relating to the North Atlantic Treaty (1949).
    Hearings on S.938, Assistance to Greece and Turkey, March 24, 1947.
    Hearings on Interim Aid Bill, November 11, 1947.
    Hearings on European Recovery Program, January 20–22, 1948.
    Hearings on NATO Pact, April 27, 1969.

HOUSE OF REPRESENTATIVES:
Committee on Foreign Affairs:
    Hearings, March 20, 1947.

Government of the United Kingdom

HOUSE OF COMMONS:
Parliamentary Debates.

FOREIGN OFFICE:
*Memorandum of Agreement between the United States and the United Kingdom
    on the Economic Fusion of American and British Zones of Occupation in
    Germany, December 2, 1946.*
*Germany: An Account of the Events Leading Up to a Reference of the Berlin Question
    to the United Nations* (CMD 7354, 1948).

Government of France

ASSEMBLÉE NATIONALE:
Débats, Discussion of German membership in NATO.

MINISTÈRE DES AFFAIRES ÉTRANGÈRES:
Documents français relatifs à l'Allemagne, 1945–1947 (1947).
*Documents de la Conférence des Ministères des Affaires Étrangères de la France,
    du Royaume Uni et de L'URSS tenue à Paris Juin 27 au Juillet 3, 1947*
    (Paris: Imprimerie National, 1947).

Government of U.S.S.R.

MINISTRY OF FOREIGN AFFAIRS:
Correspondence between the Chairman of the Council of Ministers of the U.S.S.R.
    and the President of the U.S.A. and the Prime Ministers of Great Britain
    during the Great Patriotic War of 1941–1945 (Moscow: State Political
    Book Publishing House, 1957).

Government of Canada
*Report of Royal Commission . . . to investigate the Facts Relating to and Circum-
    stances Surrounding the Communications by Public Officials and other Per-
    sons in Positions of Trust, of Secret and Confidential Information to Agents
    of a Foreign Power* (1946).

PRINTED SOURCES CITED

United Nations
Third Report of the United Nations Atomic Energy Commission to the Security Council, May 17, 1948. (Reprinted in U.S. Department of State publication, *International Organizations and Conferences,* Series III, no. 7, 1948.)
Six Power Conference on Germany, London, February 23–June 2, 1948.
   Final Report and Communiqué, published June 2, 1948, and supplementary letter of explanation, June 7, 1948.

Collections of Documents

Documents on International Affairs (London: Royal Institute of International Affairs—Chatham House, Annual).

Unpublished Papers

Papers of Bernard M. Baruch, Princeton University.
Papers of William Clayton, The Oral History Project of Columbia University.
Papers of Arthur Krock, Princeton University.
Papers of Admiral William Leahy, Library of Congress.

Periodicals and Newspapers

L'Année Politique (Paris)
Boston Globe
Daily News (Washington, D.C.)
The Economist (London)
Foreign Affairs (New York)
Izvestia (Moscow)
Look (New York)
New Republic (Washington, D.C.)
New Times (Moscow)
New York Times
P.M. (New York)
Politique Étrangère (Paris)
Le Populaire (Paris)
Pravda (Moscow)
Soviet *Information Bulletin* (Washington, D.C.)
Sunday Times (London)
Tass (Moscow)
Times (London)

Index